# RILEY
# 1½ & 2½ Litre
## *Gold Portfolio*
## 1945-1955

Compiled by
R.M. Clarke

ISBN 1 870642 503

*Cover Photograph by Vince Manocchi Courtesy of*
*Special Interest Autos*

Distributed by
Brooklands Book Distribution Ltd.
'Holmerise', Seven Hills Road,
Cobham, Surrey, England
Printed in Hong Kong

# BROOKLANDS BOOKS

## BROOKLANDS BOOKS SERIES
AC Ace & Aceca 1953-1983
AC Cobra 1962-1969
Alfa Romeo Alfasud 1972-1984
Alfa Romeo Alfetta Coupes GT.GTV.GTV6 1974-1987
Alfa Romeo Giulia Berlinas 1962-1976
Alfa Romeo Giulia Coupés 1963-1976
Alfa Romeo Spider 1966-1987
Allard Gold Portfolio 1937-1958
Alvis Gold Portfolio 1919-1967
Aston Martin Gold Portfolio 1972-1985
Austin Seven 1922-1982
Austin A30 & A35 1951-1962
Austin Healey 3000 1959-1967
Austin Healey 100 & 3000 Collection No. 1
Austin Healey 'Frogeye' Sprite Collection No. 1
Austin Healey Sprite 1958-1971
Avanti 1962-1983
BMW Six Cylinder Coupés 1969-1975
BMW 1600 Collection No. 1
BMW 2002 1968-1976
Bristol Cars Gold Portfolio 1946-1985
Buick Automobiles 1947-1960
Buick Riviera 1963-1978
Cadillac Automobiles 1949-1959
Cadillac Automobiles 1960-1969
Cadillac Eldorado 1967-1978
Camaro 1966-1970
Chevrolet Camaro & Z-28 1973-1981
High Performance Camaros 1982-1988
Chevrolet Camaro Collection No. 1
Chevrolet 1955-1957
Chevrolet Impala & SS 1958-1971
Chevelle & SS 1964-1972
Chevy II Nova & SS 1962-1973
High Performance Corvettes 1983-1989
Chrysler 300 1955-1970
Citroen Traction Avant 1934-1957
Citroen DS & ID 1955-1975
Citroen 2CV 1948-1982
Cobras & Replicas 1962-1983
Cortina 1600E & GT 1967-1970
Corvair 1959-1968
Daimler Dart & V-8 250 1959-1969
Datsun 240Z 1970-1973
Datsun 280Z & ZX 1975-1983
De Tomaso Collection No. 1
Dodge Charger 1966-1974
Excalibur Collection No. 1
Ferrari Cars 1946-1956
Ferrari Dino 1965-1974
Ferrari Dino 308 1974-1979
Ferrari 308 & Mondial 1980-1984
Ferrari Collection No. 1
Fiat-Bertone X1/9 1973-1988
Fiat Pininfarina 124+2000 Spider 1968-1985
Ford Automobiles 1944-1959
Ford Fairlane 1955-1970
Ford Falcon 1960-1970
Ford RS Escort 1968-1980
Honda CRX 1983-1987
High Performance Escorts MkI 1968-1974
High Performance Escorts MkII 1975-1980
High Performance Mustangs 1982-1988
Hudson & Railton Cars 1936-1940
Jaguar Cars 1957-1961
Jaguar Cars 1961-1964
Jaguar XK120 XK140 XK150 Gold Portfolio 1948-1960
Jaguar MK2 1959-1969
Jaguar E-Type Gold Portfolio 1961-1971
Jaguar E-Type 1966-1971
Jaguar E-Type V12 1971-1975
Jaguar XJ6 1968-1972
Jaguar XJ6 Series II 1973-1979
Jaguar XJ6 & XJ12 Series III 1979-1985
Jaguar XJ12 1972-1980
Jaguar XJS Gold Portfolio 1975-1988
Jensen Cars 1946-1967
Jensen Cars 1967-1979
Jensen Interceptor Gold Portfolio 1966-1986
Jensen Healey 1972-1976
Lamborghini Cars 1964-1970
Lamborghini Cars 1970-1975
Lamborghini Countach Collection No. 1
Lamborghini Countach & Urraco 1974-1980
Lamborghini Countach & Jalpa 1980-1985
Lancia Stratos 1972-1985
Land Rover 1948-1973
Land Rover Series II & IIa 1958-1971
Land Rover Series III 1971-1985
Land Rover 90 & 110 1983-1989
Land Rover 90 & 110 1983-1989
Lotus Cortina 1963-1970
Lotur Elan Gold Portfolio 1962-1974
Lotus Elan Collection No. 2
Lotus Elite 1957-1964
Lotus Elite & Eclat 1974-1981
Lotus Turbo Esprit 1980-1986
Lotus Europa 1966-1975
Lotus Europa Collection No. 1
Lotus Seven 1957-1980
Lotus Seven Collection No. 1
Marcos Cars 1960-1988
Maserati 1965-1970
Maserati 1970-1975
Marcos Cars 1960-1988
Mazda RX-7 Collection No. 1
Mercedes 190 & 300SL 1954-1963
Mercedes 230/250/280SL 1963-1971
Mercedes 350/450SL & SLC 1971-1980
Mercedes Benz Cars 1949-1954
Mercedes Benz Cars 1954-1957
Mercedes Benz Cars 1957-1961
Mercedes Benz Competition Cars 1950-1957
Metropolitan 1954-1962
MG TC 1945-1949

MG TD 1949-1953
MG TF 1953-1955
MG Cars 1957-1959
MG Cars 1959-1962
MG Cars 1959-1962
MG Midget 1961-1980
MGA Collection No. 1
MGA Roadsters 1955-1962
MGB Roadsters 1962-1980
MGB GT 1965-1980
Mini Cooper 1961-1971
Morgan Cars 1960-1970
The Morgan 3-Weeler Gold Portfolio 1910-1952
Morgan Cars Gold Portfolio 1968-1989
Morris Minor Collection No. 1
Olosmobile Automobiles 1955-1963
Old's Cutlass & 4-4-2 1964-1972
Oldsmobile Toronado 1966-1978
Opel GT 1968-1973
Packard Gold Portfolio 1946-1958
Pantera 1970-1973
Pantera & Mangusta 1969-1974
Plymouth Barracuda 1964-1974
Pontiac Fiero 1984-1988
Pontiac GTO 1964-1970
Pontiac Firebird 1967-1973
Pontiac Firebird and Trans-Am 1973-1981
High Performance Firebirds 1982-1988
Pontiac Tempest & GTO 1961-1965
Porsche Cars 1960-1964
Porsche Cars 1964-1968
Porsche Cars 1968-1972
Porsche Cars in the Sixties
Porsche Cars 1972-1975
Porsche 356 1952-1965
Porsche 911 1965-1969
Porsche 911 1970-1972
Porsche 911 1973-1977
Porsche 911 Carrera 1973-1977
Porsche 911 SC 1978-1983
Porsche 911 Turbo 1975-1984
Porsche 914 Gold Portfolio 1969-1976
Porsche 914 Collection No. 1
Porsche 924 Gold Portfolio 1975-1988
Porsche 928 1977-1989
Porsche 944 1981-1985
Reliant Scimitar 1964-1986
Riley 1½ & 2½ Litre Gold Portfolio 1945-1955
Rolls Royce Silver Cloud 1955-1965
Rolls Royce Silver Shadow 1965-1980
Range Rover Gold Portfolio 1970-1988
Rover 3 & 3.5 Litre 1958-1973
Rover P4 1949-1959
Rover P4 1955-1964
Rover 2000 + 2200 1963-1977
Rover 3500 1968-1977
Rover 3500 & Vitesse 1976-1986
Saab Sonett Collection No. 1
Saab Turbo 1976-1983
Studebaker Hawks & Larks 1956-1963
Sunbeam Tiger and Alpine Gold Portfolio 1959-1967
Thunderbird 1955-1957
Thunderbird 1958-1963
Thunderbird 1964-1976
Toyota MR2 1984-1988
Triumph 2000-2.5-2500 1963-1977
Triumph Spitfire 1962-1980
Triumph Spitfire Collection No. 1
Triumph Stag 1970-1980
Triumph Stag Collection No. 1
Triumph TR2 & TR3 1952-1960
Triumph TR4.TR5.TR250 1961-1968
Triumph TR6 1969-1976
Triumph TR6 Collection No. 1
Triumph TR7 & TR8 1975-1982
Triumph GT6 1966-1974
Triumph Vitesse & Herald 1959-1971
TVR Gold Portfolio 1959-1988
Volkswagen Cars 1936-1956
VW Beetle 1956-1977
VW Beetle Collection No. 1
VW Golf GTi 1976-1986
VW Karmann Ghia 1955-1982
VW Scirocco 1974-1981
VW Bus-Camper-Van 1954-1967
VW Bus-Camper-Van 1968-1979
VW Bus-Camper-Van 1979-1989
Volvo 1800 1960-1973
Volvo 120 Series 1956-1970

## BROOKLANDS MUSCLE CARS SERIES
American Motors Muscle Cars 1966-1970
Buick Muscle Cars 1965-1970
Camaro Muscle Cars 1966-1972
Capri Muscle Cars 1969-1983
Chevrolet Muscle Cars 1966-1972
Dodge Muscle Cars 1967-1970
Mercury Muscle Cars 1966-1971
Mini Muscle Cars 1961-1979
Mopar Muscle Cars 1964-1967
Mopar Muscle Cars 1968-1971
Mustang Muscle Cars 1967-1971
Shelby Mustang Muscle Cars 1965-1970
Oldsmobile Muscle Cars 1964-1970
Plymouth Muscle Cars 1966-1971
Pontiac Muscle Cars 1966-1972
Muscle Cars Compared Book 2 1965-1971

## BROOKLANDS ROAD & TRACK SERIES
Road & Track on Alfa Romeo 1949-1963
Road & Track on Alfa Romeo 1964-1970
Road & Track on Alfa Romeo 1971-1976
Road & Track on Alfa Romeo 1977-1989
Road & Track on Aston Martin 1962-1984
Road & Track on Auburn Cord & Duesenberg 1952-1984
Road & Track on Audi 1952-1980
Road & Track on Audi 1980-1986
Road & Track on Austin Healey 1953-1970

Road & Track on BMW Cars 1966-1974
Road & Track on BMW Cars 1975-1978
Road & Track on BMW Cars 1979-1983
Road & Track on Cobra, Shelby &
Ford GT40 1962-1983
Road & Track on Corvette 1953-1967
Road & Track on Corvette 1968-1982
Road & Track on Corvette 1982-1986
Road & Track on Datsun Z 1970-1983
Road & Track on Ferrari 1950-1968
Road & Track on Ferrari 1968-1974
Road & Track on Ferrari 1975-1981
Road & Track on Ferrari 1981-1984
Road & Track on Fiat Sports Cars 1968-1987
Road & Track on Jaguar 1950-1960
Road & Track on Jaguar 1961-1968
Road & Track on Jaguar 1968-1974
Road & Track on Jaguar 1974-1982
Road & Track on Jaguar 1983-1989
Road & Track on Lamborghini 1964-1985
Road & Track on Lotus 1972-1981
Road & Track on Maserati 1952-1974
Road & Track on Maserati 1975-1983
Road & Track on Mazda RX7 1978-1986
Road & Track on Mercedes 1952-1962
Road & Track on Mercedes 1963-1970
Road & Track on Mercedes 1971-1979
Road & Track on Mercedes 1980-1987
Road & Track on MG Sports Cars 1949-1961
Road & Track on MG Sports Cars 1967-1980
Road & Track on Mustang 1964-1977
Road & Track on Peugeot 1955-1986
Road & Track on Pontiac 1960-1983
Road & Track on Porsche 1951-1967
Road & Track on Porsche 1968-1971
Road & Track on Porsche 1972-1975
Road & Track on Porsche 1975-1978
Road & Track on Porsche 1979-1982
Road & Track on Porsche 1982-1985
Road & Track on Porsche 1985-1988
Road & Track on Rolls Royce & Bentley 1950-1965
Road & Track on Rolls Royce & Bentley 1966-1984
Road & Track on Saab 1955-1985
Road & Track on Toyota Sports & G T Cars 1966-1986
Road & Track on Triumph Sports Cars 1953-1967
Road & Track on Triumph Sports Cars 1967-1974
Road & Track on Triumph Sports Cars 1974-1982
Road & Track on Volkswagen 1951-1968
Road & Track on Volkswagen 1968-1978
Road & Track on Volkswagen 1978-1985
Road & Track on Volvo 1957-1974
Road & Track on Volvo 1975-1985
Road & Track Henry Manney at Large & Abroad

## BROOKLANDS CAR AND DRIVER SERIES
Car and Driver on BMW 1955-1977
Car and Driver on BMW 1977-1985
Car and Driver on Cobra, Shelby & Ford GT40
1963-1984
Car and Driver on Datsun Z 1600 & 2000
1966-1984
Car and Driver on Corvette 1956-1967
Car and Driver on Corvette 1968-1977
Car and Driver on Corvette 1978-1982
Car and Driver on Corvette 1983-1988
Car and Driver on Ferrari 1955-1962
Car and Driver on Ferrari 1963-1975
Car and Driver on Ferrari 1976-1983
Car and Driver on Mopar 1956-1967
Car and Driver on Mopar 1968-1975
Car and Driver on Mustang 1964-1972
Car and Driver on Pontiac 1961-1975
Car and Driver on Porsche 1955-1962
Car and Driver on Porsche 1963-1970
Car and Driver on Porsche 1970-1976
Car and Driver on Porsche 1977-1981
Car and Driver on Porsche 1982-1986
Car and Driver on Saab 1956-1985
Car and Driver on Volvo 1955-1986

## BROOKLANDS MOTOR & THOROUGHBRED & CLASSIC CAR SERIES
Motor & T & CC on Ferrari 1966-1976
Motor & T & CC on Ferrari 1976-1984
Motor & T & CC on Lotus 1979-1983

## BROOKLANDS PRACTICAL CLASSICS SERIES
Practical Classics on Austin A 40 Restoration
Practical Classics on Land Rover Restoration
Practical Classics on Metalworking in Restoration
Practical Classics on Midget/Sprite Restoration
Practical Classics on Mini Cooper Restoration
Practical Classics on MGB Restoration
Practical Classics on Morris Minor Restoration
Practical Classics on Triumph Herald/Vitesse
Practical Classics on Triumph Spitfire Restoration
Practical Classics on VW Beetle Restoration
Practical Classics on 1930S Car Restoration

## BROOKLANDS MILITARY VEHICLES SERIES
Allied Military Vehicles Collection No. 1
Allied Military Vehicles Collection No. 2
Dodge Military Vehicles Collection No. 1
Military Jeeps 1941-1945
Off Road Jeeps 1944-1971
V W Kubelwagen 1940-1975

## CONTENTS

**BROOKLANDS BOOKS**

## ACKNOWLEDGEMENTS

We are pleased to have Riley represented in our list once again. This Gold Portfolio replaces two earlier titles on the RM models which unfortunately went out-of-print some years ago.

Dr James Taylor a knowledgable enthusiast on RMs and a keen supporter of our series kindly volunteered to write a short introduction which will be found below. He has recently written for Motor Racing Publications 'The RM Rileys 1945-1957. 1½ Litre, 2½ Litre, and Pathfinder' which we highly recommend, as a companion to this book.

We are also indebted to the publishers of Auto Age, Autocar, Classic Car, Classic and Sportscar, Light Car, Motor, Motor Manual, Motor Sport, Practical Classics, Road & Track, Special Interest Autos, Sports Car World and Thoroughbred & Classic Cars for once again allowing us to include their road tests and other copyright stories in our reference series. Our thanks go also to David Brownell, Editor of Special Interest Autos who came to our aid at short notice with the attractive photograph for our front cover.

R.M. Clarke

It is difficult now to imagine the situation in 1945, when any new car was a major event for a car-hungry public, but the tenor of the motoring press' reports on the new 1½-litre Riley announced that autumn made clear that this car was something really special. Its elegant styling did not offend purists by breaking with tradition; its performance lived up to that expected of the Riley name; but above all, its combination of sports-car handling with saloon-car ride comfort put it into a class quite different from most of its contemporaries.

Series production got under way early in 1946, and the new saloon was complemented later that year by a 2½-litre engined model on a longer wheelbase, which immediately became one of the hottest properties around in the British motoring world. Yet despite this success, Riley could not afford to rest on their laurels. Like other manufacturers, they were under pressure to build cars for export and so to earn Britain much-needed foreign currency to help rebuild the War-shattered economy. So 1948 saw the arrival of the first left-hand-drive Rileys and of a three-seater Roadster model with the 2½-litre engine. Sadly, though, the Roadster failed badly in the North American market for which it had been conceived, and manufacture was stopped only two years after it had begun.

A similar fate befell the stylish drophead model on the 2½-litre chassis, which was introduced later in 1948 but never sold in large quantities. The need to husband resources carefully in order to remain competitive in overseas markets led to its early disappearance and, by the middle of 1951, the Riley range was reduced once more to the two saloons which had been in production from 1946-1947.

Export sales, however, were about to collapse; and the Riley's traditional styling was making it more and more of an anachronism even at home. From the autumn of 1953, the 2½-litre was replaced by the new Pathfinder model, and the 1½-litre was facelifted, to continue in its revised form until the beginning of 1955. In all, 22,913 of three Rileys were made.

Latterly known as the "RM" Rileys, after the model-code allocated to them by the British Motor Corporation of which Riley became a part in 1952, these cars very quickly attained what is now called "classic" status. A club was formed for their maintenance and preservation in 1969 — several years before the classic-car movement in Britain had really gathered momentum — and that club remains one of the very best classic-car clubs.

James Taylor

The characteristic Riley radiator is retained, but the head lamps are built into the inner wing valances to reduce wind resistance and simplify cleaning.

## SPECIFICATION

**Engine.**—12 h.p., four cylinders, 69×100 mm. (1,496 c.c.). Overhead valves at 90 degrees in hemispherical combustion chambers. Three-bearing crankshaft. Aluminium alloy pistons. S.U. carburettor Lucas coil ignition. Mechanical fuel pump. Full-flow oil filter. Cross-flow pump cooling.

**Transmission.**—Borg and Beck clutch. Four-speed gear box Synchromesh on second, third and top. Overall ratios: First 19.8, second 11.2, third 7.2, top 4.88 to 1 Enclosed propeller-shaft to spiral bevel rear axle.

**Brakes.**—Girling Hydro-mechanical in 10in. drums.

**Suspension.**—Independent front and half-elliptic rear springs.

**Steering.**—Special Riley, with 17in. adjustable steering wheel.

**Fuel Tank Capacity.**—12½ gallons.

**Leading Dimensions.**—Wheelbase 9ft. 4½in. Track 4ft. 3in. Overall length 14ft. 10in., width 5ft. 2½in., height 4ft. 9in. Ground clearance 7in.

**Tyres.**—Dunlop 5.75×16 on wide-base rims. Disc wheels.

**Weight.**—24½ cwt.

# THE BEST RILEY YET

## New 1½-litre Saloon Exhibits Remarkable Characteristics on the Road

AS most keen drivers well know, and all Riley enthusiasts are firmly convinced, the history of motoring has been enriched by many a good Riley model. These cars have always had a character of their own, upon which a definite tradition has become founded. The design has been original, and essentially progressive. The cars have always had potentialities well beyond the average of the day, and features different from the usual and especially attractive.

Witness, for example, the original Riley Nine Monaco saloon. It was the first small car which held the road like a large one; the first small car to give ample room for four people with luggage under cover in a compact and yet comfortable saloon body; the first to have a four-speed gear box with a really quiet and useful third speed, and the

only car of its time sold with an engine so well designed that although it was *par excellence* a normal car engine it was also ready to be tuned for racing purposes, and did, indeed, distinguish itself in the racing field. This was because the crankshaft was sturdy, the valve gear light, the overhead valves were inclined in a hemispherical head, and the valve ports free, and, in common with the inlet manifold, machined to smooth regular surfaces.

The Nine was the first of a remarkable series of cars. Space precludes the Riley history up to date, but many other fine models, including the pre-war 1½-litre and the Sixteen-Four, will jump to the memory. These cars had complete individuality of design. Future cars will maintain that individuality, and the first of them to be announced, the post-war 1½-litre, has an even more strikingly individual character than any previous Riley model.

No doubt the reader will have already studied the illustrations, so there is scarcely need to tell him that the appearance of the car, long, broad, and yet low, is most attractive. What may be concealed within this graceful exterior will most engender curiosity. Riley recipes

A more graceful tail than that of the new Riley is difficult to imagine. From the practical viewpoint it has the merit of providing a luggage boot of considerable capacity.

Although compact and low built, the entirely new post-war 1½-litre Riley saloon provides plenty of room for five people and amp[le]
attraction of looking graceful from any angle, as seen in other views on the preceding pag[e]

are simplicity, in conjunction with making the best possible use of what experience has already proved to be good; plenty of power and not too much weight; concentration upon those features of rigidity, weight distribution, suspension and steering which can so vitally affect the "feel" and the absolute safety of the car on the road.

Except for the engine, which is the well-known and welltried 1½-litre, the car is a new production. There are a great many details of special interest in the construction, but it is desired by the makers to withhold them until such time as cars are actually coming off the production line, which should be towards the end of September. *The Autocar* has been offered the somewhat unusual course of trying out the car on the road first, and presenting impressions of its behaviour some time in advance of describing its mechanical construction.

On all counts the performance is truly remarkable. By some means best known to themselves the Riley "backroom" boys have achieved a suspension combining a really comfortable "level" ride, with a sureness of road holding which is quite outstanding.

### Superb Roadholding in Comfort

The way this car can be taken round curves is astonishing. Not many racing cars would do better. It can be "placed" to an inch to negotiate a curve at high speed, and it proceeds with a certainty that suggests running on rails which have been banked. There is no skidding, tail wagging, outward roll, or sawing at the steering wheel. What is so surprising is that this road holding has been achieved in conjunction with a suspension which is not in the least hard, but is in fact well above the average for comfort. One estimates that this car can quite safely be taken round a sharp curve at a speed 20 per cent. faster than the average good driver would essay on a normally good car. Lest this appreciation of a supremely good cornering ability should in any way be misunderstood it is necessary to explain that a car which can be cornered exceedingly fast without risk is incomparably more safe at customary speeds than one which is verging on the uncontrollable at customary speeds. Moreover the good cornering car can be relied upon to help out the staid driver in an emergency from causes outside his control.

Some further remarks about this suspension are called for. It is of the type which deals faithfully with bad sur-

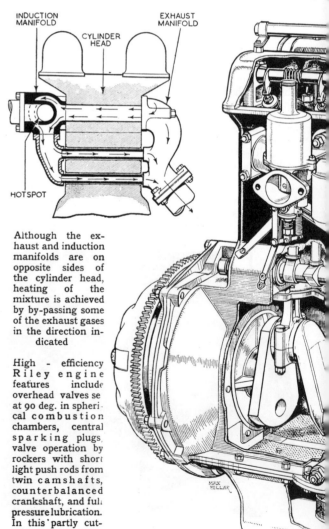

Although the exhaust and induction manifolds are on opposite sides of the cylinder head, heating of the mixture is achieved by by-passing some of the exhaust gases in the direction indicated

High - efficiency Riley engine features include overhead valves se[t] at 90 deg. in spherical combustion chambers, central sparking plugs, valve operation by rockers with short light push rods from twin camshafts, counterbalanced crankshaft, and full pressure lubrication. In this partly cutaway view colour is used to emphasise moving parts

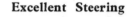

faces as well as good ones. As an example the car can be driven quite comfortably with the near-side wheels on the grass verge of a country road. Another point is that the riding is pretty well as good in the rear seats as it is in the front; it is quite possible to write legibly on a paper resting on one's knee while the car is cruising at 50 m.p.h.

To give a more definite impression of the feelings of the driver when handling this new Riley for the first time: The engine is mounted on rubber so effectively that it is as smooth running as anyone would wish, from the highest r.p.m.—somewhere about 4,500—down to a low-speed crawl on top gear. The maximum speed, by the way, we should estimate at about 80 m.p.h., lacking the opportunity to test it against the stop-watch. The engine is also flexible, and has plenty of power at low r.p.m., hence there is no need to perform a lot of gear changing in normal

driving. As applies to all Rileys, but more so than to the best ones of the past, this is a dual-purpose car. Either one can drive it peaceably and comfortably, and make a good average speed without effort, or one can take advantage of the latent possibilities afforded by its good power-to-weight ratio, use the gear box to advantage, and make play with the road holding and cornering ability, and so put up an average speed over a long run which is quite surprisingly high. The $1\frac{1}{2}$-litre is a fine engine, and will stand up to hard driving.

When a fresh driver takes over control of the car his impressions are these: First that the driving position is "typically Riley"; one sits up rather than lolls back, and the adjustable steering wheel tucks nicely in. Then the tapering bonnet and fairly narrow radiator afford excellent visibility. Carried on a tunnel, the gear lever is short, and close to the left hand. There is no need to use first gear to start. One eases in the clutch and gives a touch on the accelerator, and the car moves sweetly away. As there is synchromesh on second, third, and top, gear changing is perfectly easy—it asks for no skill, but only for deliberate movement. In a short distance one is in top gear, cruising quietly along and ready to take notice.

## Excellent Steering

At first, to one coming off a faithful pre-war car, the steering feels a shade stiff, or perhaps firm. It is a special form of steering gear, is quick in response, and has next to no backlash. Within a mile you have acquired the feel of it, and in five miles you think it is a superb sort of steering; which indeed it is. We gather that it can be set lighter if desired, but the firmness is there purposely in order to damp sudden movements on the part of the driver. There is no kick-back from the front wheels. The car follows the steering with complete accuracy, and immediately. As a result it can be steered with a notable exactness. If you decide to go round a curve one foot from the verge, the car obeys exactly, without two bites at the cherry, so to speak. It is the same at all speeds which you care to attempt, and one that has to be tried to be fully appreciated.

Before going far one naturally tries out the brakes.

ggage space. The car has the

The engine and four-speed gear box unit from the near side. Engine design has not been materially altered; 54 b.h.p. is developed. The gear box has synchromesh on second, third and top

These also are something special, the Girling hydro-mechanical. They are a revelation in braking. The pedal requires scarcely more pressure than is normally applied to an accelerator. At the very instant you touch the pedal you feel that the brakes begin to take hold. There is no lost motion, and the quickness with which you slow down the car is exactly proportional to the pressure you put on the pedal. The braking is exceptionally smooth, and as powerful as you like to make it, and one more asset to this quite remarkable car.

It might perhaps be thought that, denied as one has been for so long the experience of freely trying out a new car, there may be a tendency to be over-enthusiastic, but we feel that a similar verdict will come from every other experienced driver who handles this car in the future. Some characteristics have been built into the new Riley that have not been evident before.

As regards the ability to climb hills, the car was tried on the old Cotswold favourites, Willersey, Saintbury, and Fish. So long is it since we used them that the curves and corners have become unfamiliar. With this car it seems that it is no longer a question of how easily or otherwise the hills can be climbed, but of how fast the driver feels inclined to take them. Fish can be a top gear climb, or very fast with the use of third. Third is good enough for the steepest part of Willersey.

There is ample room for three people in the rear seat of the new Riley and deep wells provide plenty of leg room. The interior trimming is notably neat. Experience shows that the "ride" in the rear seats is as comfortable as in front. Left : The instruments and minor controls are neatly arranged in a central panel. Steering wheel "reach" is adjustable by the telescopic steering column.

Some description of the saloon coachwork, which later will be followed by a drop-head coupé, will be of interest. The body is set low on the chassis, but it has plenty of head room. The seats also are low and wide, and considerable leg room is given to the rear seat, which will take three people in comfort, by the use of fairly deep footwells. This body follows customary Riley practice in having wide doors, with four lights, and the rear doors extend to the depth of the rear seat cushion. The front seats are of the adjustable chair type. The interior trim is in excellent style and of simple good taste. At the front is a V windscreen, and the section in front of the driver is arranged to open with a winding handle. The roof is fabric covered on a perforated metal panelling, so as to save weight and avoid drumming.

The 1½-litre engine has not been altered in any material points. The construction is essentially rigid, the four cylinders being formed in one casting integral with the greater part of the crankcase, forming a solid support for a massive counterbalanced crankshaft carried in three main bearings. At the front is an enclosed distribution gear which drives a pair of camshafts, one on each side of the cylinder block. The valves are operated through overhead rockers and light short push rods. The valve ports have a through flow, on the one side to the exhaust and on the other to an inlet manifold having an S.U. carburettor.

The connecting rods are steel forgings of H section, and the pistons are of aluminium alloy with four rings. Particular care has been devoted to the lubrication system. A pump of high capacity draws oil from the crankcase and passes it under pressure through a large filter, whence it passes to the crankshaft, big-end, and camshaft bearings and to the rocker gear and timing. The cooling system also is interesting. A water pump actuated in conjunction with a fan by a triangular belt drive delivers cool water to the cylinder head, where there is a cross flow from the exhaust to the inlet side, ensuring that the regions of greatest heat receive adequate cooling. Circulation is arranged to be greater in the cylinder head than in the block.

Later there will be a 16 h.p. four-cylinder Riley engine, of 80.5 × 120 mm. (2,443 c.c.). This will be put into a car similar to the 1½-litre, and should give a phenomenal performance.                                    M. T.

# A CAR FOR THE DISCRIMINATING

## A New 1½-Litre Riley

### Independent Front Suspension, new Girling brakes, new steering, fast and with excellent acceleration, having spacious coachwork with abnormal luggage accommodation

THE new 1½-litre Riley saloon, preliminary details of which are now released, is quite the most interesting post-war car announced so far. It is definitely one that will appeal to the discriminating motorist, especially to those who cover long distances and use a car for week-end touring and appreciate the importance of generous accommodation for both passengers and luggage. It falls into that class of high-performance cars with which the Riley Company has been associated since the days of the famous Nine.

At the moment it is permissible only to give a general outline of its features and some impression, after a long afternoon's run, of its very pleasant behaviour on the road.

Just how much deviation from previous practice is needed to justify that adjective " new " may be a debatable point, but the word is warranted in this case for several reasons. First, and most obvious, as the accompanying pictures show, the body is unlike any previous Riley model. Secondly, the chassis frame is not the same as before. Thirdly, there is independent front suspension—a feature not found in any previous production Riley. And, perhaps most important of all, the whole " feel " and behaviour of this car mark it as quite distinct from all its predecessors.

### "Special Series" Performance

In addition to all that, there are changes in such important components as the brakes and the wheels. Even though the engine is the 'well-tried Riley with inclined overhead valves, it has detail modifications sufficiently potent to provide the old " Special Series " performance with only a single carburetter, and in the transmission (which retains the familiar Riley enclosed propeller shaft) as well as in the rear suspension there are minor changes.

Built low without going to extremes —the overall height is 4 ft. 9 ins. and there is 7 ins. ground clearance—with

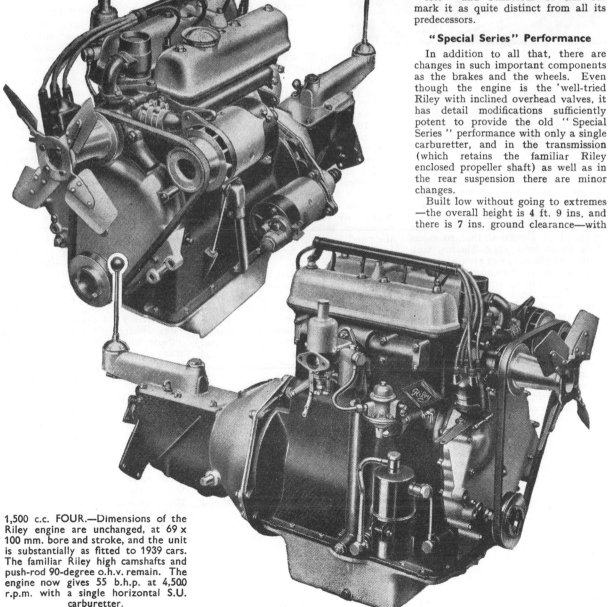

1,500 c.c. FOUR.—Dimensions of the Riley engine are unchanged, at 69 x 100 mm. bore and stroke, and the unit is substantially as fitted to 1939 cars. The familiar Riley high camshafts and push-rod 90-degree o.h.v. remain. The engine now gives 55 b.h.p. at 4,500 r.p.m. with a single horizontal S.U. carburetter.

9

DIGNITY. — The body lines of the post-war Riley blend well with the slope of a traditional Riley radiator. The vee-screen may be noted, and the new disc wheels with spring-on centre plates, of Riley design and manufacture, are quite in keeping.

CAPACIOUS TAIL.— Despite a 12½-gallon tank the tail includes a luggage compartment holding two large suit cases, plus a few small ones and golf clubs, and also has a tray for the spare wheel. This view also shows dual petrol tank fillers.

a nicely curved boot and a fixed fabric head, this Riley has attractive lines to which photographs barely do justice. Its doors, hinged on the centre pillars, are wide and expose practically the whole depth of each seat, so that entry (sometimes awkward in a low car) presents no difficulty

### Commendable Luggage Space

Body width is generous and there is ample room for three on the rear seat. In the tail is luggage accommodation of deceptive spaciousness, with a separate compartment below for the spare wheel. Despite all that, room has been found for a 12½-gallon fuel tank with dual fillers, one in each wing.

This body is of composite construction. The panels, at present of steel, are pressed (not beaten), and are carried by a timber framework.

At the front is the familiar Riley radiator shell with only such minor changes as are needed to blend with the bonnet and body lines. The well-sloped windscreen is of a shallow Vee form with dual wipers, and the driver's panel is openable. On the prototype car, the front wings are in one piece with the running boards (as shown in our illustrations), but in production these parts will be separated for ease of replacement in case of accident, although precisely the same shape will be retained.

Built largely of box sections, the chassis frame evidently is a stiff one. At the front it carries the transverse wishbones of the independent suspension system, which employs torsion-bar springs.

As to the general size of the car, its wheelbase measures 9 ft. 4½ ins. with an overall length of 14 ft. 10 ins. A somewhat unusual feature nowadays is

that the front and rear track dimensions are identical, the figure being 4 ft. 3 ins. The overall width is 5 ft. 2½ ins.

Wide-base rims are used to carry the 5.75-16 tyres, and it is interesting to find that the disc wheels with large spring-on centre covers are of Riley manufacture. The brakes, in 10-in. drums, are Girlings of the new hydro-mechanical type, in which the front shoes are operated hydraulically from the pedal and the rear shoes are connected by the well-known Girling mechanical linkage to the pedal and to the hand control, which, incidentally, is of the pistol-grip type and is located just below the facia.

A large spring-spoked steering wheel is mounted on a telescopic column adjustable for length. At the lower end there is a departure from usual British practice in the use of a pinion and tooth rack to transmit the motion of the steering wheel to the road wheels, somewhat in the manner found so satisfactory by certain Continental makers.

### Increased Power Output

As a result of development, some 55 b.h.p. is now generated at 4,500 r.p.m. by the 1,496 c.c. four-cylinder engine, which in all major features is identical with the pre-war Riley engine of this size. This very creditable output is given with a compression ratio of only 6.5 to 1 and with a single horizontal S.U. carburetter. The bore and stroke dimensions are unchanged at 69 mm. by 100 mm., and the valves are still inclined at an included angle of 90 degrees, operation being by push-rods from two separate camshafts, one on each side of the cylinders, and now driven by chain.

In unit with the engine, of course, is a Borg and Beck clutch and a synchromesh four-speed gearbox with a short, stubby "remote control" lever. The overall ratios are 4.88, 7.2, 11.2 and 19.4 to 1 forward, with a reverse of the same ratio as bottom gear.

### The Steering

On the road, our first experience was as a front-seat passenger with that able driver, Victor Leverett, at the wheel. Inclined though one might pardonably have been to attribute part of the performance to his skill and his being accustomed to the car, it was, nevertheless, obvious that the vehicle itself was something out of the ordinary—and this was confirmed later when we occupied the driver's seat. Most prominent amongst the characteristics which impressed us was the fine combination of highly accurate steering with unusually comfortable suspension on all types of road surface, and a stolid refusal to heel over in the fastest cornering.

To put these things first must not be taken as suggesting that the speed, acceleration, braking, etc., were merely normal. Far from it. Each of those qualities, too, is praiseworthy and the whole combination makes a car that undoubtedly will appeal to the enthusiast.

Inevitably, of course, there is something which might be improved. From outside, this Riley certainly is not a noisy car, but the general level of murmurous sound inside it did seem to us to be rather high by the present criterion.

The new Riley steering is out of the ordinary in more ways than one. Perhaps its great accuracy is due in part to the fact that there is virtually no back lash or lost motion at all. Anyway, for once there was excuse for the passenger who murmured the cliché about running on rails. Yet, despite this precision, there is very little castor effect, at any rate so far as the feel of the wheel indicates.

There is a popular school which holds that a steering wheel should whizz back to the straight-ahead position if it is released when coming out of a bend. This is not the time for an argument on such matters, but perhaps it may be

CONTINUED ON PAGE 51

10

# "Secret" of the Riley Twelve

## Remarkable Road Holding and Accurate Steering Obtained by Studiously Designing for Rigidity

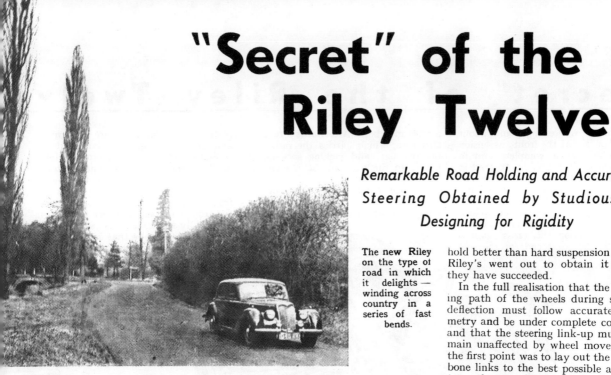

The new Riley on the type of road in which it delights — winding across country in a series of fast bends.

SOME months ago when the post-war Riley Twelve was first announced (*The Autocar*, August 24, 1945), no details were divulged concerning the construction of the chassis and the suspension. It was then stated, with good reason, as many who have since tried the car will confirm, that this new Riley held the road, was steady on corners and bends and combined stability with comfortable riding in a quite remarkable manner. The time has now arrived when the "secret" of the design can be disclosed. It is the result of a close study of rigidity and a profound attention to mechanical details. The

ultimately excellent results were not obtained in a single bound, but in a series of exploratory steps.

At the outset the design staff considered, as many experienced car users will agree, that although independent suspension of front wheels should by every theoretical sign and portent offer a considerable advance over the orthodox beam axle and half-elliptics, few independent suspension systems so far have succeeded in realising the possibilities to the full extent.

### Torsion Bar I.f.s.

So careful research was made into various systems, and one which was considered to have travelled farthest along the road to perfection was chosen for further development. It was the lateral wishbone type used in conjunction with torsion bar springs

In the earlier days of fast motoring it had become a tradition that a car would not hold the road and steer properly at high speeds unless it had hard springs with small deflection, checked by plenty of shock absorber action Modern ideas, however, are showing that this sort of suspension is not the best answer to the problem. It has become evident that flexible, comfortable, even riding suspension can be combined with a road

hold better than hard suspension gave. Riley's went out to obtain it; and they have succeeded.

In the full realisation that the floating path of the wheels during spring deflection must follow accurate geometry and be under complete control, and that the steering link-up must remain unaffected by wheel movement, the first point was to lay out the wishbone links to the best possible advantage; the second was to make the links as rigid as possible in themselves; the third to provide them with as wide a fulcrum base as possible, so that there was minimum fore and aft "give."

### The Vital Strut

The next point, perhaps the most important of all, was to provide a strut between the links on each side which was stout enough to ensure that everything remained in correct alignment. Lastly, this strut was to attach the suspension unit firmly to a really stout frame, so that the rear wheels kept relative position with the front under all conditions.

In the illustrations not only will the general disposition of the suspension system and frame be seen, but also the manner in which the points just outlined have been covered.

### 1½-LITRE RILEY SPECIFICATION

**Engine.**—12 h.p., four cylinders, 69 × 100 mm. (1,496 c.c.). Overhead valves at 90 degrees in hemispherical combustion chambers. 55 b.h.p. at 4,500 r.p.m. Three-bearing crankshaft. Aluminium alloy pistons. S.U. carburettor. Lucas coil ignition. Mechanical fuel pump. Full-flow oil filter. Cross-flow pump cooling.

**Transmission.**—Borg and Beck clutch. Four-speed gear box. Synchromesh on second, third and top. Overall ratios: First 19.4, second 11.2, third 7.2, top 4.88 to 1. Enclosed propeller-shaft to spiral bevel rear axle.

**Suspension.**—Torsion bar independent front, and half-elliptic rear springs.

**Brakes.**—Girling Hydromechanical in 10in. drums.

**Steering.**—Special Riley horizontal gear, with 17in. adjustable wheel.

**Fuel Tank Capacity.**—12½ gallons.

**Tyres.**—Dunlop 5.75 × 16in. on widebase rims Disc wheels.

**Weight.**—24½ cwt.

**Main Dimensions.** — Wheelbase 9ft. 4½in. Track 4ft. 3in. Overall length 14ft. 10in. Width 5ft. 2½in. Height 4ft. 9in. Ground clearance 7in.

**Price** (saloon), £555, plus £154 18s. 4d. purchase tax Total £709 18s. 4d.

Riley engines are usually a joy to look at, and the Twelve is no exception. Valves are operated by short push rods from high twin camshafts. Note the accessible oil filler on the near-side valve cover.

# "Secret" of the Riley Twelve

One of the interesting points about the design is that the front suspension is assembled as a complete unit in itself, which afterwards is attached to the front end of the frame. The essence of the unit is the central structure, which consists of a U-shaped cross beam built up of pressed and welded sheet steel into a stout box section. When in position this cross beam is bolted to the front ends of the side members of the frame and so forms a cross-member. Afterwards a further structure, which carries the radiator, bumper bar, and jacking sockets, is bolted to the front of the suspension unit.

The upper extremities or tips of the cross beam are joined together by a large tubular strut, so that a complete rectangular structure is formed and also a straight tubular strut is provided between the fulcrum points of the upper wishbones and a stout box-section strut between the lower wishbones. Box-section extensions from the points of the cross beam form the front wing stays; hence the wings are rigidly supported. A point about the tubular strut is that it is detachable, to facilitate withdrawing the engine forward. The engine unit can be

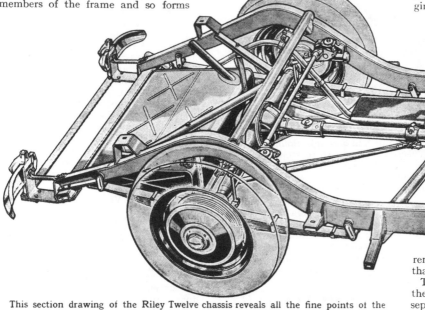

This section drawing of the Riley Twelve chassis reveals all the fine points of the design. Deep box-section side members are employed for the frame, which is braced by tubular cross-members. The propeller-shaft is enclosed in a torque tube, forming part of the rear axle structure. The remote control lever for the synchro-mesh gear box is short and sturdy; there is a telescopically adjustable steering wheel, and independent torsion bar front suspension on the wishbone principle is used. The characteristic Riley radiator is retained.

removed from the complete car in less than three-quarters of an hour.

The next point to observe is that the upper and lower wishbones are separated by considerable vertical distance, the loading on them being thus reduced as far as possible. The wishbones are of a tubular welded steel construction, and it will be observed that the fulcrum points are far apart, so that the base of each triangle is wide and the support given by the wishbones in the fore and aft sense is rigid. Although they are stiff these wishbones are not heavy, for great care has been taken to reduce unsprung weight throughout the design.

The base or fulcrum point of each wishbone is carried in Harris rubber bushes, which give just the degree of cushioning desired and avoid any need for lubrication at a point where carelessness might fail to provide it at regular intervals. The outer ends of the wishbones have bronze bearings in brackets at the top and bottom of the king pins. The king pins themselves turn in bronze bearings and rather an unusual form of thrust is provided. In the upper end of the top bracket a stainless steel sleeve is secured. In this a truncated screw thread is cut

Neat finish and elegant appearance characterise the interior Rear seats are well within the wheelbase. The steering has been removed for the purpose of the photograph, as also have the centrally hinged doors.

and a similar screw thread is cut on the upper end of the king pin. The thrust, therefore, is taken on a large screw-thread surface, and the truncation allows space for lubricant to be packed. A grease-gun nipple at the head of the pin serves these thrusts and the upper and lower king pin swivel bearings, as well as the outer wishbone bearings. So much for the linkage system.

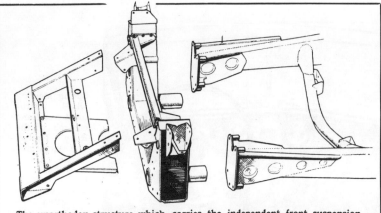

The unorthodox structure which carries the independent front suspension. A stout box-section U-member, suitably braced, forms a unit independent of the frame, to which it is bolted.

and not when it is falling. This particular form of damper has been chosen after considerable experiment. One more point is that this suspension allows the front wheels to turn through a wide arc and so gives an exceptionally small turning circle.

Steering is another highly interesting feature of this car. When the car's road performance was dealt with in *The Autocar* it was remarked that the steering was very definite and accurate, rather quick and at first sight slightly on the stiff side, but that all these features commended themselves as soon as driving experience showed what could be done with the car. The reason for the slight stiffness is the type of king pin thrust on the screw-thread principle, which has just been described. This introduces a slight initial damping effect.

### Unorthodox Steering

Reference to the illustrations will show that the steering is quite unorthodox. A track rod from each steering arm runs to the centre of the cross beam member of the chassis. There each track rod is ball-jointed to a sleeve attached to a horizontal gear slide. This slide has helical teeth cut along it and these are engaged by a helical pinion in the steering gear box to which the column is attached.

As regards the actual spring, the fulcrum of each lower wishbone is formed of a tube with an internal spline, and into the spline is engaged the end of a torsion bar, the rearward end of which is anchored in an adjustable bracket attached to a curved tubular cross-member of the main frame. These torsion bars are pre-set in course of manufacture so that the position of the wishbone linkage during assembly will be correct when the car is laden. It is, however, possible to adjust the setting of the torsion bars, and also they can be removed and the front ends entered into a different position on the splines.

A properly designed torsion bar spring is no more likely to fail than any other spring. Nevertheless, as a safety measure soft rubber snubbers are attached to the lower part of the cross beam in a position to engage a lower wishbone and so prevent a wheel from rising as high as a front wing in the event of spring failure.

Yet another interesting point about this suspension is the type of spring damper used. This is a straight telescopic hydraulic strut which runs dia-

gonally from the point of the lower wishbone to the head of the cross beam on each side. These hydraulic dampers work in one direction only; that is to say, they impose a damping effect only when the wheel is rising,

Mounting details of the Riley independent front suspension. The fulcrum of the lower wishbone is internally splined to take the end of the fore and aft torsion bar, the setting of which is adjustable. A telescopic hydraulic strut running diagonally in the wishbone parallelogram forms the spring damper

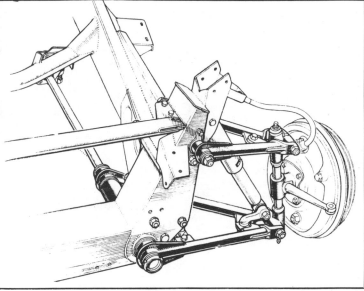

Spring steering wheel, instrument panel and controls of the Riley Twelve. The large and legible speedometer dial will be noticed. A V windscreen is fitted.

The horizontal gear is allowed a limited float opposite the pinion, and is held in close engagement by a spring-loaded plunger. This arrangement, combined with the use of helical gears, reduces backlash to a minimum, and has considerable effect in securing the accuracy of steering which is a notable feature of the car. Another point is that the steering column is the last unit to be assembled into the car, which avoids one of the common difficulties of body mounting. The column is easily dismountable.

The horizontal gear is enclosed at its outer ends in tubes, with adjustable stops, whereas in the centre it is encased in rubber boots to retain lubricant and keep out dirt. The position of the inner ends of the track rods is such as to conform to the geometry of the wishbones, so that rise and fall of the suspension does not affect alignment.

It will be seen that the main frame is of a deep box section, rising over the rear axle. The side members are connected by a series of stout steel tubular cross-members. The whole frame is built on a jig and the cross-members are welded into place. It is so stiff that if one corner of the frame is lifted well up, the doors of the body will still open or close properly.

As the 12 h.p. four-cylinder Riley engine has recently been described at length there is no need to refer to it again, except to say that the engine and four-speed gear box unit, together with dry single-plate clutch, is carried in the frame on flexible rubber mountings. Drive from the gear box is taken through a short open jack shaft to the head of a propeller-shaft enclosed in a torque tube, which forms part of the back axle structure.

The half-elliptic rear springs are underslung, and are considerably longer than have been used in previous Riley designs, and allow for an increased deflection. Front and rear suspension systems are very carefully correlated, which is the reason for the fact that the new car gives as comfortable riding in the back seats as in the front. The rear springs are controlled by Luvax-Girling self-recuperating hydraulic dampers, which are coupled by a torsion bar. The brake equipment is the Girling hydromechanical system, in which the front brakes are hydraulically operated, whilst the rear brakes are mechanically applied.

**Below :** Taking a corner in characteristic Riley style—" almost as if it wasn't there." This picture of the new model in country surroundings, reproduced by a two-colour process of printing, will fill many readers with hope and expectation of better motoring days ahead when the new cars are freely available and the last petrol restrictions have been swept away.

styled on the most modern lines, with a sleek swept-down top and a generally squat, wide, large-car appearance.  At first sight, the impression is that of a car of twice the engine size.

To describe the new model in detail.  The Riley power unit probably needs no introduction.  It is the linear descendant of the engine designed years ago for the first Riley Nine and to this day retains the distinctive basic layout which has proved so successful in competitions, records and on the road.

The engine, flexibly mounted on the frame, is a four-cylinder of 1,496 c.c., with bore and stroke of 69 mm. and 100 mm.  The power output is high—55 b.h.p. at only 4,500 r.p.m., with a moderate compression ratio of 6½ to 1.  As an indication of the unusual " urge "

# A New Riley Twelve

EVER since the news had broken that the Riley concern had a new car on the stocks for the first post-war season, expectancy and surmise have been running high—not only among the many thousands of Riley enthusiasts.  It may be stated right away that expectations will be more than fulfilled.  The new Riley Twelve is a car of distinction, an example of first-class automobile engineering and capable of excellent performance.

Its forerunner of 1939-1940, produced after the reorganization of the factory under the Nuffield banner, but with Mr. Victor Riley at its head, was a car of sound design and excellent performance.  It is not surprising, therefore, that the successor retains many of the outstanding characteristics which have been tried over years of experience in competitions of all types and in the hands of discriminating private owners.  However, the chassis has been completely redesigned around a neat, compact and sturdy independent front suspension system, which sets the keynote of the new car—supple springing, steadiness and sports-car behaviour with town-carriage manners.  The new car is undeniably Riley, but its performance marks a great step forward even over what one was accustomed to from a Riley in the past.  The car is not merely a new Riley; it is a Riley with a difference.

The famous four-cylinder o.h.v. 1½-litre engine is retained almost unchanged, although more power is now obtained.  The makers are

inclined to conservatism in regard to the maximum speed available, but it may be taken that the new Twelve is a good many m.p.h. faster than its predecessor, although it is not so much the maximum speed which impresses as the manner in which the car travels.

### A New Front End

The chassis from behind the engine to the rear is similar to previous Rileys, characterized by rigidity and absence from tail sway.  At the front it is entirely new, coupled with a new steering layout which gives remarkably sensitive but kick-free control.  The new body is

of this engine, the accompanying data panel shows that maximum torque is reached at 3,000 r.p.m. with as high a figure as 76 lb.-ft.  Bearing in mind the total weight of the saloon at 24 cwt., some idea of the possible performance can be gauged.

The clever Riley overhead valve arrangement is of course retained.  There is a camshaft on each side of the engine, carried very high up in the block and operating short push-rods to the rocker gear.  The valves are set at 90 degrees to each other in the head.  The cooling arrangements are particularly ingenious.  The incoming cool water is pumped by two ports direct to the exhaust valves (being the hottest areas).  Behind the valve seatings is a baffle system which diverts about two-

## 1½-LITRE RILEY DATA

| | | 1½-litre | | | 1½-litre |
|---|---|---|---|---|---|
| Present tax | .. .. | £15 per annum | Friction lining area .. | | 126.8 sq. ins. |
| | | | Car wt. per sq. in. (B).. | | 21.2 lb. |
| Cubic capacity .. .. | | 1,496 | Suspension : Front .. | | Independent |
| Cylinders .. .. | | 4 | Rear | | Semi-elliptic |
| Valve position .. .. | | o.h.v. at 90 degrees | Steering gear .. .. | | Riley |
| Bore .. .. .. | | 69 mm. | Steering wheel diameter | | 17 ins. |
| Stroke .. .. .. | | 100 mm. | Wheelbase .. .. | | 9 ft. 4½ ins. |
| Comp. ratio .. .. | | 6.5 | Track, front .. .. | | 4 ft. 4¼ ins. |
| Max. power (A).. .. | | 55 b.h.p. | Track, rear .. .. | | 4 ft. 4¼ ins. |
| at .. .. | | 4,500 r.p.m. | Overall length .. .. | | 14 ft. 11 ins. |
| Max. torque (A) .. | | 76 lb./ft. | Overall width .. .. | | 5 ft. 3½ ins. |
| at .. .. | | 3,000 r.p.m. | Overall height .. .. | | 4 ft. 11 ins. |
| H.P. : Sq. in. piston area (A) | | 2.37 | Ground clearance .. | | 7½ ins. |
| Wt.: Sq. in. piston area (B) | | 116 lb. | Turning circle .. .. | | 30 ft. |
| Ft./Min. Piston speed at | | | Weight—dry .. .. | | 24 cwt. |
| max. h.p. (A).. .. | | 2,950 | Tyre size .. .. | | 5.75 × 16 ins. |
| Carburetter .. .. | | S.U. horiz. H2 | Wheel type .. .. | | Disc |
| Ignition .. .. .. | | Coil | Fuel capacity .. .. | | 12½ gals. |
| Plugs : Make and type | | Champion L10S | Oil capacity .. .. | | 10¾ pints |
| Fuel pump .. .. | | A.C. mech. | Water capacity.. .. | | 13 pints |
| Oil filter (by-pass, full | | | Electrical system .. | | Lucas 12-volt c.v.c. |
| flow) .. .. .. | | Full Flow | Battery capacity .. | | 51/58 amp. hrs. |
| Clutch .. .. .. | | Borg & Beck | | | |
| 1st gear .. .. | | 19.4 | **Top Gear Facts :** | | |
| 2nd gear .. .. | | 11.2 | Engine speed per 10 | | |
| 3rd gear.. .. .. | | 7.22 | m.p.h... .. | | 624 |
| Top gear .. .. | | 4.86 | Piston speed per 10 | | |
| Reverse .. .. | | 19.4 | m.p.h... .. | | 408 |
| Prop. shaft .. .. | | Enclosed | Road speed at 2,500 ft./ | | |
| Final drive .. .. | | Spiral Bevel | min. (piston).. .. | | 61.2 |
| Brakes .. .. .. | | Girling hydro. mech. | Litres per ton-mile .. | | 2,330 |
| Drums .. .. .. | | 10 ins. | | | |

(A) With normal setting of carburetter, etc.  (B) Dry weight.

THE RIGHT HEIGHT.—The centre of gravity on the New Riley Twelve is much below that of the normal car, with consequent advantage in reducing roll on corners. At the same time, head room and floor height have not been cut down to an impracticable level.

thirds of the flow downwards to the cylinder jackets and the remaining one-third flows across the head to the inlet valves. A four-bladed fan looks after the radiator air-flow and is driven by a belt which also drives a high-mounted dynamo on the near side of the block.

Realizing that the smooth, easy-revving engine will be driven for prolonged periods at high speeds by enthusiasts, the designer has paid equal attention to engine lubrication, and oil pumped from the $10\frac{1}{4}$-pint sump is first of all circulated through a full-flow external oil filter, carried low down on the off side of the block, before being pumped to crankshaft, big-end, camshaft and valve-rocker bearings.

An A.C. mechanical pump driven off the "inlet" camshaft draws petrol from a $12\frac{1}{2}$ gallon rear tank (which has filler pipes on both sides) and supplies a horizontal H2 S.U. carburetter.

The distributor is accessibly mounted alongside the water pump with the coil close by on the off side of the engine. The battery is carried under the bonnet.

The outstanding interest in the $1\frac{1}{2}$-litre Riley is the entirely new "Torsionic" front suspension. Torsion bars parallel with the longitudinal axis of the chassis, and well within the frame

CAPACITY.—The rear luggage locker is well constituted for long distance touring, a feature aided by the forward position of the rear seats. Small parcels are carried on a tray beneath the instrument panel.

NEW FEATURE.— These illustrations show the IFS system of the Riley, comprising double wishbones of unequal length, the lower pair connected to longitudinal torsion bars which are splined into rubber insulated mountings on the frame cross tubing, The extreme front of the car is stiffened by fabricated sections as shown in the upper sketch.

width, are carried low down underneath the side members. The rear extremities are held rigidly in special mountings, while the front ends, passing through the base of a massive cradle, are free to twist, thus providing the springing action. The rear ends are adjustable for stiffness of springing and are splined so that turning to a new position restores the full range of adjustment when necessary. The torsion bars, measuring about 2 ft. 6 ins. in length, are pre-stressed on machines to remove the initial elasticity which would otherwise have to be taken up after the first thousand miles on the road.

A robust cradle in front carries the entire suspension unit, the steering layout and the radiator mounting, and is bolted up to the flat end plates of the chassis frame members as a complete assembly.

At the forward end of each torsion bar is a tubular wish-bone forming a triangle the base of which is the torsion bar itself. The apex of the triangle is anchored to the bottom of a long swivel-pin, which carries the stub-

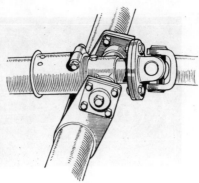

UNCONVENTIONAL.—Torque tube drive is employed together with an external universal joint, drive being taken through a trunnion bearing anchored to a frame crossmember.

Borg and Beck clutch of large diameter to a four-speed gearbox. The horizontal clutch operating lever, by the way, is fitted with a neat universal joint to accommodate any motion in the engine.

The ratios are calculated for lively motoring—4.88, 7.22 and 11.2, and 19.4 for bottom and reverse (synchromesh on the higher three). A short remote-control terminates in a business-like lever nicely placed in the driving compartment. A massive, adjustable rubber-mounting holds the back of the gearbox.

### Torque-tube Drive

The drive is taken by a short, open shaft and universals to a massive trunnion, where the drive divides and is continued through a propeller shaft enclosed in a torque-tube anchored to the banjo casing of the final drive. In addition, there are tie-rods between the banjo and the torque-tube for even greater rigidity. A small inspection trap permits examination and adjustment of the crown wheel and pinion meshing.

Girling brakes work on 10-in. drums, those on the front being operated by hydro-mechanical means and producing 60 per cent. of the braking effort. The rear braking is by mechanical means. A pistol-grip handbrake is placed to the left of the driver.

The 16-in. wheels are of the modern pressed-steel disc pattern, with small ventilators around the periphery to admit cooling air to the brake drums. The tyres are 5.75-in.

The flat petrol tank (mounted at three points on rubber) holds 12½ gallons, giving a cruising range of some 300-350 miles. Rileys, in point of fact, claim that the car will average 30 m.p.g., and are prepared to prove it on their own circuit under test conditions. The tank is fitted with twin fillers, so that the car can be refuelled either side and, when both caps are opened, can be filled very quickly.

The saloon body is extremely handsome, suggesting a sports close-coupled

axle and the steering-arm. These wishbones move with the torsion bar in accordance with road shocks. Above this pair of arms is a second pair, moving in sympathy with the sprung pair and anchored to the top of the swivel pin. These are held at the free end in a special rubber mounting needing no lubrication. Luvax telescopic hydraulic shock absorbers are mounted between the lower wish-bone "triangles" and the top of the cradle, at an angle of about 75 degrees.

### New Steering Layout

The steering is equally simple and modernistic. The long steering column terminates forward of the cradle in a small box containing a pinion in engagement with a rack (totally enclosed), which runs horizontally across the car and is wound to right or left as the steering wheel is turned. From the centre of this long rack split track-rods are connected to the steering arms, carried on the long swivel-pins of the wheels. There is an adjustable lock-stop each end of the rack. The lock, by the way, gives a turning circle of unusual merit—only 30 ft.

The chassis frame itself bears a strong resemblance in general conception to the pre-war car, apart from the entirely new front end. The side members, fully boxed for stiffness, are about 6 ins. deep and 2 ins. wide. There are six cross-bracings, three of which are stout tubular members of immense rigidity. The frame sweeps sharply upwards to clear the back axle.

Semi-elliptic springs are used at the back, carried in Harris-type rubber bushes, and the U-bolts which anchor the axle are lined with balata belting to prevent rusting. Piston-type hydraulic shock-absorbers are mounted high on the frame, and are linked by a stout anti-roll bar running right across the chassis. Four brackets are carried on each side-member to hold the body plus sockets for jacking. Two more corner sockets are fitted at the front.

Transmission is through a single-plate

INCORPOREAL.—With body removed, as in this drawing, the Riley chassis is disclosed as having box section frame members with tubular bracing and well raked steering column attached to a rack and pinion gearing mounted transversely at the front.

coupé of high power rather than a 1½-litre full-four-seater saloon. It is low, wide and rakish, with a sleek, sweeping tail and impressive frontal design. The bonnet has no louvres and is fastened by carriage-key locks.

The four-door steel body has a leather top to the roof, built over a sort of light netting of expanded steel, thus cutting weight as well as interior drumming. The well-domed wings blend neatly into the sweeping lines. The running boards are narrow, acting as serviceable steps without being wide enough to muddy trousers or silk stockings.

The interior appointments are first quality, and only useful " gadgets " are fitted. For instance, pouches behind the front seats replace the conventional door pockets, which so often become bulky with stuffed-in odds and ends. A deep shelf spans the car behind the instrument panel. The roof light is placed in the middle of the car, not at the back.

The seating is, of course, most comfortable, in fine-quality leather, and fully adjustable. An important feature is that all passengers are carried within the wheelbase, as the rear wheel arches begin behind the rear seat squab, without sacrifice of leg room. Additional foot room for rear passengers is found by placing toe boards under the front seats. We are assured that a passenger can write a letter in comfort in the back seat at 55 m.p.h. This deep, wide rear " couch " will really seat three if required.

The windscreen is of the V-type, in which the driver's half will open, leaving the passenger protected. The steering column is adjustable for rake as well as length, and the wheel is a sports type with three flexible spokes. The gear lever is nicely placed, with the hand-brake pistol-grip nearby.

The luggage boot is exceptional. Actually it will carry four suitcases—two large, two medium—two attaché cases and a bag of golf clubs! The spare wheel sits in a compartment below, accessible through a hinged panel.

The twin-bulb diffused-dip head lamps are recessed in " blisters " in the front fairing and are quickly detachable as units. The reflectors can be adjusted

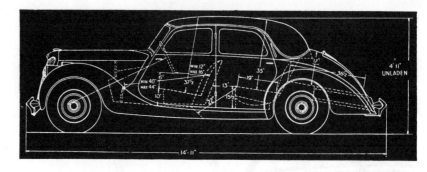

CREDITABLE COMBINATION.—This drawing (scale 1:30) shows how the forward seating position is being combined with moderate wheelbase and reasonable interior dimensions. Inter-axle seating is a feature.

in situ. There are two fog lights low down in front of the stocky, sloping radiator.

Quarter-bumpers of a modernistic, chunky design protect the four corners of the car, while a steel bar shields the rear lights and glass number-plate panel.

The Riley has a 9-ft. 4¼-in. wheelbase (14 ft. 11 ins. from tip to tail) and a track of 4 ft. 4¼ ins. It is only 4 ft. 11 ins. high, with a clear 7½ ins. under the chassis The total weight is only 24 cwt.

### Road Impressions

We were able to make only a brief test run in the neighbourhood of the Coventry factory, but that run sufficed to prove that here is, indeed, an entirely new Riley with all the old Riley attractiveness plus a new " urge " and something quite remarkable in the way of smoothness, steering and general stability The Torsionic front suspension is dead steady, yet gives a supple, easy ride free from pitching or roll. Even at high speeds over rough test surfaces the front stayed rigid as a rock. The car seems to solve the blending of a soft ride with sports-car steadiness.

The steering is high geared and free from kick. As a demonstration the car was put into a series of swift zigzags at 60 m.p.h., whereupon it wagged quickly down the road and then straightened out instantly. On another occasion, still at a mile a minute, it was

swerved up on to the grass verge, and careered along with off-side wheels on the rough. The car merely charged along at an angle with a perceptible vibration, as in an old-fashioned car on a rough road. Cornering is a delight, the Riley taking the curves at any speed as if on rails.

On normal short straights we touched 75 m.p.h. with ease and with throttle in hand. We should imagine that the maximum is on the right side of 80 m.p.h. under the right conditions. At such speeds, although the engine is revving hard, there is no drumming or vibration in the body, merely the sound of wind swishing past, and conversation proceeded in normal tones. Between 40 and 70 m.p.h. we noted really vivacious acceleration, and we should judge that the full enjoyment of this vehicle would be discovered on a long, fast cross-country run.

The brakes particularly merit a word of praise. We put them on at 75 m.p.h. several times, whereupon the car came to a standstill in a dead straight line and in a markedly short space. It is, indeed, a very safe, fast car.

In all, Rileys have produced a car which is streets ahead of anything they have constructed in the past—and that, as they say, " is something."

The price is £709 18s. 4d. (including £154 18s. 4d. Purchase Tax). The makers are Riley (Coventry), Ltd., Foleshill, Coventry.

POPULAR VIEW.—The New Riley has outstanding performance and the rear view is one that will probably be most seen by other drivers on the road.

# Riley Round Trip

## Through France and Switzerland in the New Riley Twelve

### By Grande Vitesse

WHICHEVER WAY YOU LOOK AT IT the new Riley has pleasant, modern lines and a low, compact appearance. (Snapped on N5 on the way to Sens, south of Paris.)

WHEN kind friends heard that I intended taking my brand-new 1½-litre " Torsionic" Riley right down the middle of France to Albi for the Grand Prix in that remote and heat-blistered city, and then across the Midi and Provence up into Switzerland for the Grand Prix des Nations at Geneva, followed by a little mild touring in that somewhat hilly country before striking back across France for home, they spoke up in one voice and gave as their opinion that I was obviously crazy.

"Why, old boy," they chorused in unison, "a brand-new post-war car with an entirely new chassis and with new-fangled suspension! You're simply asking for it. Didn't you know? Post-war cars fall to pieces in the first 1,000 miles and have to be rebuilt, old boy. You'll see."

Mind you, in the ordinary way I prefer to go Continental motoring on a car I know inside out rather than one which is delivered brand new seven days before I am due to cross the Channel. There was, I suppose, a faint element of risk about it, having regard to the unknown qualities of French fuel and the reputed harshness of post-war French roads. But I had looked carefully at the new Riley front springing layout, and I had gazed at the somewhat massive rear leaf springs. I had also stared at the bare chassis, with its several stiffening devices, and thought it " properly stayed and braced."

When I collected the vehicle, looking extremely brilliant without so much as a finger mark on its undeniably sleek coachwork, from the Pall Mall showrooms, Mr. Jimmy James said: "You may find it inclined to pink rather, on pool petrol, but you must remember it's pretty high-compressioned and was designed for real fuel. Just bear it in mind and make allowances, will you?"

Well, admittedly, it does pink. It pinks—let's face it—so that it is really rather a nuisance at times, when one is in a hurry and feeling easily irritated,

but if the engine is treated gently and the gearbox is used as it asks to be used, the pinking merely causes one to swear at pool petrol.

### Running-in Period

Thus, with seven days to go, I set about running-in the Riley in spare time. By the end of the week I had managed to cover a mere handful of miles. It was too soon to do even the usual 500 miles maintenance, but I drained and refilled the sump with the recommended lubricant, greased up all round, checked the back axle level, left the engine severely alone, as there was no indication of anything needing to be done, and trundled off to the coast.

In those few first miles cruising at 40 m.p.h., I realized that the " Torsionic" front suspension was really something out of the ordinary. By the time I had covered the first 100 miles in France, I realized that here was something very much out of the ordinary indeed, for I was driving a 12 h.p. 24-cwt. vehicle which rode like a large-size limousine. It ironed out the most awe-inspiring roads so that

they felt like normal roughish surfaces in England—which, frankly, they were not. Time after time I tensed at the wheel, awaiting the shock of an undodgeable pot-hole which rushed under the front end, and time after time the Riley took it with a gentle dip. I got used to it after a while, and maintained my 40-45 m.p.h. running-in speed over surfaces where instinct suggested 30-35 m.p.h. Nothing happened. There was not even a creak or a groan from the heavily loaded body.

The steering is definitely unusual. At first, I admit, the impression is one of slight heaviness. After some time it is realized that the steering is not heavy so much as remarkably firm and what I can only describe as positive. It is not heavy, because you can twiddle the wheel from lock to lock without effort, although it is quite high-geared, and there is no fatiguing feel of hauling on the steering when travelling lopsided on a steep camber or when weaving through quick successions of left and right hairpins down a mountain pass. The vehicle follows its steering, no matter what the speed or the state of the surface. There is never any sideways hop when steering fast round a sharp bend with a surface like a rough sea (and we met plenty), and the Riley follows its line as if glued to it. I know it is remarkably easy to rhapsodize about this sort of thing, but there it is—it happens. After about 1,000 miles you find you have been slowing down too much for corners and that motoring through bends on the throttle is what the Riley likes best. It does not merely hold the road; it feels as if it is digging its wheels down into it.

After the first 1,000 miles I opened up to 50-55 m.p.h. as a cruising speed (somewhere about one-third throttle), at which speed the bad stretches of road made even less impression on the springing, and quite sharp bends could be taken without any abatement of gait.

THE SIMPLON PASS, rising to 6,500 ft. in a 24-mile steady climb, failed to bring the Riley anywhere near to boiling.

THE SYNTHETIC TYRES (575 by 16), although running hot when speeds went above 60 m.p.h., gave no trouble whatsoever during 2,800 miles of Continental motoring. In the distance is Monte Leone, on the Simplon.

After 1,500 miles I thought it was about time I basted the engine a bit now and then to free it off, and at about half-throttle we cruised at 60-65 m.p.h.; 70-75 meant merely a slightly more powerful hum from under the bonnet and a speedometer 80 was held on full throttle with a little more to come had I held on a little longer.

However, bearing in mind the intense heat of the day (the exterior metal of the car was too hot to touch) and the synthetic tyres, I kept the cruising speed to between 50 and 60 m.p.h. to avoid any trouble with tyres so far from home. There was no trouble.

It is interesting to place on record that through the heat of the Midi in mid-summer, when tar melted on the roads and I dripped as I sat behind the wheel (for the draught of air from the open screen and windows felt like the breath of a furnace), the radiator thermometer remained steady at a shade over 70 degrees. When parked in the shade for an hour or more, the warmth

would not allow the water to cool off to less than 60 degrees!

### Per Ardua

From Albi to Geneva, through Auvergne, Provence, up the Rhone Valley and over the Savoy mountains, we journeyed four up, with luggage crammed everywhere we could find. The rear passengers found their ride comfortable and uncramped, and, if anything, the car seemed to bite into the road more than ever. Despite hours of steady climbing in second gear (thanks to very low octane petrol and the Riley high compression) the temperature never exceeded 80 degrees, and the rear springs never bottomed even when I hit one or two imperial crevices on mountain roads.

To cope with the great heat and the added weight, I pumped up the tyres from the standard 22 lb. front and 24 lb. rear to 24 lb. front and 26 lb. rear, this seeming to be a good idea at the time. Actually, it wasn't. Synthetic tyres heat up in themselves, and I sup-

pose that the running pressures must have gone up to over 30 lb. It was perfectly all right, except that the steering wheel began to judder and kick.

Later, on coming back from Switzerland to the coast and now travelling at 60-65 m.p.h. for long periods, as I was in a hurry, I found that the higher pressures with only two up and a bootful of luggage certainly did not suit the Riley suspension, and, in addition to kick on the steering wheel over bad surfaces, there was a new tendency for the rear wheels to hop sideways over transverse bumps or when crashing over pot-holes which were too close together.

Since getting back to England with tyres which show little signs of wear after 2,800 miles "over there" and without so much as a puncture, I let the pressures down to normal and found the suspension immediately returned to normal, and the kick and teeter disappeared wherefore I would murmur to other Riley owners—stick to the maker's recommended pressures.

Having reached Switzerland, with a glad sigh I pulled up at the first filling station and bought myself a tankful of Swiss petrol. Instantly the car came alive, after the paraffiny stuff which was French "pool." The pinking was no longer a factor. I could put my foot down with a slam at any speed in any gear, and found the car accelerate smoothly and extremely noticeably. I regret that, my stop-watch having packed up half-way through the race at Geneva, I was unable to take any timed performances from the Riley. It must suffice, therefore, to state that the car accelerates fast for a touring car of this weight. Between 60 m.p.h. and 75 m.p.h. it seems to gain a new lease of life, as it were, and the needle moves over the intervening 15 m.p.h. like the hand of a stop-watch.

### What's Bred in the Bone

There is a definite feeling about this little four-cylinder engine, bred of racing for many years, that the more you rev. it the more it revels. It seems to thrive on thrashing. You can drive it like a town carriage up to 50 or 60 m.p.h., and then, if you feel in a hurry, you can start handling it like a small racing car and the response is remarkable. The whole character of the car seems to change, and you find you are driving not a touring saloon but a sports car.

Naturally, in Switzerland, I tried a couple of passes in the short time at my disposal. First of all I took it up the Simplon from Brigue. Now, the Simplon is a steeper climb than you'd think. The first third of the way up its 24 miles of steady climbing is steep but well surfaced. The second third has appreciable straights with easy gradient over rougher roads, and the top third is rough and very serpentine. The summit, by the Hospice, is at 6,580 ft.

Before we started off we were warned that the alcohol content of the Swiss fuel would cause vapour locks as soon as the engine got really hot, and that all Swiss drivers suffered from it—sometimes in the heat of the valley roads.

After about 10 miles we overtook

ON THE WAY to Martigny for the Pass of the Grand St. Bernard (8,024 ft.) we crossed one of those picturesque Swiss gabled bridges which span ice-cold mountain torrents.

the Alfa-Romeo team on its way back from Geneva to Italy in two big Alfas and a Lancia Aprilia. They had already passed us in the Rhone Valley in a cloud of dust and a rush of wind. This time they were halted with their bonnets open, no doubt waiting for vapour locks to clear.

The Riley ran up smoothly in second and third gears, and on some of the short straights I eased it into top for half a minute or so. Bottom gear was needed on one or two of the sharper and blinder hairpins, not because the gradient demanded it but because I pictured the descending motor coach round the corner. The radiator temperature crept up to 80 degrees C., and went on creeping until the needle sat on 90 degrees. Half-way up the pass, where the gradients eased, the engine actually cooled off, and the needle went back to 80 degrees for the rest of the climb. So we never got anywhere near boiling.

We halted three or four times to marvel at the scenery and to take

IN THE RHONE VALLEY from Montreux to Brigue. This snap does give an idea of the low build of the Riley which still has ample headroom inside, although I am 6 ft. 3 ins. high. The Swiss couple came up to remark on the smart lines of the car which were admired wherever we went.

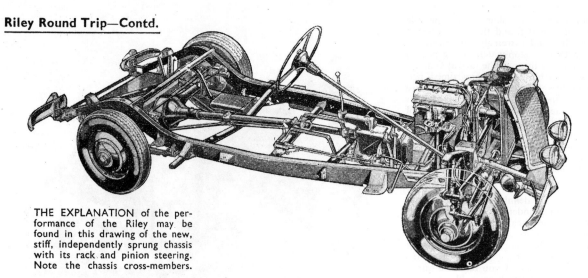

THE EXPLANATION of the performance of the Riley may be found in this drawing of the new, stiff, independently sprung chassis with its rack and pinion steering. Note the chassis cross-members.

photos, during which time, of course, the temperature rose, but each time, on the restart, it cooled off again. We reached the top, including stops, in three-quarters of an hour. No vapour locks. Except when cornering or in bottom gear for a few moments as mentioned, the speed never fell below 25 m.p.h. anywhere.

Next day, and at noon, when the sun was blistering the paintwork, I attacked the 31-mile climb of the Grand St. Bernard, from Martigny. This famous pass is higher but not so steep as the Simplon, but the surface for the final 25 miles is dust and stones and the hairpins come in rapid succession. The heat was really terrific and there was no shade, for the sun sat overhead. What breeze there was came from behind us.

The speedometer remained at between 20 and 25 m.p.h. (for I was not rushing the job). I had to use second, revving fast and easily, for most of the time, managed to get into third for about 33 per cent. of the way and came down into bottom for the worst hairpins. I had to stop several times on the long grind up, for there were no fewer than ten whacking great motor coaches on the way down, and there was no room for the Riley as well, during which time we sat in any convenient bay at intervals to let them pass.

The radiator temperature went up to 80 degrees on the lower slopes and mounted to 90 degrees for the rest of the way. At about 300 yards from the Hospice at the summit, a cow wandered across the bonnet, I took my foot off, and on the apex of the hairpin the engine died of the well-known vapour lock. We waited about a quarter of an hour, the temperature cooled off a little and we restarted without bother. This pass, by the way, rises to 8,024 ft.

Now you'll be wondering how many things fell off the car and what broke and so on. First of all, a nut fell off underneath and one of the rear torque arms, thus released at its anchorage to the torque tube, made a devil's tattoo until I got another nut fitted.

Secondly, due to the intense heat, oil seeped from the back axle out on to the rear right-hand tyre. Again a local garage renewed the oil seal and cured the only evidence of the extreme heat we encountered. Thirdly, the left-hand

## TECHNICALITIES

**Engine:** Four cylinders, 69 mm. bore. 100 mm. stroke, 1,496 c.c., rated at 12 h.p. and taxed at £15. Overhead valves operated by pushrods from two camshafts. Develops 55 b.h.p. at 4,500 r.p.m. Gives 2.37 h.p. per sq. in. of piston area. Compression ratio 6.5 to 1.
S.U. horizontal H2 carburetter, coil ignition (12-volt), Champion plugs, full-flow external oil filter.
Borg and Beck clutch, four-speed gearbox (4.88, 7.2, 11.2 and 19.4 to 1) with synchromesh on higher three ratios. Mechanical fuel pump (A.C.) Enclosed propeller shaft, spiral bevel final drive.
Girling hydro-mechanical brakes with 10-in. drums.
**Front** suspension: Riley "Torsionic" with parallel torsion bars and wing arms. hydraulic dampers. Rear: Semi-elliptic leaf springs with hydraulic dampers.
Wheelbase: 9 ft. 4½ ins.; track: 4 ft. 4½ ins.; overall length: 14 ft. 11 ins.; overall height: 4 ft. 11 ins.; ground clearance: 7½ ins.; turning circle: 30 ft.
Weight: 24 cwt.
Price: £863 5s. including Purchase Tax.

TAIL VIEW on one of the few straight roads in Switzerland — between Martigny and Sion in the Rhone Valley.

trafficator began to stick. Fourthly, the driver's window tightened up, owing to the quality of post-war felt. Fifthly, a wire shorted behind the facia board and burnt itself out—cured by getting a length of new wire locally. And that is the sum total of defects! And, mind you, this car was brand new, not run in and not "serviced" before departure.

People who really go touring will especially appreciate the boot in the tail, above the spare wheel compartment. Into this cavity we packed one large Revelation suitcase, one medium-sized suitcase, one smaller suitcase, one attaché case, one haversack (ex-Army Officer's type), one canvas "grip" bag (you know the sort I mean), one portable typewriter, two rugs, one Army blanket, and we cemented the lot together with two raincoats. In addition we added odds and ends like books, bottles of "eau mineral," a wooden box measuring 3 ft. by 10 ins. by 6 ins., containing spares and a complete spare leaf spring, neither of which was needed.

A word of praise for the Girling brakes. These adjuncts to safe motoring were given as good a pasting as brakes very well can be in actual use. They were clamped to the brake drums every few seconds for periods of an hour at a time when descending passes and they were used hard when travelling at pretty constant fifties and sixties all day. On the descents of passes in the Puy de Dome, Auvergne and the Alps they were "on" almost all the time and they got hot. They did not become feeble and there was no fading. Back in England they are still as effective as ever. They do not even require adjustment. There is no suggestion of pull one way or the other and they are capable of a real "crash stop," as I tried experimentally the other evening.

One usually attempts to sum up impressions of a car in a few graceful words. That defeats me. If asked for a quick answer, I would say: a real man's car capable of man-size performance wherever you go, with quite super-suspension for a small car which is much bigger than it looks, and a car which women will rave about.

# A New 2½-Litre Riley

*First full description of latest addition to post-war range*
*Features include 90 b.h.p. engine and independent torsion-bar suspension*
*Price of saloon £1,125 3s. 10d. (including P.T.)*

THE interest taken in the announcement of the 1½-litre Riley early this year was as great as that aroused by any post-war car yet described. Here was no "interim" model, but a true post-war design and one, moreover, that was obviously worthy of the traditions of a company which has always produced cars for the motorist who wants a machine designed around an ideal rather than a price. Its characteristics were ably summed up as representing sports-car performance with town-carriage manners.

Since that date the production models which have found their way in steadily increasing numbers into the hands of private owners have shown conclusively that the paper promise of the design has in every way been fulfilled in practice.

Now comes the news of another new Riley, a successor to the pre-war Sixteen and a model which embodies all that is making such a strong appeal in the 1½-litre type, with the added appeal of even better performance. Compared with the 55 b.h.p. of the 1½-litre engine, the new 2½-litre power unit gives an output of 90 h.p. on the brake. Just what the added 35 b.h.p. means in terms of acceleration, hill-climbing and maximum speed can well be imagined

when it is stated that the wheelbase of the new model is a mere 6 ins. greater, so that the dry weight of the complete car has increased by only 4 cwt. This additional weight is equivalent to an increase of 16.6 per cent., but, for performance purposes, must be regarded as less than that because the weight of passengers, luggage and fuel has also to be taken into account. Allowing 4 cwt. for two passengers, a small amount of luggage and a full tank, the increase comes down to 14.3 per cent. Power output, on the other hand, is greater by 63.6 per cent.

### High Speed at Low r.p.m.

Difference in flat-out performance, however, is only half the story. Equally important is the effect on cruising speeds. The greater output naturally permits appreciably higher gear ratios to be used, and these, coupled with larger tyres, bring about a very distinct reduction in engine revs. The 1½-litre, which is relatively high geared for a car of its type, has a top-gear engine speed of 3,740 r.p.m. at 60 m.p.h. With the 2½-litre, engine revs. at the same road speed come down to 3,060 r.p.m. These are mere figures. Just what they mean in practice under the strenuous conditions of high-speed long-distance

Continental touring is another story— and one that will be told in a later issue.

\* \* \*

An examination of the new car in detail reveals many points of close similarity with the 1½-litre model. In general layout (but not in all details) the chassis is identical and, as the photographs show, the coachwork and equipment are the same, apart from the longer bonnet which sets off the already well-balanced lines and makes the 2½-litre a very imposing car as well as a very attractive one.

The engine is of new design, but, as one would expect, incorporates many typical Riley features. Of 2,443 c.c., it is of the four-cylinder o.h.v. type and a noteworthy point is that a relatively long stroke in relation to the bore, which has been a feature of Riley engines for many years, is retained, the actual bore and stroke dimensions being 80.5 mm. and 120 mm. The maximum output (90 b.h.p., as already recorded) is developed at 4,000 r.p.m. and is high for an engine of this size, but no unduly high compression ratio is employed, the actual figure being 6.8 to 1. The maximum torque is 136 lb.-ft. at 2,000 r.p.m.

As one would expect, the overhead-valve arrangements characteristic of

The general arrangement of the rack and pinion steering and the independent front suspension are shown in this drawing.

Riley engines for many years, are incorporated in the new design, in which one finds the usual two camshafts disposed one on each side of the engine and located high in the cylinder block, whence only short push rods are required to operate the valves through the usual rockers. The valves themselves are disposed at 90 degrees to one another, so that their heads conform to the hemispherical combustion chambers. The latter are machined and the 14 mm. sparking plugs are centrally located between the valves.

Cooling, as one would expect with a high-efficiency engine of this kind, has been very carefully schemed to direct cool water to the hottest areas. From the base of the radiator, water is directed by a centrifugal pump via an external water pipe to two ports which carry direct to the surroundings of the exhaust valves. Thence the flow is in two directions; part of the water passes directly across the head to the inlet valves and thence to a cast-in passage along which it flows to the exit at the front; the remainder, about one-third of the total volume, is deflected downwards by a system of baffles into the cylinder jackets, where it again flows across to the opposite side and so out through the exit duct. The whole arrangement is carefully schemed to maintain as even a temperature as possible throughout the entire block and head.

### Design for Warming

For rapid warming up and maintenance of correct temperature in cold weather, a thermostat is incorporated. The pump is driven by a Vee belt, which also serves to drive the dynamo. This arrangement is, of course, conventional, but a slight variation in the case of the Riley is that the fan, instead of being mounted on an extension of the pump spindle, is mounted on a separate spindle of its own and driven at slightly reduced speed by a separate leather belt from a pulley on the pump shaft. This system has been adopted, partly to position the fan to the best advantage in relation to the radiator, and partly because it enables the fan to be put out of action in cold weather, if desired, simply by removing the belt, when the dynamo and water pump drive remain unaffected.

The three-bearing crankshaft is machined and balanced and the two camshafts are driven from its front end by a triangulated chain drive, a feature of which is an ingenious tensioner. This takes the form of a jockey sprocket mounted on a spring-loaded ratchet device, so arranged that, as chain stretch takes place, the sprocket mounting is moved along the ratchet by spring pressure and assumes a positive position where it is unaffected by reverse loads.

Aluminium-alloy pistons with four rings are employed, the gudgeon-pin bushes being of phosphor-bronze. The gudgeon pins themselves are hardened, ground and burnished.

Lubrication has obviously received the attention due with a high-output engine. A gear-type pump with an output of $3\frac{1}{2}$ gallons per minute at 3,500 r.p.m. draws oil via a gauze filter in the large ribbed aluminium-alloy sump and delivers it to a full-flow filter located on

The general design and layout of the front and rear suspension follows the lines of the well-tried post-war 1½-litre Riley. The torsional anti-roll bar at the rear and the cam adjusters for the torsion bars at the front can be seen in these illustrations.

The new Riley has the merit that its lines remain in excellent proportion when viewed from any angle.

the off side of the engine. Thence, the supply is taken to the main bearings and big ends and to the camshaft bearings, timing gear and valve rockers. A small deviation from previous Riley practice is to be noted in the oil-filling arrangements. In place of provision being made for adding oil to the sump via the overhead valve gear, there is now a large filler orifice located on the near side of the crankcase adjacent to the dip stick.

Carburation arrangements on the new engine include two S.U. horizontal H4 carburetters mounted on a cast-aluminium intake manifold incorporating a balance passage between the two instruments. Above the carburetters is a cylindrical oil-wetted air cleaner and silencer through which both instruments draw their supply via an aluminium casting connecting their intakes. The fuel supply is effected by an A.C. mechanical pump driven from the off-side camshaft, from which, also, the drive is taken for the distributor, which is accessibly placed close to the 12-volt coil.

The exhaust system is on the near side of the engine, the gases being carried away by a four-branch manifold designed to give an uninterrupted flow; thence they pass via flexible piping to the two silencers, the one of large cylindrical section running alongside the chassis frame and the second (a relatively small flat chamber) located

within the frame just forward of the rear axle.

In unit with the engine is a Borg and Beck single dry-plate clutch and a four-speed gearbox with synchromesh for all but first gear.

### Cable Control

The whole engine-gearbox unit is flexibly mounted on rubber buffers. At the rear, these are located close together on a bracket welded to one of the tubular cross-members of the chassis frame. At the front, the engine is carried by a cradle bolted to the timing case and the buffers are interposed between this cradle and two brackets welded to the sub-frame which carries the front suspension; these buffers are widely spaced and positioned relatively high in relation to the engine so that, although the unit is virtually three-point mounted, there is no tendency towards undue oscillation. Endwise movement of the unit which might take place due to the resiliency of the rubber is resisted by a cable anchorage at the rear and there is a similar (but vertical) cable anchorage at the front to prevent any vertical, as opposed to oscillatory, movement.

The appearance of the cradle, as will be noted from the illustrations, gives the impression that it is not possible to replace the belt driving the dynamo and water pump without removing

the engine from the frame; actually, this is not the case, as removal of two of the bolts, together with their distance pieces, which secure the cradle to the timing case, enables the belt to be withdrawn.

From the rear of the gearbox a short propeller shaft conveys the drive to the final propeller shaft which is enclosed in a torque tube. The rear axle, of more substantial construction than on the 1½-litre type, is of conventional spiral-bevel type.

The frame follows the general arrangement of the 1½-litre, incorporating substantial box-section side members joined by tubular cross-members. The frame is upswept over the rear axle, to which it is connected by semi-elliptic springs carried in Harris-type rubber bushes; the springs, of course, serve only to carry the weight of the car, the braking and torque reaction loads being taken by the torque tube already mentioned.

Bolted to the front end of the frame is an independent front suspension unit, which consists of a massive cradle to which are pivoted triangulated welded struts carrying the front wheels. The cradle also serves as a mounting for the rack and pinion steering and for the radiator. This construction, besides facilitating assembly in the first place, is of great benefit should the car be

The instruments are well laid out, with a background of polished woodwork and a very high standard of detail fittings.

The spare wheel is carried in a separate locker and thus leaves the large, low-loading luggage compartment free of obstruction.

# 2½-LITRE RILEY DATA

involved in an accident necessitating extensive front end overhaul.

The general layout of the front suspension is clearly shown in an accompanying illustration from which it will be seen that the torsion bars extend forward from their mountings on a cross-bar which passes below the engine unit and, at their forward ends, virtually form the base of the lower triangulated struts. Thus, upward movements of the wheels are resisted by the tendency of the torsion bars to resist twisting. It will be appreciated that the location of the rear end of the torsion bars controls the load which the whole system can carry and cam adjusters are provided at these points to enable the system to be set as required. Damping action is provided by a pair of telescopic hydraulic shock absorbers mounted diagonally between the apex of the lower triangulated struts and the upper portion of the cradle.

At the rear, piston-type shock absorbers are used and are interconnected by a torsional anti-roll bar.

Girling hydro-mechanical brakes are employed, the shoes working in 12-in. drums. In this system, of course, hydraulic operation is used on the front wheels and mechanical for the rear. The hand brake (operating on the rear wheels only) is of the pistol-grip type located to the left of the steering column which, incidentally, is of the Bluemel telescopic type.

So far as coachwork is concerned, readers who are familiar with the 1½-litre model will also recognize the new model because, except for a still better appearance achieved by the longer bonnet, the bodywork and general lines of the two cars are identical.

Notable points include the fitting of a fixed leather head supported by expanded steel netting (a feature which reduces both weight and drumming), a large rear locker (which serves both to offset the sweeping lines of the whole car and also to provide an exceptional amount of luggage accommodation), inter-axle seating, and a V-type windscreen, of which the driver can open half.

As one would expect, the interior appointments reveal both good quality and good taste. A pleasing simplicity is to be noted, yet this characteristic is not carried to the stage of austerity.

The price of this new model is £880, plus £245 3s. 10d. Purchase Tax, making a total of £1,125 3s. 10d.

| | Saloon | | Saloon |
|---|---|---|---|
| Present tax .. .. | £20 | Brakes .. .. .. | Girling hydro, mech. |
| Cubic capacity .. .. | 2,443 c.c. | Drums .. .. .. | 12 ins. |
| Cylinders .. .. .. | 4 | Friction lining area | 136.5 sq. ins. |
| Valve position .. .. | o.h.v. at 90 degrees | Brake lining area sq. in. | |
| Bore .. .. .. | 80.5 mm. | per ton .. .. | 97.5 sq. in. |
| Stroke .. .. .. | 120 mm. | Suspension .. .. | Front : Independent |
| Comp. ratio .. .. | 6.8 | | (torsion bar) |
| Max. power (A) .. | 90 b.h.p. | | Rear : Semi-elliptic |
| at .. .. .. | 4,000 r.p.m. | Steering gear .. | Riley (rack and pinion) |
| Max. B.M.E.P. .. .. | 138 lb. sq. in. | Steering wheel .. | 17 ins. |
| at .. .. .. | 2,000 r.p.m. | Wheelbase .. .. | 9 ft. 11 ins. |
| H.P.: Sq. in. piston | | Track, front .. .. | 4 ft. 4¼ ins. |
| area (A) .. .. | 2.85 | Track, rear .. .. | 4 ft. 4¼ ins. |
| Piston area: Sq. ins. | | Overall length .. | 15 ft. 6 ins. |
| per ton .. .. | 22·6 sq. in. | Overall width .. | 5 ft. 3½ ins. |
| Ft./min. piston speed at | | Overall height .. | 4 ft. 11½ ins. |
| max. h.p. .. .. | 3,160 | Ground clearance .. | 7½ ins. |
| Carburetters (A) .. | Two S.U. horizontal | Turning circle .. | R.H., 36 ft. ; L.H., 37 ft. |
| | H4 | Weight—dry .. .. | 28 cwt. |
| Ignition .. .. .. | Lucas coil | Tyre size .. .. | 6 × 16 ins. |
| Plugs : Make and type | Lodge HLNP | Wheel type .. .. | Disc |
| Fuel pump .. .. | A.C. mechanical | Fuel capacity .. .. | 12½ gallons |
| Oil filter make (by-pass, | | Oil capacity .. .. | 14 pints |
| full flow) .. .. | Tecalemit full-flow | Water capacity .. .. | 21 pints |
| Oil circulation : Galls. | | Electrical system .. | Lucas 12-volt c.v.c. |
| per min. .. .. | 3.5 galls. at 3,500 r.p.m. | Battery capacity .. | 72 amp./hrs. |
| Clutch .. .. .. | Borg and Beck, single | | |
| | dry plate | **Top gear facts :** | |
| 1st gear .. .. .. | 15.0 | Road speed per 1,000 | |
| 2nd gear (S) .. .. | 8.86 | r.p.m. .. .. | 19.6 m.p.h. |
| 3rd gear (S) .. .. | ·5.83 | Piston speed per 10 | |
| Top gear (S) .. .. | 4.11 | m.p.h. .. .. | 402 ft./min. |
| Reverse .. .. .. | 15.0 | Road speed at 2,500 ft./ | |
| Prop. shaft .. .. | Enclosed | min. (piston) .. | 62.1 m.p.h. |
| Final drive .. .. | Spiral bevel | Litres per ton-mile .. | 2,680 |

(A) With normal road settings of carburetter.    (B) Dry weight.    (S) Synchromesh.

The new Riley 2½-litre saloon is a very good-looking car. The driver can view both front wings from his seat and there is plenty of leg room for four large passengers.

# *First of the New*

# Riley

# MODELS

## *for Magnificent Motoring*

### *The RILEY 1½ litre Saloon*

Riley 'Torsionic' Independent front suspension, finger-light steering, Girling hydro-mechanical brakes, an entirely new body with a 51 in. rear seat and dust-proof luggage accommodation of unique dimensions are outstanding features of the post-war Riley car. The famous 1½ litre Riley engine with hemispherical head, inter-axle seating, four-speed gearbox, torque tube transmission—characteristics responsible for Riley individuality—are retained and, with many new refinements, blend to give MAGNIFICENT MOTORING.

RILEY (COVENTRY) LTD., COVENTRY

RUMOUR has been busy for some time past with the expected advent of the new 2½-litre Riley, and now that this new car has arrived it can best be described as "like the 1½-litre, only more so." This means that the coachwork is similar, but that an engine of 2,443 c.c., developing 90 b.h.p. in a strengthened chassis, is able to provide a road performance of a very high order. As the complete car weighs 28 cwt, the lb per c.c. figure is 1.28. The ratio of lb weight to maximum b.h.p. developed is 34.6, and the maximum output of the engine is at the rate of 36.8 b.h.p. per litre. These figures give an indication of what to expect in performance. An actual run in the car shows that, although it is entirely tractable and refined, it has an acceleration and a facility for high speed which together will swallow 100 miles in a surprisingly short time.

### Scale Differences

As might be expected, the principles which were so carefully developed for the 1½-litre have also been applied to the 2½-litre, hence the small difference existing between the two models, except in size and detail. To accommodate the larger engine the wheelbase is longer, and the frame is made of heavier section steel pressings. The gear box and clutch are of larger dimensions, the enclosed propeller-shaft and rear axle are increased in size to deal with the higher power, and the independent front suspension is more robust. In short, although the 2½-litre is like the 1½-litre, it is not the same car with just a larger engine, but a new car built to stand up to a high performance.

It will be seen from the illustrations that the longer wheelbase and longer bonnet add to the graceful nature of the new Riley appearance. The car is long, low and wide, and it looks like the flyer which it is. The bodywork is a four-wide-door four-light five-seater saloon, with the rear seat within the wheelbase and wells to give increased leg room. It has the clever dimensioning which Riley's understand so well, for they have the trick of producing coachwork which does not look bulky, but which, on acquaintance, proves to have a surprising amount of room and to pro-

vide an unusual degree of comfort on a long run. It is not only the seating arrangement that is the root of the matter, but also the seating position relative to the distribution of weight and the centre of gravity, and the nature of the behaviour of the road springs.

To return to the coachwork, the head is not metal panelled but is constructed of perforated sheet covered in fabric, giving a light structure which does not transmit drumming. At the front is a V-windscreen, which has a fixed panel on the passenger side, but an opening panel in front of the driver; thus in thick fog the driver can open the screen to see better without putting the passenger into a direct draught. This screen, because

# Now . . .
# the 90 b.h.p

_Autocar_

The new 2½-litre chassis is similar in design to the post-war 1½-litre, but more robust. Besides the rigidly designed engine the main features are a deep box-section frame with many cross-members and a rigid front end carrying a sub-assembly of independent front suspension with longitudinal torsion bar springs. This chassis is a study in modern design aimed to make a fast car entirely safe.

Built for stability, comfort, and an express performance, the 2½-litre Riley looks what it is, a car for the connoisseur.

Showing the neat and very conveniently arranged controls of the new Riley model.

of the wide body, gives the driver a clear and wide range of visibility which is unusually good. The doors, which are hinged on the centre pillar, have a considerable slope on their front and rear opening edges respectively, which adds to their operational width, and entry or egress is particularly easy. Except at the front there are no running boards, and one steps straight in or out.

The interior appointments of the coachwork are in excellent taste, and conspicuous for neatness rather than flamboyant styling, from the pleated

# 2½-litre Riley

hide upholstery to the polished walnut cappings and facia. The driving compartment bears the impress of the authorship of essentially practical motorists. At the back of the car is a long swept tail which provides a luggage container of considerable magnitude.

To appreciate fully the character of this car it is necessary to fathom the ideas behind its design. Swift travel continuously from place to place can best be accomplished if a car is not merely fast but also is essentially safe, meaning that it not only feels safe but *is* safe. Moreover, swift travel is pleasant only when the riding is comfortable, and devoid of sway and pitching over all kinds of roads; when stability is excellent, steering is accurate, noise is not noticeable, visibility is unobstructed, brakes are faithfully powerful, ventilation is available without draught, and relaxation possible for all the passengers.

Without these necessities travel can still be swift, but at the same time nerve-racking and "sick-making" to

all except the over-enthusiastic driver. With these matters in mind the design of the Riley can be reviewed.

As the evolution of cars has proceeded it has become more and more evident that the primary factor is a good stiff frame. The more flexible the suspension the greater the need to tie the structure of the vehicle together so that the wheels in all circumstances retain their relative positions. The best suspension cannot give proper stability if the frame is excessively twisting and weaving.

Hence the mechanical design of the Riley starts with its frame. This is built up of deep box-section side members, greatest in girth close to the bell housing of the power unit, straight in side elevation, but arching up and over the rear axle. At the extreme front, where the independent front suspension system is attached as a complete sub-assembly, is a dropped box-section cross-member of large size. Across the frame between and below the clutch pit and the rear of the sump is a stout dropped tube, which is not only a stiffener in a vital place for front-end rigidity, but also provides the anchorage points for the tail ends of the front suspension longitudinal torsion bars.

Below the tail end of the gear box and carrying the rear rubber mounting for the engine unit is a second cross tube. About eighteen inches behind that is a third cross tube which carries the flexible mounting for the head of the torque tube in which the propeller-shaft is enclosed. A fourth cross tube occurs about half-way be-

---

## 2½-LITRE RILEY SPECIFICATION

**Engine.**—16 h.p. rating, four cylinders, 80.5 × 120 mm (2,443 c.c.). Overhead valves, set at 90 degrees in hemispherical combustion chambers, operated by rockers and short push rods with twin camshafts. 90 b.h.p. at 4,300 r.p.m.
Three - bearing counterweighted and balanced crankshaft. Four-ring aluminium alloy pistons. Pressure feed oil system from submerged pump, with full-flow oil filter. Pump and fan water circulation with thermostat and cross flow to exhaust valve seats. Two horizontal S.U. carburettors.

**Transmission.**—Dry single-plate Borg and Beck clutch Four-speed gear box with remote control lever and synchromesh on second, third and top. Overall gear ratios 4.11, 5.83, 8.86, and 15 to 1.
Short open shaft to propeller-shaft enclosed in torque tube. Banjo type steel rear axle with spiral bevel final drive.

**Steering.**—Special Riley horizontal gear with wire-spoked telescopic wheel.
**Suspension.**—Torsion bar independent front and underslung half-elliptic rear, with Girling direct-acting front and Luvax-Girling rear cross-coupled hydraulic dampers.
**Brakes.**—Girling hydro-mechanical in multi-ribbed 12in nickel chrome drums.
**Fuel Tank Capacity.**—12½-gallon rear tank. Mechanical fuel pump.
**Electrical Equipment.**—Lucas 12-volt with automatic voltage control. High-duty coil ignition. 72 ampère-hour battery.
**Tyres and Wheels.**—Dunlop 16 × 6.oin widebase rims. Detachable steel disc wheels.
**Weight.**—28 cwt.
**Main Dimensions.**—Wheelbase 9ft 11in. Track, 4ft 4½in. Overall length, 15ft 6in; width, 5ft 3½in, height 4ft 11½in.
**Price.**—Saloon, £880, plus purchase tax £245 3s 10d, total £1,125 3s 10d.

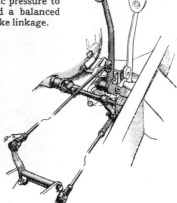

Left : How the pedal pulls on the floating master cylinder of the Girling hydro-mechanical brake set, applying hydraulic pressure to the front brakes and a balanced pull on the rear brake linkage.

Right : The clutch pedal is unaffected by movement of the power unit, being linked to a cross shaft which again is linked to a flexibly jointed shaft coupled to the clutch. The brake mechanism is omitted for clarity.

tween this, the third one, and the rear axle. Then a cross tube joins the side member arches over the rear axle, and from its centre diagonal tubes run out to the tail of the frame to steady it laterally. The component parts of this frame are welded together. At the extreme tail is a box-section cross-member.

The fuel tank is flexibly mounted low in the tail, and is of shallow lozenge shape in section, and provided with three internal baffle walls. Two filler caps are fitted.

Next in point of interest comes the independent front suspension system, which gives the quality of easy riding but at the same time ensures the directional stability. It is of the lateral wishbone type, controlled by diagonally placed Girling telescopic direct-acting hydraulic dampers. Mention has already been made of the large box-section front cross-member. Seen from the front it is shaped like a widely spaced letter U, the uprights of which carry at top and bottom the wishbone fulcrum points. This front member is bolted to the frame, and can be detached together with the suspension as a complete unit.

### Wishbone Details

The points of the uprights are coupled together by a stout detachable cross tube, on the centre of which is the cradle for the twin front rubber mountings of the engine unit. This can be withdrawn forwards out of the car if necessary. The lower wishbone on each side is of steel tube formed into a triangle with a wide base, which is hollow, mounted on Harris rubber bushes, and is splined internally to take the forward end of the torsion bar spring. Somewhat shorter in length, the upper wishbones are similar in structure and have their fulcrum points in the head of the uprights. These uprights also provide a massive support for the brackets carrying the front wings. The outer ends of the wishbones have bronze bearings in brackets carrying the top and bottom

ends of the steering king pins, which also turn in bronze bearings.

In order to obtain a large surface to take end thrust, the uppermost end of each king pin has a large screw thread cut in it, and this operates in a stainless steel sleeve internally threaded and secured in the king pin bracket. The screw thread is slightly truncated so as to allow space for lubricant to pack in from the grease gun. This suspension system is similar to that of the 1½-litre Riley, but increased in strength. Unsprung weight is kept as low as possible and the direct-acting dampers impose a minimum resistance to the rise of the wheels and a maximum to the fall.

On each side a rubber cushion snubber carried by the front cross-member engages a stop on the lower wishbone if the rise of a wheel should from any cause exceed the predestined travel. To the front of the U cross-member is bolted a triangulated outrigger structure which supports the front of the radiator and provides a rigid mounting for the front bumper. Underslung half-elliptic springs of

considerable length are used at the rear, and are controlled by Luvax-Girling piston-type recuperating hydraulic dampers, coupled by a torsion bar. These springs have Harris-flex rubber-bushed shackles.

In order to obtain a steering which is quick, light, direct and unaffected by front wheel movements a special type of gear is employed. It consists of an enclosed horizontal slide with helical teeth cut along it, engaged by a helical-toothed pinion to which the steering column is attached. This slide is mounted in its casing in such a way that it is held in close engagement with the helical pinion by a spring-loaded plunger, only a limited degree of float being allowed, and by this means backlash is avoided. A steering track rod runs from each steering arm to a ball joint attached to the slide, the rods being of a length to conform with the geometry of the suspension.

### Proved Features

The reason for the engine being left until last in this description is that the chassis has been newly designed to provide an appropriate setting for a power unit of already established excellence. The engine is a further development of the already well-known 16 h.p. Riley unit, in which a number of special features have proved their merits since the days when the famous Riley Nine—forerunner of a distinguished design—first shone into fame. This 16 h.p. engine has shown how smooth running and how powerful a relatively large sized four-cylinder can be.

The structure consists of a cylinder block in one casting with a deep-sided

Arrangement of the 90-degree valves in the detachable cylinder head, which has hemispherical combustion chambers. The valve rockers are operated by short vertical push rods from twin camshafts carried high in the cylinder block.

and rigid crankcase, carrying a large counterweighted crankshaft in three large bearings. Carried high up in the cylinder block are twin camshafts, one on each side, and chain driven. The cylinder head is detachable and contains hemispherical combustion chambers with overhead valves set at 90 degrees, and centrally placed sparking plugs. These valves are operated by rockers, housed in two cover boxes, and by short and very light push rods. The valve ports are straight, and, like the combustion chambers, are

Underside of the cylinder head, showing the valves, in the hemispherical combustion chambers, and the position of the sparking plugs.

This is the special Riley steering gear unit. Within the main assembly is a horizontal bar with helical teeth. These are engaged by a helical pinion, which is coupled to the steering wheel. A form of spring loading reduces backlash to a minimum.

machined to equal size. This valve arrangement is one of the ideals for power output.

The valve ports are on opposite sides of the engine, there is a special free-flowing exhaust manifold on one side and twin S.U. horizontal carburettors are fitted on the other side, the carburettors being provided with a common air intake chamber coupled to a large air silencer. The cooling system is carefully arranged to provide that the water circulation in the head is greater than in the block, so as to equalize temperature, and also a supply of cool water is specifically directed on to the exhaust valve seats. The engine oiling system includes the valve gear, inasmuch as the submerged pump is surrounded by a strainer and all the oil in circulation has to pass through a full-flow filter.

### Power Unit Mountings

Engine and gear box form a unit which is cradled in rubber cushions. There is a twin V-arranged mounting fairly high at the front, and a second mounting below the tail of the gear box. End-wise float of the unit is prevented by flexible cables at back and front. Incidentally, the gear lever is mounted on a rearward-projecting tunnel, which brings it conveniently

close to hand. Chassis lubrication is reduced to a minimum, and consists mainly of maintaining the oil levels in the engine, gear box, and rear axle. The other points such as hubs, fan, steering swivels and ball joints are fitted with grease gun nipples of the Tecalemit self-locking type. Accessible jack attachment is provided by square sockets at front and rear.

Naturally a car which has the performance of this one needs good

brakes. They are the Girling hydromechanical type operating in 12in multi-ribbed nickel chrome drums. With this system the front brakes are operated hydraulically and the rear brakes mechanically. The brake pedal is coupled to a floating hydraulic master cylinder, the tail of which is coupled to the mechanical linkage of the rear brakes.

### Safety Ensured

When pressure is applied to the pedal in the normal way hydraulic pressure is generated in the master cylinder and applied through the pipe lines to the front brake wheel cylinders, and at the same time an automatically balanced mechanical pull is applied to the rear brakes. If for any possible reason the front brakes should go out of action a stop in the master cylinder ensures that the rear brakes will operate. Conversely if the rear brakes go out of action a stop in the linkage ensures that the hydraulic front application is unaffected. The hand brake operates on the rear wheels only.

Within the long and graceful lines of the tail there is much room for luggage under cover. This car has a particularly graceful rear view, which is aided by the low build and the smart black and chromium wheels.

**Make**: Riley        **Type**: 2½-litre Saloon

**Makers**: Riley (Coventry) Ltd., Coventry.

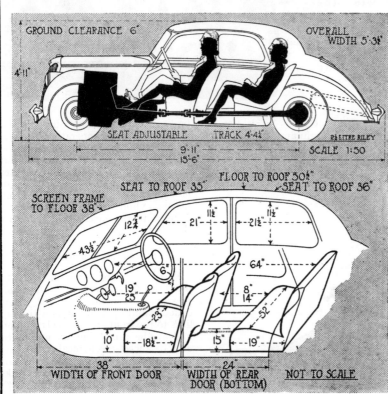

GROUND CLEARANCE 6"    OVERALL WIDTH 5'·3½"
4'·11"   SEAT ADJUSTABLE   TRACK 4'·4½"   2½ LITRE RILEY
9'·11"   15'·6"   SCALE 1:50

SCREEN FRAME TO FLOOR 38"   SEAT TO ROOF 35"   FLOOR TO ROOF 50½"   SEAT TO ROOF 36"
WIDTH OF FRONT DOOR 38"   WIDTH OF REAR DOOR (BOTTOM) 24"   NOT TO SCALE

## In Brief

Price £880.   Tax, £245 3s. 10d. = £1,125 3s. 10d.

| | |
|---|---|
| Present Tax .. .. .. .. | £20 |
| Road weight unladen .. | 28½ cwt. |
| Laden weight as tested .. | 31½ cwt. |
| Consumption .. .. | 24-26 m.p.g. |
| Speed .. .. .. | 94.8 m.p.h. (mean both ways) |
| | 72 m.p.h. 3rd. |
| | 45 m.p.h. 2nd. |

Acceleration :

     10-30 on top, 9.0 secs.
     0-50 through gears, 10.2 secs.
     0-80 through gears, 31.0 secs.

Tapley lb. per ton and gradients :
     250 lb. max. on top = 1 in 9
     370 lb. max. on 3rd = 1 in 6
     560 lb. max. on 2nd = 1 in 4

Gearing: 19.6 m.p.h. on top at 1,000 r.p.m. 62.5 m.p.h. at 2,500 r.p.m. piston speed.

## Specification :

| | |
|---|---|
| Cubic capacity .. .. | 2,443 c.c. |
| Cylinders.. .. | 4 |
| Valve position .. .. | Overhead (pushrod) |
| Bore.. .. .. | 80.5 mm. |
| Stroke .. .. .. | 120 mm. |
| Compression ratio .. | 6.8 |
| Max. power .. .. | 90 b.h.p. |
| at | 4,000 r.p.m. |
| H.P. per sq. in. of piston area | 2.85 |
| H.P. per ton unladen .. | 63 |
| Piston area per ton .. | 22.6 sq. ins. |
| Litres per laden ton-mile | 2,360 |
| Ft./min. piston speed at max. h.p. .. .. | 3,160 |
| Carburetter .. .. | Twin S.U. horizontal H.4 |
| Ignition .. .. .. | Lucas coil |
| Plugs, make and type .. | Lodge HLNP |
| Fuel pump.. .. | A.C. mechanical |
| Oil filter .. .. .. | Tecalemit full-flow |
| Clutch .. .. .. | Borg and Beck, single dry plate |
| 1st gear .. .. .. | 15.0 |
| 2nd gear .. .. .. | 8.86 |
| 3rd gear .. .. .. | 5.83 |
| Top gear .. .. .. | 4.11 |
| Reverse .. .. .. | 15.0 |
| Propeller shaft .. .. | Torque tube |
| Final drive .. .. | Spiral bevel |
| Brakes .. .. .. | Girling hydro mech. |
| Drums .. .. .. | 12 ins. |
| Friction lining area .. | 136.5 sq. ins. |
| Brake area per ton .. | 96 sq. ins. |
| Steering .. .. .. | Riley (rack and pinion) |
| Tyre size .. .. .. | 6 × 16 ins. |

Fully described in " The Motor," November 27, 1946

## Test Conditions

Milan-Como Autostrada.
Dry, moderate wind. Swiss petrol and natural rubber tyres.

## Test Data

**ACCELERATION TIMES on Three Upper Ratios**

| | Top | 3rd | 2nd |
|---|---|---|---|
| 10–30 m.p.h. .. .. .. .. .. | 9.0 secs. | 6.2 secs. | 4.0 secs. |
| 20–40 m.p.h. .. .. .. .. .. | 7.8 secs. | 6.0 secs. | 4.8 secs. |
| 30–50 m.p.h. .. .. .. .. .. | 9.8 secs. | 6.2 secs. | — |
| 40–60 m.p.h. .. .. .. .. .. | 8.9 secs. | 7.4 secs. | — |

**ACCELERATION TIMES Through Gears**

| | |
|---|---|
| 0–30 m.p.h. .. .. .. | 4.8 secs. |
| 0–40 m.p.h. .. .. .. | 7.0 secs. |
| 0–50 m.p.h. .. .. .. | 10.2 secs. |
| 0–60 m.p.h. .. .. .. | 15.2 secs. |
| 0–70 m.p.h. .. .. .. | 20.8 secs. |
| 0–80 m.p.h. .. .. .. | 31.0 secs. |
| Standing quarter-mile .. | 19.8 secs. |

**MAXIMUM SPEED : Flying Kilometre**

Mean of four opposite runs .. 94.8 m.p.h.
Best time equals.. .. .. 96.2 m.p.h.

**BRAKES at 30 m.p.h.**

0.94 g. ( = 32 ft. stopping distance) with 110 lb. pedal pressure.
0.86 g. ( = 35 ft. stopping distance) with 100 lb. pedal pressure.
0.75 g. ( = 40 ft. stopping distance) with 75 lb. pedal pressure.
0.48 g. ( = 63 ft. stopping distance) with 50 lb. pedal pressure.

**FUEL CONSUMPTION**

27.2 m.p.g. at constant 30 m.p.h.
25.0 m.p.g. at constant 40 m.p.h.
26.0 m.p.g. at constant 50 m.p.h.
25.0 m.p.g. at constant 60 m.p.h.
23.0 m.p.g. at constant 70 m.p.h.

**HILL CLIMBING (On British Pool Petrol)**

Max. top-gear speed on 1 in 15 .. 45 m.p.h.
Max. top-gear speed on 1 in 20 .. 68 m.p.h.

**STEERING**

Turning circle, Left 37 ft. ; Right, 36 ft., 2½ turns of steering wheel lock to lock.

## Maintenance

**Fuel Tank :** 12½ gallons. **Sump capacity:** 14 pints. **Gearbox oil capacity :** 2 pints. **Rear axle oil capacity:** 5 pints. **Radiator water capacity :** 21 pints. **Grease points :** 12 points. Duckham's Laminoid. 4 points (wheels) Duckham's HBB. **Plug gap :** .025 ins. to .030 ins. **Contact gap :** .012 ins. to .015 ins. **Tappets :** Inlet .003 ins. Exhaust .004 ins. (hot engine). **Front wheel toe-in. Castor angle :** 3 degrees. **Damper fluid :** Girling thin type. **Tyre pressure :** 24 lb. front and rear. **Oil filter element :** Tecalemit, renew every 10,000. **Electrical system :** Lucas 12 volt. 72 amp/hrs. CVC. **Bulbs :** all single pole. Head lamps, nearside double filament 36/36 watts ; offside 36 watts, side, tail, roof and stop lamps, 6 watts ; Ignition, panel and petrol gauge lamps, 2.4 watts ; reversing lamp, 24 watts ; Trafficators, 3 watts ; dash lamp, 2.4 watts ; fog lamp, 48 watts ; pass lamp, 48 watts.

# THE RILEY 2½-LITRE SALOON

## High performance and very fine road-holding are the outstanding features of this new car

MOTORISTS who remember the big four-cylinder 16 h.p. Riley of pre-war days have been speculating for some time as to the reappearance of this car, and wondering whether it would follow the lines of the extremely successful post-war 1½-litre model already introduced.

In theory, the 2½-litre model could hardly fail to be a success. By 1939 this engine was recognized as one of the most outstanding power units available on the British market, and if any criticism could be levelled against the chassis to which it was then fitted, it was that road-holding and suspension were hardly up to the extremely high cruising speed made possible by the 90 h.p. unit.

What has happened now is that this same engine, modified and improved in

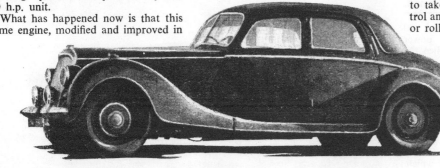

a satisfactory blend of the best British and Continental body-styling without making the smallest concession to the vulgarity of transatlantic influence.

At first the driver may find the roof-line a little low, and the wearing of a hat by a tall person might be difficult. In point of fact, this is only a temporary state of affairs, because, after some distance, the seat cushions settle and the extra headroom thus provided is just sufficient for all purposes. But perhaps the most significant point is that during a high-speed drive over some of the worst roads in Europe with three people on board, never once did anyone touch the roof with their heads,

although unexpected humps were encountered at speeds in excess of 80 m.p.h., and Continental level crossings are still notorious for their evil contours. This brings us to the most important feature of the whole car. It is increasingly obvious that, in their new independent front suspension the Riley Company has achieved a considerable technical triumph. Allied to the rack-and-pinion steering and the 9-ft. 6-in. wheelbase, the general results are something which many a racing car cannot surpass. Thus, it is possible to encounter an unexpectedly sharp bend with a film of grease and an adverse camber, at speeds far greater than would normally be considered safe, and yet to take that corner with absolute control and an entire absence of skid, sway, or roll. The driving position is admirable, inasmuch as a large portion of both front wings can be seen, and, owing to the accuracy of the steering, it is possible to place the front end within a matter of an inch or two at maximum speed on indifferent surfaces.

various details and considerably the better for the introduction of twin carburetters, has been placed in a slightly lengthened version of the new 1½-litre chassis. It was immediately obvious that this combination should produce a most exceptional motorcar, and in order to satisfy ourselves as to the durability of the new design, two of the latest Rileys were recently taken to Italy in order to carry out the fullest possible tests and maintain high maximum speeds for long periods on the Italian motor-roads.

### Highly Individual

The Riley Company have never made concessions to passing fashion if they were not convinced that such designs had technical merit. Consequently, we have grown to expect a series of highly individual motorcars, lacking occasionally the little niceties and luxuries of their competitors, but providing a feeling of breeding and stamina increasingly difficult to find in these days of quantity production. It is, therefore, most pleasing to discover that the new 2½-litre model is in many ways more "a car apart" than ever before, and 4,000 miles of hard driving did nothing to dispel this viewpoint.

From the point of view of appearance, it is undoubtedly an extremely handsome motorcar. The extra length of bonnet sets off the whole vehicle, and, with its leather-covered roof, it is obvious that the new Riley has achieved

The new Riley is well proportioned. The leather-covered roof gives the car a pleasing individuality.

Our road test took the car to Italy, via Switzerland, so that a very wide variety of conditions were encountered.

firmed by tests carried out on a sister car. In point of fact, the consumption throughout the entire speed range is excellent for so robust and comparatively unstreamlined a vehicle. As to

Timed by the Milan Automobile Club, the Riley, with rear wheels spinning on the dry road, gets away to record a remarkable figure for the standing quarter-mile.

Averaging 94 m.p.h. over the kilometre the car remained absolutely steady, despite the indifferent surface of the Autostrada.

## The Riley 2½-Litre Saloon
### —Contd.

The manufacturers' claim of 90 brake-horse represents the power delivered to the road wheels when the efficient silencers are in position, and certainly the big four-cylinder engine has a very considerable punch. A glance at the data panel will show how exceptional are the acceleration times, and particularly interesting is the standing quarter-mile timed by the Milan Automobile Club. To achieve this distance from a standstill in less than 20 seconds is something which, before the war, was confined to a select few of the world's most powerful high-performance cars, and this degree of acceleration also means that the car reaches an effortless cruising speed of between 80 and 90 m.p.h. with exceptional rapidity and a very marked

The blending of the traditional Riley radiator with such modern lines is one of the most interesting features of the car's appearance.

absence of fuss. Indeed, in trying to discover why driving fatigue is reduced to an absolute minimum in the new Riley, we came to the conclusion that the suppression, at high speed, of noise and mechanical excitement generally is the greatest contributory factor.

In all these essentials, therefore, the new Riley is an extremly good vehicle. No car ever tested by "The Motor" has been entirely above reproach, and if criticism can be levelled against the Riley, it is that neither the lights nor the horns are quite powerful enough, in view of the extremely high speed so readily obtained. The brakes on the car tested were admirable, but during a prolonged high-speed descent of an Alpine pass, a degree of fade was noticeable. This loss in efficiency only occurred after very savage treatment, and passed off within two miles or so of the end of the descent. It is possible that the brake linings may not be entirely suitable for such exceptional conditions, and the Riley Company are taking immediate steps to counter this slight criticism.

The petrol consumption figures are particularly interesting. It will be observed that the car is more economic at a steady 50 m.p.h. than at 40. This is a most intriguing characteristic of the latest engine and one which is con-

carburation in general, the Riley is fairly sensitive to temperature, and with the fan coupled up is rather over-cooled for an English winter. It is, however, a very easy matter to blank off a portion of the radiator block, and it is satisfactory that the cooling system is designed to cope with even tropical conditions without over-heating.

A good mark must be given to the manual control of the ignition, which enables a correct setting to be chosen for all grades of petrol.

It remains to be said that the finish of the car is extremely good and that the whole design of the body and its interior appointments are chosen with a view to the experienced owner-driver's requirements. The luggage boot is large; the spare wheel is housed in a separate locker in the tail. The characteristic deep foot-wells for the rear compartment make it possible for 6-ft. passengers to ride in comfort well within the wheelbase. The steering is a little on the heavy side at very low speeds, but this is a small price to pay for exceptional accuracy and control when running fast.

Summing up, this car might be described as an outstanding event in Riley history, and a very worthwhile contribution to a tradition of great motorcars emanating from their factory.

# Road-burning Riley

*GEE-GEE waxes enthusiastic concerning the qualities of what he has dubbed the—*

COVERING an event like the Highland Three Days' Trial calls for a quite exceptional motorcar. In addition to the need for getting "from here to there" as swiftly as possible, there is the actual trials route to be considered. No self-respecting journalist would attempt to describe an event of this nature without traversing most of the route taken by the competitors: in other words, the car must be fast, dead reliable, possess a good steering lock, be dependably suspended, and be economical.

The 1½-litre Riley saloon has all these attributes—and more. That altogether incredible suspension carried me safely over places which it would be highly complimentary to call tracks. Miles and miles were travelled over pieces of landscape that resembled river-beds. There were ruts by the thousand, countless bumps and boulders, and an infinite variety of potholes, generally resembling miniature craters. Add to these surface conditions a continual downpour of rain and sleet, interrupted only by snowstorms and gales, and you have some idea of the conditions under which the 1947 "Highland" was held.

Accurate steering was a necessity on some of the "roads" discovered by the trial organizers. The effects of snow and ice on the surface of the

others. Names which roll easily from the tongues of Highlanders, but often stump the Lowlanders and completely defeat the Sassenach, are commonplace in Inverness-shire.

On main roads the Riley travelled effortlessly in the middle sixties. Possibly the power-unit could be quieter, but that is a detail when it is delivering the goods. On the return journey, I accomplished a very quick piece of motoring between Hamilton and Carlisle, without being conscious that I was really hurrying. During part of that run I put 51 miles into the hour, which is a remarkable performance for a 1½-litre saloon over ordinary roads.

Altogether, the latest Riley is one of the most likeable vehicles.

It is not heavy on the E-coupons either. I found that all-over consumption, including bags of lower-gear work and high-speed cruising, was over 27 m.p.g. Conservatively driven I don't see any reason why over 30 m.p.g. should not be obtainable; but it is very difficult to keep an itching foot off the loud pedal of a road-burner such as the 1½-litre Riley.

I felt that driving over long distances could never become boring in such an interesting car as the Riley is. Despite the armchair comfort of the driving seat, I never experienced any of the drowsiness which often assails me during many continuous hours at the wheel of some closed cars. I venture to state that there are very few cars in which I would feel so free from fatigue, after reeling off the miles between dawn and sunset.

Taking it by and large, the 1½-litre Riley is an excellent proposition for people who like to get around quicker than most, in addition to owning a vehicle with all the manners and comfort of a town carriage. The decidedly generous luggage space is an added attraction to long-distance tourists, particularly those who wish to go abroad. Family men will also appreciate this very important point.

(Left) The steep and slippery Shirramore road which leads to Laggan Dam from Laggan Inn, with the majestic Grampians in the distance.

(Below) The 1½-litre Riley poses for its picture on Loch Lagganside.

(Above) A blizzard raging in the "Sma' Glen," Perthshire, on Easter Saturday.

(Right) Another Loch Laggan vista, with Ben Dearg towering, snow-capped, in the middle background.

Dalwhinnie-Laggan road are almost unbelievable. One nasty bend, partially blocked by a deep snowdrift, became narrower and narrower as each successive competing car dislodged large pieces of the drift. Tail-enders, including myself with the Riley, were left with scarcely the width of a car in which to negotiate. It isn't altogether a happy experience to crawl round a corner with one's nearside wheels an inch or two from a drop of over 100 ft.

Then there was that steep and slippery climb up to Shirramore from Loch Lagganside, which defeated many of the officials' cars. The Riley managed it by sheer power and controllability.

There was much wheel-twisting and gear-changing to reach tongue-twisting places like Muirshearlich, Blarmachfoldach, Achenadain, Crannachan and

Left: We halt at a temporary wooden bridge while an ox-cart lumbers over. The new bridge is arising from the ruins of the destroyed one.

IT had become obvious that the Geneva Show would be unusually important. A "high-level" conference decided that *The Autocar* and its sister journals *The Motor Cycle* and *Motor Transport* must deal with it adequately.

Thus it happened that three ex-R.E.M.E. types and an ex-matelot had to get to Geneva by March 11 and be back in London before 24.00 hours on March 16. It was also desired to obtain some experience of the 2½-litre Riley under Continental road conditions. So the combined—in more senses than one—operation was conceived.

Everything was "laid on" in the best Services' manner. I fixed the car papers and passages. Tommy, the "truck" man, handled finance. Harry, who professes to like two wheels better than four, saw to passports and hotels. Fergie, the artist, thought he had nothing to do, but did plenty!

In fact, he drove the Riley up to London from Coventry on Friday, March 7, when the daily press, the B.B.C., the R.A.C. and the A.A. all said there was no road open. He left Coventry at 12.30 hours, rang up from Kettering at 18.00 hours—little nearer London than when he started—but arrived, tired and triumphant, at 01.00 hours on Saturday. He had covered 157 miles on the journey instead of 90. Stout fellow, our left-handed matelot!

So we sped swiftly down to Folkestone on the Saturday afternoon over roads which were nearly clear of snow, although there was plenty at the sides, to ensure being alongside the *Invicta* at Dover for loading at 09.30 hours on Sunday. The run down whetted our appetites for long straight Continental roads where we could really let the Riley have its head.

### Pot-holes at Speed

We had a lovely calm, sunny morning for the crossing and the R.A.C. smoothed the Customs business, so that we got away from Calais at about 15.00 hours. We took the Boulogne road, N.1, and in several dips between the rolling hills we found flood water pouring across in a muddy torrent. It also became obvious that frost had played the dickens with the road surface. The trouble was that one never knew when a patch of broken surface would appear, but after we had run slap over some atrocious pot-holes at over 80 m.p.h. and found that the Riley floated over them without shock we just didn't trouble.

As we only had to make Compiègne for the night, a mere 145 miles, we cruised quietly at 60 when the surface was not too good, or at 80 if it was better. On one good stretch we pushed the needle well up in the 90s and we found it very comfortable motoring, although, with four men up and the tail full of luggage, we just bottomed once or twice over particularly bad bumps.

Slowly we trickled through Montreuil, Abbeville, Amiens and Dijon, so that the crew could see the sights. At the Hotel du Palais at Compiègne, which we reached at 18.30 hours, we were expected. While we dealt with an aperitif we were offered the menu and the choice of dishes was truly embarrassing. Over a marvellous meal we toasted

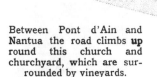

Between Pont d'Ain and Nantua the road climbs up round this church and churchyard, which are surrounded by vineyards.

Fergie, for his epic run from Coventry, in a bottle of Châteauneuf du Pape which we remember with reverence.

Our programme for Monday was first to cash travellers' cheques, and then to make for Dijon by way of Soissons, Château Thierry and Troyes. The Monday night we intended to spend in France, but somewhere near the border so that we could make Geneva easily for lunch. Unfortunately the bank at Compiègne was not opening until the afternoon, so we called at the bank at Château Thierry. There we were most courteously received, but the drill for dealing with T.C.s was a bit strange to the staff and it took some time. Then we filled up with petrol and with Harry at the wheel hit the high spots to Sezanne, where the Hotel de France had a

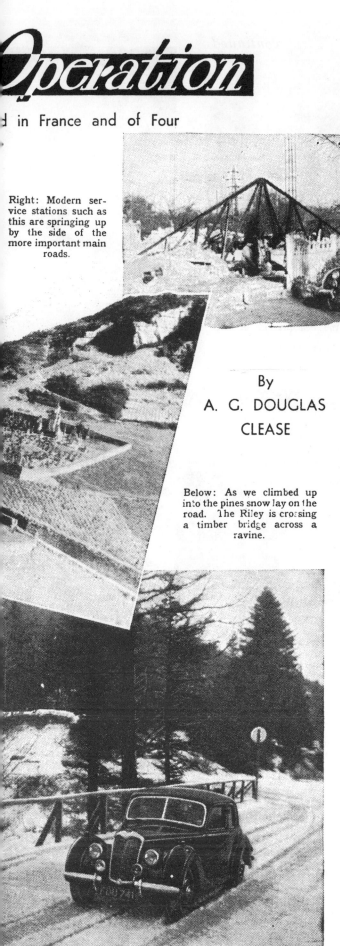

# *Operation*
## in France and of Four

Right: Modern service stations such as this are springing up by the side of the more important main roads.

## By
## A. G. DOUGLAS CLEASE

Below: As we climbed up into the pines snow lay on the road. The Riley is crossing a timber bridge across a ravine.

marvellous pre-war reputation for its excellent food. Over that lunch a veil should be drawn. It was too good to be discussed in public. But during the afternoon Harry and Fergie dozed peacefully in the rear seats, oblivious of the fact that twice the needle was up to the 96 mark. It says a lot for the suspension that the "bods in the back" could and did sleep in comfort.

But on the whole we rather pottered that afternoon, for the engine is quite tractable and flexible if one feels like that, although on both Pool petrol and French *essence* it is desirable to use the instrument board control to retard the ignition a shade. Tommy, with the aid of the Michelin Guide, navigated for me through Troyes and Chatillon-sur-Seine, where we stopped for an excellent cup of tea at the Hotel Côte d'Or.

### Fast Climbing on Third

It then struck us that we had quite some way to go to find a suitable resting place for the night and we decided on Chalon-sur-Saône. So we opened up to a cruising 80 when we could, and down N.71 we reeled off the 50-odd miles to Dijon in an hour. I knew the way through on to N.74 for Beaune and we sped past the famous vineyards which lie alongside the road with the Riley running tirelessly. The 44 miles from Dijon to Chalon took less than the hour and we accepted the Michelin recommendation of the Royal Hotel. As usual Monsieur Bibendum was right. We had large, modernly furnished rooms with spotless white bathrooms and lashings of really hot water. The Riley was in the large covered garage, travel-stained but an object of admiration to the staff.

Next morning we continued to Bourg, Pont d'Ain, and along N.84 to Nantua and Bellegarde. We enjoyed the fast climb on third through the foothills of the Juras, using second for the sharper bends—and what "get-away" it gave us! At one point, when cruising at 80-plus on a seemingly continuous straight, we were suddenly confronted by a left bend. Actually there were two separate straights in perfect alignment, with a double bend in a dip between them. As our matelot described it later, "we let go the anchors and put the wheel to port" and with a swish of tyres ran smoothly round. But the quiet remark which broke the ensuing silence was shattering—"We nearly ran out of road" said Fergie. But as a demonstration of steadiness on a bend under hard braking it was an excellent performance.

At the French Customs the car papers were soon dealt with. Passports were in order, also our money. Then

# *Combined Operation . . . . . . . continued*

The imposing Palace of the League of Nations will become the headquarters of **the** European section of UNO.
Right: Despite the snowplough the snow lay thickly on the bends of the Col de la Faucille.

we were ordered to empty our pockets on to the table, to hold our coats open and were "frisked" in true American film fashion. Our luggage was not examined. At the Swiss Customs formalities took but seconds.

Geneva we enjoyed, and were sorry we could not see more of it. But with Swiss petrol in the tank, on which full advance could be used because it contains 20 per cent alcohol, we began our return journey at 08.00 hours on Saturday. We had to reach Arras that night, 410 miles away, which left us an easy 70 miles to Calais next day.

On the climb up the Col de la Faucille snow began to fall, and by the time we were up amidst the pines it was lying on the road. A Chevrolet truck barred the way; just ahead of it a huge Latil snowplough was clearing the road. Slowly we followed the labouring plough to the summit and down the descent. Then at a road fork the plough stopped, the Chevrolet charged the virgin snow on the road ahead, and we followed in its tracks. All went well until on a particularly wet and deep patch of snow we lost both steering and driving adhesion. We were snow-borne! The wet, sticky stuff had clung to the underside of sump, gear box and chassis generally, and we were planing off the top of the snow ridge between the ruts. Actually there was snow up round the engine under the bonnet.

We carried a spade, however, and so dug ourselves out. Then with borrowed strap-on chains we got going again. The resistance of the coagulating snow was so great that we were using full throttle on second gear downhill, incredible as it may seem. All this took valuable time, and not until noon were we clear of the snow. Then we began to motor seriously.

It is rather extraordinary that we got snowed up on la Faucille, although Fergie had managed to get through 157

Snow had fallen thickly since midnight and the big Latil snowplough towed a "dead" plough behind it as it cleared the road up la Faucille.

miles of snow on his way up from Coventry, and the explanation probably lies in the different nature of the snow. On la Faucille it was unusually wet and sticky and clung to everything, whereas in England it had been dry and powdery. Probably we should have been wise to reduce tyre pressures a little, as on the run from Coventry they had been let down to 18 lb per sq in. For fast running, however, they should be at 24 lb per sq in and we had taken considerable pains before leaving Geneva to get the pressures just right and were, therefore, loth to let the tyres down if we could avoid it. Two cars following us had no trouble, but then of course we had reduced the depth of snow through which they were running.

105 it went, the maximum reading and, with the crew urging it on excitedly, hard up against the stop, where we kept it for between two and three miles. That was on the first good stretch, quite level, and to prove that it was no accident we did it again a few miles farther on.

It was good to find the Univers at Arras undamaged and flourishing. After an excellent dinner we watched the guests arriving for the annual *soirée* of a local horse-breeding society. As they jockeyed for position with their cars in the courtyard we were glad that the Riley was safely locked up. At one moment we counted five cars all reversing and converging, but at the critical moment someone shouted "*assez*" and a crash was miraculously averted. The festivities went with a swing until 06.00 hours, but we had comfortable rooms in a quiet wing and were undisturbed.

## We Finish in a Gale

On Sunday we made a pilgrimage to two of the British military cemeteries near Arras, lunched early in the town, and ran swiftly to Calais. There is quite a lot of *pavé* on this road, and it was good to see that some of the biggest, narrowest and roughest paved villages are being by-passed. The crossing was reasonably smooth, although the sea was rising nastily as we entered Dover Harbour, but the boat train from Paris had been delayed, and so the boat was late and we were getting anxious about our time-table. However, we left Dover at 20.30 hours and found ourselves battling with a terrific gale as we sped London-wards. Showers of leaves blew over us and sizeable branches just missed us. At 23.00 hours we completed our combined operation with one hour in hand, thanks to the gallant Riley.

There is one point worth mentioning, for it should be remembered by those who may make a tour to Switzerland this year. That is, one must not take more than 4,000 French francs out of France. We had been warned of this and yet we had to bear in mind that we had to return across France on a Saturday and Sunday, and the French banks, we were told, close at 11.00 hours on Saturday. Our jugglings with travellers' cheques and French francs had, therefore, to be really skilful. We also had to watch the petrol coupon position, but having left England with a full tank and taking care to leave Switzerland with a full tank also, we managed it with one or two coupons in hand.

| Hour | Miles | Total | Av. Speed |
|------|-------|-------|-----------|
| 1st | 39 | 39 | 39.0 |
| 2nd | 50 | 89 | 44.5 |
| 3rd | 46 | 135 | 45.0 |
| 4th | 48 | 183 | 45.75 |
| 5th | 49 | 232 | 46.4 |
| 6th | 50 | 282 | 47.0 |
| 7th | 48 | 330 | 47.14 |
| 8th | 48 | 378 | 47.25 |
| 8½ | 20 | 398 | 46.8 |

We followed N.5 to Dijon, then N.74 to Langres, N.19 to Chaumont, N.67 to Joinville and St. Dizier, N.4 to Chalons-sur-Marne, N.44 to Reims and Cambrai, and finally N.39 to Arras. Our log read as above.

Possibly those figures give a falsely low idea of the car's great capabilities, but an average of nearly 47 m.p.h. for practically 400 miles swift travelling, especially as there were many slow sections, through numerous villages with rough *pavé*, through large towns, and over temporary bridges, and quite a number of halts. It is a pity that we did not keep a more detailed log, because some of the half-hour mileages were around a 60 m.p.h. average. Once at least 10 km. were covered in five minutes—an average of 75 m.p.h.

It was on this return trip that we found two stretches of road of excellent surface. Putting the Riley flat out, we watched the needle climb quickly round the dial to 90, and continue more slowly to the 100. Still it went on, 101, 102, the engine pulling strongly and the car riding as steadily as at half the speed. Up to

Leaving the hotel at Geneva on the start of the return journey.

## DATA FOR THE DRIVER

### 2½-LITRE RILEY

PRICE, with four-door four-light saloon body, £880, plus £245 3s. 10d. purchase tax, total, £1,125 3s. 10d.

RATING : 16 h.p., four cylinders, overhead valves, 80.5×120 mm., 2,443 c.c. TAX, £25.

BRAKE HORSE-POWER : 90 at 4,300 r.p.m.  COMPRESSION RATIO : 6.8 to 1.

WEIGHT, without passengers : 29 cwt.  LB. PER C.C. : 1.33.

TYRE SIZE : 6.00 × 16in on bolt-on steel disc wheels with wide-base rims.

LIGHTING SET : 12-volt.  Automatic voltage control.

TANK CAPACITY : 12½ gallons : approx. fuel consumption range, 20–25 m.p.g.

TURNING CIRCLE : (L.) 37ft ; (R.) 36ft. MINIMUM GROUND CLEARANCE : 6⅛in.

MAIN DIMENSIONS : Wheelbase, 9ft. 11in.  Track, 4ft 4½in (front and rear). Overall length, 15ft 6in ; width, 5ft 3in ; height, 4ft 11in.

WEATHER : Dry, mild, wind fresh.

### ACCELERATION

| Overall gear ratios | From steady m.p.h of | | |
|---|---|---|---|
| | 10 to 30 | 20 to 40 | 30 to 50 |
| 4.11 to 1 | 10.8 sec | 10.4 sec | 10.9 sec |
| 5.81 to 1 | 7.3 sec | 7.6 sec | 8.3 sec |
| 8.85 to 1 | 5.3 sec | 5.9 sec | — |
| 15.00 to 1 | — | — | — |

From rest through gears to—

| | | | |
|---|---|---|---|
| 30 m.p.h. | .. | .. | .. 6.4 sec |
| 50 m.p.h. | .. | .. | .. 13.3 sec |
| 60 m.p.h. | .. | .. | .. 18.8 sec |
| 70 m.p.h. | .. | .. | .. 26.7 sec |

Steering wheel movement from lock to lock : 2⅓ turns.

Speedometer correction by Electrical Speedometer : 10=12 ;  20=22 ; 30=31 ; 40=40 ; 50=50 ; 60=60 ; 70=69.5 ;  80=80.

Speeds attainable on indirect gears (by Electrical Speedometer)—

| | | | M.p.h. (normal and max.) |
|---|---|---|---|
| 1st | .. | .. | 20–25 |
| 2nd | .. | .. | 36–43 |
| 3rd | .. | .. | 55–70 |

Acceleration figures are the means of several runs in opposite directions.

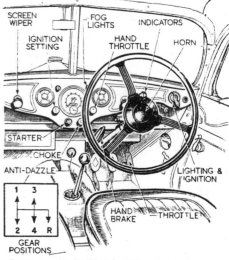

SCREEN WIPER — FOG LIGHTS — INDICATORS — IGNITION SETTING — HAND THROTTLE — HORN — STARTER — CHOKE — ANTI-DAZZLE — LIGHTING & IGNITION — HAND BRAKE — THROTTLE — GEAR POSITIONS

*Current model described in " The Autocar " of November 29, 1946.*

---

TESTING of this car on the road was undertaken with the keenest sense of anticipation, for already the broadly similar 1½-litre has been winning a reputation for itself, and it was clear from the specification of the 2½-litre, when it was announced towards the end of 1946, that this was likely to be something remarkable in cars.

Extensive, indeed intensive, trial of this model has resulted in expectations being even exceeded. As a whole this is an outstanding car of the present time. To start with, it is as new a car in design and appearance as has yet come into production from any British factory since the war, although the 16 h.p. 2½-litre four-cylinder engine is basically a type that was well proved before the war.

It is not easy in comparatively few words to give a picture of this machine. To some extent the accompanying performance figures and other data which have been obtained tell the story, but, as always, not the whole of it.

This Riley has a magnificent all-round performance, including a very high maximum speed. It provides with moderate engine capacity and a comfortable four-seater saloon body the kind of performance for which not many years ago at least 3½ litres would have been necessary. The effect of the car as a whole is to provide a refreshing re-minder that the sports car of years ago is not dead as regards some of the best points belonging to that type, but with, in addition, the advantages of modern design, especially as regards suspension.

For covering journeys in the shortest possible time by road this car has few equals, for it has no particular speed at which it is "best," and it can be cruised as fast as road and traffic conditions permit up to an easily attained rate of 80 m.p.h., where there is at least 10 m.p.h. in reserve. The highest reading obtained in this country was 90 by a speedometer of extraordinary accuracy as tested by *The Autocar's* electrical master speedometer.

Such abilities would be worth little, in fact would be a menace, if with them did not go superlative features of control. This car's suspension, besides affording an extremely high degree of riding comfort, is such as to tie it down to the road for fast cornering and under braking, enabling curves to be rounded at speeds which represent the maximum of many another car on the straight. The brakes, which are the Girling hydro-mechanical system, perform wonders in dealing safely with the high rates at which the driver to whom such a car appeals finds himself habitually handling it where conditions permit him to do so.

There is firmness in the suspension but not harshness. It irons out road inequalities, an ability which it has had particular opportunities of displaying during the test with so many instances as there are at present of damage to road surfaces from the winter frosts. One can tell, sometimes from audible evidence under extreme conditions, that shocks are being received by the suspension, but the level riding is seldom disturbed, and back-seat passengers travel in an extraordinary degree of comfort even when speeds are being held between 60 and 90 m.p.h. It will be remembered that the front wheels are independently sprung, by means of torsion bars.

The steering is exactly suited to the performance. In common with the suspension, if two dissimilar components can be compared, it has firmness but is not heavy or tiring, though at low speed the driver has definitely to steer round sharp corners against strong self-centring caster action.

On fast bends, however, he does little more than bear on the wheel to take the car round in a smooth sweep, and it goes exactly where he desires to place it.

It is perhaps some indication of the kind of car this is that the inclination was felt to cover with it more than 1,000 miles in less than a week of comprehensive testing, which included special journeys for the purpose of ascertaining this remarkable car's average speed capabilities on English roads. As recounted in the last issue, it so happens, too, that at about the same period a similar car was taken by a member of *The Autocar* staff to Switzerland with three passengers and luggage. Thus from the two experiences, Continental and home, a complete picture has been gained of the latest Riley's behaviour.

### Average Speed Performances

Performances on the Continental run included average speeds in excess of 46 m.p.h., including stops, over nearly 400 miles, but many people will be more interested in what the car can do on our own more restricted roads. Conditions having been selected as far as possible, over a favourable route, it was established that the Riley can make running time averages even in England of the order of 50 m.p.h. in safety. The average over 199 miles, counting running time only, was 47.76 m.p.h., or 43.42 m.p.h. in overall time. Quarter-hour readings were obtained showing averages rising, as road conditions improved, from 45 m.p.h. up to 56 m.p.h., whilst the best half-hour gave 29.5 miles or an average of 59 m.p.h., but conditions then intervened and the hour run in question finished with a total of 51 miles covered in sixty minutes.

It will be noticed that a maximum of 70 m.p.h. is available on third gear and over 40 on second. On top gear 60 m.p.h. is obtained without any effort at all. After experience has been gained of the car at higher speeds this seems little more than an ambling gait. Safety is the keynote of this very fast car's behaviour at all times.

With so high-efficiency an engine of no great size some disadvantages might be expected at the lower end of the scale, and it is true that in traffic and in by-way motoring extensive use of the gear box is desirable, since the characteristics of the engine are such as to suggest a change to third at appreciably below 20 m.p.h., though in point of fact, as a test figure, the engine will pull smoothly at 12 m.p.h. on top gear. The engine is essentially of sports car character, but not intractable or noisy or rough. In fact as a whole it is smooth, though possessing a certain hardness that is in many ways attractive. Perhaps above all, there is the impression of the 2½-litre Riley being thoroughly up to its work and of the engine being able to withstand really hard work.

With such performance as is available on the indirect gears it can be handled as a "gear box" car, though the engine takes hold strongly in accelerating at about 25 m.p.h. on top. On present petrol there is some pinking, and sometimes a tendency to run on after switching off, though the pinking can be minimized by means of a setting control on the instrument board without serious detriment to the performance. It was noticed that on the good Swiss petrol the example taken abroad displayed neither pinking nor running on.

The gear change is a delightful one with a vertical remote control lever in exactly the right position, and synchromesh on top, third and second, which works extremely well. First gear makes itself audible. The other gears are pleasantly subdued, but not silent.

Considering the work that they are so frequently given the brakes, as already indicated, deserve the highest praise. The pedal action is not heavy, and straight-line safe braking without pull on the steering is obtained at all times, including occasions when a corner is being taken fast and need for braking arises. The clutch action is smooth for starting without special care being taken. There is fair room for the left foot off the clutch pedal during normal driving, though an ideal position is not attained.

One of the first impressions concerns the excellent forward visibility, again in the old style. The driver can see both wings, a point which adds greatly to confidence. The large spring-spoked steering wheel is raked at just the right angle and is telescopically adjustable.

Immediate starting from cold is obtained with the hand throttle—an unusual and welcome fitting nowadays—opened to a fast tick-over position. The choke can be closed almost as soon as the engine fires. A radiator thermometer is a welcome fitting on the instrument board.

Good support is given by the seats, front and back. For the upholstery cloth edged with leather is used. The rear seat passengers are placed low. Arm rests are not provided at the centre or the sides, nor is a sliding roof fitted, which some owners will regret. The body is well finished, but interior heating and de-icing equipment is not included. The head lamp beam is capital for fast driving.

The battery is really accessible beneath the bonnet; the tools also are carried there, including a very effective portable hydraulic jack which is applied with the utmost ease to sockets at front and rear. A great deal of luggage space is provided.

Measurements are taken with the driving seat at the central position of fore and aft adjustment. These body diagrams are to scale.

# ◄ *Riley* ► 1½ LITRE . . . . . . .

## —again contributing toward better Motoring

*It is almost fifty years since Mr Percy Riley built his first car, and during that fifty years the firm of Riley has become famous, both on and off the race track.*

Pioneers of the small high performance four cylinder engine, Riley cars have always been outstanding in both design and performance, and in their new 1½ litre model, have incorporated all the finer features gained during their long experience.

The new car is undeniably Riley, but its performance marks a step forward even over what one was accustomed to expect from a Riley in the past.

### DESIGN.

The new body is styled on the most modern lines, with a sleek swept down top and a squat, wide, big car appearance. At the front the familiar Riley radiator is retained,, the headlamps are built in, and neat external fog lights are fitted. The doors, hinged on the centre pillar, are wide and expose practically the whole depth of each seat, making entry easier than usual on such a low car.

The tail sweeps back to a spacious luggage compartment which accentuates the graceful body lines of the car.

### POWER LAYOUT.

The famous Riley four cylinder overhead valve engine is retained almost unchanged, although considerably more power is now obtained. Flexibly mounted in the frame, the 12 h.p. engine produces 55 b.h.p. at 4,500 r.p.m. which gives some idea of the performance of the car.

The engine has a camshaft high up on each side of the block, and these operate short push rods to the rocker gear.

The most outstanding breakaway from past Riley practice is in the front suspension. The "Torsionic" independent suspension consists of parallel independent torsion bars, with Harris bushings which do not require any lubrication or maintenance. Normal semi-elliptics are provided at the rear.

The steering is new and of the horizontal rack and pinion type. There is a four speed gear box with synchro mesh on second, third and top, and a remote control racing type gear lever mounted in the centre.

The Girling hydro-mechanical brakes operate on 10 in. drums and produce 60 per cent. of the braking effort. A pistol grip hand brake is fitted.

### PERFORMANCE.

As might be expected of this Riley, the road performance is outstanding. The engine is smooth and flexible. Like all Rileys this is a dual purpose car, and one can either drive it peacably and comfortably, or else use its terrific potentialities as a sports car.

It can corner like a racing car and can be "placed" to an inch even at very high speed; yet at its cruising speed of 50 m.p.h. it is superbly comfortable.

It is capable of speeds of 75–80 m.p.h. and yet gives a performance of 30 m.p.g. at normal speed.

Like previous Rileys, this is a car for the connoisseur, but particularly ones like me who still have the urge to own a sports car but are a but too old for the discomforts that usually accompany it. This is a comfortable sports car indeed!

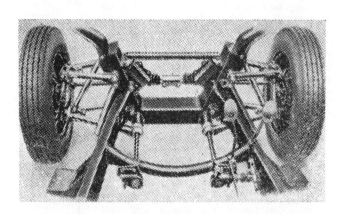

Parallel torsion bars replace the orthodox front springs.

¾ FRONT VIEW OF THE NEW RILEY 1½ LITRE SALOON

## INTERIOR.

The interior is simply and beautifully finished, and is more roomy than any previous model. Seats are low and wide, giving ample accommodation for five large adults. The upholstery is in leather, the instrument panel and all cappings in polished walnut.

*The sprung telescopic steering wheel is comfortably raked, and the windscreen gives excellent visibility. Instruments simply and neatly laid out in the centre of the panel, and underneath, a wide shelf is provided.*

*Price is £1,181 plus tax.*

## SPECIFICATIONS.

**ENGINE.**
12 h.p. four cylinders, 69 x 100 mm. (1,496 c.c.). Overhead valves at 90 degrees in hemi-spherical combustion chambers. Three-bearing crankshaft. Aluminium alloy pistons. S.U. carburetter. Lucas coil ignition. Mechanical fuel pump. Full-flow oil filter. Cross-flow pump cooling.

**TRANSMISSION.**
Borg and Beck clutch. Four speed gear box. Synchromesh on second, third and top. Overall ratios: First, 19.8; second, 11.2; third, 7.2; top, 4.88 to1. Enclosed propellor shaft to spiral bevel rear axle.

**BRAKES.**
Girling Hydro-mechanical in 10 in. drums.

**SUSPENSION.**
Independent front and half-elliptic rear springs.

**STEERING.**
Special Riley, with 17 in. adjustable steering wheel.

**FUEL TANK CAPACITY.**
12½ gallons.

**LEADING DIMENSIONS.**
Wheelbase 9 ft. 4½ in. Track 4 ft. 3 in. Overall length 14 ft. 10 in., width, 5 ft. 2½ in., height 4 ft. 9 in. Ground clearance 7 in.

**TYRES.**
Dunlop 5.75 x 16 on wide-base rims. Disc wheels.

**WEIGHT.**
24½ cwt.

No. 1338

1½-LITRE

RILEY

SALOON

# *The* Autocar ROAD TESTS

## DATA FOR THE DRIVER

### 1½-LITRE RILEY

PRICE, with four-door four-light saloon body, £675, plus £188 5s purchase tax. Total £863 5s.

RATING : 11.9 h.p., 4 cylinders, o.h.v., 69 × 100 mm, 1,496 c.c. TAX (1947), £15.

BRAKE HORSE-POWER : 55 at 4,500 r.p.m. COMPRESSION RATIO : 6.75 to 1.

WEIGHT, without passengers, 24 cwt 1 qr. LB. PER C.C. : 1.82.

TYRE SIZE : 5.75 × 16in on bolt-on steel disc wheels.

LIGHTING SET : 12-volt. Automatic voltage control.

TANK CAPACITY : 12½ gallons ; approx. fuel consumption range, 25-29 m.p.g.

TURNING CIRCLE : 30ft (L and R). MINIMUM GROUND CLEARANCE : 7½in.

MAIN DIMENSIONS : Wheelbase, 9ft 4½in. Track, 4ft 4½in (front and rear).
Overall length, 14ft 11in ; width, 5ft 3½in ; height, 4ft 11in.

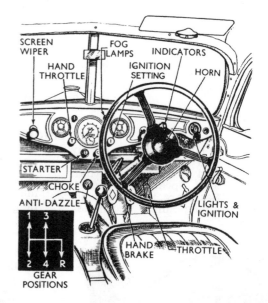

| ACCELERATION | | | |
|---|---|---|---|
| Overall gear ratios | *From steady m.p.h. of* | | |
| | 10 to 30 | 20 to 40 | 30 to 50 |
| 4.89 to 1 | 12.7 sec. | 13.3 sec. | 15.3 sec. |
| 7.23 to 1 | 8.6 sec. | 9.5 sec. | 12.0 sec. |
| 11.20 to 1 | 6.4 sec. | — | — |
| 19.42 to 1 | — | — | — |

From rest through gears to:—

| | | |
|---|---|---|
| 30 m.p.h. | .. .. | 7.8 sec. |
| 50 m.p.h. | .. .. | 19.0 sec. |
| 60 m.p.h. | .. .. | 31.2 sec. |

Steering wheel movement from lock to lock : 2¼ turns.

Speedometer correction by Electrical Speedometer : 10 (car speedometer) = 8 ; 20 = 18.5 ; 30 = 28.5 ; 40 = 37.5 ; 50 = 47 ; 60 = 54.5.

Speeds attainable on indirect gears (by electrical speedometer)

| | | M.p.h. (normal and max.) |
|---|---|---|
| 1st | .. .. .. | 14–21 |
| 2nd | .. .. .. | 30–36 |
| 3rd | .. .. .. | 48–54 |

WEATHER : Dry, warm ; wind negligible.

Acceleration figures are the means of several runs in opposite directions.

*Current model described in " The Autocar " of February 22, 1946.*

---

IT is possible to take a national pride in the fact that so very good a car in the overall sense as the 1½-litre Riley is produced in this country. This, indeed, is a first-rate example of a type of car which can be said to be peculiar to the British motor industry and which is made better here than anywhere else in the world. The qualities that make it so desirable in an experienced British motorist's eyes are exactly those to appeal to owners in other countries, among them economy of running, comfort of the suspension, and a remarkable accuracy of control which, allied with other features such as a really rigid frame, gives the car an extremely high safety factor.

By no means least, the Riley is modern, with its torsion bar independent front suspension and an external appearance which takes the eye and yet is not gaudy. The frontal treatment in particular shows a concession towards present tendencies, in the building-in of the head lamps, yet the characteristics of a "real car" are retained.

The present occasion is not the first on which *The Autocar* has had road experience of the 1½-litre Riley, but it has afforded a more long-distance opportunity than hitherto of judging the car and of forming opinions which can come only from living with a car in everyday conditions for a time. A very high opinion indeed has been formed of this car, and not for a few features or for its spirited performance alone, but because of a combination of points of appeal in the design and general arrangement

and in its behaviour on the road. The result is to make one feel strongly that here is a car well designed and honestly and soundly built, which should give an owner excellent service, and which has such qualities as to lift motoring far above the plane of transport alone.

There is performance in plenty for most requirements as regards the top end of the speed range and decided life in the acceleration ; the figures coldly measured by stop-watch come as something of a favourable surprise when one remembers that an engine of only 1½ litres is pulling a saloon body of generous size for four people and not a featherweight, cramped for space. Further, it possesses a suspension of exceptional merit in both the comfort afforded and the stability provided for cornering and holding the car four-square to the road at speed. It feels completely safe, and passengers, as well as the driver, have the impression of travelling in a train as regards the better features of railway travel. In addition it is a suspension remarkably effective in taking the sting out of really bad surfaces such as are found away from the big towns in overseas territories. Passengers with experience of many cars describe the rear seat riding as altogether exceptional for the absence of shock and for the fact that they are not thrown sideways during fast cornering, even though a central arm rest is not fitted.

From the first moment of starting the engine in the garage in the morning, throughout a day's run with all

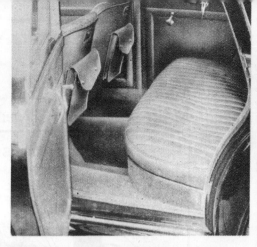

its variety of conditions—traffic, speed on the clear stretches, and climbing—this Riley conveys the suggestion as strongly as it is possible for it to be conveyed of robustness and efficiency. Also one senses quality not only in things that can be seen, but beneath the surface, too.

The Riley firm are second to none in length of experience of building a high-output 1½-litre four-cylinder engine, and a remarkably good unit they produce. This engine will rev freely and still remain smooth, and even at its limit of performance on top gear it still makes no fuss, and consequently no sense of strain is induced in the driver or passengers. On level ground, with no help from the wind, a speed of 74 m.p.h. was recorded on *The Autocar's* master speedometer; perhaps 3 or 4 m.p.h. beyond that creditable figure could be gained under more helpful conditions. The car quickly gets up into the 60s and holds the speed well, but such is the engine's behaviour that within the limit available, the road conditions and the driver's ideas of the moment are alone the factors governing the speed which shall be used.

## An All-round Appeal

It is not a function of this Road Test to make comparison with the 1½-litre's more powerful and longer-wheelbase companion, the 2½-litre, a Road Test of which *The Autocar* has already published. It may, however, be remarked by one who has sampled the two cars under similar conditions, with a lapse of time between the tests, that the 1½-litre comes as no disappointment for, as already indicated, it has enough sheer performance to make it interesting to drive and, in conjunction with its qualities of road holding, to give it 40 m.p.h. averaging capabilities without tiring the occupants or making the driver work hard. It is a capital all-rounder, by which is meant that besides being able to travel fast it is tractable and flexible, and in fact shows these qualities to a remarkable extent. It can be handled largely on top and third gears in traffic, yet be started smoothly from rest on second gear, and climb all but the more unusual kind of hill on third gear. Second gear sufficed to take it comfortably up a 1 in 6½ gradient on which baulking by other traffic occurred and a fast approach was prevented. An ignition setting control is provided, and with this moved towards the retarded position pinking on the present petrol is virtually eliminated without noticeable loss of performance.

The steering is quite high geared, but is not heavy, and gives the driver an exceptional accuracy of control which, coupled with the fact that the riding is about as stable and

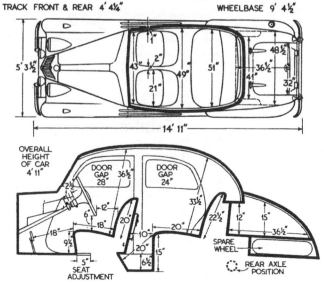

TRACK FRONT & REAR 4' 4¼"    WHEELBASE 9' 4½"

Full use of the available width is made in the rear seat by the absence of elbow rests, and good leg room is provided by means of wells, which incorporate comfortably sloped foot rests. The wallet-type pockets are practical.

even-keel as that of a saloon car is ever likely to be, leaves him unconcerned at what other people on the road may do, for gaps can be shot with complete certainty. Little indication is given by the car's behaviour of what is the ideal speed at which a driver strange to it should take fast bends. It can be cornered with minimum movement of the wheel with a feeling of complete balance, and the safety margin in this as in other connections is wide. The Girling hydro-mechanical brakes do their full share in maintaining this margin, and throughout the test never at any time left the driver with the uneasy suggestion of being near the point of " running out of brake."

The gear change is among the excellent features, with synchromesh on second, third and top of an effectiveness which seldom lets the driver over-ride it and grate teeth. On the infrequent occasions when he does do this, he usually realizes that his clutch technique has been at fault. The lever itself is vertical and all its movements are silkily smooth yet positive. The hand-brake control, of pull-out type under the instrument board, is handy enough to reach and out of the way as regards forming an obstruction, but a pull-up lever between the front seats would be preferred. That remark, plus the fact that a perfect off-the-clutch position is not found for the left foot, and the personal point that it is regarded as a pity that the car is not fitted with a sliding roof, are, indeed, the only adverse comments to be offered, other than on points of detail which arise on every car, and on which opinion is to some extent a matter of individual inclinations. As regards a sliding roof, it is realized, of course, that overseas this fitting is apt to be more a disadvantage than an asset, whilst even in this country by no means every motorist is partial to it.

The driving position brings the driver close up to the spring-spoked wheel, which is telescopically adjustable, and he has extremely satisfactory vision through the deep V windscreen. An average-height driver can see enough of the near-side wing to be useful, and does not notice the central strip of the screen frame as an obstruction to vision. The section of the screen in front of the driver can be opened out. A very good rearward view is given by the mirror, though on a much reduced scale. The horn note is strong but not raucous. The off-side head lamp beam was set too close to the car, reducing the range more than was ideal for fast night driving, but in spite of the built-in principle the beam is readily adjustable.

A luggage boot of very considerable carrying capacity rounds off a body of excellent lines and practical features. The engine is neat and well finished, with its main auxiliaries accessible. It started and warmed up from cold with less use of the mixture control than is general; a hand throttle is fitted for the benefit of those who still like to warm up before moving off. Among the instruments is that now rare but valuable provision, an engine water thermometer. Twin petrol tank fillers make filling up easy from either side and the tank is of a generous size as regards range without replenishing.

Measurements are taken with the driving seat at the central position of fore and aft adjustment. These body diagrams are to scale.

# The Motor Road Test No. 12/47

**Make:** Riley **Type:** 1½-litre Saloon

**Makers:** Riley (Coventry) Limited, Coventry

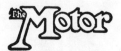

## Dimensions and Seating

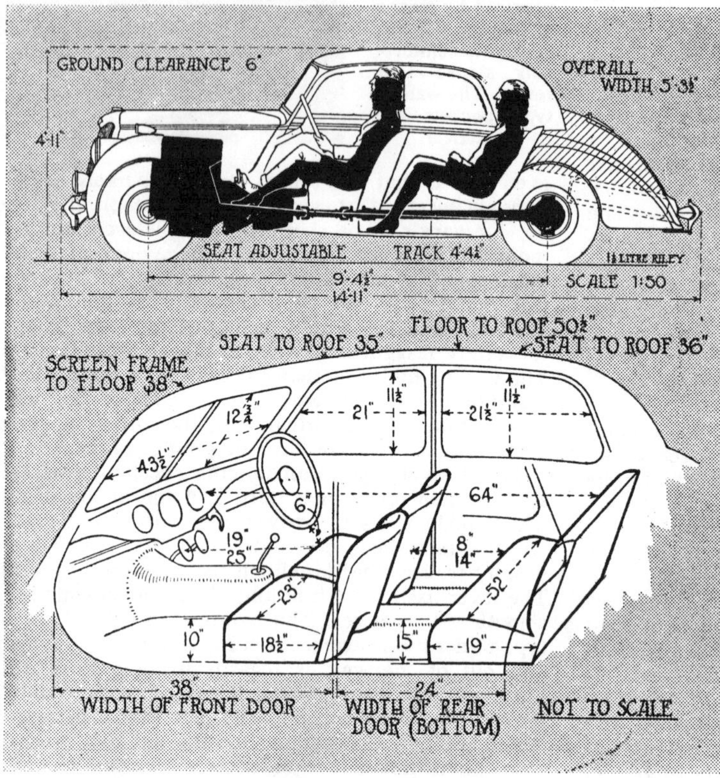


## Test Conditions

Fine, warm, light wind, dry concrete. Pool petrol and natural rubber tyres.

## Test Data

**ACCELERATION TIMES on Two Upper Ratios**

| | Top | 3rd |
|---|---|---|
| 10–30 m.p.h. | 12.9 secs. | 8.3 secs. |
| 20–40 m.p.h. | 13.2 secs. | 8.6 secs. |
| 30–50 m.p.h. | 13.9 secs. | 10.5 secs. |
| 40–60 m.p.h. | 17.1 secs. | — |
| 50–70 m.p.h. | 23.0 secs. | — |

**ACCELERATION TIMES through Gears**

| | |
|---|---|
| 0–30 m.p.h. | 6.0 secs. |
| 0–40 m.p.h. | 10.7 secs. |
| 0–50 m.p.h. | 16.5 secs. |
| 0–60 m.p.h. | 25.1 secs. |
| 0–70 m.p.h. | 38.7 secs. |
| Standing quarter-mile | 23.0 secs. |

**MAXIMUM SPEEDS**

**Flying Quarter-mile**

| | |
|---|---|
| Mean of six opposite runs | 78.0 m.p.h. |
| Best time equals | 81.8 m.p.h. |

**Speed in Gears**

| | |
|---|---|
| Maximum speed in 3rd gear | 54 m.p.h. |
| Maximum speed in 2nd gear | 35 m.p.h. |

**BRAKES at 30 m.p.h.**

0.90 g. (=33.5 ft. stopping distance) with 95 lb. pedal pressure.
0.52 g. (=58.0 ft. stopping distance) with 75 lb. pedal pressure.
0.35 g. (=86.1 ft. stopping distance) with 50 lb. pedal pressure.
0.20 g. (=151.0 ft. stopping distance) with 25 lb. pedal pressure.

**FUEL CONSUMPTION**

Overall consumption (driven hard) for 603 miles, 23 gallons, equals 26.2 m.p.g.
35.9 m.p.g. at constant 30 m.p.h.
32.5 m.p.g. at constant 40 m.p.h.
29.5 m.p.g. at constant 50 m.p.h.
26.4 m.p.g. at constant 60 m.p.h.
21.6 m.p.g. at constant 70 m.p.h.

**HILL CLIMBING**

Max. top gear speed on 1 in 20 .. 55 m.p.h.
Max. top gear speed on 1 in 15 .. 45 m.p.h.
Max. gradient climbable on top gear, 1 in 12.8 (Tapley 175 lb. per ton).
Max. gradient climbable on 3rd gear, 1 in 8.4 (Tapley 265 lb. per ton).
Max. gradient climbable on 2nd gear, 1 in 5.9 (Tapley 375 lb. per ton).

**STEERING**

Left-hand lock .. 30 ft.
Right-hand lock .. 30 ft.
2¼ turns of steering wheel, lock to lock.

## Miscellaneous

Rear springs are rubber bushed. Inner mountings of front suspension struts are also rubber mounted. Front shock absorbers are the sealed type. Engine oil S.A.E. 20 for extreme cold condition (under 32 degrees F.). Steering gearbox lubricated with Duckham's Laminoid Soft each 30,000 miles. (No grease nipple fitted—cover to be removed.)

## In Brief

| | |
|---|---|
| Price: | £675 0s. 0d. plus purchase tax £188 5s. 0d. = £863 5s. 0d. |
| Capacity | 1,496 c.c. |
| Road weight unladen as tested | 24¾ cwt. |
| Front/rear weight distribution | 12¼ cwt./12½ cwt. |
| Laden weight as tested | 27¾ cwt. |
| Fuel consumption | 26-28 m.p.g. |
| Maximum speed | 78.0 m.p.h. |
| Maximum speed on 1 in 20 gradient | 55.0 m.p.h. |
| Maximum top gear gradient | 1 in 12.8 |
| Acceleration | 10-30 on top: 12.9 secs. 0-50 through gears: 16.5 secs. |
| Gearing | 16.0 m.p.h. in top at 1,000 r.p.m. 61.2 m.p.h. at 2,500 feet per minute piston speed. |

## Specification

| | |
|---|---|
| **Engine:** | |
| Cylinders | 4 |
| Bore | 69 mm. |
| Stroke | 100 mm. |
| Cubic capacity | 1,496 c.c. |
| Piston area | 23.2 sq. ins. |
| Valves | o.h.v. (short push rods) |
| Compression ratio | 6.7 to 1 |
| Max. b.h.p. | 55 |
| at | 4,500 r.p.m. |
| B.H.P. per sq. in. piston area | 2.37 |
| Piston speed at max. b.h.p. | 2,960 ft./min. |
| Carburetter | S.U. Model H.2 |
| Ignition | Lucas coil |
| Sparking plugs | Champion L10S |
| Fuel pump | A.C. mechanical |
| Oil filter | Full-flow |
| **Transmission:** | |
| Clutch | Borg and Beck, single plate, 8 ins. diameter |
| Top gear | 4.89 |
| 3rd gear | 7.23 |
| 2nd gear | 11.2 |
| 1st gear | 19.42 |
| Propeller shaft | Torque tube drive. Short intermediate shaft between torque tube and gearbox |
| Final drive | Spiral bevel |
| **Chassis:** | |
| Brakes | Girling hydro-mech. |
| Brake drum diameter | 10 ins. |
| Friction lining area | 126.48 sq. ins. |
| Tyres | 5.75 ins. by 16 ins. |
| Steering gear | Rack and pinion (helical gears) |
| **Performance Factors:** (At laden weight as tested) | |
| Piston area, sq. in. per ton | 18.7 |
| Brake lining area, sq. in. per ton | 102 |
| Litres per ton-mile | 2,270 |

Fully described in "The Motor," February 27, 1946

## Maintenance

**Fuel tank:** 12½ gallons. **Sump:** 10 pints, S.A.E. 30. **Gearbox:** 2 pints, S.A.E. 140. **Rear axle:** 2¾ pints, 140. **Radiator:** 13 pints (complete cooling system). **Chassis lubrication:** Grease gun, 16 points Duckham's Laminoid Soft. **Ignition timing:** 8 degrees B.T.D.C. fuel advance. **Spark plug gap:** .030 in. **Contact-breaker gap:** .012 to .015 in. **Tappets** (hot/cold): Inlet, .003 in.; exhaust, .004 in. **Front wheel toe-in:** Nil. **Camber angle:** 1 degree. **Castor angle:** 3 degrees. **Tyre pressures:** Front, 22 lb.; rear, 24 lb. **Brake fluid:** Girling hydraulic fluid **Shock absorber fluid** (rears only): Luvax Girling fluid. **Battery:** Lucas 12-volt, 58-amp./hr. **Lamp bulbs:** Single pole Lucas, 36-watt head, 6-watt side and tail, 24-watt reversing.

# The Riley 1½-litre Saloon

## Tireless Performance and Excellent Road-holding Combine With All-passenger Comfort and Good Visibility

TIGHT TURN.—The small turning circle of 30 ft. is particulary useful for town driving and parking.

FEW post-war designs have had a better reception than was accorded to the 1½-litre Riley on its first announcement early last year; and few have created greater respect in the hands of private owners in the intervening period.

One has only to drive this model a few miles to appreciate some of the reasons for this. Perhaps the greatest of them all was summed up by the sub-heading to our original description—" sports car behaviour with town carriage manners."

Every enthusiastic motorist appreciates high performance, but nowadays it is not even every enthusiast who appreciates the penalties that so often used to go with it. With the Riley the user makes no sacrifice in the interests of a very crisp performance, excellent road-holding and steering that is amongst the most accurate we have tried.

On the score of appearance, also, this Riley has a universal appeal, because it has lines which will offend none. Aerodynamically, the shape of the car is good, but not extreme, and its general lines are such as to satisfy modern thought without offending conservative tastes which cling to the classic line in external styling

FORWARD POSITION. — Rear-seat passengers sit well forward of the rear axle and two deep footwells provide adequate leg room. Pockets for maps and small articles and disappearing ashtrays are fitted to the back of the front seats.

One further attraction of this car may be mentioned at the outset. The 1½-litre Riley is not one of those models, sometimes encountered, which create a very favourable first impression, but which one tends to "find out" as the miles pile up. Closer acquaintance (we covered close on 750 miles with the test model) merely served to endear it the more.

One reason for this is that the average speed potentialities of the car are greater than its mere performance figures suggest, creditable as the latter are. Its combination of road-worthy qualities (which will be analysed individually later) give both driver and passenger a sense of mental and physical serenity which makes long journeys less tiring and high average speeds less exacting. A point which has to be borne in mind, too, is the fact that the essential stability and controlability of the car call for less interruption in the driver's normal cruising speed when obstructions and corners are encountered than is the case with a car which has less of the thoroughbred about its steering and suspension.

The acceleration and speed figures given in the accompanying data panel tell their own factual tale regarding performance. It remains to add that the engine has that indefinable quality of willingness about it which invites the driver to make full use of its potentialities and never promotes qualms as to whether it is being over-driven. The standard of silence and smoothness are not exceptional and the driver is, in fact, conscious that he is handling a machine, but the way that machine behaves is thoroughly satisfying and restful.

### High Cruising Speeds

A cruising speed of 60-65 m.p.h. is entirely effortless and the former figure is reached quickly and held easily. Another detail of performance which was notable during the performance tests was the consistency with which the car behaved on various runs, a point which suggests maintenance of tune over long periods.

Engine performance is allied to a transmission system which includes a gearbox and axle providing a good standard of silence, whilst the gear change itself (synchromesh on all except first gear) is positive in action and responds well to rapid treatment on those odd occasions when ultimate acceleration through the gears is required. The only occasions when we experienced any protest were partly of our own making through not depressing the clutch pedal to the full extent of its rather long travel. This may have been partly due to the particular pedal adjustment of the car tried (which was such that the clutch did not free fully until the pedal was completely depressed), but, even so, a shorter clutch travel would undoubtedly make driving more pleasant. Another minor criticism concerning the clutch pedal is that its position in relation to the clutch and gearbox housing leaves little room for the driver's left foot except on the pedal itself.

Reference has already been made to the excellent road-holding and cornering qualities of the Riley, qualities which result from the combination of a suspension system incorporating torsion bars and wishbones at the front and semi-elliptics at the rear, together with a rack-and-pinion steering mechanism and good weight distribution. The outcome is a ride which is steady at all speeds, and although, perhaps, a little on the firm side on bumpy cobbles, is never harsh. As for steering, the rack-and-pinion system gives light operation and extreme accuracy, with no trace of kick-back through the steering wheel. For town driving and parking, the layout earns additional praise by reason of the unusually small turning circle of only 30 ft.

## Good Layout

The layout of the controls (apart from the minor criticism already registered regarding the clutch pedal) is, on the whole, excellent. The spring-spoke steering wheel, with its extensible column, is capable of adjustment to the ideal position for any driver, and stubby remote-control gear lever and pistol-grip hand brake are nicely placed where the hand can slip easily from one to the other.

A slight alteration in the hand-brake angle, however, would remove the risk of a driver catching his knuckles on the tip of the pistol-grip when the gear lever is moved into a forward position with the hand brake applied. This, however, is only a minor criticism, and so also is the suggestion that a better place might be found for the foot dipper switch, which at present calls for the left leg being raised to reach it.

The layout of the facia board is pleasant and the use of polished walnut for the board itself a welcome change from plastics and painted metals. In addition to the usual dials, instruments include a water temperature thermometer, whilst the board also houses two minor controls, which will appeal to the discerning driver, in the shape of a screw-out hand throttle and a manual advance and retard knob.

The latter is of particular advantage in this era of poor petrol, because it has enabled the manufacturers to avoid performance sacrifices in the interests of eliminating pinking by enabling the driver readily to overcome any tendencies (and they are not very pronounced) in this direction.

## Seeing Clearly

Driving comfort is aided also by first-class visibility. Not only can the driver see the whole array of wing tips, lamps and radiator top but, owing to the pronounced slope of the windscreen and the fact that he sits close to it, he also suffers far less than usual from the inevitable blind spot created by the windscreen pillars. For fog-driving (or ventilation), the driver's half of the screen, which is of the Vee type, can be swung open. A further detail in favour of good visibility is the use of a driving mirror of the reducing type, which enables a small mirror to be used, thus causing a minimum obstruction of vision whilst still giving an adequate view through the rear window.

In addition to the opening windscreen pane, ventilators at the side of the scuttle are a further aid to keeping the interior fresh.

Driver comfort is matched by passenger comfort, the rear seats, in particular, being exceptionally comfortable. So far as the front passenger is concerned, a forward, sliding, individual seat is used, and the manufacturers could make a distinct improvement in passenger comfort here by shaping it to conform more nearly to the old-fashioned bucket type. This does not imply any fault in the existing seat, which is very comfortable indeed; it is simply that the alteration would give the front passenger that little lateral support on corners which would make a big increase in comfort when the driver happens to be exercising the fine cornering qualities of the car to the full. The driver himself has the steering wheel to hold, but the front passenger is very apt to find himself sliding sideways on the cushion.

Luggage accommodation takes the form of a large rear locker with a very big platform area above the spare wheel which enables a substantial quantity of baggage to be carried. For odds and ends, there is a parcel tray beneath the facia board and very useful patch-type pockets on the backs of the front seats, besides a small shelf behind the rear squab. Other items of equipment include a pair of "pass lamps," an easy jacking system by means of a detachable jack which engages with special sockets under the bumper over-riders at front and back, visors for driver and passenger, a bonnet locked by a carriage-type key, twin filler caps for the 12½-gallon fuel tank, and all the usual instruments and fittings.

When we handed the car back, there was a distinct feeling of parting with a friend, for the Riley has an individuality —and a typically British individuality at that—which makes it anything but "just another car," and the thought was irrepressible that it will be a bad day for the British motor industry if its like ever disappears in a misguided worship of standardization.

COCKPIT VIEW.—Layout of the driving compartment shows careful planning. The large instruments are easy to read, hand brake and gear levers are well placed and the extensible steering column provides the correct steering wheel location for drivers of varying heights.

AID TO VISION.—The section of the V-screen in front of the driver is made to open up and provide a clear view for fog-driving.

# for Magnificent Motoring

"The longer wheel-base and longer bonnet add to the graceful nature of the new Riley appearance. The car is long, low and wide and looks the flyer it is ..... The interior appointments of the coachwork are in excellent taste and conspicuous for neatness rather than flamboyant styling."

vide "The Autocar"

**90 H.P. 2½ litre Saloon £880** plus £245. 3s. 10d. Purchase Tax

**1½ litre Saloon ... £675** plus £188. 5s. 0d. Purchase Tax.

*Riley- as old as the industry- as modern as the hour*

RILEY (COVENTRY) LIMITED, COVENTRY

LONDON SHOWROOMS: "RILEY CARS" 55-56, PALL MALL, S.W.1

*Some Impressions of the*

# 1947 1½-LITRE RILEY SALOON

*Excellent Performance and Road-holding. Driving Characteristics that Appeal to the Enthusiast.*

ONE of the most popular post-war makes is the Riley, either in 1½-litre or 2½-litre saloon form. Consequently, we awaited eagerly an opportunity to test one of these cars, which became possible a few months ago when we collected a 1½-litre model from the showrooms of Jimmy James, Ltd.

Unfortunately, early in the test, while accelerating hard in 3rd gear, No. 2 exhaust valve stuck open and, although it was easily freed, the engine seemed to lack power thereafter. Consequently, although we covered an appreciable mileage in the Riley at high speeds, we refrained from taking any performance figures, returning the car to the manufacturers for servicing before attempting runs against the stop-watch. Alas, the present restrictions on the use of petrol have made a resumption of our acquaintance with the Riley out of the question, but we have decided that our general impressions may be of interest, as this is one of the most talked-of and popular of modern cars.

From the driver's seat both front wings are easily seen, and the pedals are well placed, although there isn't a lot of room beside the clutch pedal or on the foot rest provided. The seats are very comfortable and leg room is entirely generous. The windscreen is in two sections, only that before the driver opening, but the central pillar and door pillars do not affect visibility, and the driver's panel winds out fully horizontal.

Very useful is the full-width parcels shelf that runs below the instrument panel. From left to right the genuine wood facia carries: pull-out ash-tray, wiper control for passenger, combined ammeter and 100 lb./sq. in. oil gauge, panel lamp switch, screw-type hand throttle below, 95 m.p.h. Jaeger speedometer with clock, starter, choke and ignition advance and retard controls below, spot-lamp switch, combined water thermometer and fuel gauge, wiper control for driver, screen winding handle, Lucas ignition and lamps switch, and ignition tell-tale window. The spring-spoke steering wheel has the horn push in its hub. The horn, as on many modern cars, was rather more purposeful than polite, while the facia lighting was too bright for continual use after dark.

The rear-located direction indicators worked well, controlled from the wheel centre, and an effective interior lamp was provided, with its switch on the driver's side of the car. The central mirror was rather small. The rear seat accommodates three persons in comfort, but the interior is a trifle spartan, lacking as it does door pockets or "pulls." Admittedly there is a pocket on the back of each bucket front seat, but somehow we prefer to carry books and maps, etc., in the doors. Entry and exit does not contort the driver and he finds gear lever and hand-brake lever well placed; the rigid gear lever is spring-loaded to the high ratio side of its invisible gate.

Going round the Riley, the good lines and pleasing finish of which need no emphasis, one finds sensible fuel fillers and half-bumpers and a useful tow-bar at the rear. The rear locker is really accommodating and the spare wheel is carried beneath it. The tools live under the bonnet and are rather a motley collection; the starting handle inserts easily and normally stows under the rear seat. The bonnet is in two sections and four carriage-type locks have to be manipulated before all is revealed. The tyres are Dunlop 5.75 by 16 E.L.P.

Turning to the driving aspect of the Riley, the clutch action is fairly light and its engagement pleasantly positive, but the treadle accelerator needs fair pressure. Very soon the car is cruising effortlessly at an indicated 60 m.p.h., and it readily goes up to 70 m.p.h. with little extra effort. There is a good deal of engine noise and wind roar at these speeds, but a very good feature is that, no matter how many windows are open, no rush of air enters the body, so that one rides in comfort, adequately ventilated, yet with loose papers or parcels intact on the seats.

On "Pool" petrol the engine naturally pinks unless the ignition control is used intelligently. This pull-out control can be fairly easily operated by left fore-finger and thumb, but functioned rather stiffly and could, with improvement, be transposed with the hand-throttle control. That such a control is provided at all, however, stamps the designer as someone who appreciates enthusiasts' requirements. This observation gains further moment when one comes to consider the gear change. Although synchro-mesh is provided we were unaware of this until we returned the car and congratulated a salesman on a really good "crash" box. We had made double-declutch and clutchless changes up and down with equal facility; indeed, it pays to ignore the self-aids and really enjoy yourself on what is unquestionably an accommodating gearbox, once the driver has become used to the fairly long lever travel and restrained himself from trying to effect absolute snap-changes. The gears, like the transmission, are commendably quiet on drive and over-run. Slight vibration is transmitted through the gear lever.

The steering is heavy and inclined to be flabby at traffic-speeds, and, on the car tested, pulled somewhat to the near side. But at higher speeds it becomes light and very accurate and there is strong castor action. Slight return motion is felt through the wheel at times, but the column is absolutely rigid. Telescopic adjustment is provided and the ratio is

*The 1½-litre Riley Saloon.*

[*Motor Sport Copyright*]

such that 2¼ turns take one from one generous lock to the other. The car generally corners and handles in a safe and excellent fashion and really fast cornering gives rise to preliminary warning from the tyres before the tail slides. Front i.f.s. is by torsion bars. Although providing a comfortable ride, the suspension is not unduly supple, so that under cornering or heavy braking the car remains stable.

The Girling hydro-mechanical brakes are entirely adequate to the performance and, moreover, are a pleasure to use, being silent and truly progressive for a moderate pedal pressure, yet fully able to lock the wheels. For motoring at night the Lucas lighting, as we expected, is, again, entirely adequate, although the foot dipper control is most awkwardly placed on the propeller-shaft tunnel. The hand-brake holds the car well and releases nicely.

Oil pressure varies with engine speed, from 40 to 65 lb./sq. in., and the water temperature did not exceed an indicated 70 degrees C., although the engine ran-on badly after switching off. The facia clock has an irritatingly loud tick.

As we have said, we did not take performance figures, so we were unable to check the speedometer readings, and the folowing speed figures *need to be studied with this in mind.* Acceleration is a trifle sluggish from really low speeds,

but the engine begins to pull well from about 35 m.p.h. in top gear and, as we have observed, 60 m.p.h. is the normal cruising speed. In normal driving one would change-up at approximately 15, 25 and 40 m.p.h. on the indirect ratios, but extreme readings of 22 m.p.h. in 1st,

37 m.p.h. in 2nd and 58 m.p.h. in 3rd were obtained before bad valve bounce intervened. An indicated 60 m.p.h. in 3rd gear was possible without undue distress from beneath the bonnet. The maximum indicated speed attained was 70 m.p.h., but another driver saw 80 on the speedometer under favourable conditions. The

weight, unladen, with about two gallons of fuel, was 23½ cwt. Fuel consumption came out at 18 to 19 m.p.g. over a mileage of 300, driving hard, but the car was obviously out of tune, a tappet refusing to hold its setting after an exhaust valve had stuck down, and water collecting in the plug recesses. The fuel gauge was not particularly accurate, incidentally. In spite of this lack of tune the car always started impeccably after a night in the open.

After the Editor had covered 212 miles in the Riley he handed it over to the proprietor of MOTOR SPORT, who decided to use it for a quick journey to the coast from his home and back, over a route he knew exceedingly well. On a run of 57 miles the Riley showed a saving of nine minutes compared to a popular " Ten " driven hard by its owner, who obviously knows it far better than he knew the Riley. The speedometer showed 72-75 m.p.h. for appreciable distances, and 80 was recorded on two separate occasions.

In conclusion, the 1947 1½-litre Riley is contributing its bit to the present Crisis, offering as it does fast, safe, yet economical transport to V.I.P.s, and making mouths water on the export front. The price, including purchase tax, is £863 5s. 0d., and the dimensions are 5 ft. 3½ in. by 14 ft. 11 in., with 4 ft. 4½ in. track and 9 ft. 4½ in. wheel base.

## A Car for the Discriminating—Contd.

APPRECIATED features to be noted in this view are the sweeping wings, the large rear window and a graceful stern.

CONTINUED FROM PAGE 10
mentioned here that any such self-centring effect must require a corresponding expenditure of force by the driver when turning the wheel in the first place, and holding it on corners.

Another pleasing feature of the new Riley steering is that it is free from kick. This might not be expected in a mechanism which (unlike the worm gear, for instance) has no claim to irreversibility, but it can be obtained simply by correct geometry in the steering layout. In this case, that is presumably the explanation. However that may be, the fact is that only on one particularly vile stretch of road was there even the slightest sign of kick at the steering wheel.

With such steering, one can safely take what would be liberties in other circumstances, and, in this, the smoothly powerful and well-balanced Girling brakes are a comforting ally. Consequently, rapid cornering and " swerving the curves " occurred fairly

frequently during that afternoon's run, and this established quite clearly that the Riley 1½-litre, with no anti-roll bars or other such aids to an upright life, simply does not roll. There have, of course, been other cars of which that is equally true, but very few indeed of them have managed it with a suspension so soft and comfortable as this, and on that point there is the somewhat remarkable fact to record that the back seats (almost over the axle) actually provide a rather more comfortable ride than do the front ones.

### Good Climbing

As to performance, this was not a formal road test and no times were taken; but there is no doubt that, when the occasion arises for that to be done, the figures will be very gratifying to those responsible for the design and development of this car. With only a nominal " Twelve " engine to propel

a car weighing some 26 cwt., plus four adult male occupants, nothing very startling would normally be expected. Yet, in fact, this proved to be a distinctly lively car.

Perhaps as good an indication as any of its performance was provided on a Cotswold incline, the sort of road that not many years ago would have imposed an absolute maximum of 50 m.p.h. on a saloon of this engine size. With the Riley cantering up it happily on half throttle at 60 by an apparently accurate speedometer, the pedal was pressed right down and in a matter of seconds (not many of them, either), the needle was up to 70.

And this was done with the utmost gentility. No sign of a " pink " then or in the possibly more searching test of accelerating on top gear from about 12 m.p.h.

Altogether this is a car to lighten the life of a motoring journalist. It justifies, indeed it inspires, enthusiasm.

MOTORING THE NEW MODELS
. . by H. C. HASTINGS

# The 1½-Litre Riley

THIS month I was able to achieve a little ambition that I have nursed for a considerable time, namely, to give the 1½-litre Riley an extended test and see for myself whether, on closer acquaintance, this car really lives up to the fine reputation it has achieved and to my brief impressions registered during a short run early this year.

Far from falling short of expectations, the Riley, like most really good things, seemed better and better on longer acquaintance. Several hundred miles at the wheel confirmed my previous opinion that this model is

(Right) A 30-ft. turning circle makes the 1½-litre Riley one of the most manœuvrable cars on the market. (Below) Rear-seat passengers are assured of a comfortable ride. The interior furnishing is carried out in real leather. Note the provision of satchels on the back of the front seats. (Bottom) The facia panel is typical of a style adopted on the majority of high-grade British cars.

TRADITIONAL: The latest Riley, despite modern treatment of the front-end, still retains its essentially Riley character by the use of a "real" radiator.

is difficult to define but easy for a driver to appreciate.

Its performance in terms of actual figures is recorded in the accompanying data panel, and these figures, whilst very creditable in themselves, hardly do justice to its average-speed propensities because the car is one of those which always feel so essentially safe. The torsion-bar front springing provides suspension that is, perhaps, slightly on the firm side when travelling slowly over bumpy cobbled roads but which, even under these conditions, gives a remarkably steady ride. On the open road, and in particular under winding twisty conditions, all trace of this firmness disappears, yet there is never a suspicion that the front end of the car is anything but rock steady.

These qualities are coupled with a rack and pinion steering system which gives an almost unique combination of lightness and sensitivity with complete absence of kick-back through the steering wheel. Braking (of the Girling hydro-mechanical type) is entirely adequate for the car's performance, and the layout of the controls has obviously been planned by a designer who drives himself and knows what is required.

Despite the sleek lines, passenger accommodation at both front and rear is extremely comfortable and the rear seat width of 51 ins. enables three to be carried on occasion. Likewise, luggage accommodation and space for incidentals have also been well planned, with

very useful pockets attached to the backs of the front seats and a full-width parcel tray fitted beneath the facia panel.

The panel carries a comprehensive range of instruments, details which appeal to the discerning driver including a radiator thermometer and hand ignition control. This fitting is particularly useful at the present time, as it means that the manufacturers need make no concessions to the questionable quality of present-day petrol, but that the slight pinking which results in certain circumstances can easily be overcome by retarding the spark.

The gear change, effected by a nicely placed remote control lever, is positive and foolproof, provided that the driver remembers to depress the clutch pedal to the full extent because the last quarter-inch of the rather long travel is important. Of the pistol-grip type, the hand brake is thoroughly adequate and is placed close to the gear lever, where the driver's left hand can quickly slip from one to the other. Further good points from a driver angle are the telescopic steering column, the provision of a winder to open the driver's half of the Vee-type windscreen and a seating position which gives a good view of both front wings.

Perhaps the best way to describe the Riley is to say that it is essentially a driver's car, but one in which the mental and physical comfort of the passengers and the needs of both town and country motoring (even to the provision of a 30-ft. turning circle) have received equal attention—a car, in fact, which will delight the enthusiast.

## IN BRIEF
### THE 1½-LITRE RILEY

**Engine.**—Four-cylinder, o.h.v. (push-rod), 69 mm. by 100 mm., 1,496 c.c., 55 b.h.p. at 4,500 r.p.m. S.U. horizontal carburetter. A.C. fuel **pump.**

**Transmission.**—Borg and Beck clutch, enclosed prop. shaft, spiral bevel final drive. Gears, 4.88, 7.22, 11.2 (synchromesh), and 19.4 to 1.

**General.**—Torsion-bar i.f.s. semi-elliptic rear springs. Girling hydro-mechanical brakes. Dunlop tyres, 16 by 5.75 ins. Lucas 12-volt c.v.c. electrical equipment. Wheelbase, 9 ft. 4½ ins.; track, 4 ft. 4½ ins.; ground clearance, 7½ ins.; turning circle, 30 ft.; turns of steering wheel, lock to lock, 2¼. Unladen weight (as tested), 24¾ cwt.

**Performance.**—Touring maximum (mean timed ¼-mile after ¾-mile run), 75 m.p.h. Speeds in gears, 54 m.p.h. (third), 35 m.p.h. (second). Acceleration, 0-50 (through the gears) 12½ secs.; 20-40 m.p.h. (top), 13.2 secs.; 30-50 m.p.h. (top), 13.9 secs. Gradient climbable in top, 1 in 12½. Petrol consumption (40 m.p.h. cruising), 29.6 m.p.g.

**Price.**—£675 plus £188 5s. purchase tax (£863 5s.).

definitely one of the outstanding post-war designs.

Perhaps the most noteworthy thing about it is that it just asks to be driven hard, to be accelerated briskly in its gears, to be taken round corners in a way that would be foolish on some cars and downright suicidal on others, and to be allowed to cruise swiftly and effortlessly under all conditions.

I would not say that the Riley is the smoothest or the most silent 1½-litre car I have driven, but there is a certain willingness about its performance which

# A Three-seater

# SPORTS RILEY

## A Striking New Open Model for Export on the 2½-litre Chassis

STANDARD HEIGHT.
—A feature of the new Riley is the fitting of robust American-style bumpers which are set at the standard trans-atlantic height. Both this illustration and that above accent the roomy luggage space in the swept tail, which also houses a 20-gallon fuel tank.

MARKET research in the export field has shown that the demand overseas for open sports models represents a very fruitful outlet for British manufacturers. In the U.S., in particular, there is a valuable market for such cars, since they represent a type not catered for in the catalogues of the big American manufacturing groups. Britain is already catering for this demand to a considerable extent so far as small sports cars are concerned, but the market for the rather larger open car which provides body space more in line with American ideas is almost untapped.

Appreciating this fact, Riley (Coventry), Ltd., are entering the field with a full three-seater sports model on a slightly modified edition of the already famous 2½-litre chassis, and the prototype (illustrated on this page) is even now in Geneva, whence it has

been driven by the general manager, Mr. Jack Tatlow, in a personal investigation of Continental reactions.

The 2½-litre chassis, with its 90 b.h.p. o.h.v. four-cylinder engine and independent torsion-bar front suspension, is used in basically unaltered form, but certain minor changes are being incorporated to make it even more suitable for overseas needs.

Notable amongst these are the use of a 20-gallon petrol tank, a steering-column gear change, and the stiffening-up of the front and rear ends of the chassis frame. The reason for this last alteration is interesting; it has been effected (principally with U.S. needs in view) to enable massive American-style bumpers to be fitted and for no dire results to arise when they are subjected to American-style use!

These bumpers, incidentally, are not only full-width affairs of very robust

construction, but are specially reinforced at points liable to impact, and are provided with two pairs of over-riders on each side. They are, moreover, fitted at the standard U.S. height of 18 ins., and are well curved at their extremities to give full wing protection.

At the front, apart from the slightly American air lent by these bumpers, the lines of the new model are pure Riley. At the rear the boot is carried down in a graceful sweep of distinctly trans-atlantic suggestion, which at once provides luggage space of truly exceptional proportions and gives a very imposing appearance. The whole car, in fact, has an unusual air of sleek roominess that is entirely pleasing.

### High Performance Forecast

This suggestion of speed and space is in no way false. As readers will recall, the standard saloon model, when tested by "The Motor" soon after its introduction, showed itself capable of a maximum mean speed of 94.8 m.p.h., with a rest to 80 m.p.h. acceleration time through the gears of a mere 31 secs. The new three-seater, lighter and (with the screen folded flat) appreciably smaller in frontal area, should have no difficulty in materially improving on these already oustanding figures.

As for the space considerations, the fact that the width across the bench-type seat is 54 ins. and that the designer had at his disposal a 9-ft. 11-in. wheelbase when planning leg room, speak for themselves. Actually, the seat has

THREE ON ONE.—The bench-type front seat holds three people comfortably with plenty of leg space due to the fitting of a steering-column gear change.

an adjustment range of 5 ins., so that tall or short can be accommodated in equal comfort.

The hood is both practical and of good line when erected, and disappears entirely beneath a cover behind the seat when furled, whilst the side screens are housed in the same spot when not in use. Hood material is in a shade to match the real leather upholstery, and both, in turn, match the wheel colour. Various colour combinations will be available, the choice on the prototype being a particularly happy combination of cream body and scarlet upholstery, hood and wheels.

The exceptional size of the boot has already been mentioned, and an interesting detail in connection with it

is that the twin filler caps for the large rear tank are housed within it close to its rear edge, where they are normally out of sight and secure from the attentions of thieves. In order, however, to avoid any possibility of petrol fumes reaching the luggage, the caps are covered by a hinged fume-tight lid, and arranged so that any fuel splashed over through careless filling drains away direct on to the road.

Other details include a facia panel very similar to the standard design, with a wax finish for the real walnut panelling to make it proof against tropical sun; large rear-hinged doors; direction indicators recessed into the body sides aft the door; a telescopic steering column and an exceptionally large,

steeply raked fold-flat screen, which provides first-class visibility, the latter aided by the low bonnet, which gives a full-width view of the front wings.

In all, this new Riley is a car which should have a strong appeal the world over and particularly in America, where it will provide the room to which users in that continent are accustomed, coupled with the attractions of open-car motoring and a performance which will enable it to show off the excellent lines of its tail even to the high-powered cars of the States.

For the present, it will be a case of overseas buyers first. When the time comes for it to be offered to British motorists, a long waiting list will not be long in forming.

# Three-seater 2½-litre

BRITISH sports cars are playing a vital part in the export drive. American buyers, particularly, are keenly interested in our high-performance cars, and there is undoubtedly a steady market for our sporting vehicles across the Atlantic.

Realizing this, Riley (Coventry), Ltd., has produced a special export three-seater open car on a slightly modified version of their very fast 2½-litre chassis. An example of the car made a late appearance at Geneva.

Basically, the normal chassis remains unaltered, but some minor changes have been effected to meet certain overseas needs. Left-hand drive is featured along with low-geared steering. Other modifications include the use of a 20-gallon rear petrol tank, a gear lever mounted on the steering column and the strengthening of the frame at the front and rear ends, to enable robust American - style bumpers to be fitted—and used.

The new export Riley: an open three-seater on the 2½-litre chassis.

Riley re-enter the open-car market with a—

The new car is essentially Riley in appearance, but the bonnet line and radiator have been lowered by 1½ ins. The tail half, which incorporates a

luggage boot of unusually large dimensions, is styled in graceful, sweeping lines.

Within the boot are housed the two filler caps for the fuel tank. These are covered by a hinged, fume-tight lid.

The seating accommodation of the new model provides a high standard of comfort and roominess, the width across the bench-type seat being 54 ins. Ample leg room for drivers of all heights is catered for by a seat adjustment of 5 ins. and the provision of a telescopic steering column.

The hood and side curtains, when not in use, are stowed in a concealed position beneath a cover behind the seat. The hood material is toned to match the leather upholstery and the wheels. Various colour combinations will be available.

Other features include direction indicators, recessed into the body, and a large, fold-flat windscreen. The lighting equipment is designed to conform to all overseas requirements.

With the hood folded and neatly concealed, the smooth lines of the Riley are uninterrupted.

A sight to gladden the sportsman's heart—the traditional British open sports car returns under the ægis of the Riley company and with a 2½-litre engine.

# NEW SPORTS 2½-LITRE RILEY

## Smart Open Three-seater Specially Designed for the Overseas Market

EVERYBODY who is wise on motoring matters in this country knows by now that the 2½-litre Riley "goes like a bomb." There are enough enthusiastic owners about to spread the news. In fact the average speeds which they claim are getting very near to traditional fishermen's stories. There is no doubt, however, that this Riley is genuinely a very fast car, and an eminently roadworthy one as well. Saloons and coupés, however, are not everyone's choice, and the announcement that an open three-seater sports version is going into production will be very welcome. The only regrettable aspect is that the first claim of export will not leave much hope for the home enthusiast at present.

Substantially the chassis of the new sports model is the same as that of the 2½-litre saloon, with its 90 b.h.p. four-cylinder o.h.v. engine, independent front-wheel suspension of the torsion bar type, stiff box-section frame, and the one hundred and one touches that long experience of fast cars has given Rileys. There are, however, one or two points of difference. The first cars will have left-hand steering, with consequent rearrangement of controls, and the gear lever will be mounted on the steering column below the wheel. This is because the bench-type front seat is wide enough to take three people. Another point is that the special rack and pinion steering has been amended slightly to give a lower

effective gearing, and so make the steering lighter to conform with overseas preference.

As will be seen from the illustrations, the car looks longer and lower than ever; this is because the radiator and bonnet line has been dropped 1½ inches. The body has very shapely lines, and the characteristic Riley front appearance has been maintained. As the car has to operate in countries where bumpers are used for bumping, the bumper equipment has been very considerably strengthened up, and carried well round the wings. Four stout over-riders are fitted at each end, and these have stout button-shaped stops which will prevent opposition bumpers from riding over and hooking.

### Good Weather Protection

Wide doors with cut-aways for elbow freedom give access to the front compartment, in which is the single and comfortable bench seat the full width of the wide body. Behind the seat is a fairly large and shallow recess into which the hood can be folded completely out of sight and concealed beneath a cover. Detachable side panels are also stowed in the same area, and when the hood is up and the side panels are in place the occupants of the car are completely protected from bad weather. The long tail of the body provides a luggage boot of prodi-

gious capacity. The lid of this conceals the twin fillers of the fuel tank, which contains 20 gallons—enough for nearly 500 miles.

The windscreen can be folded flat for competition driving, and, as the scuttle has an upswept rear edge, wind is deflected over the heads of the occupants. The top of the bonnet is locked from inside the car. The lighting equipment conforms with most overseas requirements, with dip and switch head lamps, and twin independent fog lamps. The first sample has been completed just too late to appear in the Geneva Show, although it will appear in Geneva before the show ends. Finished in cream with red leather upholstery and a red hood to match, it looks extremely smart and attractive.

Hefty bumpers wrap well round the wings to afford real protection, and substantial over-riders assist in this respect.

As a closed car the Riley will provide weatherproof motoring, whilst the hood does not detract from the rakish appearance of this low-built model; the bonnet line has been lowered by 1½in.

# GENEVA ROAD

## The Story of Four Men in a Car Making Work a Holiday on a Journey Through France

### By A. G. Douglas Clease

WHEN the first post-war Salon at Geneva was held last year I led an expedition there. The tale was told under the title "Combined Operation" in *The Autocar* of April 11, 1947, and was so well received that I am encouraged to relate the story of a similar trip this year.

Again the car was a 2½-litre Riley, but my own and not a works car, and there were changes in the crew. Driver and navigator were the same, myself and P. M. A. (Tommy) Thomas, Technical Editor of *Motor Transport*, but assistant-navigator-cum-purser was Max Millar—head artist of *The Autocar* and not the cheeky chappie—and fourth man was W. E. (Young Bill) Banks of the photographic staff.

Now, much of the fun of "going foreign" is planning the trip beforehand. At least it is to Tommy and me. Not for us a route prepared by the R.A.C. or A.A.; we so much enjoy getting out our own, with the help of Michelin and an extensive knowledge of the Continent. So early in February we went into a huddle. We really planned the return journey first, to make everything fit in with "press arrangements," which are akin to the laws of the Medes and Persians.

We had to be back in London on Sunday, March 14, and the earlier the better. So we decided to leave Geneva on the Friday afternoon, in time to cross the frontier into France and reach the Royal Hotel at Châlon-sur-Saône for the night. Then on the Saturday we would run the 400 miles to Dunkirk, following more or less the same fast route as last year through Dijon, Langres, Rheims and Arras, and catch the night ferry to Dover.

For the outward journey we would cross on the Sunday night ferry from Dover, sleep on board until a reasonable hour, and then proceed south via Paris, Fontainebleau, Auxerre and down N.6 to Châlon-sur-Saône, or Beaune, or Bourg—there are plenty of *les bonnes tables*—for the night, continuing to Geneva next day. But wherever we spent the night we wanted to call at Châlon-sur-Saône to park surplus French francs with M. Vachet at the

The old gateway of the little town of Moret on N.5B. This town lies about 50 miles south of Paris.

Royal Hotel, to provide for our return journey on Saturday when the banks might not be open. One can take only a restricted amount of French currency out of France into Switzerland.

A few days before we started a complication arose. The ferry schedules were altered temporarily and we should have to turn out on arrival at Dunkirk at about 03.30 hours. Plans were recast. We ought to clear customs by 05.00 at latest and so make Paris for breakfast, just over 170 miles, at 09.00. Why not, therefore, go farther south, towards Chambery, and then turn north to Geneva through Aix-les-Bains and Annecy? It would give us a sight of the distant Alps, and provide plenty of subjects for young Bill to photograph.

We put the project to Max and young Bill. Max was a little dismayed at the idea of such a short night, early start, and long day, but Bill, who had not motored abroad before, was in the mood to agree to anything. The trip was worked out in detail, route, distances, and E.T.A. at various points. We should need a petrol "letter of credit," which we would obtain in Paris.

At last Sunday, March 7, rolled round and we "rendez-voused" at Dorset House at 16.00 hours. We had previously carried out a luggage-stowing rehearsal, and less than five minutes was occupied in getting suitcases aboard. The run to Dover was uneventful, but swift. Max summed it up in three words—"What a car."

We dined well *chez* Graham Lyon, the White Cliffs Hotel, drove to the ferry berth, and went through passport and currency controls, and customs quickly and smoothly with the help of the R.A.C. Then we just drove aboard up a ramp into the garage, and turned in. Just as easily as that; no cranes.

At 03.00 Monday the steward routed us out with tea. We shaved and felt better. After a bacon and egg breakfast we thought we might even live through the day. We were ashore at 03.45 and then ensued a dreary wait for the customs. At last we got the *carnet*, our luggage was not examined, and we were off at 05.25.

Looking back towards Switzerland through the *Défile de l'Ecluse.* On the left is seen Fort l'Ecluse with below it a bend of the Rhône which passes beneath a fine modern concrete viaduct. The Riley in the foreground is almost immediately over the mouth of the railway tunnel.

Getting through Dunkirk and out on N.16 is like looking for a black kitten in a coal house. Luckily at last a clerk from the shipping office wanted a lift home, so we packed him into the back with Max and Bill, and he put us on the route nationale. But in the first half-hour we had covered only eight miles. The road was wet and slippery,

When a stone was thrown up by the wheels and lodged between the torsion bar and the sump so firmly that it could only be dislodged with a hammer it resulted in horrible noises suggestive of the most dire trouble.

so only 19 miles were put into the next half-hour. This, added to our late start, had thrown out our schedule and we made it worse by missing a turning and finding ourselves running into Armentières. Then, while cutting across to Béthune, we suddenly found ourselves halted and surrounded by a possé of gendarmes and *douaniers.* Apparently smugglers and black market men use that road, but the fact that we were English was enough explanation. We were waved on with broad grins exchanged.

## The Pace Quickens

It was my brainwave to breakfast at the Univers at Arras ; and how good the ham and eggs were. Refreshed, we put 45 miles in the hour despite indifferent roads, and 44 miles in the next, with 24 in the next half-hour. This brought us to Paris about noon, and by the time we found 2, Rue Paul Cézanne, for the petrol "letter of credit" and our way out on N.7 it was 1300 hours. A stop for petrol as we left Paris, and then down the good fast road we really got cracking, cruising at 80 m.p.h. on the smooth surface, whereas 60 had been our cruising gait on the indifferent more northerly roads. For the first time we got the three figures, to the joy of the crew. No wonder we covered 30 miles in 30 minutes and reached the famous Auberge du Grand Veneur at Barbizon before it was too late for lunch.

And what a lunch! The "hunting lodge" atmosphere, with the huge log fire and the spits turning slowly in front of it, driven by a windmill in the hot updraught in the big chimney, the deft white-coated waiters, the wide choice of good food and good wine—all delighted my companions whose first visit it was, and earned me great kudos for knowing the place.

Lunch, a few words with our host, M. Johner, and a photograph took a couple of hours. With nearly 200 miles to Châlon-sur-Saône and the time 15.40 it was necessary to step on it to arrive at a reasonable hour. But the road through Sens and Joigny, where we joined N.6, was still good, except through villages, and in spite of stopping in response to young Bill's wails for photographs we put 24 miles in the first half-hour and 30 into the next, following on with two 40s in the next two hours and 37 in the last 55 minutes into Châlon-sur-Saône. In the day's run we had covered 421 miles in 14 hours, of which three had been given to meals, one to dodging about Paris, and goodness knows how long to Bill's cameras. But we were all fresh and untired, thanks to the Riley's excellent suspension and road holding. In fact, we gave each other five minutes for a wash before we met for an aperitif in the bar. Then to dinner, which included a *coq au vin* amongst other good things. It was warm enough to stroll round without hats or overcoats afterwards. And so to bed.

### Fright of Our Lives

By ten o'clock next morning, on our way to the bank, the sun was so hot that as we looked in an optician's window we saw smoke rising from a velvet curtain behind a row of lenses. We summoned *le patron* quickly and pointed it out. He dived back into his shop and took action with a speed *formidable*. Max opined that we had done our good deed for the day.

It was 11.00 by the time we had loaded up, filled the tank, and got going. We warmed up the engine carefully before giving it much throttle, and then lost no time on the bit of N.6 that was left to us, for at Tournus we knew the chances were that N.75 through Bourg and Pont d'Ain would not be too smooth. We were right, and when we turned east along N.504 for Belley the road was not one for speed.

About six miles before we got to Belley we had a shock. The Riley "felt" peculiar to Tommy and me in the front

Langres is an excellent example of an old fortified town which is entered from the direction of Dijon through this imposing gateway.

seats. We thought we were "on the rim," but, when I hopped out to see, all tyres were sound. And as I switched the engine off in stopping I fancied I heard a rumble. I started up again—and instantly switched off.

We looked at each other in dismay! What could such a devastating "thump, thumpity thump" portend? I got the starting handle out and turned the engine over. All

On the road between Belley and Aix-les-Bains. We wondered why the garden on the rocky summit above the tunnel should have a gateway in such a peculiar position.

At the summit of the Col de Bertiand (2,450ft) looking down over the valley of the Ain with the hills thrown in bold relief by the setting sun.

was smooth and quiet. I switched on and started—and switched off horrified! Big-ends? Main bearings?

Then Tommy had a brainwave. "Engine mounting?" he queried. I looked at the front—O.K. I lay down and looked underneath. A stone was lodged on the torsion bar. I tried to move it, but found it jammed tight between torsion bar and crankcase. Hope began to rise as I called for a hammer. It took quite an effort to dislodge it.

I switched on, pressed the starter—the engine ran smoothly!

We felt we really needed an aperitif when we pulled up at the Hotel Pernallet at Belley, followed by a good lunch. We had both. The log entry reads simply "What a lunch."

French road engineers make skilful use of tunnels such as these encountered on the journey from Belley towards the Col du Chat and Aix-les-Bains.

After Bill had aired his cameras we pushed on through Yenne and over the Col du Chat. The view from the summit was superb, over Lac du Bourget, with Aix-les-Bains on the far shore and snow-clad peaks in the mist on the horizon. So Bill became O.C. and we stopped thereafter at his merest nod as we trickled on to Aix, Annecy, and by the St. Julien customs into Geneva.

Our return journey took us out of Switzerland by St. Génis, Collonges, Bellegarde and Nantua, whence we followed N.79 over the Col de Bertiand. We got through the customs very quickly and smoothly, so had time to stop for photographs of Fort l'Ecluse overlooking the Rhone and the railway, and again on the top of the Col, which is about 2,450ft above sea level. The Riley swept up in a fast third gear climb.

Soon we were through Bourg and back in Châlon-sur-Saône, where the Royal had kept us our same rooms. It was young Bill's birthday, so we made it a festive occasion. He was persuaded to join me in *escargots*, and went happily to bed with a snail shell and a collection of corks as souvenirs. Tommy and I and M. Vachet sat up a little longer and settled the troubled affairs of the world.

## Last Lap

On Saturday we really had to motor, and the log shows that we kept up an average of over 40 m.p.h., including stops for petrol, photographs and long drinks, for it was really hot and thirst-making. Having stopped for an hour and a half in Rheims we hurried a bit over an excellent fast stretch and covered 31 miles in 30 minutes, and 10 miles in the next seven minutes. The speedometer 100 was again attained and held for some distance.

Arras was reached at 20.00 hours and we stopped for our last meal in France. As we came out from the restaurant we found a rear tyre flat, but the crew dealt expeditiously with that, and despite a rising mist we found our way through Hazebrouck and Cassel without much trouble. At Dunkirk we could see the ferry boat but could *not* find the way to her. At last we managed it and were soon through the formalities, to drive aboard and turn in.

At Dover we could not stay aboard, but the customs were operating, so we went through, without trouble, and started for London. As the sun rose so did the mist, but with an occasional rest for a few seconds for our eyes we carried on and drew up at Dorset House at 09.30 hours, tired, but happy. And as we all agreed, "What a car!"

# The 1½-litre Riley

BEARING one of the oldest names in the Industry, the marque Riley has always been notable for an individuality which lifts it out of the rut of contemporary design. To say that it is not so much what a Riley does as the way it does it, is to repeat a remark which has been made many times in the past.

Now that we are well into the post-war era, the individuality of the Riley is, perhaps, even more notable than before, because the latest product at once pleases the driver of progressive ideas without upsetting his opposite number with strong leanings towards the vintage era of motoring.

These remarks apply equally to the 1½- and 2½-litre models, but it is of the smaller car that I write here. I recently covered a few hundred miles at the wheel of one of the 1949 editions and, as usual, found myself dropping rapidly into the Riley style of motoring and ending the experience with regret, for the Riley is a car which makes its driver at home the moment he takes the wheel and endears itself more and more as acquaintance improves.

The 1949 type differs little from its forerunner, which, being also a true post-war design, was thoroughly modern. All that the manufacturers have done, in fact, is to review the initial post-war model in the light of two years' usage and introduced detail changes that seemed desirable.

As a result, driving amenities are even better than before and one takes the wheel with a feeling of immediate confidence. The seating position is at once comfortable and planned for good control and everything seems to be just where one expects to find it—or if not, it can readily be made so, as the front seats are individually adjustable and the steering column is telescopic.

The makers have not adopted the popular idea of a steering-column gear change and the need for it does not exist, for there is no question of seating three in the front, and room for two is thoroughly adequate. Thus, the remote-control lever does not get in the way and is, on the other hand, a joy to use, with its short travel and very positive action.

Positive, in fact, is the operative word in respect of all the controls of this car. By some standards, the steering might be classed as rather on the heavy side; against that, there is no suggestion of sponginess, the response is immediate and the accuracy reassuring at all times and a delight when one is making full use of the very brisk performance that goes with this car.

Braking, too, is well up to performance requirements and the Girling Hydro-mechanical system combines light pedal pressure with progressive response.

All-round visibility takes one back to the days when all good sports cars gave their drivers a view of the full front wing span; a point which will also be appreciated by many is that the driver's half of the Vee screen can be opened for ventilation, fog or icing. Upward vision is, perhaps, rather more restricted than with some cars.

With the performance characteristics of the 1½-litre Riley, I can safely leave the figures given in the accompanying data panel to speak for themselves, except to remark that an outstanding feature of the Riley is not merely how fast it goes or how soon it reaches maximum or cruising speed, but how well it retains those speeds over give-and-take roads. Its steering, cornering, road holding and braking are all of an order which enable the user to confine reductions in speed for road or traffic conditions to a bare minimum and both peace of mind and average speeds benefit enormously in consequence.

The engine, moreover, never seems to tire and a genuine 60-65 m.p.h. cruising speed can be maintained indefinitely. At this, as at other speeds, the engine is not completely silent, but the slight mechanical noise present merely serves to remind the driver that he is in control of a very efficient and willing piece of machinery—never to annoy him.

Suspension characteristics combine a moderately firm ride with absolute steadiness under all conditions and a significant point is the excellent rear-seat ride, which was remarked on by more than one passenger.

To these desirable features can be added generous luggage accommodation, comprehensive equipment, first-rate finish all round, and sleek, external lines.

(Above) Facia panel of the Riley. The panel switch on the extreme right is the "dipper." (Right) Commodious luggage accommodation is a feature.

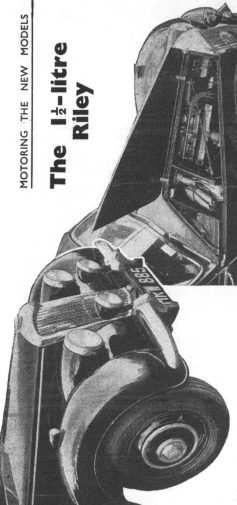

(Above) The 1½-litre Riley front-end. Note how the twin pass lights have been raised to comply with new regulations. (Right) The bonnet tops are hinged for access to the four-cylinder,1,496 c.c. (69 mm. x100 mm.) engine.

### THE 1½-LITRE RILEY

**Performance.**—Touring maximum (mean timed quarter-mile after three-quarter-mile run), 74.5 m.p.h. Speeds in gears, 54 m.p.h. (third); 35 m.p.h. (second). Acceleration, 0-50 m.p.h. (through the gears), 16.7 secs.; 20-40 m.p.h. (top), 12.4 secs.; 30-50 m.p.h. (top), 15.1 secs.; 40-60 m.p.h. (top), 17.3 secs. Gradient climbable in top, 1 in 12½. Unladen weight (as tested), 24½ cwt. Petrol consumption (40 m.p.h. cruising), 28.2 m.p.g. **Price**, £675, plus £188 5s. 0d. purchase tax (£863 5s. 0d.).

The Riley in the depths of Glen Etive. This road, leading off the Glencoe highway near Kingshouse Hotel, was the worst in surface, and offered the wildest scenery, of the whole trip. Views of the Glencoe mountains and the Buchaille Etive Mor group "from the back," most of them between 3,000 and 3,600ft, are very impressive, from viewpoints quite different from those afforded by the main road. This road ends at the pier at Lochetivehead and has to be retraced. Even with i.f.s. it is a 20 m.p.h. maximum road, and much of it slower.

TO the Southerner dependent upon the present standard petrol ration the "real" Scotland is unfortunately out of range unless the car is sent by train or sea. To one who has long held that the magnificent scenery which the Highlands offers should be seen by everyone who calls himself a tourist it is indeed ironical that it should be possible for the Englishman to travel by car to the South of France, for instance, and yet, at the moment, not to tour the Scottish Highlands from a South of England base. Fortunately, however, for those concerned such motoring is possible to large numbers of car owners in Northern England, as well as to the Scots themselves, of course. On the line of thought which prompts one who at times becomes a little weary of eulogies of post-war Continental motoring and menus to make the suggestion, "See Scotland First," it is also to be wondered how many Scottish and North of England car owners have themselves never found the best of the Highlands.

Without being able to claim, under present conditions, to have gone exactly where I should have chosen if entirely free from current restrictions, I have recently been fortunate enough to combine business with holiday in about a fifty-fifty ratio and re-discover some of the beauties, ruggedness and charm of a country which is unlike England, and even North Wales, to an extent that those who have not gone far past the Border would scarcely credit. It is not my object to detail a tour of Scotland; the accompanying map will give a good indication of the route covered. Rather is it my aim to remind others, as I was reminded, of places that I had long wished to revisit and to try to convey the appeal of a country which has so much that is worth seeing, and which can be seen without language difficulties or currency restrictions—and which, to touch upon an ever-present subject of these times, can provide some good food.

This return to Scotland possessed a particular piquancy for me personally in that I was last there in September, 1939, and at Fort Augustus, well up in the Highlands, learned of the war starting. In the gloom that then descended, magnified in those circumstances as we sped homeward by the grim splendour of Glencoe, it seemed hardly possible that touring in Scotland would again be enjoyed; and in the years that followed those prospects looked even fainter. Thus to cross the Border again in a good car—a 1½-litre Riley and incidentally from the same organization as the two cars which had carried myself and colleagues southward on that day, nearly nine years ago, when the bottom seemed to have dropped out of everything that we cherished—had more significance than the bare fact would suggest.

The northward run to Oban—the Great North Road, A1, being joined just below Eaton Socon, after skirting London north-westward—was divided about equally by an overnight halt in northernmost Yorkshire, and continued on the second day on an unorthodox route by ignoring the Scotch Corner to Carlisle road and taking B6277 through Teesdale to Alston in Cumberland, then by B6292 to Brampton, the western trunk route to Scotland being regained at Gretna, after short-circuiting Carlisle.

This route, though on "slower" roads than the accepted one after leaving A1 at Scotch Corner, is direct enough, as the map at once shows, and has excellent surfaces. It gave mile upon mile without sight of another car, offered fine moorland panoramas along the Pennines, and, in

# TESTING GROUND

By H. S. Linfield

*Conditions Which in Many Respects Correspond to Those Overseas Provide the Opportunity of Seeing a Modern High-efficiency British Design to Advantage*

addition, the magnificent High Force waterfall, near Middleton-in-Teesdale, which was in full foamy brown spate in the wet early summer, and which was not equalled of its kind by anything seen in Scotland on this particular trip. On this section, as also on some main roads in Scotland, it was possible to coast in neutral for a mile or two at a stretch, by reason of the long-distance view ahead and the absence of baulking traffic.

Glasgow was avoided by taking the Erskine chain ferry, down-Clyde. To avoid becoming involved in Glasgow proper and to find the ferry provides an exercise in route finding, and we made one mistake which brought us into busy, industrial-looking Hamilton, too near the Glasgow network to be pleasant. Once Paisley is reached the way to the ferry is well marked, however. The service is good, the drive on and off is perfectly easy, and, in contrast with most Scottish ferries, the charge is low—ninepence for the car and a penny for passengers.

On the other side of the Clyde one begins to feel almost at once that one is really in Scotland and becomes impatient, especially on behalf of passengers who have not been this way before, for the first sight of Loch Lomond, the " bonny " banks of which are followed for many miles on the route northward to Tarbet and Crianlarich. Evening, I consider, is the best of all times to run beside Loch Lomond and we were fortunate to have sunshine.

## Weather Contrasts

All that day we had gone into and out of rain and sunshine. Before crossing the Clyde we had noticed ahead an ominous storm-filled sky, an angry deep yellow in the early evening. We missed the actual sequel to this harbinger of weather trouble, but saw the results, not many miles north of the Clyde, where there was evidence of a cloudburst, with mud washed down from the banks spread thick on the road and the surface broken up in places. We were to hear, too, on arrival at Oban that it had rained from 10 a.m. to 6 p.m. that day, yet we had been comparatively fortunate. The changes of weather experienced over so relatively short a journey, less than 300 miles for the day, are often interesting.

(Right) High Force, near Middleton-in-Teesdale, Durham, seen en route to Scotland, via Alston. Nothing to compare with this fall, in full spate in a wet June, was found elsewhere. (Below) Easdale, south-west of Oban, once a slate-quarrying centre. Reference to older maps shows Easdale as a small island in the middle distance, but the name is now given to the village on the larger island of Seil—an island only by virtue of the narrow Clachan Sound

Beyond Loch Lomond and Crianlarich, then Tyndrum, where the northward route is left, I had entirely forgotten the road westward to the coast at Oban, last seen in 1933. This road, A85, is one of those good examples of Scottish main roads modernized and realigned between the wars, which does not mean that it is straight for long at a time. As elsewhere, and notably through Glencoe, one sees every now and then, close to this largely new road, short, overgrown stretches of the old road, and realizes what a corkscrew affair it must have been, just as the minor Highland roads are to this day. In the late evening we ran through the Pass of Brander without properly appreciating that it was the pass, which we had been expecting, though we had remarked on the likeness of the screes flanking Loch Awe at one point to the still more impressive screes of Wastwater, in the English Lake District.

## No Car Worries

Arrival at Oban completed 570 miles for the two days of motoring; not so many years ago one had chosen to make the more distant Inverness in one hop from London. The Riley, unmentioned in detail so far, had been thoroughly unobtrusive except as a first-class means of long-distance transport. In other words, it had given not a single second's worry, had put its 40 miles-plus into any hour for which it had been kept going continuously, and, a great asset on a long run, had needed only one fill-up of petrol between Surrey and Oban, by reason of possessing a 12½-gallon tank. The oil level on the dipstick had not budged a fraction, yet the car had run for mile upon mile at 55 to 60 m.p.h. further south on the favourable stretches of A1, and on the fast Lockerbie-Abington section over the Border, higher at times, with always a reassuringly unblinking oil pressure reading around 50 lb per sq in at speed and a water temperature not exceeding 70 deg C. Next morning the engine started instantly, as it did throughout the fortnight of its being in my hands, and sounded in every way perfect.

One of the main objects of this trip was to select a medium-sized British car of modern design, as the Riley is, and observe it under conditions involving long-distance runs on the to-and-fro journeys, and to test it generally,

The deep-spanned Clachan Bridge, on the Oban-Kilninver-Easdale road, south-west of Oban. Clachan Bridge is noted in guide-books as "the only bridge over the Atlantic." It spans the narrowest part of Clachan Sound, an arm of the sea, which separates the island of Seil from the mainland of Argyll. It must be admitted that, though the bridge is unusually steep, it otherwise gives the impression of being just another bridge!

especially the suspension, under conditions offered by the Scottish Highlands. In a number of respects these correspond quite closely to conditions in the less highly developed territories overseas. That remark applies not only to road surfaces, but also to sparseness of population and distances between filling stations and sources of service.

In many parts of Scotland—one might include all the Highlands—one feels for such reasons far more dependent upon the reliability of one's car than applies in the infinitely more built-up Midlands and South. It is possible to see some of the best of the scenery without going over bad road surfaces—Glencoe's "new" road is an outstanding example. Apart from exceptions such as Tornapress (Pass of the Cattle), a good deal farther north, which I should have liked to revisit, hills in the Highlands are not nearly so steep as in Devon, though they are often long. The Highlands, except for the most remote areas, are not inaccessible by car. On the other hand, it is easy to find roads which would be decidedly unpleasant unless a car had a really good suspension system, coupled with accurate steering and powerful brakes, and in general they are hardly roads for the novice.

### I.f.s. Seen to Real Advantage

It so happened that I had never been into the Highlands before in a car with independent front suspension. One remarks on the benefits of i.f.s. on ordinary roads; over routes such as Scotland can provide if the main roads are left one quickly realizes the advantages of such a suspension and can appreciate what a good i.f.s. such as the Riley's torsion bar system means to some owners overseas. The reconstructed Scottish main roads are as near perfect in surface as any to be found in Britain, but others are not as good as they may appear at first sight and would be felt with ordinary springing. It is when you take a road such as that through Glen Lonan, starting from Taynuilt, in the shadow of the 3,600ft Ben Cruachan, or, still more

so, the Glen Etive road from the Glencoe highway near Kingshouse Hotel that you appreciate what a genuine Highland road is like.

Glen Etive shows one a real Highland mountainscape in sheer solitude, and the route has to be retraced, as there is no way out of the glen by car other than by returning over the same road. In both glens, more markedly in Etive, the loose stone surface is bad but not appalling; it worries one more as regards tyres than springs. The chief difficulty, again principally in Etive, is ruts-cum-raised central section. We covered nine of the eleven miles to the head of Loch Etive before deciding to give it best at a closed gate, with memories of too many gates to deal with in Glen Lonan a few days previously, and thoughts of an overdue dinner very much in mind. There was no impression of treating the Riley roughly in either glen, though admittedly the speed is automatically kept very low by the succession of acute blind corners, every one of which contains "possibilities." One may not have met another car for miles, but it is obviously never safe to assume even in so remote a spot that one has the road to oneself.

Even in the wild fastnesses of Etive, the grandeur of which was increased by lowering clouds around the over-3,000 feet summits, we met one car and a sidecar on the return journey and, strange sight, saw a trim 4½-litre Bentley parked in a bay, tonneau covered against rain, and doubtless left by an angling addict.

If you spend time motoring in such country you come to value as never before features of a well-designed and well thought out, solidly built car, such as the Riley has proved itself to be. It is worth a great deal to feel confidence in your car, as we had come to do, when travelling, for example, at 9 p.m. away from Glencoe on the fine ribbon of road which replaced the sinuous old road. There can be no similar road in Britain, so nearly perfect in surface and alignment, offering such grand scenery and yet so lonely for the thirty miles or so down to Tyndrum, where either one can turn right for the thirty-five miles again to Oban or continue southward to Crianlarich and Loch Lomondside. It does not really get dark in this part of Scotland in June, and certainly it is light enough to read outside at 10.45 p.m., but we felt infinitely alone there even on a Saturday evening, and help seemed far away if your car should fail you.

Glen Orchy. This road (B8074), from Dalmally to Bridge of Orchy, on the new Glencoe road, follows the rocky and swift River Orchy, and offers fine scenery of a remote nature without being difficult or of car-damaging surface.

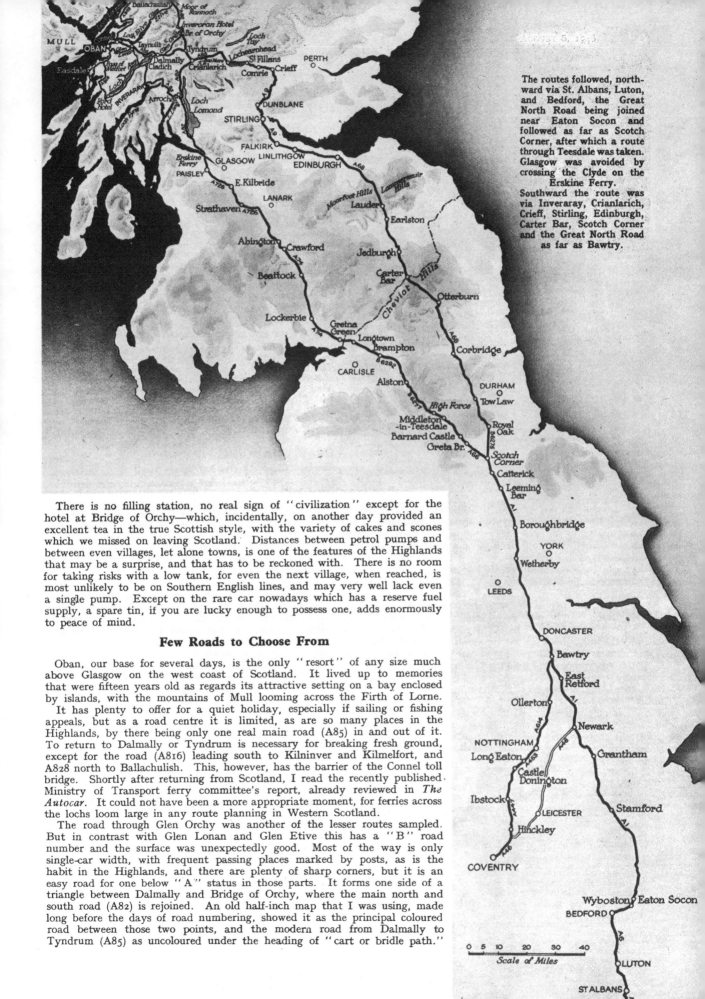

The routes followed, north-ward via St. Albans, Luton, and Bedford, the Great North Road being joined near Eaton Socon and followed as far as Scotch Corner, after which a route through Teesdale was taken. Glasgow was avoided by crossing the Clyde on the Erskine Ferry. Southward the route was via Inveraray, Crianlarich, Crieff, Stirling, Edinburgh, Carter Bar, Scotch Corner and the Great North Road as far as Bawtry.

There is no filling station, no real sign of "civilization" except for the hotel at Bridge of Orchy—which, incidentally, on another day provided an excellent tea in the true Scottish style, with the variety of cakes and scones which we missed on leaving Scotland. Distances between petrol pumps and between even villages, let alone towns, is one of the features of the Highlands that may be a surprise, and that has to be reckoned with. There is no room for taking risks with a low tank, for even the next village, when reached, is most unlikely to be on Southern English lines, and may very well lack even a single pump. Except on the rare car nowadays which has a reserve fuel supply, a spare tin, if you are lucky enough to possess one, adds enormously to peace of mind.

## Few Roads to Choose From

Oban, our base for several days, is the only "resort" of any size much above Glasgow on the west coast of Scotland. It lived up to memories that were fifteen years old as regards its attractive setting on a bay enclosed by islands, with the mountains of Mull looming across the Firth of Lorne.

It has plenty to offer for a quiet holiday, especially if sailing or fishing appeals, but as a road centre it is limited, as are so many places in the Highlands, by there being only one real main road (A85) in and out of it. To return to Dalmally or Tyndrum is necessary for breaking fresh ground, except for the road (A816) leading south to Kilninver and Kilmelfort, and A828 north to Ballachulish. This, however, has the barrier of the Connel toll bridge. Shortly after returning from Scotland, I read the recently published Ministry of Transport ferry committee's report, already reviewed in The Autocar. It could not have been a more appropriate moment, for ferries across the lochs loom large in any route planning in Western Scotland.

The road through Glen Orchy was another of the lesser routes sampled. But in contrast with Glen Lonan and Glen Etive this has a "B" road number and the surface was unexpectedly good. Most of the way is only single-car width, with frequent passing places marked by posts, as is the habit in the Highlands, and there are plenty of sharp corners, but it is an easy road for one below "A" status in those parts. It forms one side of a triangle between Dalmally and Bridge of Orchy, where the main north and south road (A82) is rejoined. An old half-inch map that I was using, made long before the days of road numbering, showed it as the principal coloured road between those two points, and the modern road from Dalmally to Tyndrum (A85) as uncoloured under the heading of "cart or bridle path."

# HIGHLAND TESTING

**Last week the author described impressions of revisiting the Scottish Highlands after an interval approaching ten years, owing to the war. He recently took there a current series 1½-litre Riley saloon on an extended test under conditions which in some ways are more arduous and revealing than can be imposed anywhere else in Great Britain. This is the concluding article.**

AMONG high spots of the journeys based on Oban was, unexpectedly, the Pass of Kintraw, beyond Kilmelfort, south of Oban, where the surrounding heights are modest, with 1,000ft as the maximum and where the hills rather than mountains are green and not awesome ; yet the pass itself has more of the atmosphere of a climb worthy of such a label than most other passes that were encountered, and includes a couple of near-hairpin bends. To the right as one climbs is Loch Craignish, a sea loch ; beyond are the Inner Hebridean islands of Scarba and Jura, and farther out still is the chain known as the Isles of the Sea, or the Garvelloch Isles, with more suggestion in the distance of open Atlantic than is usually offered in this part of Scotland.

In an entirely different category were the rugged, remote impressiveness of Glen Etive, already mentioned, and, of course, the giants of Glencoe. Always previously I had run through Glencoe north to south, from Ballachulish. This time the opportunity was taken of reversing the direction. The evening in question suited the " Glen of Weeping," with low cloud down to the higher peaks and no sunshine, and I strongly recommend the northward trip. The magnificence of the setting increases as one runs down the glen, as, on a lesser scale, the downward run is more impressive at Cheddar Gorge, in Somerset. In the other direction there is the effect of wanting to look back for much of the time.

As a tiring road to drive over, without, in my opinion, adequate scenic return for the effort expended, at all events on a rather grey evening such as we had for it, I shall remember the run along the east side of Loch Awe, from Ford to Port Sonachan and then Dalmally, follow-

ing the loch closely for nearly twenty-five miles and with never a straight three hundred yards, I should think.

During all this the Riley had still used no engine oil, but preparatory to the run south it was given a thorough chassis lubrication, the rear brakes were taken up slightly, but not the front hydraulically operated set, as they did not need adjustment, and a quarter-pint of oil was added to the rear axle. This work was carried out by an enthusiastic and most capable man in a quite small garage in Oban, who, by his very approach to the job and his subsequent handling of it, typified a picture of the first-class mechanic whom one so often finds in Scotland. To be fair, however, he was a " naturalized " North Countryman. He impressed me in the first instance by asking for the makers' instruction book and lubrication chart, whereas if you offer any such guidance to some garage men a certain resentment may result.

## No Real Oil Consumption

The Riley, I felt, thoroughly deserved this attention, and day after day it had behaved faultlessly, with not even the minor irritations that are always a nuisance and that can be a positive threat to peace of mind when far from the home or factory base. Only because it seemed almost unnatural for even a new engine to use no oil at all did I put in a largely unnecessary pint before starting south ; this brought the level over the top mark on the dipstick and the oil was still above level—and clean looking —at the end of the journey after a further 500 miles, in spite of continuous fast motoring on the homeward run.

It was while carrying out a Road Test of the 1½-litre last autumn that I was smitten with the wish to put this model to a more extended test under conditions that would give it a chance of still better displaying its sound qualities. A more satisfactory choice could not have been made. It is not too big a car for the narrow roads and has an admirable steering lock ; it cruised at 60 m.p.h. or so on the journey to and fro, showing the strongest possible thoroughbred qualities in its ability to keep hard at work

Conditions Which in Many Respects Correspond to Those
Overseas Provide the Opportunity of Seeing a Modern High-
efficiency British Design to Advantage :—Part II.

By

## H. S. Linfield

Loch Tulla, reached by an offshoot from the modern Glencoe road at Bridge of Orchy. The road, about two miles long, has to be retraced, as it leads only to Forest Lodge, though it would appear that its continuation formed the old Glencoe road over Black Mount. The other, eastern, end of Loch Tulla is seen when the new road is being followed.

one always seems to need to take for a journey covering a fortnight or so, including two tins of petrol, could be stowed in the really roomy luggage boot. Only, as with any car, did I wish for a sliding roof, to enable the full value to be obtained from every hour of sunshine, besides increasing the view in mountainous country ; and, an old point of criticism, a more comfortable position for the left foot off the clutch pedal. But I must admit that this item was not so actively in mind after the first long day spent at the wheel as it was at first.

For several reasons the return journey was not started on the principle of selecting the shortest route. Edinburgh was to be visited, for one thing, whereas via Glasgow gives the shortest distance to the south. Visits to Scotland are too rare under present conditions to let any chance pass of taking in scenery and paying visits that lie reasonably on one's route while one is up there. In particular I wanted to see the new Rest and be Thankful road between Inveraray and Tarbet, finished only during the war. Preceding it, from Cairndow, is a section of switchback road, mainly straight, with a perfectly good surface, incidentally coloured red, but causing a fast car almost to take off on the brows if the driver is tempted to open the throttle !

### Farewell to Scotland's Best

After the descent of Rest and be Thankful to Loch Long, at Arrochar, and Tarbet, we duplicated part of the original outward journey alongside Loch Lomond, as far as Crianlarich, there to swing east and take in Loch Earn from Lochearnhead, a lovely sylvan stretch with a Scottish lake showing itself in a green and leafy setting as compared with the bare grandeur further north and west. We began to feel from Crianlarich, and still more after Loch Earn's banks had been left at St. Fillan's, that the " real " Scotland was being lost. Yet on this last afternoon we had still seen remains of snow on the 3,863ft Ben More;

" Frontier "—but no international complications ! England-Scotland at Carter Bar on the run south from Edinburgh. This road reaches 1,371ft over the Cheviots.

What happens to the surroundings of the best-known Scottish loch, Loch Lomond, in the interests of development, so necessary to the Highlands. The scene shows installation of hydro-electric plant between Tarbet and Ardlui, where for a short distance the lovely lochside scenery is ruined.

without becoming hot and bothered or losing tune, and the way in which it sat down on the road at speed and cornered fast without a trace of roll was just as one wished. One knew exactly where one was with the steering, and the gear change, with a longish but rigid remote-control lever and excellent synchromesh, was a delight to use. Other features especially valuable for country such as the Scottish Highlands were the big petrol tank already mentioned, and twin horns loud enough to be heard round the innumerable blind corners.

Comfort of riding in the wide back seat was another strong point, and it was vastly appreciated that considerable luggage for two, plus the many items that

Above : Looking down Glen Croe from the new Rest and Be Thankful road, between Inveraray and Arrochar. The famous old road is seen winding through the valley ; it is to be used next year for a speed hill-climb organized by the Royal Scottish A.C.

Left : Pass of Kintraw, on the Oban-Kilmelfort-Kilmartin road (A816). Although the surrounding hills are modest in altitude more effect of a pass is obtained here than in most places except in the rugged North-west Highlands. The hills rise sheer close to the road to give this impression. There are good views of Loch Craignish, a sea loch, and of the islands of Scarba and Jura.

elsewhere, and especially, of course, on Ben Nevis, of which we had the best view from a MacBrayne steamer on the way to Fort William, there had been a good many bens still bearing snow in mid-June.

Comrie and Crieff brought us back to fair-sized inhabited areas once more, and even after Oban, which is in fact a larger town than either, it was strange to our eyes to see people in numbers once again, shopping and going about the everyday affairs of a country town. Stirling recalled realities to us with still more of a jar—and then the process was completed by Edinburgh, which personally I always like being in, in contrast with Glasgow, and which never seems difficult as regards traffic or finding one's way.

The Scots we found almost universally pleasant and courteous, to an extent, in fact, which led to certain odious comparisons being made within twenty-four hours of crossing the Border again, although I am not suggesting that habitual rudeness is encountered in casual contacts farther south. The difference lies, at least partly, in the fact that, for instance, one never seems to enter a Scottish roadside hotel without someone being at hand or quickly appearing to greet you in a pleasant manner that is far from being overdone, and to offer service willingly, whereas elsewhere it is, shall we say, not always so. I will leave

it at that, adding only that on this particular journey there was a notable example of exceptional treatment in a North of England hotel.

Except that there are not enough hotels for the busiest season in the more remote and desirable areas, the Highlands are well equipped psychologically for an increase in the tourist industry, the importance of which is now being fully recognized in Scotland. The Scots understand the art of making you feel at home, and they have good food to offer, especially, it was our own experience, in hotels away from the towns. Early June seems soon enough in the year to visit the Highlands ; the season then is late spring rather than summer and various forms of seasonal activity have only just begun.

Memories of good hotels and food on this trip include especially the Allan Breck, an attractive modern white place with its name from R. L. Stevenson's " Kidnapped," in a beautiful setting overlooking Loch Linnhe, not far south of Ballachulish ferry, on the road from Connel Bridge. Dinner and the atmosphere there were so good that we went out of our way to return another evening. Then lunch, though cold, was good at the Argyll Arms at Inveraray, and teas at various places were almost universally appetizing. Perhaps best remembered of these

Corran Esplanade, Oban. Beyond are the island of Kerrera, separated by the Sound of that name, and the mountains of Mull. One of the MacBrayne steamers which provide many trips to the nearby islands and to Fort William is seen coming in.

In Glen Orchy, beside the fast-flowing River Orchy. This road (B8074) offers "remoteness," yet is easy to drive over and has a quite good surface, though it is only single-car width. It provides an interesting and mileage-, if not time-, saving link between Oban, Dalmally and Glencoe, avoiding Tyndrum.

was our first Scottish tea, on the way north, at the Crawford Hotel, at Crawford, between Lockerbie and Abington.

Below the Border, on the run south, I especially commend the Percy Arms, at Otterburn, some thirty-five miles north of Newcastle-on-Tyne, just off A68. Without previous reservation we arrived at 9.30 p.m.; a good cold supper was produced and arrangements were made to ensure an early start for us—before 8.30 a.m.—as was necessary to fulfil the next day's programme.

Even with Highland scenes so fresh in mind there was great appeal in the Border country, which is perhaps seen to the best advantage of the wide Cheviot vistas on the route taken, by Jedburgh, over Carter Bar and so to Otterburn. There is something to hold one about this history-steeped country and to make one want to return to explore.

### A Good Alternative to A1

This route from Edinburgh had been deliberately chosen to avoid the normal A1 main route via Berwick-on-Tweed, just as the Carlisle road was ignored on the run up in favour of Teesdale and Alston. A rather remarkable long-distance continuity of road numbering had been noticed when studying the map, A68 running from just south of Edinburgh, out of Scotland by Jedburgh, over Carter Bar and then leaving Newcastle well to the east and giving a nearly enough true south line, missing all the towns, including Darlington, until it joins A1 a little north of Scotch Corner.

In the morning, from Otterburn, A68 indeed proved very direct, although some unexpected rights and lefts are involved here and there in following its well-marked course. Because of "switchbacks" and a certain amount of climbing which would be put down as steep in the south, it is not a really fast road in terms of the cruising speed that can be used, but directionally it is good and I feel sure that it must save time as compared with the delays of the dreary Newcastle—Durham—Darlington route.

We were in Boroughbridge for coffee in little more than two hours, with 92 miles in the bag. Thence to Coventry, where the run ended, with 250 miles covered by 3 in the afternoon, was just a journey—fast and satisfying, the Riley still holding its 60 m.p.h. without fuss and frequently pushed round to 70 on A1 and the still fast stretches that offered after leaving it at Bawtry for Nottingham. A

better line, I felt on studying the map afterwards, would have been to continue on A1 as far as Newark and then on A46 via Leicester, for our route became decidedly confused for a time south of Nottingham, and we were somewhat surprised to find ourselves in Castle Donington—*the* Donington, of course.

Before I finally leave Scotland as a subject let me make plain that I do not fall into the error of supposing that only the Western Highlands are Scotland from the touring point of view. Nor do I claim to have "done" the Highlands in ten days. To say nothing of the far north-west, there is Perthshire, which I happen to know less well, and also, as I know from other visits, much of the Lowland country south of Edinburgh is thoroughly good—and not so "low" as regards scenic effects.

A last word concerning the car; it finished, as it began, entirely in one piece, with no measurable oil consumption, no rattles or bits working loose and with everything working, though considerably more run-in than at the beginning. Petrol consumption, including everything—fast running and miles of climbing, much strictly unnecessary use of the gears when cornering and for extra acceleration—worked out at 25-26 m.p.g. Half a day's check over and changes of oil, it being a new car, plus chassis lubrication, brake adjustment to correct the effect of new linings settling down, and it would be fit for anything. We parted with regret and with a great and increased respect formed for the 1½-litre, as honestly built a car as can be found and a thorough pleasure to handle.

### True British Quality

It had stood up to some really hard work without flagging and it could not fail to impress anyone who values obvious engineering quality in a car, added to external amenities that leave no room to regret the absence of this or that in the equipment—always as a personal view, which is by no means universally shared, excepting a sliding roof! Its feeling of solidity gives confidence and somehow makes it feel bigger than it actually is. Confidence was the word that summed up impressions of the car after many hours spent in it; and we had been with it through a good deal of wild, lonely country—conditions under which there is no more valuable thing than to have faith in one's car to finish the journey.

SLEEK 1½.—The 1½-litre Riley saloon remains substantially unchanged for 1949, but there are detail modifications to engine air ntake and front brake assemblies. The external covers for the bonnet locks have now been removed and, at the rear, the exhaust tail pipe now points straight back, as on the 2½-litre model

# Rileys Improved in Detail

## Increased Power and 2LS Brakes on 2½-Litre Model

NO sweeping changes have been made in the Riley range for 1949 This was, of course, to be expected, since all three models are true post-war designs. The 1½-litre saloon was, in fact, one of the first completely new designs to appear after the cessation of hostilities; the 2½-litre saloon, on a basically similar but slightly lengthened chassis, appeared a few months later and the three-seater sports

model on the latter chassis was intro duced in March this year.

In addition, a drop-head coupé is now being introduced on the 2½-litre chassis, and an example of this model will be exhibited at the Motor Show.

Outwardly, all represent an extremely attractive blend of modern line and classic styling, whilst, mechanically, they combine traditional Riley features —such as hemispherical combustion

chambers with inclined valves operated by short push rods from high camshafts —with recent innovations such as torsion-bar independent front suspension. The result is a range of cars of distinctly above-average performance (maximum speeds on "The Motor" tests of the 1½-litre and 2½-litre saloons were 78 m.p.h. and 94.8 m.p.h. respectively) and outstanding cornering and road-holding qualities.

### RILEY DATA

| Model | 1½-litre | 2½-litre | Model | 1½-litre | 2½-litre |
|---|---|---|---|---|---|
| **Engine Dimensions:** | | | **Transmission (contd.)** | | |
| Cylinders .. .. | 4 | 4 | Prop. shaft .. .. | Enclosed | Enclosed |
| Bore .. .. | 69 mm. | 80.5 mm. | Final drive .. .. | Spiral Bevel | Spiral bevel |
| Stroke .. .. | 100 mm. | 120 mm. | **Chassis Details** | | |
| Cubic capacity | 1.496 c.c. | 2,443 c.c. | Brakes .. .. | Girling hydro-mech. | Girling hydro-mech. |
| Piston area .. .. | 23.2 | 31.6 | | | (2LS on front) |
| Valves .. .. | O.H. (at 90 degrees) | O.H. (at 90 degrees) | Brake drum diameter | 10 ins. | 12 ins. |
| Compression ratio | 6.8 to 1 | 6.8 to 1 | Friction lining area | 126.48 sq. ins. | 136.5 sq. ins. |
| **Engine Performance:** | | | Suspension, front .. | Independent (torsion | Independent (torsion |
| Max. b.h.p... .. | 55 | 100 | | bar) | bar) |
| at | 4,500 | 4,500 | Suspension, rear .. | Semi-elliptic | Semi-elliptic |
| Max. b.m.e.p. .. | 128 | 136 | Shock absorbers .. | Girling | Girling |
| at | 2,500 | 2,500 | Wheel type .. | Pressed disc | Pressed disc |
| B.H.P. per sq. in. | | | Tyre size .. .. | 5.75 x 16 | 6.00 x 16 |
| piston area .. | 2.37 | 3.17 | Steering gear .. | Riley rack and pinion | Riley rack and pinion |
| Peak piston speed ft. | | | Steering wheel .. | 17 ins. | 18 ins. |
| per min. .. .. | 2,960 | 3,500 | **Dimensions:** | | |
| **Engine Details:** | | | Wheelbase .. .. | 9 ft. 4½ ins. | 9 ft. 11 ins. |
| Carburetter .. | S.U. (H2-type) | Two S.U. (H4-type) | Track, front .. | 4 ft. 4½ ins. | 4 ft. 4½ ins. |
| Ignition .. .. | 12-volt Lucas coil | 12-volt Lucas coil | Track, rear .. .. | 4 ft. 4½ ins. | 4 ft. 4½ ins. |
| Plugs: make and type | Champion L10S | Champion NA8 | Overall length .. | 14 ft. 11 ins. | 15 ft. 6 ins. |
| Fuel Pump .. .. | A.C. Mech. | S.U. Electric | Overall width .. | 5 ft. 3½ ins. | 5 ft. 3½ ins. * |
| Fuel capacity .. | 12 gals. | 12½ gals. * | Overall height .. | 4 ft. 11 ins. | 4 ft. 11 ins. * |
| Oil filter (make, by-pass or full flow) | Full flow (Wilmot Breeden) | Full flow (Tecalemit) | Ground clearance.. | 7½ ins. | 7 ins. |
| Oil capacity .. | 10 pints | 14 pints | Turning circle .. | 30 ft. | 36 ft. |
| Cooling system .. | Pump, fan and thermo-stat | Pump, fan and thermo-stat | Dry weight .. | 24¼ cwt. | 28 cwt. |
| Water capacity .. | 13 pints | 21 pints | **Performance Data:** | | |
| Electrical system .. | Lucas 12-volt | Lucas 12-volt | Piston area, sq. in. | | |
| Battery capacity .. | 58 amp./hr. | 63 amp./hr. | per ton .. .. | 19.1 | 22.6 |
| **Transmission:** | | | Brake lining area, sq. | | |
| Clutch .. .. | Borg and Beck | Borg and Beck | in. per ton .. | 104 | 97.5 |
| Gear ratios: Top .. | 4.89 | 4.11 | Top gear m.p.h. per | | |
| 3rd .. | 7.23 | 5.83 | 1,000 r.p.m. .. | 16 | 19.5 |
| 2nd .. | 11.2 | 8.86 | Top gear m.p.h. at | | |
| 1st .. | 19.42 | 15.0 | 2,500 ft./min. | | |
| Rev. .. | 19.42 | 15.0 | piston speed .. | 61.2 | 62.1 |
| | | | Litres per ton-mile, | | |
| | | | dry .. .. | 2,320 | 2,680 |

* **Note.** Data given for the 2½-litre type refers to the saloon. The specification of the three-seater sports model differs in the following respects :—Fuel capacity, 20 gals. ; width, 5 ft. 6 ins. ; height, 4 ft. 7 ins. ; weight, 26½ cwt.

Externally, the 1949 models are virtually indistinguishable from their predecessors; only the very observant will notice the omission of the small plated covers which used to conceal the carriage-type locks on the bonnet sides or notice that the exhaust tail pipe of the 1½-litre model now points straight backwards (as on the 2½-litre car) instead of at an angle as before. This, incidentally, removes what used to be the only distinguishing clue to the identity of the two saloons when viewed from the rear.

Most notable alterations to the 2½-litre type concern the engine and brakes. In the former, inlet valves which are larger in diameter (but of the same weight as before owing to a more concave formation of their heads) are fitted and this alteration has resulted in a very considerable increase in power, the engine now developing 100 b.h.p. at 4,500 r.p.m. So far as brakes are concerned, the latest Girling Hydro-mechanical system with two leading shoes on the front has been adopted.

### Brakes and Maintenance Improved

In the 1½-litre, there has also been a slight change in the front brakes which are now of the Girling Hydro-mechanical HNS1 type, with the upper pull-off spring of the single leading shoe now attached to an anchorage on the back plate instead of to the trailing shoe. The 1½-litre engine is substantially unchanged but a detail maintenance improvement has been obtained by altering the angle of the carburetter air-intake elbow and the mounting of the air-cleaner to provide better accessibility to the carburetter dash-pot and also to allow the inlet valve cover to be removed without disturbing the air-cleaner.

On all models, the gearbox tunnel has been narrowed to provide increased foot room and slight modifications have

been carried out to provide a lower floor level. Another useful detail alteration is the elimination of the previous carriage-type locks which secured the bonnet-top and the substitution of an internal arrangement of catches controlled by knobs each side of the glove-tray.

### Attention to Details

Considerable attention has been paid to making the cars both waterproof and dustproof and the opening section of the V windscreen is now provided with an additional rubber edging to provide a double seal. A rubber seal has also been provided on the doors, whilst improved dust and draught excluders are fitted to the pedals.

Coachwork improvements include the fitting (above the centre of the facia board) of an additional ash-tray at the front, the provision of folding arm-rests to the rear seats, and the substitution of a hand-dipper button closely adjacent to the steering-wheel rim on the off-side of the facia board in place of the previous foot-dipper. In addition, an interior heater and de-misting system (with a selector knob on the facia board which enables hot or cold air to be directed to the interior in general, to the screen only, to the front passenger only, or to the driver only as required), is now available as an optional extra. Externally, the cars differ in the use of a new plastic known as Melloroid for the head of the saloon models, this material having been developed for its resistance to wear and blemish.

We have recently been able to inspect and handle on the road the export model 2½-litre with left-hand drive and open 2/3 seater body. This car maintains the Riley tradition of an open sports model and all who have enjoyed the special Riley qualities in this type of car in the past will find them present

in an even more developed form in this model. Using the same axle ratio as is employed on the saloon car, the acceleration figures are naturally considerably improved and, so far as maximum speed is concerned, special tests have been made in Belgium as there are no roads in this country on which the car can be properly timed at its full speed.

This model will be the subject of a " Motor " road test in due course and meantime some details of its construction will be of interest.

The body has a wide bench-type seat permitting three to be carried in reasonable comfort, or even four if a child were a member of the party. The entire stern of the car is devoted to a very large luggage space and provision of a twenty-gallon fuel tank will be welcomed by all long distance motorists. Certain modifications have been made to the steering gear following upon the transfer to left-hand drive, and we found the motion to be direct yet with almost complete freedom from reaction from the road wheels. The handling of the car was particularly good on fast bends.

Although the body is of professedly sporting type with a fold-flat screen, a very " solid " hood is provided with which the side screens make a close fit. Although, therefore, it would be an exaggeration to put this car in the convertible coupe class, it has nevertheless very full weather protection and the top can be easily raised or lowered. It will be appreciated that a bench-type seat has been fitted in conjunction with a steering column gear lever, and, although it is not easy to fit this mechanism to a four-speed gearbox, the Riley change which comes to the right hand is satisfactory in itself and certainly greatly increases the overall utility of the car.

THREE-ABREAST TOURER.—"Certain modifications have been made to the steering gear . . . and we found the motion to be direct yet with almost complete freedom from reaction from the road wheels. The handling of the car was particularly good on fast bends. . . ."

# RILEY MODIFICATIONS

### Minor Changes to Models of Proved Excellence

THAT the 1½- and 2½-litre Rileys are outstanding cars in a number of ways—for instance, their road holding and stability, their comfortable suspension, their general behaviour and their performance—is a matter of common knowledge to the car-loving public. They were, and still are, advanced designs. It is interesting therefore to record that since their first appearance there has been no need for alteration except in the smaller details. In the interim one or two minor modifications have gradually been embodied, largely as the result of widening experience of the cars in all conditions and in many countries.

### Two-leading-shoe Front Brakes

For example the 2½-litre is a very fast car, capable of close on 100 m.p.h. When it was used in exacting trials, and over Alpine passes, it was found that an improvement in the braking system would be beneficial, so the recent models now have the latest Girling hydro-mechanical system with two leading shoes on the front wheels.

Tall people were apt to criticize the head room in the saloon body, so the floor of the car was redesigned so as to lower its level, and more head room was thus gained without loss of comfort, good appearance or ground clearance. Experience in many climates brought about an improved method of sealing the windscreen against water and dust percolation by means of a new type of recessed rubber edging. Attention was also specially paid to the exclusion of dust

and draught from the interior of the coachwork, and effective seals have been added to the door openings and places where controls pass through the front bulkhead.

Another point is the adoption of fasteners for the top sections of the bonnet, operated from inside the car, which means that the bonnet is automatically locked when the body is locked. There is a small plunger, one on each side of the glove shelf, which unlocks the adjacent part of the bonnet when it is pulled outward. These catches are spring-loaded and re-engage automatically when the opened bonnet is pressed down. On long journeys some

drivers found it awkward to find a rest for the left foot away from the clutch pedal. On the later models the gear box tunnel has been reduced in width so as to leave room for the foot.

Both sizes of engine have received careful attention and research, and although it has not been found necessary to make any major alterations, the power has been further improved and refined. The 2½-litre has been given inlet valves of increased size and is now able to develop 100 b.h.p. at 4,500 r.p.m. Accessibility of the carburettor on the 1½-litre

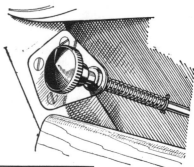

One of the new remote controls for the bonnet, which still opens in two sections from a lengthwise central hinge.

A fine example of British engineering, the 2½-litre Riley engine and gear box. With its two carburettors and the larger inlet valves it now develops 100 b.h.p.

engine has been improved by a slight change in the shape of the intake elbow.

Provision is now made for the fitting of an air heating plant as an optional extra. By means of a small enclosed fan and radiator hot or cold air can be admitted to the interior of the car, to the driver only, the front passenger only, or to the windscreen for de-misting. To improve driving comfort the head lamp dipper switch has been moved from the floor and placed on the facia panel in the form of an easily located and operated push button. A folding armrest of an improved type and considerable width is now fitted to the rear seat. Finally a new plastic called Melleroid has been adopted for the head covering of all models. This material is hard wearing and resistant to blemishes.

Earlier in the year an open sports three-seater on the 2½-litre chassis was introduced, with a view to catering for overseas markets, the U.S. in particular. At present this model, which was described in *The Autocar* of March 19 last, is for export only, indeed, and is supplied with left-hand controls. It provides seating for three on a very wide adjustable one-piece seat, and the tail of the body is devoted to luggage space.

A steering column gear change has been adopted for the 2½-litre sports three-seater, here seen with left-hand steering for export.

# *The Autocar* ROAD TESTS

## DATA FOR THE DRIVER

### 2½-LITRE RILEY SPORTS THREE-SEATER

**PRICE,** with open three-seater body, not quoted in Great Britain. Export only at present.

**RATING :** 16 h.p., four cylinders, overhead valves, 80.5 × 120 mm, 2443 c.c.

**BRAKE HORSE-POWER:** 100 at 4,500 r.p.m. **COMPRESSION RATIO:** 6.85 to 1.

**WEIGHT,** without passengers : 27 cwt 2 qr. **LB per C.C. :** 1.26.

**TYRE SIZE :** 6.00 × 16in on bolt-on steel disc wheels.

**LIGHTING SET :** 12-volt. Automatic voltage control.

**TANK CAPACITY :** 20 gallons : approximate fuel consumption range, 20-24 m.p.g.

**TURNING CIRCLE :** (R) 36ft ; (L) 37ft. **MINIMUM GROUND CLEARANCE:** 7in.

**MAIN DIMENSIONS :** Wheelbase, 9ft 11in. Track, 4ft 4½in (front and rear). Overall length, 15ft 6in ; width, 5ft 6in ; height, 4ft 7in.

**Left panel — controls:** LIGHTS & IGNITION, SCREEN WIPER, PANEL LIGHT, FOG LAMPS, INDICATORS, SCREEN WIPER, HAND THROTTLE, CHOKE, STARTER, HAND BRAKE, BONNET LOCK, ANTI-DAZZLE, GEAR LEVER, IGNITION SETTING, PUSH IN FOR R

### ACCELERATION

| Overall gear ratios | From steady m.p.h. of | | |
|---|---|---|---|
| | 10 to 30 | 20 to 40 | 30 to 50 |
| 4.11 to 1 | 10.2 sec | 10.2 sec | 10.8 sec |
| 5.83 to 1 | 7.0 sec | 7.4 sec | 8.0 sec |
| 8.86 to 1 | 5.0 sec | 5.3 sec | — |
| 15.00 to 1 | — | — | — |

| From rest through gears to :— | | | | sec. |
|---|---|---|---|---|
| 30 m.p.h. | .. | .. | .. | 5.9 |
| 50 m.p.h. | .. | .. | .. | 14.0 |
| 60 m.p.h. | .. | .. | .. | 19.0 |
| 70 m.p.h. | .. | .. | .. | 28.0 |
| 80 m.p.h. | .. | .. | .. | 38.3 |

Steering wheel movement from lock to lock : 3 turns.

Speedometer correction by Electric Speedometer :—

| Car Speedometer | Electric Speedometer | Car Speedometer | Electric Speedometer |
|---|---|---|---|
| 10 | = 10 | 60 | = 58 |
| 20 | = 20 | 70 | = 66.25 |
| 30 | = 29.75 | 80 | = 76 |
| 40 | = 39 | 90 | = 85.75 |
| 50 | = 48 | | |

| Speeds attainable on gears (by Electric Speedometer) | | | M.p.h. (normal and max.) |
|---|---|---|---|
| 1st | .. | .. | 21-26 |
| 2nd | .. | .. | 40-44 |
| 3rd | .. | .. | 60-65 |
| Top | .. | .. | 98 |

**WEATHER :** Dry, warm ; fresh wind.

Acceleration figures are the means of several runs in opposite directions.

*Current model described in " The Autocar " of March 19, 1948.*

THIS open model on the 2½-litre Riley chassis represents a return to an open car in the modern style by a firm which through the years has usually offered open sports cars in addition to closed models. The current three-seater was designed with a view particularly to the American market and under present conditions it is unfortunately purely an export model, to the extent that no home market price is quoted for it. The price overseas varies, of course, on different markets, but it is understood that it is closely comparable with that of the 2½-litre saloon.

No attempt has been made to provide a car with a very much higher maximum speed than that of the fleet saloon, and the same gear ratios are used. Characteristically, the body is solidly built and there is thus no very great saving of weight over the saloon. With the latest engine, developing 100 brake horse power, the test results show that the acceleration performance is in some respects better than that of the saloon previously tested by *The Autocar*. An impression is certainly gained of the all-round performance being brisker than the saloon's.

It is intended purely as a two-three-seater of sporting character and additional seats are not provided in the tail of the body, which is devoted to a luggage locker of truly vast capacity. By the use for the first time on a Riley of a steering-column gear change the full benefit of a one-piece type of seat is gained as regards useful width avail-

able and ease of getting in and out by either door. This open model feels every bit as "solid" on the road as the closed car in spite of the absence of the stiffening effect of a steel roof, a fact which emphasizes the rigidity of the box-section frame which forms its foundation. The export nature of this model was stressed by the fact of the car undergoing test being fitted with left-hand drive.

So well-known is the behaviour of the 2½-litre Riley saloon, which has proved so successful in the post-war period, that it was no surprise to find that the natural cruising speed is in the region of 75 m.p.h., and this is a thoroughly comfortable rate on a top gear of 4.11 to 1. The genuine maximum available closely approaches 100 m.p.h., with a fine surge of acceleration available on second and third gears. But it can be treated a good deal as a top gear car, for the engine proves decidedly more flexible at low speed than earlier examples, and picks up strongly ; the pinking that occurs under such conditions on the petrol at present available in Great Britain would probably be absent on fuels of higher octane value obtainable elsewhere.

This car's averaging capabilities on a journey are altogether exceptional, and it puts its 45 miles or so into an hour with consummate ease even over the usual English roads that constantly provide handicaps in the shape of bends and speed limits. One can readily visualize the car

This view shows the three-seater in the enclosed state. The side screens are efficient draught and rain excluders. When the hood is down the wide windscreen can be folded flat on the scuttle, a position which may appeal in hot climates and in which condition the car was tested for maximum speed.

flying across France, for example, at a 50-plus average, or again between cities in South Africa or Australia, where 500-mile hops are a commonplace, and at the same time taking in its stride the deteriorations of road surface by virtue of the excellent qualities of its torsion bar front suspension and long half-elliptic rear springs.

## Unhurried Speed

At 50 to 60 m.p.h. this car seems hardly to be moving, and on occasions when the driver may not be specially trying to hurry he is apt to receive a surprise on glancing at the speedometer to find that the needle is sitting between 70 and 75 when he had not been consciously thinking of speed and had supposed that he was doing around 65 m.p.h. Speeds up to about 85 m.p.h. are obtained really readily on stretches of road such as are found fairly frequently in England, and from the performance table it will be observed that the Riley reached a genuine 80 m.p.h. in a mean time substantially below two-thirds of a minute, from a standing start. For the ultimate speed to be seen it needs appreciable space in which to build up the revs, and the occasion offered as part of this test to time the car over the Belgian road where Lt. Col. Goldie Gardner recently broke class records. A total run of approximately six miles was available and the speedometer reached a reading of just over 100 m.p.h. during two electrically timed kilometre runs, the average of which gave 97.98 m.p.h. This was with the hood down and screen flat. The fuel used would be somewhat superior in octane value to un-alloyed Pool.

Above all is the factor of safety always associated with Rileys and seen in very high measure in this model. The car sits firm and square on the road, takes corners on an even keel even when high speeds are being held, and gives the driver every possible impression that he is closely in touch with its control through the steering and is able to

put it just where he wants on the road. The steering is firm and not in the least spongy and has good castor action. A degree of heaviness for low-speed turning can be excused in the light of this steering's admirable qualities for fast driving with the utmost confidence. Such is the feeling of complete safety afforded that even in darkness nearly 100 miles can be put into a little more than two hours over typical English roads.

The brakes, too, are in keeping ; they are of the Girling hydro-mechanical type with two leading shoes in the front drums. Without being at all fierce at any time they deal faithfully with the high speeds of this car and do not require heavy pressure on the pedal. As regards both power available and the way in which the braking efficiency is maintained under continued hard use, the latest brakes are a decided improvement upon the braking experienced on the earlier 2½-litre Riley.

## Driving Position

The new gear change works well of its kind and has the important point that there is a positive stop against the unintentional engagement of reverse. A knob on the end of the lever has to be pushed in before reverse gear can be selected. In all respects, both in the driving compartment and under the bonnet, the left-hand drive fits in well, and as the steering wheel is placed as far as possible over to the left the full width of the wide front seat is made available. Naturally the car will be supplied with right-hand drive for countries with the same rule of the road as in Great Britain. The driver's foot positions are comfortable and he has an excellent view outwards over the handsomely long bonnet—which is lower than on the saloon—and also he has a proper view of both front wings. At speed there was some flapping from the hood against its frame, but a lined version in future production will overcome this point, and an improved arrangement of the

Left : Deep bumpers with massive overriders somewhat alter the front appearance of the three-seater in comparison with the saloon. At both front and rear the bumpers curve round to protect the sides of the wings. The bonnet line is lower than on the saloon. Right : The hood, in an attractive plastic material, is neat and goes entirely out of sight when down.

driving mirror will give a better view behind with the hood up.

It is easy to raise and lower the hood, and with it down a beautifully quiet, swift form of travel is experienced, a sensation in motoring which, indeed, could hardly be bettered in fine weather. As has already been indicated, there is nothing at all flimsy about the open body and one has the feeling of sitting well down in it. Nor, curiously enough, does the driver experience any disadvantage through not having a separate seat with a rounded back rest to support the shoulders, this no doubt being largely because the lateral stability of the car is such that there is extremely little tendency for the occupants to be thrown sideways during fast cornering. Good protection against draught and rain is given by the side screens, which attach to the doors by quick-action fastenings.

The concession which the current Rileys make to present-day fashion in the enclosing of the head lamps in faired tunnels, though they are not built into the wings, strikes one as being ample, and one has a feeling of pleasure and relief that the front-end appearance remains typically British and yet not old-fashioned by current standards. The bonnet remains of the type opening in two sections, but is now released by means of a remote-control knob at each side of the driving compartment.

### Over 400 Miles Without Refuelling

A petrol tank of 20-gallon capacity gives a cruising range of around 450 miles without refilling, according to the speeds that are used, and there are twin fillers concealed by the lid of the luggage compartment, which can be locked. To obtain the total fuel reading a switch on the instrument panel is pressed, the reading given by the gauge being, as it were, in two sections, of which twelve gallons are indicated in the usual way when the ignition is switched on, and the remaining quantity, which is consumed first, upon depression of the switch mentioned.

Starting from cold was immediate with very brief use of the choke for the twin carburettors, and the engine quickly attained working temperature. The subsequent reading of the thermometer fitted on the instrument board seldom exceeded 70 deg C.

Mention of the average speeds obtained under night conditions suggests sufficiently the kind of beam given by the head lamps ; both have double-filament bulbs, the beams being deflected downwards for anti-dazzle purposes—a

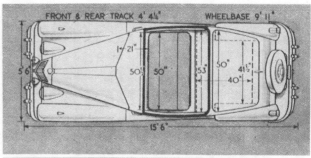
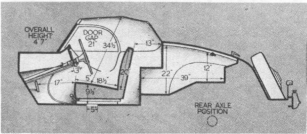

Measurements are taken with the driving seat at the central position of fore and aft adjustment. These body diagrams are to scale.

system which seems to worry some oncoming drivers in this country. Jacking is conveniently carried out at two points in front, where sockets are provided, and at a point on each side just ahead of the rear wings. The bumpers which this model carries have been designed particularly to cope with American conditions. The way in which they are wrapped round to protect the vulnerable wing corners low down is very practical, and these bumpers are noticeably more solid than is often the case.

As a whole this car gives the strongest possible impression, always associated with the Riley *marque*, of efficient design in the first instance, and honest workmanship and construction. With its high performance, its useful seating capacity and its quite exceptional luggage space, it should have an especial appeal to those overseas who want a car of character capable of covering big distances fast and tirelessly to the driver and passengers, more particularly, of course, in countries where the weather remains settled for long periods. It would have a considerable appeal, too, at home among connoisseurs if economic conditions permitted this model to be sold here.

Left : The tail is used entirely for luggage and fuel tank space. A truly enormous luggage-carrying capacity is provided, it will be observed. The twin fillers for the 20-gallon tank are inside the boot lid. A fishtail on the end of the exhaust pipe gives the engine a subtly " sports " note. Right : The bonnet opens in two sections, as on the Riley saloon models, and is released by means of a control at each side of the driving compartment.

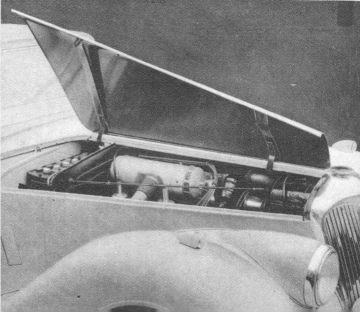

# The 1½-litre Riley

THE basic design of the Riley engine has not changed a great deal for many years, the chief difference being that chain-driven camshafts are now employed as opposed to gear drive on the earlier models. However, many less obvious modifications have been made to enable the new 1½-litre unit to develop 55 b.h.p. at 4,500 r.p.m.

This four-cylinder engine has a bore and stroke of 69 mm. and 100 mm. respectively (1,496 c.c.). The cylinders are cast en bloc with the crankcase, being made of nickel-chrome cast iron. Beneath this is bolted the ribbed aluminium-alloy 10-pint capacity sump. The cast-iron cylinder head with straight-through inlet and exhaust ports, has machined, hemispherical combustion chambers and centrally situated Champion sparking plugs. Compression ratio is 6.7 to 1.

Silicon-chrome overhead exhaust and inlet valves having 1 7/16-in. diameter heads are inclined at an angle of 45 degrees to the vertical in the cylinder head. They are operated from two chain-driven, three-bearing camshafts, through hollow, mushroom - type tappets, short push-rods and pressure-lubricated rockers. Rocker gear is protected from dirt and made oil-tight by means of aluminium covers with laminated cork gaskets. The inlet camshaft has a spiral gear machined in situ at its centre for the oil-pump drive. At the front end is a gear drive for the distributor. Timing wheels are enclosed by an aluminium cover.

Lo-ex special aluminium alloy is used for the high-compression, split-skirt pistons, each of which has three 2-mm.-wide compression rings and one 5/32-in.-wide oil ring. Floating gudgeon

pins in phosphor-bronze bushes are secured by circlips.

Carbon steel, one per cent. nickel and heat treated, is employed for the H-section connecting rods which measure 8 ins. between centres. Big-end bearings are white metal run directly on to the rods.

The crankshaft, which is made of one per cent. chrome-molybdenum, heat-treated steel, runs in three white metal bearings, the front main bearing being 2⅛ ins. long, the centre 1 7/16 ins. and the rear 2⅜ ins. End thrust is taken on the rear bearing. Standard crankpin diameter is 1.875 ins. and the main journal diameters are: front and rear 1.75 ins., centre 2.75 ins. At the forward end of the crankshaft is the main timing wheel, keyed in position and clamped

by the hand-starter dog, which is keyed and locked by a taper pin. An oil thrower is located between the timing wheel and the starter dog.

Engine bearings are pressure fed with oil from a gear-driven, self-priming pump of generous capacity, situated in the sump and enclosed by a fine-mesh strainer. A full-flow filter is incorporated in the lubrication system. The dipper-rod is on the near side of the engine just forward of the exhaust outlet pipe. The oil filler orifice is on the near-side rocker cover. From here, the oil reaches the sump via passages in the cylinder head and block. Minimum permissible oil pressures when running in top gear are: 19 lb. per sq. in. at 15 m.p.h., 22 lb. at 20 m.p.h., 26 lb. at 30 m.p.h. and 35 lb. at 50 m.p.h. On the off side of the crankcase, in a central position just above the top of the sump, is an oil pressure release valve. To increase the oil pressure, the adjusting screw should be turned clockwise.

Cooling water is circulated by a centrifugal pump mounted on the front of the cylinder head with a thermostat above it. "Cross-flow" cooling has been applied to the cylinder head to ensure a direct supply of cool water to the exhaust valve seats. The fan is carried on an extension of the water pump shaft, the whole being driven by a V-belt from the crankshaft. Capacity of the cooling system is 13 pints.

An A.C. mechanical fuel pump, actuated by an eccentric on the inlet camshaft, draws petrol from a 12½-gallon rear tank and supplies it to a single horizontal S.U. carburetter bolted to the inlet manifold on the off side of the engine.

Twelve-volt Lucas special equipment is standardized. Manual control for ignition advance and retard is featured in addition to the automatic system.

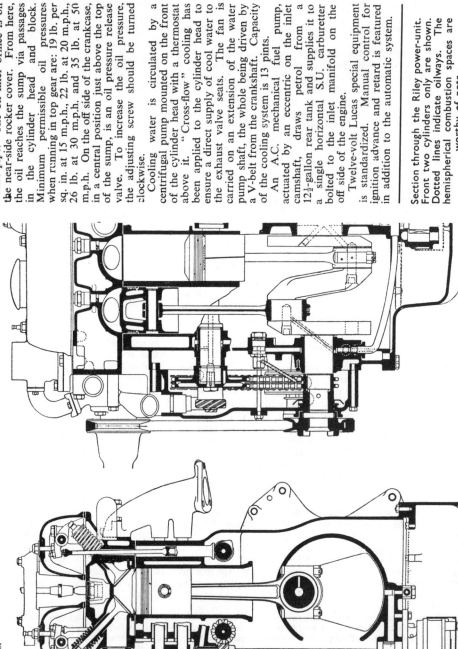

Section through the Riley power-unit. Front two cylinders only are shown. Dotted lines indicate oilways. The hemispherical combustion spaces are worthy of note.

Diagrammatic, head-on view of the Riley 1½-litre engine, showing the disposition and angle of the valves, also the high located camshaft with short push-rods.

Restrained and yet not dated in its appearance, the Riley has impressive and well-balanced proportions. The roof, which has no sliding section, is covered in a grained plastic material.

## DATA FOR THE DRIVER

### 2½-LITRE RILEY SALOON

**PRICE,** with four-door saloon body, £958, plus £266 17s 2d British purchase tax. Total (in Great Britain), £1,224 17s 2d.

**RATING :** 16 h.p., 4 cylinders, overhead valves, 80.5 × 120 mm, 2,443 c.c.

**BRAKE HORSE-POWER :** 100 at 4,500 r.p.m.  **COMPRESSION RATIO :** 6.9 to 1.

**WEIGHT :** 28 cwt 2 qr 7 lb (3,199 lb).  **LB per C.C. :** 1.31.  **B.H.P. per TON:** 70.05.

**TYRE SIZE :** 6.00 × 16in on bolt-on steel disc wheels.  **LIGHTING SET :** 12-volt.

**TANK CAPACITY :** 12½ gallons : approximate fuel consumption range, 18-24 m.p.g.

**TURNING CIRCLE :** 36ft (L. and R.).  **MINIMUM GROUND CLEARANCE :** 7in.

**MAIN DIMENSIONS :** Wheelbase, 9ft 11in.  Track, 4ft 4½in (front and rear).
Overall length, 15ft 6in ; width, 5ft 3½in ; height, 4ft 11½in.

### ACCELERATION

| Overall gear ratios | From steady m.p.h. of | | |
|---|---|---|---|
| | 10 to 30 | 20 to 40 | 30 to 50 |
| 4.11 to 1 | 10.4 sec | 10.7 sec | 11.9 sec |
| 5.83 to 1 | 7.5 sec | 7.7 sec | 8.4 sec |
| 8.86 to 1 | 5.4 sec | 5.7 sec | — |
| 15.00 to 1 | — | — | — |

From rest through gears to :—  Sec.

| | | | | |
|---|---|---|---|---|
| 30 m.p.h. | .. | .. | .. | 5.9 |
| 50 m.p.h. | .. | .. | .. | 13.0 |
| 60 m.p.h. | .. | .. | .. | 18.4 |
| 70 m.p.h. | .. | .. | .. | 27.1 |
| 80 m.p.h. | .. | .. | .. | 38.8 |

Steering wheel movement from lock to lock : 2¼ turns.

### Speedometer correction by Electric Speedometer :—

| Car Speed-ometer | Electric Speed-ometer | Car Speed-ometer | Electric Speed-ometer |
|---|---|---|---|
| 10 | 10.5 | 60 | 56 |
| 20 | 20.5 | 70 | 64.5 |
| 30 | 29.75 | 80 | 73 |
| 40 | 38 | 90 | 83.5 |
| 50 | 47.5 | | |

| Speeds attainable on gears (by Electric Speedometer) | M.p.h. (normal and max.) |
|---|---|
| 1st .. .. .. | 17–27 |
| 2nd .. .. .. | 35–46 |
| 3rd .. .. .. | 57–67 |
| Top .. .. .. | 92 |

**WEATHER :** Dry, mild ; wind negligible.

Acceleration figures are the means of several runs in opposite directions.

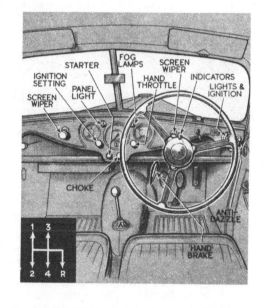

*Described in " The Autocar " of November 29, 1946*

---

SINCE it was introduced in 1946 the 2½-litre Riley has been establishing a great name for its performance and handling qualities. From the outset it was apparent that with its high-output 2½-litre four-cylinder engine, designed for efficiency on lines which Riley's have so well understood for many years, this car provided with roomy saloon comfort one of the very highest all-round performances available in any car of the present time. If one additionally considers the fact that the list price in Great Britain is under £1,000 and, therefore, the car does not incur the double-rate purchase tax, it is probably true that in this fine example of British specialist car is offered the highest performance available today at the price at which it sells.

When it was introduced the present range of Rileys looked modern, yet without a hint of extremist tendencies ; today, when styling, sometimes in exaggerated forms, has come very much to the fore, these cars still do not look dated, and the discerning type of motorist appreciates the clean-cut, unequivocal lines. In the more recent examples of the model improvements have been incor-

porated in the natural course of evolution—still more power has been extracted from the very willing twin-camshaft engine, yet it has been made smoother and more tractable at the lower end of the speed range ; in the course of development braking has been improved in keeping with the needs of so very fast a car, and, still more recently, a number of bodywork refinements have been incorporated.

It is a car for the real motoring enthusiast, the type of driver who wants to go far and fast, who appreciates and can obtain the utmost from steering, braking and handling qualities all designed to fit exactly the demands made on a car when high averaging is required. Most important of all, perhaps, is the safety factor which accompanies the performance.

In very few cars, past or present, can one feel so keenly as with this Riley that it is ambling along a good main road at 60 to 70 m.p.h. By ambling is meant that there is no sense of mechanical effort or suggestion of moving quickly, yet this rate represents to very many people a *maximum*, seldom if ever used in other cars. The fact that at such a speed there is a good 20 m.p.h. in reserve

"Tunnelled" head lamps, which the Riley has had since the current series was first introduced after the war, are this car's main concession to modern styling, and many people who appreciate "real" cars remain grateful that it goes no farther along the path of fashion. The lower pair of lamps is separately switched as fog lamps.

In tail view the car is clean and well balanced, with a wide luggage locker lid. Beneath the bumper overriders will be noticed the sockets (normally filled by a rubber plug) into which a very easily operated pillar jack is conveniently applied. These sockets are repeated at the front.

means a great deal. The driver is affected psychologically by the thought, knowing that he is not pressing the car, and on the mechanical side it gives the ease of running which can come only from having a considerable margin in hand. No car in existence feels more solid or safer, or sits down more squarely on the road, or is under better control than this Riley right through the speed range, up to and over an honest 90 m.p.h. Bends are taken fast by scarcely more than bearing on the wheel—there is no conscious effort in the process—and on the straight at speed the driver need no more than rest his hands lightly on the wheel, applying the merest guidance to keep the car on its course. A thoroughly rigid foundation in the shape of a well-designed frame is a large part of the Riley's exceptional feeling of tautness and stability.

The road-holding, the accuracy of steering that any experienced driver will recognize to be fully implied in such praise of roadworthiness cannot be obtained without some disadvantages. The torsion bar suspension, to give the effects described, is firm to the point of letting road surface variations be fairly noticeable, and the fairly high-geared rack and pinion type of steering is not as light at low speeds as some systems which do not have to cope, on occasion, with 90 m.p.h. These, however, are points which one accepts in weighing up the car as a whole.

With many excellent Rileys of the past clearly in mind one expects this car to have an engine which can be given the hardest work without flagging, and once again in the present test has this been shown to be so. Within the limitations imposed by British roads and traffic conditions some very hard driving has been put in on this 2½-litre, yet never did the engine water thermometer exceed a reading of 70 deg C, and never did the oil pressure show a falling off. A full-flow pressure oil filter in the engine lubrication system and 14 pints of oil in the sump help to inspire confidence when high speeds are being maintained.

British roads cramp this car, but certainly it can make

the very best use of them, as witnessed by average speed performances recorded, examples being 53 miles in one hour, 54 miles in another, and 56.5 miles in yet another, the last forming part of a run over an admittedly selected favourable route during which 74.5 miles were covered in 77 minutes, and 102 miles in two hours exactly.

Opportunity did not present of seeing a speedometer reading higher than 99, on a stretch of road on which the car did not have a completely clear run, and where it was still accelerating when the brakes had to be used. The instrument had an appreciable optimism at the higher rates, in contrast with that of the last car of this model tested by *The Autocar*, but certainly the reading quoted means a figure genuinely exceeding 90 m.p.h.

Such average speed recordings as have been mentioned were obtained when, frankly, the driver was trying. Another almost as impressive part of the performance is the way in which hour readings of 45 and 46 miles can be put up without exceeding, say, 70 m.p.h.—results which are usually considered creditable. With the Riley, to average 50 in the hour is almost a commonplace and only mileages beyond that figure assume special interest. Such is its calibre.

From the comfort point of view the suspension is extremely effective and a remarkably good back seat ride is given, it being very noticeable that there is no tendency for passengers to be thrown sideways when bends are being taken at the speeds the car's rock-steady stability invites. The driving position is a good one in that the big spring-spoked steering wheel is in a position for full power of control; indeed, it would be surprising and disturbing if it were otherwise on such a car. The wheel is

A bonnetful of compact and efficient machinery: The bonnet opens in two sections from a central hinge, the release catches being now inside the driving compartment. On the right side of the engine are seen the twin S.U. carburettors and, mounted on the bulkhead, the electric fuel pump and the fluid

reservoir for the hydraulically operated front brakes, also the tools. On the left side are the accessible battery and the radiator filler. The sparking plugs are easily reached between the twin covers of the valve rocker gear, which is operated by short push-rods from two high mounted camshafts.

Combined leather and cloth upholstery was used in the car tested, but all-leather is now being provided in cars for the home market as well as in those for export. The section of the V windscreen in front of the driver can be opened. At the rear will be noticed the deep central folding arm-rest, and

on both front and rear doors the elbow rests, which have a sponge rubber foundation. In the rear compartment, where width and leg room are good, footwells are used, at either side of the propeller-shaft tunnel. The seating is very comfortable, with plenty of support for the legs and back.

slightly off-set to the left and is telescopically adjustable on the column. One's left leg is not as comfortable as it could be, although improvement has been made in this direction, partially meeting a long-standing criticism of a very good car. Driving vision is virtually perfect, and the now all but unique complete view afforded of both front wings helps enormously to give confidence. Head room has been increased in this low-built car by comparison with the earlier examples. The windscreen pillars are wide enough to be a little obstructive at times.

Brakes are the Girling hydro-mechanical system operating hydraulically on the front wheels and through mechanical linkage on the rear. They are set a big task on a car of this performance and no particularly light weight, but they cope with requirements in a manner which inspires confidence. The way in which the brakes can be "laid on" at all speeds without upsetting stability is a great part of the car's strong safety factor.

## Acceleration Uphill

The gear change is by the now increasingly uncommon central vertical remote control lever, and especially in such a car one values its positiveness. The synchromesh is smoothly effective for all ordinarily fast changing, full depression of the clutch pedal being desirable. Gear changing in relation to hill-climbing takes on a different significance from the normal. This car will fly over a main road slope at a steady 80, where the road is clear, accelerating all the way, and it is only through a baulk or for something quite severe in gradients that one has to think of gear changing as an aid to climbing. A usual hill of 1 in 6½ gradient was taken at a minimum speed of 30 m.p.h. on third gear, second being required, however, in kindness to a high-compression engine for rounding an acute corner at the summit.

Flexibility and tractability at low speeds about town are noticeably improved over the earliest 2½-litres. No longer does one feel that it is desirable to drop to third below about 25 m.p.h., and to start on second gear and then use the top-and-third method of driving suffices for ordinary running around, there being no suggestion that the car is fierce or difficult to handle in the way that the old-type sports car could be. On the other hand there is appreciable pinking, which can be lessened for low-speed running by means of an ignition setting control on the instrument board. On the present quality of British petrol pinking was also noticeable at really high speed in this engine, while accelerating between, say, 70 and 80. One sighs for fuel of higher octane value, as available in some countries, which would eliminate this distressing tendency, or largely reduce it. The engine started from cold with the barest use of the choke.

As regards detail amenities, the new elbow rests on the

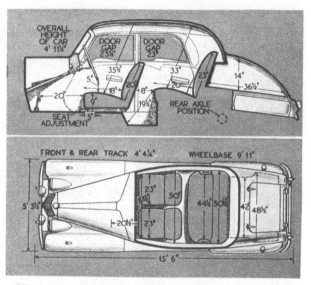

Measurements in these scale body diagrams are taken with the driving seat at the central position of fore and aft adjustment.

doors are worth having, the twin horns give a good, powerful note, and there is a useful shelf in the front compartment for oddments. A good rearward view is given by the driving mirror. There is a rear window blind with an easily operated control. The anti-dazzle control consists of a push-button switch on the right of the facia, an unusual but convenient method, as the switch can be operated without entirely removing the right hand from the wheel. A reversing light operates in conjunction with the gear lever. An interior heater with de-misting and de-icing provision is available as an optional extra (£25), but this equipment was not fitted on the car tested.

Showing the really capacious luggage locker, the lid of which is held open by a self-locking strut. A petrol filler cap is provided in each rear wing, thus avoiding the necessity for placing the car on the " right " side of a pump.

# The Motor Road Test No. 12/49

**Makers:** Riley Motors Ltd., Abingdon-on-Thames, Berks.

**Make:** Riley **Type:** 1½-litre Saloon

## Dimensions and Seating

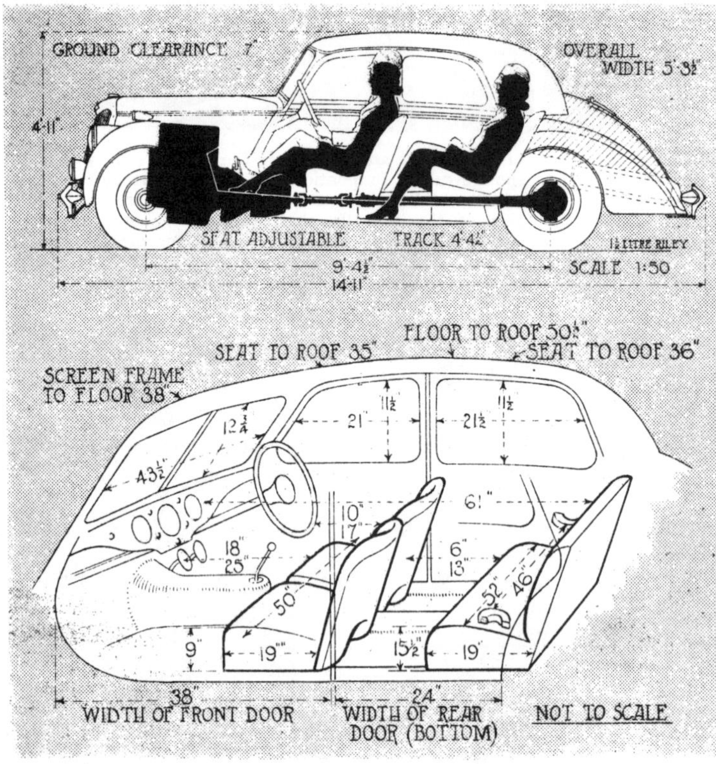

GROUND CLEARANCE 7"
OVERALL WIDTH 5' 3¾"
4' 11"
SEAT ADJUSTABLE
TRACK 4' 4½"
1½ LITRE RILEY
9' 4½"
14' 11"
SCALE 1:50
FLOOR TO ROOF 50½"
SEAT TO ROOF 35"
SEAT TO ROOF 36"
SCREEN FRAME TO FLOOR 38"
WIDTH OF FRONT DOOR
WIDTH OF REAR DOOR (BOTTOM)
NOT TO SCALE


## Test Conditions

Cool, showery, moderate wind, concrete surface, Pool grade petrol.

## Test Data

**ACCELERATION TIMES on Two Upper Ratios**

| | Top | 3rd |
|---|---|---|
| 10-30 m.p.h. | 13.1 secs. | 8.1 secs. |
| 20-40 m.p.h. | 13.8 secs. | 9.4 secs. |
| 30-50 m.p.h. | 16.3 secs. | 11.3 secs. |
| 40-60 m.p.h. | 22.1 secs. | 17.3 secs. |
| 50-70 m.p.h. | 36.6 secs. | — |

**ACCELERATION TIMES Through Gears**

| | |
|---|---|
| 0-30 m.p.h. | 7.6 secs. |
| 0-40 m.p.h. | 13.1 secs. |
| 0-50 m.p.h. | 20.1 secs. |
| 0-60 m.p.h. | 32.6 secs. |
| 0-70 m.p.h. | 53.3 secs. |
| Standing quarter-mile | 24.8 secs. |

**MAXIMUM SPEEDS**

**Flying Quarter-mile**

| | |
|---|---|
| Mean of four opposite runs | 77.8 m.p.h. |
| Best time equals | 80.4 m.p.h. |

**Speed in Gears**

| | |
|---|---|
| Max. speed in 3rd gear | 60 m.p.h. |
| Max. speed in 2nd gear | 38 m.p.h. |

**BRAKES at 30 m.p.h.**

0.93 g (= 32⅓ ft. stopping distance) with 130 lb. pedal pressure.
0.78 g (= 38½ ft. stopping distance) with 100 lb. pedal pressure.
0.60 g (= 50 ft. stopping distance) with 75 lb. pedal pressure.
0.37 g (= 81½ ft. stopping distance) with 50 lb. pedal pressure.
0.20 g (= 150 ft. stopping distance) with 25 lb. pedal pressure.

**FUEL CONSUMPTION**

Overall consumption for 153 miles, 5½ galls. =27.8 m.p.g.

32.5 m.p.g. at constant 30 m.p.h.
32.5 m.p.g. at constant 40 m.p.h.
30.5 m.p.g. at constant 50 m.p.h.
25.0 m.p.g. at constant 60 m.p.h.
19.5 m.p.g. at constant 70 m.p.h.

**STEERING**

Left- and right-hand lock, 30 ft.
2½ turns of steering wheel, lock to lock.

**HILL CLIMBING**

Max. top gear speed on 1 in 20, 44 m.p.h.
Max. top gear speed on 1 in 15, 34 m.p.h.
Max. gradient climbable on top gear, 1 in 14½ (Tapley 155 lb. per ton)
Max. gradient climbable on 3rd gear, 1 in 9¼ (Tapley 240 lb. per ton)
Max. gradient climbable on 2nd gear, 1 in 6½ (Tapley 335 lb. per ton)

## In Brief

Price. £714 plus purchase tax £199.1.8 equals £913.1.8.

| | |
|---|---|
| Capacity | 1,496 c.c. |
| Road weight unladen | 24½ cwt. |
| Front/rear wt. distribution | 50½/49½ |
| Laden weight as tested | 28 cwt. |
| Fuel consumption | 27.8 m.p.g. |
| Maximum Speed | 77.8 m.p.h. |
| Maximum speed on 1 in 20 gradient | 44 m.p.h. |
| Maximum top gear gradient | 1 in 14½ |
| Acceleration, 10-30 on top | 13.1 secs. |
| 0-50 through gears | 20.1 secs. |

Gearing 16.1 m.p.h in top at 1,000 r.p.m. 61.5 m.p.h. at 2,500 ft. per minute piston speed.

## Specification

**Engine**

| | |
|---|---|
| Cylinders | 4 |
| Bore | 69 mm. |
| Stroke | 100 mm. |
| Cubic capacity | 1,496 c.c. |
| Piston area | 23.2 sq. ins. |
| Valves | Pushrod o.h.v. (2 camshafts) |
| Compression ratio | 6.8/1 |
| Max. power | 55 b.h.p. |
| at | 4,500 r.p.m. |
| B.h.p. per sq. in. piston area | 2.37 |
| Piston speed at max. b.h.p. | 2,960 ft./min. |
| Carburetter | S.U. horizontal |
| Ignition | 12 v. Lucas coil |
| Sparking plugs | 14 mm. champion L10S |
| Fuel pump | A. C. Mechanical |
| Oil filter | Full Flow |

**Transmission**

| | |
|---|---|
| Clutch | Single dry plate |
| Top gear | 4.89 |
| 3rd gear | 7.23 |
| 2nd gear | 11.2 |
| 1st gear | 19.4 |
| Propeller shaft | Divided, rear half in torque tube |
| Final drive | Spiral bevel |

**Chassis**

| | |
|---|---|
| Brakes | Girling hydro-mech. |
| Brake drum diameter | 10 ins. |
| Friction lining area | 126.5 sq. ins. |
| Tyres | 5.75 x 16 Dunlop |
| Suspension: | front, torsion bar I.F.S rear, semi-elliptic leaf |
| Steering gear | Rack and pinion |

**Performance factors** (at laden weight as tested)

| | |
|---|---|
| Piston area, sq. ins. per ton | 16.6 sq. ins. |
| Brake lining area, sq. ins. per ton | 90.5 sq. ins. |
| Litres per ton-mile | 1,990 |

Fully described in "The Motor," September 22, 1948.

## Maintenance

**Fuel tank:** 12½ gallons. **Sump:** 10½ pints, S.A.E. 30. **Gearbox:** 2 pints, S.A.E. 140. **Rear axle:** 2¾ pints, S.A.E. 140. **Radiator:** 13 pints. **Chassis lubrication:** by grease gun to 16 points. **Ignition timing:** static 8° B.T.D.C. fully advanced. **Spark plug gap:** 0.030 in. **Contact breaker gap:** 0.012—0.015 in. **Tappets:** inlet 0.003 in., exhaust 0.004 in. **Front wheel toe-in:** nil. **Camber angle:** 1°. **Castor angle:** 3°. **Tyre pressures:** front 22 lb., rear 24 lb. **Brake fluid:** Girling. **Shock absorber fluid (rear only):** Luvax Girling piston type. **Battery:** 12-volt, 58 amp-hour. **Lamp bulbs:** 12-volt single pole, 36-watt headlamps, 6-watt side and tail lamps.

Ref. B /15/49.

# The RILEY 1½-Litre SALOON

## A Car which is Different, Offering Economical Speed and Flexible Roll-free Suspension

TYPICALLY English is the description which almost inevitably is applied to the Riley 1½-litre, a car which cannot be closely compared with products of any other country. It is a car the ancestry of which can be traced back over a long period of years, and which in new post-war form has earned ever-increasing popularity.

Handsome appearances the Riley certainly has; good looks which have been attained with the absolute minimum of ornament. Its long, low lines are matched by a restrained yet effective interior treatment, which uses leather and polished wood in preference to the fabrics and plastic mouldings of quantity-production models.

The whole character of the Riley, as regards both its proportions, its coachwork details and the sturdiness of its chassis, contributes to make the car somewhat heavy in relation to its engine size. Nevertheless, the 1½-litre must be regarded as fast for its size and very reasonably economical, facets of its performance which, together, reflect high engine efficiency and good wind-cheating lines.

In the period which has elapsed since the post-war Riley was announced, early in 1946, few changes have proved necessary. Small refinements have brought details up to Riley standards of longevity, and the latest cars carry minor identification features, externally negative in so far as no bonnet locks are now visible, internally positive in that front and rear armrests are now provided. The whole car, in fact, may be said to be at a high-water mark of development as a reliable and economical vehicle for fast long-distance travel.

Silence and smoothness, particularly at low speeds, must be admitted as falling rather below the standards set by modern cars of lower performance. The highly efficient four-cylinder engine produces appreciable vibration when idling, and some mechanical noise, per-haps emanating from the drive to twin camshafts, is evident at town speeds. Given its head on the open road, the car feels happier, and although not silent, appreciable wind noise arising apparently from door hinges when the front windows are closed, it seems altogether tireless. Backed by years of racing experience, the unusual power unit seems to operate safely at substantially higher sustained piston speeds than are often thought desirable.

### Sporting Power

Willingness to run at high speeds has involved some slight sacrifice of low-speed engine performance. In top gear, snatch is completely absent down to 15 m.p.h., and the engine will pull vigorously down to even lower speeds on demand, but at any speed below 45 m.p.h. there is vigorous pinking on Pool-grade 70-octane petrol if the throttle is opened fully without some use of the manual ignition timing control. Nevertheless, the willingness to run at high speeds is there; not so much the sort of flashy performance which invariably gets ahead of all others when the lights change to green as the sort that encourages one to point the bonnet towards really distant parts of the world.

A willing engine in a not-so-light car needs the right sort of gearbox, and the Riley unit measures up well to requirements. Like the engine, it is not dead silent, yet does not mind being worked hard, and a short, rigid central lever set well back within the driver's reach just asks to be used. The car starts from rest comfortably in second gear if desired, but all four ratios are high enough to be really useful in ordinary brisk driving. There is synchromesh mechanism to ease changes into all gears except bottom, of a type which is not uncheatable but which is adequate to make leisurely downward gear-changes a push-through action and to cover up lack of precision in ordinary driving. As regards acceleration from rest, the test figures recorded do not perhaps do full justice to the car, for while the clutch of the test car behaved perfectly in normal driving, it slipped if any attempt was made brutally to exaggerate the rapidity of departure from rest or of upward changes of gear.

The all-round riding and handling qualities of the car merit very high praise, full advantage having been taken of the low build of the car to combine sports-car stability with touring-car riding comfort. On the one hand, there is a really high standard of comfort for low-speed driving over rough surfaces, be they urban cobble-stones or rural tracks. On the other hand, the front-seat occupants continue to ride smoothly when the car is driven really fast.

CLASSIC LINE.—Good looks which do not depend on superficial ornamentation characterize the Riley 1½-litre, latest of a thoroughbred line.

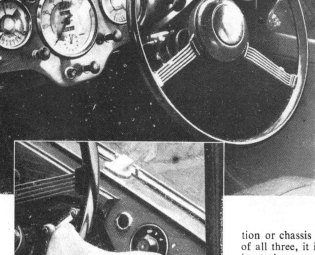

NEAT AND PRACTICAL. The spring-spoke steering wheel has two ranges of adjustment for position, and the wood facia carries an accessible finger-tip switch for headlamp dipping (see inset).

Cornering is delightfully roll-free, a quality which is particularly appreciated when S-bends are negotiated, and only on acute corners does tyre howl arise if inflation pressures are correct. Torsion-bar stabilizers, when mounted at the rear of a car, are not always contributions to the most desirable of handling characteristics. In this case, however, the car being normally virtually roll-free, the effect is simply to introduce an innocuous amount of oversteer during really fast cornering, a gentle tendency for the tail to drift outwards, which warns that the limit of tyre adhesion is being approached.

Rear-seat occupants do not travel in such tranquillity as the driver and front passenger. It is difficult to explain why this is, since the driver is never conscious of the slightest pitching or snaking tendency, but in the back of the car there is evident a markedly greater amount of vertical and lateral movement.

**Stability at Speed**

Steering on the Riley is by a rack-and-pinion gear, but does not share all the characteristics commonly associated with this design. There is high gearing by 1949 standards, 2½ turns taking the wheel from extreme to extreme of a commendably taxi-like lock, but a negligible amount of road shock is transmitted to the driver; the amount of castor action provided is very adequate. The steering effort required for manœuvring in town is rather above average, but, on the other hand, despite the car's straight-running stability on the open road, it can be steered into and out of fast-moving traffic columns more by thought than by perceptible effort or motion of the steering wheel.

A point which requires special mention is the relative insensitivity of the Riley to deflection from its course by wind. Whether this results from aerodynamic characteristics, weight distribution or chassis design or a combination of all three, it is at times very comforting to have confidence that, even at top speed, sudden wind gusts or patches of shelter will not cause the car to veer off its course.

The Riley body is quite definitely a four-seater, with appropriate accommodation for touring luggage. The front seats are individually adjustable, and armrests form handles by which the doors may be pulled shut. The rear seat is of sufficient width to accommodate three people if necessary, but the floor footwells and folding central armrest emphasize that two should be the normal complement. An unexpected complaint came from passengers on their first rides in the car to the effect that on slamming the rear door the armrest mounted on it was apt to give an unexpected blow on the hip; any regular passenger would, of course, sit well inside the car before slamming the door. The rear seat can house normally tall passengers in adequate comfort, but were it possible to extend the footwells farther forward, the extra toe-room would be appreciated. For touring, the view from the rear seats suffers somewhat from the four-light layout of the low-set body.

The driving position, appropriate to a car which is at its best when vigorously handled, is very comfortable for a driver who is alertly sitting up to his work. A ledge on the gearbox cover provides a rest for the left foot in a position such that the left knee is bent slightly, but also such that the foot is instantly available for clutch operation. The steering column is telescopic, and a modest range of vertical adjustment is also available.

Driving vision is good, the bonnet appearing long, but its lowness leaving both side lamps in full view. The external radiator cap, it may be mentioned, is a dummy, but the concealed filler, oil filler and dipstick are all grouped on the near side of the power unit. A detail which the keen owner would soon change is the driving mirror, which though well placed, is rather limited in area.

Lighting arrangements do not attract much attention during the long days of summer, but the Riley headlamps appeared to give rather longer beams than are sometimes associated with present-day inbuilt units. Dipping is by the usual twin-filament system, and a separate switch controls a pair of wide-beam fog lamps.

Cold starting is even more difficult to test in summer, but nights spent out-of-doors in rain were followed by faultless morning starts—a hand throttle allows the engine to be set to a fast idle when cold, no interconnection between choke and throttle being used. Despite the economical running of the engine, it was outstandingly willing to pull well and dispense with mixture enrichment almost immediately after being started from cold.

Door pockets, nowadays all too rare, were appreciated, but like the shelf below the facia, were disappointingly small in capacity. The luggage locker, however, proved well able to swallow up large cases, although its sloping floor induced petrol tins to slide backwards if the door was not closed quickly. The separate door of the spare wheel shelf has a catch which is only accessible when the luggage compartment is unlocked. A petrol tank giving over 300 miles' range will be appreciated by Continental tourists or night travellers, and duplicated filler caps allow it to be vented for quick filling.

Uniquely British in its appearance and general character, the Riley 1½-litre is a sturdily built car which is economical yet can cover long distances very quickly when traffic conditions permit. It is planned to appeal to a specialized taste, and does, in fact, appeal very strongly to a large number of keen owner-drivers.

EXTRA AMENITIES. Armrests and ashtrays are provisions for occupants of the low-set rear seats.

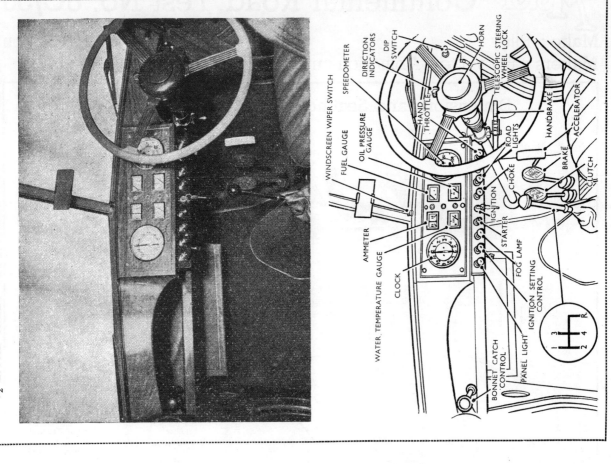

*AT THE WHEEL, No. 12 in the series written by members of the staff of " The Light Car," deals with—*

# The 1½-Litre Riley

THE lay-out of the controls and instruments of the 1½-litre Riley saloon is in keeping with the tradition of the marque. Being a high-performance machine, with sporting characteristics, it requires something extra in the way of general equipment as compared with the normal family saloon. Years of racing and competition experience have provided Riley engineers with the data necessary to equip their products in a manner which will delight all those who regard motoring as something more than merely a means of transport.

Apart from the provision of a 100 m.p.h. speedometer, in place of a 90 m.p.h. instrument, the interior lay-out of the 2½-litre and 1½-litre cars is identical. A detachable veneered walnut shield covers the centre of the facia panel, providing unusual accessibility to all instruments. Rectangular gauges showing oil pressure, fuel level, ammeter reading and water temperature are flanked by a large-dial speedometer and matching clock. If desired, a revolution counter can be fitted as an extra. Warning lamps for head lights, ignition and heater (if fitted) are provided in the centre of the panel. The instrument dials have a gold finish, and the facia arrangement is completed by garnish rails, also in veneered walnut, into which ashtrays are sunk. All windows are framed in walnut.

Directly below the facia panel are the lighting, starting and ignition switches, together with separate screw-out controls for throttle and ignition setting. The normal, pull-out control is used for the choke (S.U. carburetter). A hand-operated dipping switch is located on the extreme end of the panel, on the driver's right. The switch for the dual Lucas windscreen wipers will be found above the facia panel, just behind the centre pillar of the Vee-type screen. To prevent unauthorized interference with the engine, the bonnet locking catches

are controlled from inside the glove compartments.

The fully sprung steering wheel has a pearl plastic rim. The steering column is telescopic and, together with the fully adjustable seat gives a wide variety of driving positions. Both front seats are of the bucket-pattern, and armrests are recessed into the door panels. Upholstery is carried out in fine quality soft hide. Dual sun visors fold flush in the roof head when not in use.

Provision is made for the installation of radio and heating, both of which can be supplied as extras. The former is mounted neatly below the centre of the facia panel. On pre-1950 cars, the driver's portion of the Vee-type screen was fully opening, but this has now been abandoned in the interests of a completely leak-free screen. Careful attention has been paid to the exclusion of draughts, water and road grit from the interior, generous use being made of rubber sealing equipment. Effective "concertina-pattern" excluders are fitted to the pedals.

The stubby remote control gear lever is located immediately in front of the seats, in the centre of the floor, and the pistol-type handbrake projects from under the facia panel on the off side of the steering column.

Although the Riley is an extremely low-built machine, there is a surprising amount of headroom for all occupants. Visibility, too, is excellent, it being possible to see both near and off-side wings from the driver's seat. It says a great deal for the foresight of the Riley designers, that this car, announced in 1945, is, basically, being continued practically unchanged for 1950.

**Make : Riley**  **Type : 2½-litre Saloon**

**Makers : Riley Ltd., Abingdon-on-Thames, Berks**

## Dimensions and Seating

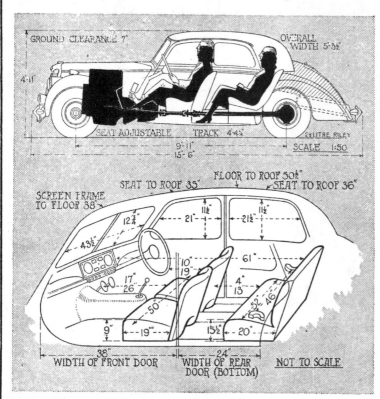

GROUND CLEARANCE 7″ — OVERALL WIDTH 5′-5½″ — 4′-11″ — SEAT ADJUSTABLE — TRACK 4′-4½″ — 2½-LITRE RILEY — 9′-11″ — 15′-6″ — SCALE 1:50

SEAT TO ROOF 35″ — FLOOR TO ROOF 50½″ — SEAT TO ROOF 36″ — SCREEN FRAME TO FLOOR 38″ — WIDTH OF FRONT DOOR 38″ — WIDTH OF REAR DOOR (BOTTOM) 24″ — NOT TO SCALE

## In Brief

Price £958, plus purchase tax £266 17 2
equals £1,224 17 2.

| | |
|---|---|
| Capacity .. .. .. | 2,443 c.c. |
| Unladen kerb weight .. | 29½ cwt. |
| Fuel consumption .. | 19.6 m.p.g. |
| Maximum speed .. .. | 90.1 m.p.h. |
| Maximum speed on 1 in 20 gradient .. .. .. | 75 m.p.h. |
| Maximum top gear gradient | 1 in 11.2 |

Acceleration,
| | |
|---|---|
| 10-30 m.p.h. in top. .. | 9.7 secs. |
| 0-50 m.p.h. through gears | 11.9 secs |

Gearing,
19.5 m.p.h. in top at 1,000 r.p.m.
62.1 m.p.h. at 2,500 ft. per min. piston
speed.

## Specification

**Engine**
| | | | | |
|---|---|---|---|---|
| Cylinders .. | .. | .. | .. | 4 |
| Bore .. | .. | .. | .. | 80.5 mm. |
| Stroke .. | .. | .. | .. | 120 mm. |
| Cubic capacity | .. | .. | .. | 2,443 c.c. |
| Piston area | .. | .. | .. | 31.6 sq. ins. |
| Valves .. | .. | .. | .. | O.H. (at 90°) |
| Compression ratio | .. | .. | .. | 6.8 : 1 |
| Max. power | .. | .. | .. | 100 b.h.p. |
| at | .. | .. | .. | 4,500 r.p.m. |
| Piston speed at max. b.h.p. | | | | 3,500 ft. per min. |
| Carburetter | .. | .. | Two S.U. (H4 type) |
| Ignition .. | .. | .. | 12-volt Lucas coil |
| Sparking plugs | .. | .. | Champion NA8 |
| Fuel pump .. | .. | .. | S.U. electric |
| Oil filter .. | .. | Full-flow Tecalemit |

**Transmission**
| | | | | |
|---|---|---|---|---|
| Clutch .. | .. | .. | Borg and Beck |
| Top gear (S.) | .. | .. | .. | 4.11 |
| 3rd gear (S.) | .. | .. | .. | 5.83 |
| 2nd gear (S.) | .. | .. | .. | 8.86 |
| 1st gear | .. | .. | .. | 15.0 |
| Propeller shaft | .. | .. | Enclosed |
| Final drive .. | .. | .. | Spiral bevel |

**Chassis**
| | | |
|---|---|---|
| Brakes | Girling hydro-mech (2LS on front) | |
| Brake drum diameter | .. | 12 ins. |
| Friction lining area | .. | 136.5 sq. ins. |

Suspension :
| | | |
|---|---|---|
| Front | .. | Independent (torsion bar) |
| Rear | .. .. | Semi-elliptic |
| Shock absorbers | .. .. | Girling |
| Tyres | .. .. | 6.00 × 16 |

**Steering**
| | | |
|---|---|---|
| Steering gear | .. | Riley rack and pinion |
| Turning circle | .. .. | 36 ft. |
| Turns of steering wheel, lock to lock .. | | 2¼ |

**Performance factors** (at laden weight as tested)
| | | |
|---|---|---|
| Piston area, sq. ins. per ton | .. | 19.15 |
| Brake lining area, sq. ins. per ton | .. | 83 |
| Specific displacement, litres per ton-mile | | 2,270 |

*Fully described in " The Motor," September 22, 1948.*

## Maintenance

**Fuel tank :** 12½ gallons. **Sump :** 14 pints, S.A.E. 30 (to 0°C.), S.A.E. 20 (to −18°C.), S.A.E. 10 (below −18°C.). **Gearbox :** 2 pints, S.A.E. 140 (to −12°C.), S.A.E. 80 (below −12°C.). **Rear axle :** 4 pints (as gearbox S.A.E.). **Steering gear :** Pack with grease. **Radiator :** 21 pints (1 drain tap), at base R.H.S. **Chassis lubrication :** By grease gun every 1,000 miles to front suspension (8 points), intermediate shaft (2 points), prop. shaft trunnion (1 point), water pump (1 point). Each 5,000 miles to wheel bearings. **Ignition timing :** 4° to 8° B.T.D.C., full advance. **Spark plug gap :** .025 in. to .030 in. **Contact-breaker gap :** .012 in. to .015 in. **Valve timing :** I.O. 17° B.T.D.C., I.C. 43° A.B.D.C. ; E.O. 45° B.B.D.C., E.C. 20° A.T.D.C. **Tappet clearances** (hot) : Inlet .003 in., exhaust .004 in. **Front-wheel toe-in :** Nil. **Camber angle :** 1°. **Castor angle :** 3°. **Swivel-pin inclination :** 11°. **Tyre pressures :** Front 24 lb., rear 24 lb. **Brake fluid :** Girling. **Lamp bulbs :** All single-pole. Head lamps, nearside double filament, 36/35 watts ; offside, 36 watts ; side, tail, roof and stop lamps, 6 watts ; ignition, panel and petrol-gauge lamps, 2.4 watts ; reversing lamp, 24 watts ; trafficators, 3 watts ; dash lamp, 2.4 watts ; fog lamp 48 watts ; pass lamp, 48 watts. Ref. B/25/50

## Test Conditions

Dry, moderate winds ; Belgian Premium petrol.

## Test Data

**ACCELERATION TIMES on Two Upper Ratios**

| | | Top | 3rd |
|---|---|---|---|
| 10–30 m.p.h. .. .. .. .. .. .. | | 9.7 secs. | 7.3 secs. |
| 20–40 m.p.h. .. .. .. .. .. .. | | 10.6 secs. | 7.6 secs. |
| 30–50 m.p.h. .. .. .. .. .. .. | | 11.85 secs. | 8.3 secs. |
| 40–60 m.p.h. .. .. .. .. .. .. | | 13.45 secs. | 10.05 secs. |
| 50–70 m.p.h. .. .. .. .. .. .. | | 15.95 secs. | — |
| 60–80 m.p.h. .. .. .. .. .. .. | | 21.75 secs. | — |

**ACCELERATION TIMES Through Gears**

| | |
|---|---|
| 0–30 m.p.h. .. .. .. | 4.65 secs. |
| 0–40 m.p.h. .. .. .. | 7.55 secs. |
| 0–50 m.p.h. .. .. .. | 11.9 secs. |
| 0–60 m.p.h. .. .. .. | 16.85 secs. |
| 0–70 m.p.h. .. .. .. | 24.3 secs. |
| 0–80 m.p.h. .. .. .. | 36.75 secs. |
| Standing quarter-mile .. | 21.1 secs. |

**MAXIMUM SPEEDS**
**Flying Quarter-mile**

| | |
|---|---|
| Mean of four opposite runs .. | 90.1 m.p.h. |
| Best time equals .. .. | 90.9 m.p.h. |

**Speed in Gears**

| | |
|---|---|
| Max. speed in 3rd gear .. | 73 m.p.h. |
| Max. speed in 2nd gear .. | 50 m.p.h. |
| Max. speed in 1st gear .. | 27 m.p.h. |

**FUEL CONSUMPTION**

31.5 m.p.g. at constant 30 m.p.h.
26.25 m.p.g. at constant 40 m.p.h.
24.5 m.p.g. at constant 50 m.p.h.
21.5 m.p.g. at constant 60 m.p.h.
18.75 m.p.g. at constant 70 m.p.h.
15.5 m.p.g. at constant 80 m.p.h.
Overall consumption for 178 miles, 9.08 gallons
=19.6 m.p.g.

**WEIGHT**

| | |
|---|---|
| Unladen kerb weight .. .. | 29½ cwt. |
| Front/rear weight distribution | 51/49 |
| Weight laden as tested .. | 33 cwt. |

**INSTRUMENTS**

| | | |
|---|---|---|
| Speedometer at 30 m.p.h. | .. | Accurate |
| Speedometer at 60 m.p.h. | .. | 11½% fast |
| Speedometer at 90 m.p.h. | .. | 6 % fast |
| Distance recorder | .. | 3 % fast |

**HILL CLIMBING** (at steady speeds)

| | |
|---|---|
| Max. top-gear speed on 1 in 20 .. | 75 m.p.h. |
| Max. top-gear speed on 1 in 15 .. | 65 m.p.h. |
| Max. gradient on top gear .. | 1 in 11.2 (Tapley 200 lb./ton) |
| Max. gradient on 3rd gear .. | 1 in 8.4 (Tapley 265 lb./ton) |
| Max. gradient on 2nd gear .. | 1 in 5.7 (Tapley 395 lb./ton) |

**BRAKES at 30 m.p.h.**

0.31 g. retardation (=97 ft. stopping distance) with 30 lb. pedal pressure.
0.43 g. retardation (=70 ft. stopping distance) with 50 lb. pedal pressure.
0.72 g. retardation (=42 ft. stopping distance) with 100 lb. pedal pressure.
0.78 g. retardation (=38.5 ft. stopping distance) with 140 lb. pedal pressure.

# The RILEY 2½-litre Saloon

## A high-performance car of marked character and unusual stability

THE testing of high performance cars on Continental roads can be justified not only by the requirements of safety during time trials at upwards of 80 m.p.h., but also because the longer distances and higher average speeds possible abroad are of great assistance in bringing out the good and, let it be admitted, some of the bad points of any given type.

The four-cylinder 2½-litre Riley was the second British car to be the subject of a run of this kind, upon which report was made in "The Motor" of December 18, 1946. On that occasion a total distance of some 4,000 miles was covered and on the recent test of the current, basically unchanged model the distance was over 2,000 miles. These embraced almost every condition likely to be encountered by the car user in Europe or the U.S.A. For some days the car was driven in London, many miles were covered on special motor roads at high average speeds, mountainous country was experienced in Switzerland and Italy, and very fast main road motoring was indulged in not only on the straight sections of the French roads but also on the more twisting sections at the base of the French Alps and the narrow, poorly surfaced roads of Southern Germany. The car was driven in every condition from one-up to more than fully loaded with four persons and a great weight of luggage. The predominant conclusion from these trials is that the 2½-litre Riley is a car of exceptional character, having a number of unusually meritorious features coupled with a few points which may be legitimately the target of criticism. Overriding everything else is the feeling of astonishment that so much usable road performance can be offered for so relatively low a price. Not only is the maximum speed on the right side of 90 m.p.h., but the usable road speed may be reckoned at anything

GRAND TOURIST.—A test extending across five European countries allowed the 2½-litre Riley to reveal its speed and stamina. It is seen above at Aix-les-Bains.

between 70/80 m.p.h. Although the piston speed is admittedly high in these circumstances the engine is so stiff in construction that it runs smoothly, coolly and with every air of enjoyment. The performance did not vary a hair's breadth during the entire course of our test, and figures quoted in the data table were taken at the end of 2,000 miles of hard driving and with cross wind which gave no assistance to speed in one direction. The fact that the four times taken for a quarter-mile stretch showed a maximum variation of one per cent. is significant of the car's character as a whole, and in this connection it must be put on record that the steering of the car gives the driver a complete feeling of confidence in all circumstances.

### Widely Varying Roads

Road surfaces in Europe vary far more than they do in this country; to give some examples, there is the flat, smooth, concrete of the German Autobahn, the rough and sometimes highly cambered pavé of France, the relatively smooth, but highly polished, roads of Italy which can be exceedingly slippery in the wet, and the very potholed surfaces of some of the frontier roads where war damage has not yet been made good. The Riley was taken over all of these both in dry and wet conditions, and not only did the driver

feel that he had complete control of the vehicle but this confidence was also imparted to the passengers. The low centre of gravity and absence of roll contribute in part to this freedom from worry, but the steering gear itself, with rack and pinion mechanism almost entirely free from backlash and with very strong self-centring action, also plays its part. Even on the roughest roads there was only slight reaction on the steering wheel, but it must be conceded that a good deal of muscular effort is needed on the rim particularly at low speeds in the traffic, whilst parking the car can be very heavy work indeed. At over, say, 40 m.p.h., however, the steering appears to be markedly lighter and there is no doubt it is in the speed ranges of 40/80 m.p.h. that this

car makes its greatest appeal. The suspension by torsion bar at the front and leaf springs at the rear is firm but sufficiently flexible to absorb the shocks of motoring at high speeds over rough roads without inconvenience to the driver and front-seat passenger, although conditions in the rear seat are definitely not so favourable and a marked motion of the radiator shell and front wing shows that whilst the fore part of the frame is adequately

UNOBSTRUCTED.—The deep locker accommodates a large quantity of luggage and is not obstructed by the separately mounted spare wheel. The dual filler caps are a great advantage.

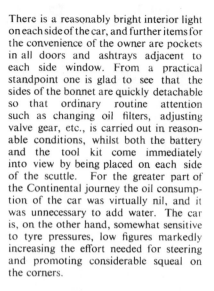

FOR THE DRIVER.—An adjustable steering column, remote gear control, and facia panel carrying accurate and clearly calibrated instruments are points of appeal to the keen driver.

## Riley Road Test - - Contd.

stiff for English conditions it permits a degree of torsional flexibility under the more severe conditions of Continental travel.

This fact, coupled with the fairly high muscular effort called for in driving, brings to mind the fact that the Riley embodies many of the characteristics typical of the vintage type of car including very marked ability to cover many miles in the hour without effort. On the road south from Avallon to Challon an average of rather over a mile a minute was sustained for an hour and distances of between 50/54 miles in the hour could readily be attained on the Continent and approached under favourable conditions in this country. It is unfortunate that on the car tested the braking system developed a minor but baffling defect, and it is possible that the figures quoted in the data panel taken before many miles had been run are less satisfactory than the best of which the design is capable.

### Minor Modifications

Turning from the mechanical aspects of the car to those of the body, there have been few changes since the car was last road tested, but amongst them have been the abolition of the opening window for the driver, a new instrument panel which bears both tachometer and speedometer dials, and a unit supplying hot or cold air to the interior of the body and the back of the windscreen. All the hot air can, if necessary, be diverted to the screen slots, and although the installation would scarcely be adequate for overcoat-free motoring in a really cold climate it supplies a ready method of supplying fresh air to the interior with a useful degree of warmth in ordinary mild weather motoring.

Although now well-known, the lines of the car continue to command admiration. Many competent judges think the 2½-litre Riley with its relatively long bonnet one of the best combinations of the modern trend with British tradition, but a penalty for the low roofline has to be paid in limited visibility. Although the Riley is one of the rare modern cars in which both sides of the front end are in plain view, the depth of the windows is circumscribed, and the rear seat occupants in particular see but little of the surrounding country. Similarly, the slope of the tail severely limits the volume of luggage which can be put under lock and key, but if the owner is willing to run with the lid raised but a few inches, and secured to the bumper by an elastic cord, the carrying capacity is practically doubled.

### Drivers' Details

The instruments can clearly be read both by night and by day, and there are warning lights which tell the driver when the heater fan motor is running and when the headlamps are in the high beam position. The latter indicator was a good deal too bright on the car tested, but it is believed that this matter has had attention on current production cars. Two foglights are supplied, operated by a separate switch, and in this connection it should be mentioned that there are now eight similar switches placed in a row below the instruments. Although neat, this arrangement can be confusing at times, and with an engine that is octane-sensitive one would enjoy a more refined advance and retard mechanism than a push-pull control on that side of the panel which is remote from the driving position with a right hand steering column. This control is, of course, supplementary to the automatic advance and retard, even so it can be used with advantage.

A wide parcels tray is placed beneath the instrument panel, and this is most useful for carrying guide books and similar items; smaller objects such as matchboxes and film containers, on the other hand, can sometimes get trapped behind the conduits leading air to the base of the windscreen.

FOR THE PASSENGERS.—Comfortable bucket seats hold the driver and front passenger steady during fast driving, and the rear seats have ample footroom in deep floor wells.

There is a reasonably bright interior light on each side of the car, and further items for the convenience of the owner are pockets in all doors and ashtrays adjacent to each side window. From a practical standpoint one is glad to see that the sides of the bonnet are quickly detachable so that ordinary routine attention such as changing oil filters, adjusting valve gear, etc., is carried out in reasonable conditions, whilst both the battery and the tool kit come immediately into view by being placed on each side of the scuttle. For the greater part of the Continental journey the oil consumption of the car was virtually nil, and it was unnecessary to add water. The car is, on the other hand, somewhat sensitive to tyre pressures, low figures markedly increasing the effort needed for steering and promoting considerable squeal on the corners.

### Average Consumption

The fuel consumption may be considered normal in relation to the power of the engine, and the average speeds attained, but especially on a car of this kind a range of little over 200 miles on one filling is insufficient, and it should also be noted that for quick replenishment it is imperative to remove the caps on both fillers. These minor criticisms do not seriously detract from the merit of the Riley, and it is legitimate to take into account the extraordinarily trouble-free running which has been characteristic of the model since its introduction. Engines which have covered between 40/50,000 miles with nothing more than routine attention are common amongst Riley owners and this is all the more remarkable in that the top gear ratio is sufficiently low to provide top gear acceleration between 10/30 m.p.h. in under 10 seconds, whilst the exceptional briskness of the car when full use is made of the gear-box is well exemplified by the 0/50 acceleration time of just under 12 seconds.

For the long-distance, hard-driving motorist who wishes to travel fast with complete confidence and safety and to be free from expensive maintenance bills, the Riley 2½-litre is a car which can be very thoroughly recommended.

*A 1½-litre light car is the subject this month of an out-of-the-ordinary test run report, by the Editor.*

# Riley Roulade

THE word "roulade" means rapid movement. It seems appropriate as part of the title of this medley of impressions, because the story is bound up with a kind of tip-and-run journey, which I made recently between London and "Rest and Be Thankful"—the Royal Scottish Automobile Club's hill-climb venue in Argyll, some 30 miles, as the crow flies from Glasgow. The crow, of course, has the advantage of direct flight; by road the distance is, perhaps, 10 or 12 miles longer, for the highway winds in and out along the western bank of Loch Lomond.

The car was a 1½-litre Riley and, as for the expedition as a whole, I may sum it up by saying that the speedometer "trip" recorded 955 miles for the double journey, including local runs from Tarbet, that the tool bag was never unrolled and that the petrol consumption worked out at a shade under 32 m.p.g.

Now the car wasn't spared and the country between Scotch Corner and Hamilton is not conducive to petrol economy; further, many miles were covered in torrential rain, which, here and there, converted the road into a miniature watersplash; and across Bowes Moor on the outward run it blew heavens hard as well. So I stress that figure of 32. It really means something —especially with petrol at over three bob a gallon.

The comfortable cruising speed was round the sixty mark, but the needle needed little persuasion to move on towards the seventies. The acceleration gives you an "appreciable" push in the back and "top-gearalising" is one of the most delightful attributes of this outstanding motor carriage made by the Nuffield Organisation.

Let me instance that long drag upwards, which begins when you leave Penrith going South—miles and miles of it; or the tiring stretch associated in the minds of all of us with the name Beattock. Half throttle was all the Riley insisted upon for country like this—thus always leaving a margin for the extra emergencies or passing·slower traffic.

There are some tricky sections, too, on these cross-country stretches: sudden dips in the road followed by blind corners. If you are not careful you find yourself drifting to the wrong side of the "strict and narrow," unless you have the right kind of steering and road-holding. For that the Riley earns full marks. The brakes were efficient too, but for really businesslike results they required fairly heavy pressure.

The delightfully smooth clutch and the silence of the gearbox warrant special mention. Seldom these days can a motor scribe use the old *cliché* and say that the gear lever falls readily to hand: finger-tip control has altered all that—except in cars like the Riley, where the hand still "falls," onto a stiff, stubby little lever, which is just where you feel it ought to be. The hand brake is worked by a pistol grip under the instrument panel. It is not my fancy, I'd like to see a "fly-off" lever on the Riley: something you could use for driving operations as well as parking; but that's merely a personal point of view.

## Comfortable Fast Cruising

Comfort? One hundred per cent. I did the trip in roughly four-hour stretches, putting 40 odd miles behind me in each hour. No trace of aches or pains—not even in the place where I sit down—and that's saying something, as many of my readers who have had to endure the agonies of badly-sprung cushions will confirm. Yes, a fine all-rounder, this 1½-litre Riley. A car that has a pedigree and lives up to it.

Here, my Passenger (who has been looking over my shoulder) reminds me that she kept a log concerning road conditions and isn't this the place to say something about it before I run out of type space?

Agreed.

We chose the familiar route to the North—via Grantham and Doncaster to Scotch Corner; then forking left to Penrith, and Carlisle. The temptation to swing off to the right at Abington in the direction of Stirling so as to by-pass Glasgow was resisted. I have a soft spot in my heart for Glasgow. Its pedestrian population is bent on suicide, but that is a thing apart.

En route to Dumbarton you can either go plumb through the centre of the city (and raise your hat courteously as you pass Kelvin Hall) or you can forego the doubtful attraction of miles of traffic and make for Great Western Avenue—a modern highway of the arterial kind.

### Traversing Glasgow

My Passenger has her own pet route but there are others, of course. She opines that it is best to make Glasgow Cross (by either of the two roads from Hamilton) thence into Argyll Street, where turn right up Buchanan Street; cross Sauchiehall Street into Cow-caddens Street, which leads into City Road. Then, when you come to a fork take the right-hand road—and you're there.

More in sorrow than in anger, my Passenger records that the reconstruction of the road between Alconbury and Stilton, which was begun before the war, has made no further progress, and that this part of the route to the north has "a general air of neglect." She warns fellow travellers to keep a look out for the 'no-passing sections on the Wansford by-pass and also north of Stamford, and she notes the fact that at a traffic-light stop in Newark " an old and respectable gentleman knocked on the window of the Riley and asked if we were going to Sutton-on-Trent: of which place I had no knowledge, and said so."

"In Lockerbie where we were slowing down for the lights" (the log continues) "a man who appeared to be in a state of coma, trickled out of a narrow side turning and got hooked up with the rear near-side quarter bumper of the Riley, which latter was bent. He drove on without stopping—but not it appeared, in a day-dream any longer. We stopped to examine. Damage fortunately very slight." Then another warning: "Keep a sharp look out for sheep and the like between Luss and Balloch and over the higher stretches of the moors." And, finally (on the homeward run): "Approaching 'The White Horse,' Eaton Socon. Could do with a drink."

The response to this appeal in writing, held up in mute supplication under my very nose, had the desired effect; and as we were on the last lap of our near-1,000-mile journey, we raised our glasses to the success of our Riley Roulade. Rapidly and right comfortably had it whisked us from London to Scotland and back.
F.J.F.

# *Judgement upheld...*

*At London's Law Courts & Inns of Court you see the Riley very much in evidence.*

*Men of keen judgement choose this car for the pleasures of motoring—the perfect mannered response, the exhilarating power for long cross country runs.*

*For over 50 years Riley has been the first choice of discriminating motorists.*

 *for Magnificent Motoring*

100 h.p. 2½ litre Saloon      1½ litre Saloon

*Riley—as old as the industry—as modern as the hour*

**RILEY MOTORS LIMITED, Sales Division: COWLEY, OXFORD**

*London Showrooms:* "RILEY CARS" 55-56 PALL MALL, S.W.1.

*Overseas Business:* Nuffield Exports Ltd. Oxford and 41 Piccadilly, London, W.1.

# 3,000 Miles With a 2½-Litre Riley Drophead Coupe

*T. G. Moore, at one time Managing Editor of " Motor Sport," tells of his Experiences with a much-discussed British Car.*

SPORTS-CAR drivers appear to be divided into two camps, those who favour the flexible springing and easy riding which characterise many of the post-war models, and those who prefer the firmer ride and the more direct steering of the vintage and pre-war eras.

My own problem was to find a modern replacement for a pre-war 3½-litre car, with similar performance, greater economy and the advantage of i.f.s. The post-war 2½-litre Riley appeared to possess all these characteristics, and when the drophead model was announced I decided to take the plunge.

I was lucky in obtaining delivery of one of the first coupés to be released for the home market, and though the car seemed rather small in comparison with my old car, I felt well satisfied with the lines and the general finish. The tan-coloured hood affords a pleasant contrast to the medium green of the bodywork and the light brown leather upholstery and body trim. The facia board and the window rails are finished in walnut veneer, with two useful interior lights. No door pockets are fitted but there is a parcel shelf under the facia board running the whole width of the car. The v-shaped windscreen, unfortunately no longer fitted with a panel which can be opened, gives a wide field of view, and both front wings are visible from the driver's seat. All controls come readily to hand, and the steering column is adjustable for length.

First impressions of the car on the road were rather unfavourable, as the steering was very heavy and the springing harsh. There was, however, a steady improvement in both these respects after the first 500 miles. The engine was partly run-in when delivered, and it required considerable restraint to keep the speed down to 40-45 m.p.h. The engine loosened up steadily as the miles went up, but best results were not obtained until the car had done 3,000 miles.

With 600 miles on the " clock," my wife and I took the Riley over to the Continent and there covered over 2,000 miles, touring in Holland, Germany and Denmark. The neat lines and compact appearance of the car made a good impression everywhere we went. School-children in all three countries seemed to be intrigued by the three letters on the number-plate and also on the A.A. plaque. In towns and villages everywhere we were, indeed, greeted by chants of " M-M-N, G-B-M."

Fast straight roads in all three countries gave one a good opportunity of appreciating the car's wide speed range. With the hood down there was no more effort or impression of speed at 80 m.p.h. than at 40, and the engine is well silenced at all speeds. With the hood up there is a fair amount of wind noise at speeds over 70 m.p.h., probably caused by the external hood-irons, which project from the otherwise smooth lines. The highest speed attained under substantially neutral conditions was a speedometer 94 m.p.h., which I estimate as an actual 87–88 on the road. With high-octane fuel or the addition of a proportion of benzol other owners tell me they get a genuine 90 m.p.h. The speedometer was 4 m.p.h. fast at 60 m.p.h. and 6 m.p.h. fast at 80 m.p.h.

Most of the main roads encountered were in good condition, but we struck an unpleasant section of treacherous pavé, known to British Army drivers as " Black Cobbles," between Hanover and Hamburg. We stopped here to give help to a Dutch driver whose Citroën had been swept off the road by a skidding lorry, and then set off as fast as we dared to the nearest town in order to call up an ambulance. Most cars were keeping their speed down to a steady 30 m.p.h. on the slippery wet roads, but with the Riley it was possible to exceed 55 m.p.h. without getting into difficulties.

Back once again in England, the emphasis turned from smooth high-speed touring to general handiness on twisting and often congested roads. Here too the Riley showed up well. The car corners steadily and holds the exact line required, helped occasionally by a touch of throttle to neutralise the under-steering tendency of the suspension. The gears are ob-viously there to be used, and make it easy to attain a high average speed, with an encouraging surge of power from 3,000 r.p.m. upwards.

The top-gear performance is quite reasonable for a four-cylinder sports car, and the engine pulls smoothly down to 20 m.p.h. On " Pool " one cannot expect much acceleration from that speed, but from 40 m.p.h. one gets a good response without bothering to change down. A local main road hill with two bends and a gradient, according to Tapley, of 1 in 13, can be climbed comfortably in top gear.

The valve gear tends to be noisy if not kept properly adjusted, and there is a certain amount of engine movement when the engine is idling. On the road these effects are no longer noticeable, and from 40 m.p.h. onwards, except for a mild engine period at 2,200 r.p.m. (45 m.p.h. in top gear), the engine is as smooth as a " six."

The engine will run up to over 5,000 r.p.m. without valve bounce, but it is wise to keep down to the maker's suggested maximum of 4,700 r.p.m. At these revs. the maximum speeds in the gears are 24, 41, 63 and 90 m.p.h.

A rev.-counter can be supplied at extra cost, and would prove a good investment for anyone who intends getting the full performance out of the car.

In the Continental countries already mentioned, the petrol is, if possible, slightly worse than English " Pool," and the Riley pinked freely whenever the throttle was used at all vigorously. On returning to England

*The Riley in a summer setting.*

[*Photograph by T. G. Moore*]

the local service station adjusted the contact breaker to give a slightly smaller gap, which has reduced the trouble without apparent falling-off in the performance. "Running-on," a fault common in post-war high-efficiency engines, is still irritating, and it seems that nothing can be done about it on present-day fuel.

One of the best features of the car is the gearbox, with its short, stiff lever only six inches below the rim of the steering wheel. Synchromesh is fitted on top, third and second gears, but does not interfere with double-declutching. Third to top is a semi-racing change when required, and a quick snick from top to second is a great help in getting clear of traffic congestion. On earlier " 2½s " the clutch tended to drag, causing grating noises if the pedal was not fully depressed. This trouble has been overcome on the latest models, and the clutch frees itself with a short movement.

The brakes are quite adequate to the speed of the car. A fair amount of force is required to get the full effect, but in use they have proved reliable, with no tendency to swing. The braking distance from 30 m.p.h. was 33 feet.

As has already been said, the suspension is firm, and the car can be cornered really fast without any trace of rolling, and without any tendency to hop on corrugated surfaces. Springing is if anything improved with four passengers or the equivalent weight of luggage. Tyre pressures are rather critical and need to be checked weekly.

The steering is high-geared, about 2⅓ turns from lock to lock, and combined with a strong castor action and wide-section tyres makes for heavy work when parking or on a long, fast journey over twisty roads. You get quite a jar through the steering wheel if you hit a pot hole at speed, but minor irregularities and corrugations are not felt. On balance, the feeling of control and directness between the steering wheel and the road more than compensates for the extra exertion on corners, and enables the driver to place his car exactly where he wants it alike at full speed on the straight and on fast bends.

The driving position is comfortable, with all controls within easy reach and with ample head room. In summer the front of the car gets warm, even with the hood open, particularly so the driver's left foot, which rests on a platform on the clutch casing. For some obscure reason scuttle ventilators are not fitted on the coupé body, but can be obtained from the makers. The alternative is to have an air-conditioning outfit installed.

The back seat is wide enough to seat three people at a pinch, and is fitted with a movable central arm-rest. Leg room is quite reasonable, but the centre of the floor is obstructed by the propeller-shaft tunnel. Head room for a six-foot passenger in the back seats is about one inch. Separate winding windows in the rear quarters give a good field of view even with the hood erected.

A useful assortment of instruments is provided, grouped on a compact panel on the dashboard. A rev.-counter with a small clock embodied in the dial can take the place of the large clock fitted as standard. The water temperature keeps

steady at 75–80 degrees. Oil pressure drops to about 40 lb./sq. in. during fast running, but the oil consumption remains constant at 2,500 m.p.g. The petrol gauge with its three indications of " full," " half," and " empty " is unreliable for the last quarter of its range. The instrument lighting is unnecessarily strong, and the warning light for the " high " position of the head-light beam was positively dazzling until I modified it with some of my wife's nail varnish.

The head lamps give a driving light sufficient for a safe 65 m.p.h. The near-side light is fitted with a two-filament bulb, which supplies the dipped beam. A similar lamp can be fitted into the off-side head lamp, and thus by plugging in or

THE 2½-LITRE RILEY
DROPHEAD COUPE

*Engine :* Four cylinders, 80.5 by 120 mm. (2,443 c.c.). R.A.C. rating, 16.06 h.p.
Valves : Overhead at 90 degrees. Push-rod-operated from two camshafts.
Ignition : Lucas coil.
Carburetters : Two S.U., Type H.4.
Petrol pump : S.U. electric.
Electrical system : Lucas 12 volt.
*Clutch :* Single dry-plate.
*Gearbox :* Four-speed-and-reverse.
*Ratios :* Top : 4.11 to 1
    3rd : 5.83 ,, ,,
    2nd : 8.86 ,, ,,
    1st : 15.0 ,, ,,
Speed at 1,000 r.p.m. in top gear : 19.5 m.p.h.
*Suspension :* Front wheels : Torsion bars with transverse links. Rear wheels : half-elliptic.
*Steering :* Rack and pinion.
*Brakes :* Girling. Front wheels : two-leading shoe hydraulic. Rear wheels : mechanical.
*Tyres :* Dunlop 6.00 by 16.
*Wheelbase :* 9 ft. 11 in.
*Track :* 4 ft. 4¼ in.
*Weight :* 28 cwt.
*Ground Clearance :* 7 in.
*Acceleration on " Pool " Petrol :*
  0–50 m.p.h. 13.6 sec.
  0–60 ,, 18.6 ,,
  0–70 ,, 26.5 ,,
*Price :* Drophead coupé : £995. plus £227 2s. 9d. purchase tax.
*Makers :* Riley Motors, Ltd., Abingdon-on-Thames, Berkshire.

out one of the connections in the wiring harness one can change in a few seconds from one dipping beam to two, a great convenience when visiting the Continent. The fog-lights are wired to a three-way switch, allowing one or two to be used as required.

Petrol consumption varies widely in accordance with the way in which the car is driven. Steady running at 40–45 m.p.h. gave 26 m.p.g., high-speed touring at 60–80 m.p.h. brought it down to 19–20 m.p.g., while fast local runs in hilly country reduced it further to 15 m.p.g. The tank holds 12½ gallons, but the inaccuracy of the gauge makes it unwise to exceed 200 miles before refilling.

The drophead body proved a great joy when touring abroad. The hood can be

folded down in less than a minute, and fits flush into a well behind the back seat. When putting it up I had at first some trouble in hooking it back in position, but found that by first tensioning one of the external hood-irons it fitted readily into place. The windscreen is supported by an extension of the front body panels, which come far enough back to house a pair of sun-visors. The hood is located on the windscreen panel by a rubber-bushed pin, and locked in position by two substantial carriage catches. The hood was well tested in some of the heavy thunderstorms encountered in Denmark, but remained watertight under all conditions.

When the hood is down it occupies part of the luggage boot. With the boot lid closed there is only room for one large suitcase and a number of smaller packages, but by fitting straps and running with the lid half open the capacity could be greatly increased. My own solution is to cover the back seat with a canvas sheet tailored to fit, which allows six substantial suitcases to be carried well within the car's wheelbase. The spare wheel is carried in a separate compartment.

Four external jack sockets are fitted to the chassis, and so wheel-changing can be carried out with the minimum of disturbance and dirt.

A last word on maintenance. Although the bonnet is pretty full of engine, the accessories, coil, petrol pump and so forth are so placed that they can readily be reached by opening one or other of the top bonnet panels, and valve clearances can also be checked without difficulty. The two top panels, and if necessary the side panels also, can be removed, giving access to all parts of the engine. The oil-filler and the dip-stick might with advantage have been extended higher up, but with care can be reached without soiling the clothes. Chassis maintenance is confined to the eight greasers on the steering and the front suspension, one on the water pump and the three nipples on the transmission. These latter are best tackled with the car over a pit or on a garage lift.

After four months' use under varied conditions I find that the Riley does provide what I want, a very useful turn of speed and a good response to driving technique on the open road combined with easy starting, simple maintenance, and an absence of fussiness in traffic. As a dual-purpose car it would be hard to beat, and at present-day prices offers distinctly good value for money.

♦♦♦♦♦♦♦♦♦♦♦♦♦♦♦♦♦♦♦♦♦♦♦♦♦♦♦♦♦♦♦

## A 100-M.P.H. TRACK ?

The Motor Industry Research Association is emphatic that Britain needs a track where sustained speeds of 100 m.p.h. can be accomplished. So it proposes to spend £150,000 on modifying the Lindley Proving Ground into a suitable track, asking the tax-payer to contribute £50,000 *via* the Government. What a pity the Industry took no steps to save Brooklands, which cost the country nothing, but the late Mr. H. F. Locke King some £250,000 of his own money in 1906/7.

## No. 39: 1947 2½-litre Riley Saloon

## No. 15: 1948 1½-litre Riley Saloon

| Price, new: £880 plus £245 3s 10d purchase tax.<br><br>Secondhand: £895. | Acceleration from rest through gears to 30 m.p.h. 7.0 sec.<br><br>To 50 m.p.h., 14.1 sec.<br>To 60 m.p.h., 19.2 sec.<br>20-40 m.p.h. (top gear), 11.1 sec.<br>30-50 m.p.h. (top gear), 11.6 sec. | Petrol consumption 20-22 m.p.g.<br><br>Oil consumption 1,000 m.p.g. approx. | Speedometer reading: 19,950.<br><br>Car first registered June, 1947. |
|---|---|---|---|

| Price, new: £863 5s<br><br>Secondhand: £1,395 | Acceleration from rest through gears to 30 m.p.h., 7.4 sec.  To 50 m.p.h., 17.8 sec.<br><br>20-40 m.p.h. (top gear), 12.1 sec. | Fuel consumption range: 25-29 m.p.g.<br><br>Oil consumption 2,500 m.p.g. approx. | Speedometer reading: 16,669.<br><br>Car first registered: December, 1948. |
|---|---|---|---|

RILEYS are, and always have been, cars for the enthusiastic motorist rather than simply a means of transport. The present 1½-litre and 2½-litre models are not massively slab-sided to pack in a maximum number of passengers; nor do they bow to the modern tendency of heavily chromiumed ornamentation. They are logical, clean-lined successors to their famous forerunners. The 2½-litre, of which a 1947 example was provided for test by B. J. Hunter, Ltd., 22-26, Cricklewood Broadway, London, N.W.2, is renowned for very high performance, four-seater comfort and, like the 1½-litre, refinement. The car tested certainly provided these features, and, since it is possible to gauge public reaction to various cars tested in succession, it may be said that this one was widely admired. It is one of those models that many people really covet.

The black cellulose was good and well polished, and most of the chromium plating was sound. Some areas, however, particularly on the bumpers, had become rather dull. The brown upholstery and carpets were good, and the polished wood facia and window surrounds had been excellently preserved.

Performance was good by Riley standards and, of course, outstandingly good compared with that of other cars generally. The central gear lever, and still perfect sychromesh, enabled quick changes to be made and the full power to be used for fast acceleration. In performance, in fact, the car was deceptive, sitting so firmly on the road that the miles were covered in safety, but at remarkably high speed. The high geared steering was naturally heavy at low speeds, the car being at its best on long, fast journeys.

The engine itself was in a healthy condition but, as is known with this model, not particularly quiet. On the car tested the bearings of the fan pulley had failed; not a serious fault, but one causing a rather loud clanking reminiscent of the noise associated with worn timing gears on older pre-war models. A criticism of this particular car, again not serious, was that the brakes were in need of adjustment to take up the pedal free travel.

Being almost exactly five years old, the car showed what is to be expected from a model of this quality after it has really seen some service. On the debit side the total was minor faults in the chromium, the two mechanical points just mentioned, a slight rattle in one door and in the steering wheel centre, and a squeak that, rather mystifyingly, occurred only at night and then not on left-hand bends! The water temperature did not rise above 70 deg. C, the tyres were good, the engine always started easily, the instruments (without a rev counter on this 1947 model) were unusually comprehensive, and fog lamps were fitted as standard.

IN considering used cars it is necessary always to relate age, condition and price. In the 1948 1½-litre Riley saloon submitted for test by W. Mumford, Ltd., Abbey Garage, St. Andrew Street, Plymouth, one has to remember that although relatively new by present-day standards the car is nevertheless nearly three years old. With this in mind it may be said that the car was outstanding. In theory some sign of age should have been in evidence, but in fact the car might recently have left the factory. Externally the chromium plating and dark green cellulose were unblemished. The pale upholstery, green roof lining and carpets fell into the same category, and the facia was without any crack or scratch in its french-polished surface.

Opening the bonnet revealed the shine of the rocker box covers, from which no oil escaped, and the whole engine gave the appearance of each component having been cleaned with individual care. The under-bonnet locker held a complete set of tools in a roll, a tyre pump, jack and wheelbrace. Matching these under the facia was a complete set of instruction literature.

It is not perhaps surprising that an engine built with the Riley tradition behind it should be none the worse for some 16,000 to 17,000 miles. In this case the loosening up of the engine resulted in acceleration figures which were a measurable improvement on those obtained when the new car was tested in 1947.

The engine started at once and pulled with very little use of the mixture control. The gear box invited use but the unit was sufficiently smooth and flexible to permit pulling away in top gear from really low speeds. Throughout the test the power unit gave the impression of having a mind of its own and that that mind had been made up to work. Never was there any feeling that the car was being overdriven and frequently, when the speeds rose to over a true 70 m.p.h., it was decided to ease off to avoid taking advantage of an unprotesting engine.

Steering was always precise, no measurable wear being present in the mechanism. Because of its high gearing it naturally tended to be heavy at manoeuvring speeds, but it had the corollary of great accuracy on the open road. The suspension was unimpaired by age or use, being firm to the extent of a bump in the road being felt as a bump. Its stability, the steering, and this firmness combined to make the car feel very safe. The brakes were powerfully adequate for all occasions although pedal travel was excessive, suggesting the need for adjustment. Oil pressure at 30 m.p.h., with the engine hot, was 30lb, and 20lb when the engine was idling. All the instruments and accessories worked properly, the range including a speedometer with separate trip mileage indicator, oil pressure, water temperature and fuel level gauges, an ammeter, clock, two fog lamps, an interior light and panel lighting. Front tyres were getting near the bald stage, the rear were good and the spare was virtually new.

### SPECIFICATIONS

| | |
|---|---|
| Arrangement and number of cylinders | 4 in line |
| Valve Arrangement | inclined ohv, 2 cams in block |
| Compression Ratio | 6.8:1 |
| Horsepower | 100 at 4500 rpm |
| Bore: 80.5 mm, Stroke: 120 mm, | |
| Displacement: 2443 cc | |
| Transmission: 4 speed, Ratios (15, 8.86, 5.83, 4.11:1) | |
| Dry Weight | 3220 lb. |
| Overall Length | 186 in. |
| Overall Width | 63.5 in. |
| Number of seats | 2 front, 2 rear |

### PERFORMANCE

| | |
|---|---|
| Standing ¼ mile | 19.6 sec. |
| Flying ¼ mile: | |
| Upwind | 86.5 mph |
| Downwind | 105.2 mph |
| Average | 94.9 mph |

### SPEEDOMETER

| Actual Speed | Speedometer |
|---|---|
| 39.3 | 40 |
| 57.5 | 60 |
| 77.6 | 80 |

Because the Riley is one of the oldest and most respected British cars, and because there is always a note of sincere admiration in the Britisher's voice when he mentions the racing history of Freddy Dixon and the fabulous Riley "Nines" of the late twenties and early thirties, *Road and Track* thought it worth while to persuade Karl Christian of Gough Industries to turn one of the 2½ litre sedans over to the staff for testing.

The Riley is definitely not Everyman's car but falls more into the category of a connoisseur's piece . . . a specialist's conveyance.

Probably few cars in the world today will equal the Riley in fast, long distance transport—particularly those anywhere near the same engine capacity and price. Its 2443 cc engine allows what seems to be effortless cruising at well over an honest 75 mph—and this on a nearly accurate speedometer.

#### The Engine

Developed by Riley in 1926 (when that family of coachbuilders, chassis designers, and engine creators was totally independent), the four-cylinder power plant remains (with the exception of periodic refinement), much the same: hemispherical cumbustion chambers, twin cams set high in the block, large over-head, inclined valves and large polished ports.

Long stroke engines are out of vogue today. The latest engineering theories advocate short strokes and low piston speeds. Yet the Riley, contrary to what would be expected, has a reputation for a remarkably long life.

Below forty-five mph the car feels heavy and sluggish (a feeling belied by 0-60 clocked times). It is obviously geared and cammed for long fast hauls. Some engine and tappet noise is clearly apparent at low speeds (from the exhaust side); however, as any Riley owner knows, the car begins to come to life

when it passes the 55 mph mark . . . it begins to smooth out . . . catch its stride, so to speak. Also known to Riley owners is the slow breaking-in of the Riley. When new, it is tighter and rougher than many. At 5000 miles the car feels "ready to go", while at 10,000 it has begun to loosen up and run properly. From England and Europe, owners' claims of 60/80 thousand miles without overhaul appear to be the rule rather than the exception.

Riley uses a high pressure gear-driven oil pump which pushes the oil (at 50 lbs. pressure) thru a full-flow filter (replaceable-cartridge type) and the capacity is nearly nine quarts of 30 weight oil. This amount of lubricant may seem a headache during the 3000 mile changes recommended by the manufacturer, but it pays off under duress of heat and high speed travel. The large, finned, cast-aluminum sump keeps the oil cool and prevents its breaking down.

Twin carburetion (S.U., type H4) is stock on all Rileys. Economy and ease of starting is maintained by the hot-spot manifold. Most of the water for engine cooling is directed thru the cylinder head and around—where most of the cooling is needed.

#### The Chassis and Suspension

A glance at the underside of the Riley is reassuring, particularly when the construction is compared to existing American cars. The impression one gets is of sturdiness thruout. The frame is huge box section with dropped tubular cross members, giving a low center of gravity, and great rigidity.

The rear suspension by half elliptic springs and airplane type shock absorbers gives a firmer than normal ride at low speeds but a delightful freedom from roll on corners.

Front suspension is an engineer's dream—the tubular struts and A frames pleasant to

the eye. Torsion bars carry stress from the independent front suspension to the first cross member immediately aft of the engine, where chassis rigidity is high. Thus, calculated steering geometry is maintained to a high degree.

Appealing to the owner/maintainer is the easy method of front wheel alignment and simple torsion bar adjustment. The front wheels run with no toe-in, which lack of angle is easily maintained by loosening, setting and re-tightening the track rods. The torsion bars have a set screw which adjusts the tension, making it quite simple to keep the front end of the car running true.

#### Coachwork and Styling

Adherents of the modern envelope-body school will feel that the Riley is old fashioned in concept. Connoisseurs will as fervently cling to its (as Nuffields put it) rare combination of classic and modern. The car has "sure-nuff" front fenders (score one for the classic fans) and both of them are visible from the driver's seat (score two). Also visible on each side of the narrow radiator shell is the ground immediately in front of the car, making it simple to avoid chuck holes and bits of flotsam which may turn up on the highway from time to time.

There is a serious blind spot to the rear and to each side, but which may be overcome by the fitting of twin side-view mirrors on the front fenders.

The air stream over the car is smooth because of the flowing lines of the Riley—and living room intensity conversation may be maintained at high speeds without difficulty. The only indication of wind noise is the slight whisper of the outside hinges on the doors . . . hinges which incidentally are equipped with grease nipples—another boon to the owner who likes to fuss with his car.

A fair amount of luggage may be carried in the rear compartment and the spare tire has a shelf of its own beneath the rear deck, making it possible to remove this fifth wheel without disturbing the luggage.

Fine leather and wood combine to make the interior luxurious without being ornate and the seating arrangement is comfortable. Arm rests front and rear are welcome to passenger and driver alike. The instrument panel is simply arranged and easy to read, tho the optional tachometer might be used (by some) more than the large electric clock; and the speedometer should be moved to the position the clock now holds, for easier reading on the left-hand-drive export models. The hand-operated ignition control, mounted on the dash is a helpful addition in to-day's varying octane fuel situation.

One of the best features of the Riley (and we hear this gimmick is regrettably passing from the English automobiling scene) is the ring and pull-cord on the head liner adjacent to the driver's head. A pull on the ring and a semi-transparent blind covers the read window, spelling sure defeat to the high-beam boys who follow you mile after mile all the while refusing to dim their lights.

The steering wheel is adjustable for height and distance from the driver, while the twin bucket front seats have a wide range of positions to suit driver and passenger individually.

Wells in the floor of the rear passenger compartment are a wise thought, giving low seating *and* roominess for the rear passengers' feet.

### Steering

And now we come to the big argument about the Riley. An owner's wife expressed enthusiasm for the 2½ litre, eliciting amazement from a local Riley dealer—he had met few women who actually liked the Riley. It is true, the car steers heavily around town, partly because of the low number of turns lock to lock (2⅓) and partly because of the spring loads in the rack and pinion steering.

The former of the two reasons makes for extreme road-worthiness and accuracy at high speeds—even on rough roads, and the latter (spring loading) was done with the Riley designers' eyes wide open.

In keeping with the reputation of long life, Rileys have evolved a steering gear box which needs lubrication only every 30,000 miles. This means a grease packed steering gear box; and when the mornings are cold . . . the grease is thick. Result: heavy steering.

Rack and pinion steering, common to many European and British cars, gives highly accurate steering and delightful feather touch in controlling a car—with two disadvantages: (1) road shock is transferred into the steering wheel, making bumpy roads doubly unpleasant, and (2) a good percentage of the road shock is also transmitted to the rack and pinion unit—causing inordinate wear.

The spring loads in the Riley rack and pinion unit, are meant to counteract these two disadvantages—with heavy steering at low speeds as a result. It is a simple matter to remove the springs if light steering is desired, but the two aforementioned disadvantages reappear.

### Handling

The Riley may be driven 85/95 mph over rough, pitted, corduroy roads with very little loss of control. In fact, at one point, over such a road (which slowed American traffic to 50 mph) a *Road and Track* test driver removed his hands from the wheel at nearly 100 mph, whereupon the car "drove itself" straight as a die for a couple of hundred yards.

In corners, the Riley is remarkable. The factory recommends 24 lbs sq in. as tire

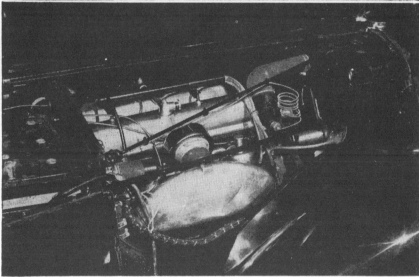

pressure, which (like practically all factory recommended tire pressures) is too low for anything but straight line travel. 30/32 lbs sq in. were kept in the Riley tires during the tests, making the ride fairly unpleasant at low speeds on anything but first class roads; but also making the sedan rock steady in really fast corners. One of the staff, while taking mountain curves at 65 or 70 mph with perfect control, expressed the doubt that his XK-120 would comport itself any better—which is saying something when the Riley's weight (3300 lbs, ready for the road) is considered.

### Brakes

. . . Another point at which Riley practice and the average driver part company. Heavy pedal pressure was required on the model tested. Even then the car wouldn't stop quickly enough and this seems a fairly typical complaint. Why this should be so is difficult to determine. The brakes are two leading shoe, hydraulic front and mechanical rear, but are 12 inches in diameter and ribbed for cooling—certainly and efficient enough set-up for good stopping. Still, the fact remains that more braking power is necessary in a 100 mph car.

The drums have normal adjust nuts on the inner surface, plus centering set screws for the purpose of seating each brake shoe flat against the drum. It is quite possible that proper adjustment of these nuts and screws give the highly efficient braking claimed by the factory. If not, then the cause

of the trouble would seem to lie in the brake lining material itself.

### Notes and Comments

Riley has sleek lines . . . looks like good breeding. Overall height . . . 4' 11½" . Foot ventilators leak cold air at night, even when closed, but have been improved as of latest Earl's Court Show. Padded top: nice idea. . . . metal under padding drilled with half-inch holes, to dampen vibrations which may creep into top. Foot rest for driver's left foot comes in mighty handy . . . Nuffields should use this on their MG. Ash trays in doors for driver and three passengers, but driver's ash tray (when open) gets in the way when left hand reaches for dashboard dip-switch. Side panels on hood (bonnet) easily removed to tune carburetors, etc. . . . car could use oil bath air cleaner in dusty regions . . . the "silencer" on delivered models gets in the way of the throttle linkage. Fan belt looks difficult to replace—it isn't, not if you know how. *Two* mufflers! One of them 40 inches long! Good idea, as there is practically no back pressure, but the long muffler has a tendency to scrape in sharp pitched driveways and would probably drag in the snow in the Middle West. If you like to take care of a car and drive it a long time, the Riley is the car for you. Should sell for $700.00 more if other imports are any criterion. Riley won't do for the average American and his wife, but for the connoisseur . . . the individual . . . he'll call it a true thorobred . . . and, of course, it is.

# The 1½-Litre Riley

FOR many years past there has been a large and enthusiastic band of motorists for whom the phrase "Once a Riley owner," is far more than a sales slogan. For them it is a literal truth; after several hundreds of miles at the wheel of the latest 1½-litre model it is not difficult to understand why.

This delightful machine has the qualities of the sports car with the amenities of the town carriage. It is fast, firm in suspension, free from roll on corners and comfortable to the point of luxury. It has, as the estate agents say, all modern conveniences, such as heating, radio, leather upholstery and walnut panelling. It also has rack and pinion steering (which, in the opinion of many drivers, cannot be bettered) and independent front suspension by torsion bars providing roadholding of a very high order indeed.

The 1,496 c.c. engine follows previous Riley practice in that it has inclined overhead valves operated by short pushrods. The two camshafts are mounted high on opposite sides of the block. Maximum power-output is 55 b.h.p. at 4,500 r.p.m. It is not a silent engine, but it is powerful, willing and tireless, responding vigorously to a touch on the throttle pedal.

In running trim (and including 12 gallons of petrol) the latest Riley turns the scales at 26 cwt. It is evident, therefore, that the four-speed gearbox is meant to be used, both in traffic and in cross-country driving. The gearchange operation itself is quick and silent, considerably assisted by the central position of the short, positive-action gear-lever. The clutch is light and smooth, but the space allotted to the left foot beside it is somewhat restricted.

steering column. An attractive feature is the positioning of the dipswitch on the facia panel within easy reach of the right hand.

Rear seat passengers are accommodated on a deep bench-type seat with central folding armrest. There are map pockets and armrests on all the doors and ashtrays for each occupant. A second loudspeaker is installed at the back of the car for the benefit of rear passengers. There is plenty of luggage space in the long, sweeping tail. The 1½-litre Riley is a car in which one feels immediately at home. Forward and rearward vision is unusually good. The

In its latest form the very handsome 1½-litre Riley has full-width bumpers at the front. Twin fog-lamps are standard fittings.

The driving position is excellent. The fully-adjustable bucket seats are well-sprung and raked to give the driver the control and vision he needs. The gold-lacquered instruments are centrally mounted on a rectangular walnut panel, with the various

wing-mounted sidelights furnish admirable lines of sight and the low seating position confers a sense of control too often absent in the modern car.

Steering is heavier than is customary to-day, but it is accurate and altogether free from any tendency to wander. On the model tested rather too much road shock was transmitted to the steering wheel at speeds above 70 m.p.h. The Girling brakes, which are operated hydraulically at the front and mechanically at the rear, were well up to the speed of the car.

In town and country the Riley is fun to drive. Although its acceleration up to 50 m.p.h. is adequate rather than spectacular, above that speed the car forges ahead in the most stimulating manner. Under favourable conditions 80 m.p.h. can be reached, no mean figure for a relatively heavy saloon car of only 1½-litres capacity.

A fair cruising speed appeared to be in the region of 60-65 m.p.h., and over long distances, 50 miles can be covered in the hour without the sensation of undue haste.

The 1½-litre Riley is distinguished by its high performance, firm roadholding and high-quality finish. On each of these counts it more than justifies the enthusiasm of the owner who seeks comfort in his leisure moments and speed with safety when time presses.

Restyling of the spare wheel and luggage compartments was introduced at the recent Earls Court Show. Note the petrol filler caps in each wing and the enlarged bumper area.

## IN BRIEF

**Engine.**—4-cyl., o.h.v. twin camshaft, 69 mm. by 100 mm. (1,496 c.c.), 55 b.h.p. at 4,500 r.p.m. Single S.U. carburetter, A.C. mechanical petrol pump. Compression ratio, 6.8 to 1.

**Transmission.**—Divided propeller shaft, rear half enclosed in torque tube. Spiral bevel final drive. Clutch, Borg and Beck single dry-plate. Gears, 4.89, 7.23, 11.2 (synchromesh) and 19.42 to 1. Reverse, 19.42 to 1.

**General.**—Suspension, front: independent by wishbones and torsion bars parallel with frame sides; rear: underslung, semi-elliptic springs. Shock absorbers, telescopic hydraulic. Brakes, Girling hydro-mechanical. Tyres, Dunlop, 5.75 by 16. Electrical equipment, Lucas, 12-volt, c.v.c.

**Dimensions, etc.**—Overall length, 14 ft. 11 in.; width, 5 ft. 3½ in.; wheelbase, 9 ft. 4½ in.; track, 4 ft. 4½ in.; clearance, 7 in.; turning circle, 30 ft; turns of wheel from lock to lock, 2¾. Weight (in running trim), 26 cwt.

**Performance.**—Touring maximum (measured quarter-mile after three-quarter-mile run), 76.36 m.p.h. Speeds in gears, 24 m.p.h. (first), 40 m.p.h. (second), 56 m.p.h. (third). Acceleration: 0-50 m.p.h. (through the gears), 18.1 secs.; 20-40 m.p.h. (top gear), 12.2 secs.; 30-50 m.p.h., 13.9 secs.; 40-60 m.p.h., 17.4 secs.; 50-70 m.p.h., 26.8 secs. Gradient climbable in top, 1 in 10.6. Petrol consumption (40 m.p.h. touring), 30.4 m.p.g.

**Price.**—£750, plus £418 3s. 4d. purchase tax (£1,168 3s. 4d.).

**Manufacturers.**—Riley Motors, Ltd., Cowley, Oxford.

**switches below them.** A shallow, full-width parcel tray extends across the scuttle, beneath which is the Radiomobile control panel. The handbrake is of the "umbrella-handle" type alongside the adjustable

Interior finish of the Riley is of high quality. The seats are leather covered and walnut is used on the facia panel and window fillets. Seats and steering column are adjustable.

# Rear Axle and Suspension Changes Featured on 1953 Models

SHARING rear-axle and suspension changes with the smaller model, the 1953 2½-litre Riley also has engine accessibility improved by the repositioning of front-end accessories.

## 1953 CARS

# RILEY

RILEY cars have been produced from the very beginnings of the British motor industry and products bearing this name have traditionally embodied features of great technical interest. Although the main layout of Riley cars of 1953 does not differ greatly from preceding models, both in maximum speed and all-round performance on the road, they continue to meet standards far above normal.

The engines are remarkable in that they continue to employ cylinder heads having valves inclined at 90 degrees which are operated from two camshafts, these shafts, however, being placed high up in the crankcase and working in conjunction with the pushrods and rockers. The result is to give many of the advantages of a twin overhead camshaft engine, a slight increase in the mass of the valve gear being compensated for by the ability to remove the cylinder head without interfering with the valve timing.

With large ports, and inlet and exhaust manifold on opposite sides of the head, the engines have a naturally high breathing power which is reflected in high output (36-40 b.h.p.) per litre, and, perhaps not less important, excel-lent water circulation around the valve seats and sparking-plug bosses.

The current Riley engines are constructed with 1½- and 2½-litre swept volume and both have rather high stroke : bore ratios and hence higher than average piston speeds. On the other hand, the main casting and the crankshaft are in each case designed to give quite exceptional solidity and despite the theoretical objections to high piston speed, it has been found in practice that these power units have exceptionally long life.

### Hypoid Bevel Introduced

The four-speed gearbox with remote central gear lever to which either of these power units are attached is unchanged, but for 1953 an entirely new rear axle will be used, the adoption of which has also involved modifications of the rear suspension. During the inter-war and post-war years Riley cars have been amongst the minority employing torque-tube drive and on post-war models the rear axle has been located by a trunnion bearing mounted on a cross-member placed a short distance behind the gearbox. A short open shaft with two universal joints was placed between the nose of the torque tube and the main gear shaft.

In the new axle the spiral bevel gears are replaced by hypoid bevels giving an offset between the propeller shaft line and the half-shaft axis, and it is also fixed to the rear springs which now propel the car in the Hotchkiss fashion.

The propeller shaft itself remains of two-piece construction, the trunnion having been replaced by a rubber-mounted centre bearing. The rear springs have been suitably modified in the light of their new function and, corresponding with the change in axle type, the final gear ratio of the 1½-litre model has been lowered, being now 5.125 in place of 4.89 : 1. The engine speed and litres per ton-mile are thereby increased by circa 7 per cent.

A minor modification to the 2½-litre car has been effected at the front end of the engine where the dynamo, water pump and fan have been redisposed so that they may now be driven by a single belt, the fan now sharing a common shaft with the water pump.

## ═══ Riley Specifications ═══

### 1½-litre

**ENGINE.—Dimensions:** Cylinders, 4; bore, 69 mm.; stroke, 100 mm.; cubic capacity, 1,496 c.c.; piston area, 23.2 sq. ins.; valves, o.h.v.; compression ratio, 6.8 : 1. **Performance:** Max. b.h.p., 55 at 4,500 r.p.m.; b.h.p. per sq. in. piston area, 2.37. **Details:** Carburetter, S.U.; ignition, coil; plugs (make and type), Champion L10S; fuel capacity, 12½ galls.; oil filter (make), Wilmot-Breeden full flow.

**TRANSMISSION.—**Clutch, Borg and Beck; overall gear ratios: top, 5.125; 3rd, 7.58; 2nd, 11.75; 1st, 20.3; rev., 20.3; three-piece open propeller shaft; final drive, hypoid. gears.

**CHASSIS DETAILS.—**Brakes, Girling hydraulic; friction lining area, 126.48 sq. ins.; suspension: front, Riley " Torsionic " independent (torsion bar); rear, semi-elliptic; shock absorbers, Girling; tyre size, 5.75-16.

**DIMENSIONS.—**Wheelbase, 9' 4½"; track: front and rear, 4' 4¼"; overall length, 14' 11"; overall width, 5' 3½"; overall height, 4' 11"; ground clearance, 7½"; turning circle, 30'; dry weight, 24¼ cwt.

**PERFORMANCE DATA.—**Top gear m.p.h. per 1,000 r.p.m., 15.26; top gear m.p.h. at 2,500 ft./min. piston speed, 58.4; litres per ton-mile, dry, 2,360.

### 2½-litre

**ENGINE.—Dimensions:** Cylinders, 4; bore, 80.3 mm.; stroke, 120 mm.; cubic capacity, 2,443 c.c.; piston area, 31.9 sq. ins.; valves, o.h.v.; compression ratio, 6.8 : 1. **Performance:** Max. b.h.p., 100 at 4,500 r.p.m.; b.h.p. per sq. in. piston area, 3.17. **Details:** Carburetters, twin S.U.; ignition, coil; plugs (make and type), Champion NA8; fuel capacity, 12½ galls.; oil filter (make), Tecalemit full flow.

**TRANSMISSION.—**Clutch, Borg and Beck; overall gear ratios: top, 4.11; 3rd, 5.83; 2nd, 8.86; 1st, 15.0; rev., 15.0; three-piece open propeller shaft; final drive, hypoid gears.

**CHASSIS DETAILS.—**Brakes, Girling hydraulic; friction lining area, 136.5 sq. ins.; suspension: front, Riley " Torsionic " independent (torsion bar); rear, semi-elliptic; shock absorbers, Girling; tyre size, 6.00-16.

**DIMENSIONS.—**Wheelbase, 9' 11"; track: front and rear, 4' 4½"; overall length, 15' 6"; overall width, 5' 3½"; overall height, 4' 11"; ground clearance, 7"; turning circle, 36'; dry weight, 28 cwt.

**PERFORMANCE DATA.—**Top gear m.p.h. per 1,000 r.p.m., 19.5; top gear m.p.h. at 2,500 ft./min. piston speed, 62.1; litres per ton-mile, dry, 2,680.

EXPOSED.—Seating within the wheelbase is a Riley feature made plain in this picture, which shows the doors removed. Good-quality fittings and furnishings are allied to seats which combine comfort and support.

# *Everybody notices a* Riley

Riley

**for**

**Magnificent**

**Motoring**

1½ litre Saloon   2½ litre Saloon

The Riley draws admiring glances wherever it goes. It is "craftsman built" in every detail—a car of remarkable character. In its long, low lines, suggestive of speed, you get a hint of its racing heritage. But a glance cannot reveal all the qualities which have made the Riley so much admired by enthusiastic motorists all over the world. You need to sit at the wheel of a Riley to appreciate one of the most responsive and exciting cars ever built. It is a car that reflects your success and sound judgment.

Write to Riley Motors Ltd., for specifications and the name of your nearest Distributor.

RILEY MOTORS LIMITED, SALES DIVISION, COWLEY, OXFORD

London Showrooms: RILEY CARS, 55-56 PALL MALL, S.W.1 Overseas Business: Nuffield Exports Ltd., Oxford & 41 Piccadilly, London, W.1

By

MICHAEL

BROWN

# *INTERIM ASSESSMENT*

## AN ANALYTICAL APPRECIATION OF A BRITISH QUALITY CAR AFTER 10,000 MILES

OPINIONS can be correctly judged only with a knowledge of the holder, but even the professional extrovert (or journalist) hesitates to lay bare his personality in so many blatant words. Yet without some knowledge of an owner his opinion of a car is worth little; how to get over the difficulty? Ah, well, readers may have weighed me up by now; if not, I cannot help them (unless they are astrologically inclined, in which case they may look up Sagittarius). I labour this point because the individual opinion of a car must be taken at its worth, whether the opinion is good or bad. If I, Bill Jones, say that the Sportsmobile is a marvellous car, the correct retailing of that comment is "*Bill Jones thinks that* the Sportsmobile is a marvellous car."

Ten thousand miles have now appeared on the recorder of my 1½-litre Riley. I have been across the Atlantic three times; one-third of the way round the world, not far towards the moon. It is a milestone mileage, and I feel that I now know my car. The first proud thrill has gone, the deeper affection has taken its place. The virtues are now balanced by the shortcomings and the car is a round personality, liked for its weaknesses as well as its strength.

Rileys are, indeed, strong meat. In the wrong hands they are wasted, like hundred-yard sprinters in a sack race. Seated beside such a driver the enthusiast writhes and dismounts at the earliest opportunity. Behind the wheel he can transform the car into the complement of himself, and between them passage from A to B is an efficient procedure; nothing is wasted, not even the extra fuel that goes with high revs and speed, for he has had his gallon's worth in exhilaration. For that he must, primarily, thank the Riley brothers' engine which powered the famous Nine, and of which the 1½-litre contemporary unit is a logical descendant.

It is a long-stroke (100 mm) four-cylinder with hemispherical combustion chambers and overhead valves operated by short push-rods from twin high-mounted camshafts. Aided by a compression ratio of 6.8 to 1, this design gives a maximum b.h.p. of 55 at 4,500 r.p.m., by which time the piston speed has reached 2,970 ft per min. This rapid reciprocation is translated into rotary motion by a three-bearing counterbalanced crankshaft; the rest is transmission.

For the moment, only the gear ratios matter of this part of the mechanism. Overall, they are, in the 1952 model: Top 4.89 to 1, third 7.23, second 11.2, and bottom 19.42 to 1. The resulting road speeds are quoted in Table I.

Enter Bill Jones. How do these figures react on this particular owner? I find that I change up at about 3,500 r.p.m. if I am pressing on (occasionally 4,000 r.p.m. from third into top), and at about 3,000 r.p.m. when I am in no hurry. Don't ask me why, because I cannot tell you, and it would make an interesting discussion finding out why one instinctively changes at certain r.p.m. figures on a certain car. The Riley is nowhere near valve bounce at these figures, so that particular limitation does not enter into it.

With such habits, third seems a trifle low on the normal load of one up, and on long Continental runs—when the driver gets attuned to continuous high speed—top gives the same impression regardless of load. But of that more later, because another factor intrudes.

The allegation might be made that the feeling arises only because I am afraid to rev the engine sufficiently; if so, the fear is in line with common sense, because maximum b.h.p. is developed at 4,500 and maximum torque at 2,500 r.p.m. (78 lb ft). The efficient working range of the engine, then, is roughly between these figures, though it gets hold in no uncertain manner at 2,000 r.p.m. when the torque curve is building up to the peak.

### Agreeable Noise

Contemporarily speaking, the unit is, I suppose, noisy. Again, Bill Jones likes it, because the noise is made up of two components, mechanical and intake. The valve gear is audible, as is the timing chain, and as the foot goes down this noise is overridden by the throaty roar of inrushing air. Described thus, it sounds like bedlam, but in fact is just right for the acute aural selection of r.p.m. in high-speed gear changes, though it means an adjustment of volume control for the slow movement of the *Pathétique*, for instance. Farther up the speed scale wind noise probably overrides all others, but that far up one is going quite fast and noise does not matter, the brain being concentrated on driving to the elimination of extraneous customary noises (for the benefit of my critics I do not use a radio at that speed).

This is no engine to undertake the job of accelerating from six to sixty in top gear, being quite lumpy low down. For that one might partly blame the single carburettor, probably unfairly, although I think that continual supervision by the magician with S.U.s can make a difference to that virtuous carburettor, which I like above all for its simplicity. The tendency to stall is usually present, and the engine is a slow warmer-up and thus sensitive to the correct viscosity of oil in the dash-pot. With too thin an oil there is a cough in cold weather until everything is warmed through, the piston moving up too quickly, reducing the air velocity and weakening the mixture.

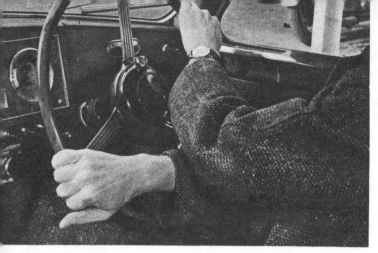

The driving position used in the Riley permits the author to cross hands when locking over in either direction. (Note the hand dip-switch just to the left of the wrist-watch.)

## INTERIM ASSESSMENT . . . . . . . . . continued

However, the particular position is only just possible, the left arm being fully extended when engaging bottom gear.

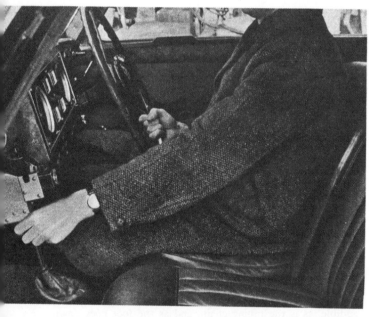

The oil-pressure gauge is the crucial instrument in warming-up. Long after the coolant temperature has settled in the neighbourhood of 175 deg F the oil pressure is unduly high. The sump contains Duckham's Q5500, which has special low-temperature characteristics, but even so it takes ten miles of motoring at judicious speeds before the pressure drops to the car's normal figure of about 50 lb per sq in at 40 m.p.h. The big ribbed aluminium sump is the reason for this. No further data can yet be given regarding the oil for the simple reason that neither sump nor head have yet been removed. I do not believe in taking engines to pieces unnecessarily. Riley's ignition setting seems to me conservative in view of the ignition hand control fitted, and when better fuels arrive I shall reset it. The engine rarely pinks, and is not easily made to pink. Where the pulling of a hand control retards the spark it seems to me that the ignition *should* be set to cause fairly frequent pinking, otherwise the control is usable only when the wise driver would change down anyway.

With one's own car one introduces various reservations for equally varied reasons. Only rarely do I demand maximum acceleration from the car, but I take, instead, my full

measure of high-speed cruising. To climb up to cruising speed gradually is good sense; it slaps down traffic impatience and is thus good for the immortal soul (or the blood pressure); it pays due regard to a not outstanding power-weight ratio, and it avoids hammer blows on the piston crown with whatever they imply in terms of engine wear (I have a theory that they mean a lot in this context). A high cruising speed is good for such an engine for several well-known reasons; additionally, the nearer an owner can get to making his engine a constant-speed unit the farther away is likely to be a rebore.

The car imposes another limit on acceleration, in any case, apart from these, for the gear box synchromesh is slow, although the box itself "feels" admirable. Moreover, the clutch pedal must go right down in order that the linings shall clear. The change is therefore a leisurely one; in fact, for better or worse I double de-clutch all the time on down changes, with the feeling that I am slightly faster than if synchronization is waited for. The lever is 8in long and makes its right angles with the precision of a geometry student; no rubber here. I make it work; I have the customary idiotic enjoyment in making it do so. The confession is frank. I also like "The Archers." Why shouldn't I? President Roosevelt relaxed with thrillers.

Beyond the box is my particular Riley's Achilles' heel, because it is not free of transmission vibration; indeed, the works have "had a go at it." At 4,500 r.p.m. on top gear *something* is telling me that the shaft is finding those revolutions hard to keep up with. The pre-1953 model has an intermediate shaft and a torque tube, and the reason may therefore be one of several. It is a long propeller-shaft, but simple whip, one would think, could be taken up by shortening the propeller-shaft and lengthening the intermediate, though at some point angularity of the universals gets too much for it. The shaft may be out of balance, and this would be transmitted to the torque tube and through the flexible (but not very) intermediate mounting at which that terminates at the forward end. Whatever it is, the transmission stops me from "caning" the machine; at 4,500 r.p.m. the speedometer needle has moved above 70 m.p.h. and the car is, in fact, getting along at an indicated 72. Fast enough, I say, for a personally owned 1½-litre.

### Superb Suspension

The suspension is a joy, my one small criticism of it being that I, speaking personally as Bill Jones, do not like the initial plunge into slow potholes that is fashionable nowadays and that is a matter of damper valve orifices. For me the old-time patter, thanks. But for cornering this suspension is superb, and my guess is that the roll axis and the centre of gravity are not very far apart. I have deliberately made the car break away on a greasy surface, and am satisfied that it does so in an orthodox manner, back wheels first, and that the resultant slide is capable of precise control. On dry roads I do not care to approach the car's breakaway point, cheerfully acknowledging that Fangio and Ascari have a lot on me there. On a wavy straight the aforesaid softness results in limited pitch, but where suspension matters—on corners—the Riley gets alpha plus.

Naturally, then, the steering is excellent, for the two go together. There is just sufficient understeer for the wheel to tug at the driver's hands (a matter, I believe, of increased lock resulting in increased castor action as compared with an oversteering car), and quite apart from the stability that goes with this is its suggestion of the stress under which a fast-cornered car is labouring. It is as well that a driver should be reminded of this as a curb on recklessness. The understeer persists throughout the bend, not changing to oversteer halfway round, a disconcerting characteristic of some cars. Steering is high-geared, and, seated well back, I rarely shift hands on the rim, although a right angle involves cross-hands. The steering is, of course, rack and pinion, and therefore virtually no motion is lost. I would like to think of something against the steering, because perfection in this department is a rarity, but it must be conceded, by me at any rate, to the Riley.

Driving seat visibility is superb; you may scan your tin oceans for landmarks if you like; I'll take a craggy radiator and side lamps. I *know* where I'm going.

As an owner, I do not use the brakes as a real aid to performance unless time demands it, thus saving the linings for emergency. The car has the hydro-mechanical system. "Too much depends on the compensator," object my engineering friends. All I can say is that I like the sense of security the dual system gives me, and that these brakes work. Considerable pressure is called for on the pedal to

**Table 1 : R.P.M. and ROAD SPEED**

| R.P.M. | M.P.H. | | | |
|---|---|---|---|---|
| | First | Second | Third | Top |
| 1,000 | 4.0 | 8.0 | 10.5 | 16.0 |
| 1,500 | 6.0 | 11.7 | 16.0 | 24.0 |
| 2,000 | 8.0 | 15.6 | 21.3 | 31.7 |
| 2,500 | 10.0 | 19.6 | 26.5 | 39.5 |
| 3,000 | 11.7 | 23.5 | 32.0 | 47.5 |
| 3,500 | 13.7 | 27.5 | 37.4 | 55.5 |
| 4,000 | 15.7 | 31.5 | 42.7 | 63.8 |
| 4,500 | 18.0 | 35.6 | 48.3 | 72.0 |
| 5,000 | 20.0 | 40.0 | 54.0 | 80.0 |

get maximum retardation, which suits me in that I prefer not to play with power through the fingertips. If I am going to pull over a ton of metal to a standstill in a reasonable distance I think I should have some indication of what I am doing; this is a similar personal quirk to that which finds virtue in the pull of the steering wheel on corners. The clutch is similarly perceptible in the pressure it needs, the throttle positive through a linkage that is well designed in its relation of the engine speed to the arc of movement.

Seated one day at the organ . . . the driver of the Riley ought not to be ill at ease, although this particular one can find room for criticism in the driving compartment. The completeness of the instrumentation is a virtue; oil gauge and thermometer are there, as well as full-beam telltale and heater blower tell-tale, the latter in a white glare that required subduing right away. I changed the clock for the combined rev counter and clock that now flanks the panel on the left, matching the speedometer on the right. Both are visible clearly, but in fact I use the rev counter all the time. The instruments are not what I call instruments, and I think with nostalgia of the Weston dials which I scanned during the war years; however, a battery of comparable instruments would probably raise the cost of the Riley by a hundred or two, and I must admit that they are hard to justify. None the less it is time stylist and engineer got together in this particular department. I can barely glance at a thermometer that reads only 90, 175 and 212 deg without a sneer; shades of Negretti and Zambra!

The row of switches may be criticized with more reason and less personal faddism, taking only the centre ones as an example of bad layout. To the left of the ignition switch is the starter, a press button operating a solenoid. Next to it is the fog lamp (pull and twist). On the right is the choke (pull), and next to that the main light switch (pull and twist). They are all too close together for the gloved hand to search with confidence. In the dark, therefore, it is easy to choke the engine in an effort to shed some light ahead, and it is easy to press the starter button when extinguishing a fog lamp. Having parted recently from an M.G. that was well arranged in such matters I suggest that someone at Abingdon has a peep round the corner of the 1¼-litre shops. And while we are being disarmingly rude, let Bill Jones say that he reckons nought of hand dipping switches, for two reasons: (a) I like both hands on the wheel rim for as much of the time as possible; (b) I do not drive at "ten to two," mobile police notwithstanding. The Riley switch is on the facia just by the right-hand screen pillar.

The switch controls head lamps that are not good enough

for this particular Bill Jones; they suffer the faults outlined in a recent leading article. I am continually being forced to brake on straight road dips by a cut-off that is much too close; at the same time I get the normal flashbacks that confront the double-dipped driver. Put me down amongst those who regard the horizontal cut-off as misapplied ingenuity—and I am being purposely moderate in that comment.

For the interior I bless the good taste that went into it and the fact that it seats four (five at a pinch) but only TWO in front. It has the footwells and obtrusive tunnel of the low-built saloon, which I accept gladly for the sake of that magnificent stability. Passengers "coo-er" appreciatively as they settle down, which is music in the owner's ears. The owner wonders who left the facia undertray unfinished so that maps and spectacle cases get mixed up with the electric wiring and the heater ducts, but that is a small point. Items that are appreciated specially include the readily accessible battery; Windtone horns; hand throttle; panel light rheostat; adjustable steering column; twin fuel filler caps; laminated glass screen; the thorough heating system and the radio. My wife and I often say that if there were a folding bed we could *live* in the car.

Externally, I find the shape satisfying in the extreme, but the finish unimpressive. After that one is descending to

Instrument layout on the 1½-litre. On the left is the combined rev counter and clock, matched on the right by the speedometer. The square dials are (top) ammeter and fuel gauge ; (bottom) thermometer and oil pressure gauge. The three tell-tales between them are (top) full beam lamps ; (centre) ignition ; (bottom) heater fan, covered by a square of green Cellophane. Switches, left to right, are : Panel light rheostat, ignition hand control, fog lamps, starter (ignition switch), choke, head and side lamps, heater rheostat, and, behind the wheel rim, the hand throttle. Below the switch panel is the radio.

the trivia, the occasionally used features like the jack (the excellent Bevelift, by the way) and the spare wheel stowage, a not too successful method. The owner does not bother too much about such details, preferring to stand back and view his ownership from a large perspective.

What does he see? This one sees a car that is the answer to a youngster's dreams; I never thought to possess one one day. Since then I have become critical and probably bigoted, but even so the 1½ has lived up to the expectations retained through all those years. There are times when, on top of my form, I make the 1½ transport me a couple of hundred miles to the best of its abilities. We get together on the job and, at the end of such a run, I am away up with the Archer himself in the heavens.

Actually I am an easily pleased owner, delighted with his new toy, but you know what I mean.

**Make :** Riley.     **Type :** 1½-litre Saloon (series R.M.E.)

**Makers :** Riley Motors Ltd., Abingdon on Thames, Berks

## Dimensions and Seating

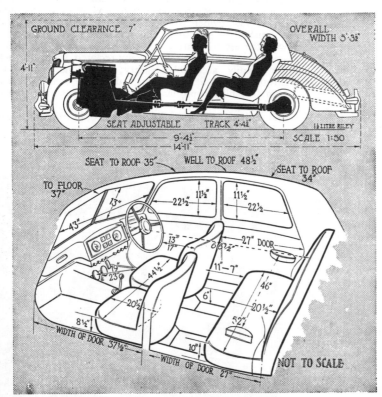

GROUND CLEARANCE 7"
OVERALL WIDTH 5'3½"
4'-11"
SEAT ADJUSTABLE    TRACK 4'-4¼"
1½ LITRE RILEY
9'-4½"
14'-11"
SCALE 1:50

SEAT TO ROOF 35"
WELL TO ROOF 48½"
SEAT TO ROOF 34"
TO FLOOR 37"
13"
43"
22½" — 11½" — 11½" — 22½"
13"/17"
8½"/9½" — 27" DOOR
50"/23"
44½"
11"–7"
46"
6"
20½"
20½"
52"
8½"
WIDTH OF DOOR 37½"
10"
WIDTH OF DOOR 27"
NOT TO SCALE

## In Brief

Price : £860 plus purchase tax £479. 5. 6. equals £1,339. 5. 6.

| | |
|---|---|
| Capacity | 1,496 c.c. |
| Unladen kerb weight | 25½ cwt. |
| Fuel consumption | 24.2 m.p.g |
| Maximum speed | 74.8 m.p.h. |
| Maximum speed on 1 in 20 gradient | 55 m.p.h. |
| Maximum top gear gradient | 1 in 13.5 |

Acceleration
10-30 m.p.h. in top    11.9 secs.
0-50 m.p.h. through gears    17.2 secs.

Gearing : 15.4 m.p.h. in top at 1,000 r.p.m., 58.7 m.p.h. at 2,500 ft. per min. piston speed.

## Specification

**Engine**

| | |
|---|---|
| Cylinders | 4 |
| Bore | 69 mm. |
| Stroke | 100 mm. |
| Cubic capacity | 1,496 c.c. |
| Piston area | 23.2 sq. in. |
| Valves | Inclined O.H.V. (pushrods and 2 camshafts) |
| Compression ratio | 6.8/1 |
| Max. power | 55 b.h.p. |
| at | 4,500 r.p.m. |
| Piston speed at max. b.h.p. | 2,950 ft. per min. |
| Carburetter | S.U. horizontal type H2 |
| Ignition | 12-volt coil |
| Sparking plugs | 14 mm. Champion L10S |
| Fuel pump | AC mechanical |
| Oil filter | Full-flow |

**Transmission**

| | |
|---|---|
| Clutch | Borg & Beck s.d.p. |
| Top gear (s/m) | 5.125 |
| 3rd gear (s/m) | 7.585 |
| 2nd gear (s/m) | 11.74 |
| 1st gear | 20.37 |
| Propeller shaft | Divided open |
| Final drive | 8/41 hypoid bevel |

**Chassis**

| | |
|---|---|
| Brakes | Girling hydraulic (2 l.s. front) |
| Brake drum diameter | 10 ins. |
| Friction lining area | 126.5 sq. ins. |

Suspension :
| | |
|---|---|
| Front | Torsion bar & wishbone I.F.S. |
| Rear | Semi elliptic |
| Shock absorbers : | Telescopic hydraulic |
| Tyres | Dunlop, 5.75 × 16 |

**Steering**

| | |
|---|---|
| Steering gear | Rack and pinion |
| Turning circle | 33 feet |
| Turns of steering wheel lock to lock | 2 |

**Performance factors** (at laden weight as tested)
| | |
|---|---|
| Piston area, sq. in. per ton | 16.0 |
| Brake lining area, sq. in. per ton | 87 |
| Specific displacement, litres per ton-mile | 2,010 |

*Fully described in "The Motor", October 15, 1952.*

## Test Conditions

Cold, dry weather with little wind. Smooth tarmac surface with patches of ice. Pool petrol.

## Test Data

**ACCELERATION TIMES on Two Upper Ratios**

| | Top | 3rd |
|---|---|---|
| 10-30 m.p.h. | 11.9 secs. | 8.1 secs. |
| 20-40 m.p.h. | 12.7 secs. | 8.3 secs. |
| 30-50 m.p.h. | 14.6 secs. | 10.4 secs. |
| 40-60 m.p.h. | 20.0 secs. | — |

**ACCELERATION TIMES Through Gears**

| | |
|---|---|
| 0-30 m.p.h. | 6.7 secs. |
| 0-40 m.p.h. | 11.3 secs. |
| 0-50 m.p.h. | 17.2 secs. |
| 0-60 m.p.h. | 29.5 secs. |
| Standing Quarter Mile | 24.1 secs. |

**FUEL CONSUMPTION**

34.5 m.p.g. at constant 30 m.p.h.
31.5 m.p.g. at constant 40 m.p.h.
27.5 m.p.g. at constant 50 m.p.h.
22.5 m.p.g. at constant 60 m.p.h.
18.0 m.p.g. at constant 70 m.p.h.

Overall consumption for 459 miles, 19 gallons =24.2 m.p.g.

**HILL CLIMBING** (at steady speeds)

| | |
|---|---|
| Max. top gear speed on 1 in 20 | 55 m.p.h. |
| Max. top gear speed on 1 in 15 | 42 m.p.h. |
| Max. gradient on top gear | 1 in 13.5 (Tapley 165 lb./ton). |
| Max. gradient on 3rd gear | 1 in 9.3 (Tapley 240 lb./ton). |
| Max. gradient on 2nd gear | 1 in 6.8 (Tapley 325 lb./ton). |

**BRAKES at 30 m.p.h.**

0.98 g retardation (=30¾ ft. stopping distance) with 220 lb. pedal pressure.
0.75 g retardation (=40 ft. stopping distance) with 150 lb. pedal pressure.
0.56 g retardation (=54 ft. stopping distance) with 100 lb. pedal pressure.
0.29 g retardation (=104 ft. stopping distance) with 50 lb. pedal pressure.
0.12 g retardation (=250 ft. stopping distance) with 25 lb. pedal pressure.

**MAXIMUM SPEEDS**
Flying Quarter-Mile

| | |
|---|---|
| Mean of four opposite runs | 74.8 m.p.h. |
| Best time equals | 76.3 m.p.h. |

Speed in Gears
| | |
|---|---|
| Max. speed in 3rd gear | 58 m.p.h. |
| Max. speed in 2nd gear | 40 m.p.h. |

**WEIGHT**

| | |
|---|---|
| Unladen kerb weight | 25½ cwt. |
| Front/rear weight distribution | 51/49 |
| Weight laden as tested | 29 cwt. |

**INSTRUMENTS**

| | |
|---|---|
| Speedometer at 30 m.p.h. | 1% fast |
| Speedometer at 60 m.p.h. | 4% fast |
| Distance recorder | 2% fast |

## Maintenance

**Fuel tank:** 12½ gallons. **Sump :** 10 pints, S.A.E. 30 Summer, S.A.E 20 winter. **Gearbox:** 2 pints. S.A.E. 90 gear oil. **Rear axle :** 2½ pints, S.A.E. 90 hypoid gear oil. **Steering gear :** Add grease every 30,000 miles. **Radiator :** 13 pints (3 drain taps). **Chassis lubrication.** By grease gun every 1,000 miles to 13 points. **Ignition timing:** 8° B.T.D.C. static (full manual advance). **Spark-plug gap:** 0.025 in. **Contact Breaker gap:** 0.012-0.015 in. **Firing order:** 1-2-4-3. **Valve timing:** I.O. 9° B.T.D.C.: I.C. 45° A.B.D.C.: E.O. 56° B.B.D.C.: E.C. 20° A.T.D.C. **Tappet clearances** (hot): Inlet 0.003 in., exhaust 0.004 in. **Carburetter jet needle:** Normal, No. 3; weak, V2; rich, B7. **Front wheel toe-in:** Nil (wheels parallel with 1½ in anhedral on lower wishbones. **Camber angle:** 1°. **Castor angle:** 3°. **Tyre pressures:** Front 22-24 lb., Rear 24-26 lb. **Brake fluid:** Girling. **Battery:** 12-volt, 51 amp. hr. **Lamp Bulbs:** Lucas 12-volt. Headlamps No. 354 (42/36 watt); Side, tail, stop, interior lamps No. 207 (6 watt); reversing lamp No. 57 (36 watt): Foglamps No. 162 (36 watt.)

Ref. B/15/52.

# The RILEY 1½-litre

## A Popular British Sports Saloon, Now Offering Improved Acceleration and Better Rear-seat Riding

C AR manufacture is very much an international business nowadays, with the industries of Britain, America and Continental Europe sending their products all over the world, and a consequence of this has been a tendency for the cars built in different countries to grow steadily more alike in character. A refreshing exception to this tendency is

**LONG AND LOW.—** Classic sports saloon lines are combined with moderate air resistance and useful interior roominess, a new detail being the enlarged rear window of curved glass.

the Riley 1½-litre saloon which we have recently tested in its improved 1953 form, progressive modernizing having left this car still essentially British in both appearance and character. In an age of standardization, it is an individualist's car, with faults which can be criticized but also with highly likeable characteristics to arouse enthusiasm in the right type of owner.

Re-designed very thoroughly at the end of the war, with a completely new body and chassis propelled by a well-tried power unit, the Riley has since that time been changed only in relatively inconspicuous respects. At the recent Motor Show, it appeared with a different type of rear axle and suspension, specification features newly incorporated including a hypoid bevel final drive giving a slightly lower top-gear ratio, an open Hardy Spicer divided propeller shaft, and splayed telescopic rear shock-absorbers. Also on the car which we have been driving was a curved glass rear window of usefully enlarged area, and by comparison with the Riley which we tested three years ago there are other alterations such as a re-designed instrument panel and a fresh-air heating and ventilating system.

The gradual process of development which this car has undergone makes comparisons inevitable, especially as keen owners of ever. the most durable cars eventually become interested in replacing them with later models. Since our last

test report on a Riley 1½-litre was published in June, 1949, the change most calculated to influence performance has been the adoption of a 5.125 : 1 ratio hypoid bevel final drive in place of the previous 4.89 : 1 spiral bevel gearing. In general, it may be said that this change has had the expected result, giving appreciably more acceleration at the expense of slightly reduced maximum speed, a result very appropriate to present-day conditions of ever-increasing road traffic congestion.

The loss which has had to be accepted amounts to just under four per cent., a drop in mean timed speed from 77.8 m.p.h. to 74.8 m.p.h. In return for this, an improvement in top-gear acceleration which amounts to approximately nine per cent. throughout the 10-50 m.p.h. speed range has been secured. Overall petrol consumption figures are difficult to compare precisely, but our steady speed tests show that the latest car is only eight per cent. heavier on fuel than its predecessor at 70 m.p.h. cruising speed,

**LARGE AREA.—**Sloping down towards the rear, the luggage locker has a large area of flat rubber-covered floor.

whilst below 35 m.p.h. the latest car actually shows improved fuel economy figures—rising to 34½ m.p.g. at 30 m.p.h. There is also evident a very marked improvement in through-the-gears acceleration times, more than 15 per cent. in the case of the 0-50 m.p.h. figure, much of this improvement resulting from a new clutch which engages positively after even the most hurried of upwards gear-changes. Pulling power on hills in top gear also benefits from the new gearing, much as does top-gear acceleration, and there are on the other hand very slightly lower attainable speeds in the indirect gears as well as in top gear.

### Accent on Roadworthiness

The other recent change concerning which comparisons may be drawn is the revised rear suspension layout, and here there is unquestionable advantage to report. In particular, the rear-seat passengers now enjoy a very much better ride than before, and no sacrifice of handling qualities is evident—the only adverse result which may be suspected from abandonment of the torque tube seems to be a possible very slight loss of traction on slippery mud or wet grass surfaces.

Roadworthiness in its widest sense is certainly one of the main virtues of the Riley 1½-litre, which is both comfortable and controllable under widely varying circumstances—appearances may suggest that it is designed primarily for main roads, but in fact its suitability for use in undeveloped parts of the world seems to be

limited only by a relatively long tail overhang.

Rack and pinion steering is undoubtedly seen to the very best advantage on this car. An almost complete absence of sponginess or lost motion is commonly associated with such a mechanical arrangement, and in this instance there is also a pleasing freedom from friction, despite which there is only a very modest amount of road reaction to be felt at the wheel during fast driving. Associated with this steering is a suspension system which always keeps the car very close to an even keel, regardless of hard cornering or braking, the overall effect being that narrow and winding roads slow the car down very little indeed. The brakes, as may be seen from the test results, require unusually high pedal pressures to produce their maximum effect, but in normal driving they respond to quite moderate pedal pressures and there is no lack of emergency stopping power.

Whereas extremely far-forward engine mountings are currently fashionable, the Riley continues to have its power unit set slightly behind the front hubs, the weight being concentrated rather more within the wheelbase than on many cars. This weight distribution, which reduces the moment of inertia of the vehicle, undoubtedly contributes to the quick responsiveness of the steering, but also contributes to riding characteristics which may best be described by saying that the Riley follows road undulations rather more closely than do some "flat ride" cars of today. A remarkably happy combination of spring strengths and shock-absorber settings (the front springs are torsion bars, and the rear springs semi-elliptic) provides extremely comfortable riding over a wide range of speeds and surfaces, without exaggerated spring movements taking place.

The Riley power unit is of rather unusual layout, although some of the features which it has inherited from the Riley 9 of 1926 are now appearing on other types of car. Four cylinders have inclined overhead valves in hemispherical combustion chambers, valve operation being by pushrods and rockers from two chain-driven camshafts in the cylinder block. By present standards, the piston stroke is unusually long, but in fact the engine runs entirely effortlessly up to the 4,500 r.p.m. at which its best power output is developed, and has an enviable reputation for longevity. Although similar engines have frequently been used in racing, the single-carburetter version fitted in this car is completely docile down to 10 m.p.h. in top gear. Hard frost during our test did not interfere with instant engine starting from cold.

Control over the four-speed gearbox is by a central remote-control lever of the traditional sports-car type, and as has been mentioned already the clutch is now far more positive in action than on preceding cars of this model which we have sampled. The gearchange is not, however, as sweet-acting and easy as we have come to expect on a Nuffield-built car. The car will start readily from rest in second gear, but for quick acceleration first gear is markedly preferable: a 1½-litre touring car fitted with sturdy coachbuilt bodywork, bringing its weight up to 1¼ tons, cannot be expected to provide dazzling acceleration, but this car is certainly no sluggard, as the test results printed on the data page confirm.

## Comfort for Four

The close-coupled four-seater sports-saloon body fitted to this car is an extremely pleasing representative of a traditional British style, modernized but not changed in character. In the front, there are two individually adjustable seats, with back-rests shaped to give lateral support, and there is a very good forward view of the road ahead over a long tapering bonnet flanked by a pair of clearly visible side-lamps. Very ample elbow room for two people is provided, and the sharply raked steering wheel has a telescopic adjustment for column length. One criticism of the driving position concerns the pedal layout, reasonably narrow driving shoes being advisable, and a rather far-back rest for the left foot not matching the rather far-forward pedal movements required for the accelerator and clutch. Wisely, a press-button control on the facia panel (conveniently adjoining the steering wheel rim) has been used for headlamp dipping. At night, however, we did not like the glare from three warning lamps on the polished walnut facia panel; we considered the dimmest setting of the rheostat-controlled facia lighting to be too brilliant for many occasions, and we found the impressive array of eight very similar unlighted control knobs below the instrument panel unnecessarily confusing. A wet-weather grouse concerns the wide area at the centre of the vee windscreen not swept by the wiper blades.

The rear seating is very comfortable, but although wells provide ample foot-room, the available knee-room is limited if the front seats are adjusted to suit moderately tall people. Behind these seats in turn, there is a really capacious luggage locker, and a big petrol tank with a sensible-size filler on each side of the car. The provision of an interior light on each side of the body, each with its switch accessible from front or rear seats, is a convenient detail, and reasonable stowage for maps and the like is provided in front-door pockets and on a shelf beneath the instrument panel. The dual sun visors which unfold out of recesses in the roof lining are neat but slightly less practical than the usual, simpler variety, and the "dimming" rear-vision mirror goes well with the enlarged rear window.

The optional extra Radiomobile radio installation fitted to the test car worked very well indeed, the dual speakers (a downward facing one below the facia, and an upward facing one behind the rear seat) giving very good reproduction. Another optional item on the car submitted for test was a fresh-air interior heating installation, but our appreciation of certain refinements in this (such as a rather-too-concealed control allowing the driver and the front passenger to receive differing amounts of warm air) was overshadowed by the fact that its maximum heat output proved inadequate even for British winter conditions.

Apart, however, from details, the Riley 1½-litre is a medium-sized quality car which gives a remarkable impression of solidity, this impression including all the detail fittings as well as the basic structure. The latest refinements considerably enhance the already strong appeal of this model to many keen motorists.

**BRITISH FURNISHING.**—Bucket seats upholstered in leather, and the polished walnut used for door fillets and the facia panel, may be seen in these photographs, which also show the telescopically adjustable steering wheel and short central gear lever.

The Riley has a distinctive appearance that retains familiar characteristics of the breed. The front wings terminate in full-length running boards and ventilators are fitted in the scuttle side panels.

## No. 1483 : 2½-LITRE RILEY SALOON

SOMETIMES a car manufacturer hits on a particular feature of design which proves so good that it is retained over the years and passed on from model to model; the Riley engine is a case in point. This unit was very much ahead of its time, and featured hemispherical combustion chambers and inclined valves operated by rockers and push rods from twin side camshafts. Through the years, engines of this basic design were produced in various sizes, the most famous being the Riley Nine, a four-cylinder of very robust construction that was able to stand up to the stress of competitions and racing. It must also be remembered that it was a Riley engine from which was developed the E.R.A., which in its pre-war heyday did a lot to fly the British flag in racing. Yet the post-war range of Rileys are by no means racing cars, but are in fact fully equipped saloons with an air of detail finish and equipment that satisfies the requirements of the house-proud car owner. None the less, the background and breeding of previous decades have left their mark.

The 2½-litre Riley, then, is a car with a robust engine capable of withstanding a great deal of hard work without losing its tune. Further, not only is it robust, but also it is a car for a chassis-conscious owner-driver, as its specification includes very many desirable features such as a " wheel at each corner," independent front suspension by means of torsion bars, and rack and pinion steering, to name only a few. Since this model was last tested the final drive has been modified, and a two-piece open propeller-shaft has replaced the torque tube. Also both front and rear brakes are now hydraulically operated.

So much for its background and specification. Considering the size and weight of the car, the road performance is very good; for example, the mean maxi-

────────DATA────────

**PRICE** (basic), with saloon body, £1,055. British purchase tax, £587 12s 2d. Total (in Great Britain), £1,642 12s 2d.
Extras : Radio £34 12s 10d. Heater £27 10s.

**ENGINE** : Capacity : 2,443 c.c. (149 cu in). Number of cylinders : 4.
Bore and stroke : 80.5 × 120 mm (3.169 × 4.725 in).
Valve gear : overhead, push rods and twin side camshafts.
Compression ratio : 6.6 to 1.
B.H.P. : 100 at 4,400 r.p.m. (B.H.P. per ton laden 58).
Torque : 134 lb ft at 3,000 r.p.m.
M.P.H. per 1,000 r.p.m. on top gear, 19.5.

**WEIGHT** (with 5 gals fuel), 30 cwt (3,356 lb).
Weight distribution (per cent) 51.2 F ; 48.8 R.
Laden as tested : 34½ cwt (3,868 lb).
Lb per c.c. (laden) : 1.58.

**BRAKES** : Type : F 2-leading shoe. R Leading and trailing.
Method of operation : F, Hydraulic. R, Hydraulic.
Drum dimensions : F, 11in diameter, 2½in wide. R, 11in diameter, 2½in wide.
Lining area : F, 93.9 sq in. R, 89.2 sq in. (106 sq in per ton laden).

**TYRES** : 6.00-16in.
Pressures (lb per sq in) : F, 24 ; R, 24.

**TANK CAPACITY** : 12½ Imperial gallons.
Oil sump, 14 pints.
Cooling system, 21 pints (plus 1½ pints if heater is fitted).

**TURNING CIRCLE** : 36ft 0in (L and R).
Steering wheel turns (lock to lock) : 2¾.

**DIMENSIONS** : Wheelbase 9ft 11in.
Track : 4ft 4½in (F and R).
Length (overall) : 15ft 6in.
Height : 4ft 11½in.
Width : 5ft 3½in.
Ground clearance : 7in.
Frontal area : 20.85 sq ft (approx.).

**ELECTRICAL SYSTEM** : 12-volt. 63 ampère-hour battery.
Head lights : Double dip, 42-36 watt.

**SUSPENSION** : Front, Independent by wishbones and torsion bars.
Rear, Half-elliptic.

## ─────── PERFORMANCE ───────

**2½-LITRE RILEY SALOON**

**ACCELERATION** : from constant speeds. Speed, Gear Ratios and time in sec.

| M.P.H. | 4.1 to 1 | 5.814 to 1 | 8.835 to 1 | 14.949 to 1 |
|---|---|---|---|---|
| 10—30 .. | 11.1 | 7.9 | 5.5 | — |
| 20—40 .. | 11.0 | 7.7 | 5.6 | — |
| 30—50 .. | 12.0 | 7.8 | — | — |
| 40—60 .. | 11.9 | 8.7 | — | — |
| 50—70 .. | 14.7 | 10.8 | — | — |
| 60—80 .. | 17.0 | — | — | — |

From rest through gears to :

| M.P.H. | sec |
|---|---|
| 30 .. | 5.3 |
| 50 .. | 12.0 |
| 60 .. | 16.4 |
| 70 .. | 23.0 |
| 80 .. | 34.3 |

Standing quarter mile, 20.8 sec.

**SPEED ON GEARS :**

| Gear | | M.P.H. (normal and max.) | K.P.H. (normal and max.) |
|---|---|---|---|
| Top .. | (mean) | 94.0 | 151.2 |
| | (best) | 94.0 | 151.2 |
| 3rd .. | .. | 60—70 | 97—113 |
| 2nd .. | .. | 36—46 | 58—74 |
| 1st .. | .. | 20—26 | 32—42 |

**TRACTIVE RESISTANCE** : 25.8 lb per ton at 10 M.P.H.

**TRACTIVE EFFORT :**

| | Pull (lb per ton) | Equivalent Gradient |
|---|---|---|
| Top .. .. | 200 | 1 in 11.1 |
| Third .. | 280 | 1 in 7.9 |
| Second.. | 400 | 1 in 5.5 |

**BRAKES :**

| Efficiency | Pedal Pressure (lb) |
|---|---|
| 87 per cent | 100 |
| 72 per cent | 75 |
| 55 per cent | 50 |

**FUEL CONSUMPTION :**
20.8 m.p.g. overall for 349 miles (13.6 litres per 100 km.)
Approximate normal range 20—23 m.p.g. (14.1-12.3 litres per 100 km.)
Fuel : Belgian Premium grade ; approximately 80 octane.

**WEATHER** : Dry ; slight cross wind.
Air temperature 30 degrees F.
Acceleration figures are the means of several runs in opposite directions.
Tractive effort and resistance obtained by Tapley meter.
Model described in *The Autocar* of October 10, 1952.

**SPEEDOMETER CORRECTION : M.P.H.**

| Car speedometer .. .. | 10 | 20 | 30 | 40 | 50 | 60 | 70 | 80 | 90 | 98 |
|---|---|---|---|---|---|---|---|---|---|---|
| True speed .. .. | 7 | 17 | 28 | 37 | 47 | 57 | 67 | 76 | 86 | 94 |

The long, low sleek lines of the Riley can be appreciated in this view and the two-colour body style (a black fabric covered top and grey cellulose on the particular car tested) is particularly suited to this type of car. There is a plated strip at the waistline, which increases the impression of length. The direction indicators are fitted well back, just behind the rear doors.

The familiar Riley radiator grille and diamond shaped badge have been retained on the post-war range of cars. Jacking points are placed below the front bumpers.

mum speed of 94 m.p.h. more than meets the requirements of a very large number of potential owners, if only for the reason that speeds in excess of 90 are often very difficult to use. This speed is also accompanied by brisk acceleration, particularly if the gears are freely used. The engine—a big four with hemispherical combustion chambers—is designed for power output to some extent at the expense of smoothness; this is particularly noticeable on the present Pool fuel, on which the engine is very prone to pinking. However, on Belgian premium grade fuel (approximately 80 octane), as used during the performance testing on the Jabbeke road, no pinking was experienced; yet it is interesting to note that the use of the superior fuel did not show any gain in maximum speed.

The gear ratios are well chosen, but the box is a little more masculine than it is usual to find today, and it is quite easy to beat the synchromesh if a snappy change is made. On the other hand, the remote control lever is positive and well placed, and conveys a sense of solidity that is seldom found in the steering column counterparts. The clutch does not possess all the present-day refinements, as the pedal is relatively heavy to operate and has a quite large range of movement. During the performance tests it did not seem to have the amount of bite associated with heavy spring pressures, which in turn often result in large pedal travels. For normal operation, however, apart from some heaviness noticeable in traffic, the clutch is satisfactory and progressive. To ensure quiet gear changes it needs to be pushed right down.

To those used to the extreme softness of some of the modern suspensions the Riley may appear to provide a somewhat refined "vintage ride." Whilst it does not follow a transatlantic tendency towards sick-making softness, neither is it harsh, for the proportions of the wheelbase

relative to the size of the car and the layout of the suspension result in a vehicle that is pitch-free and comfortable to ride in over all types of surface, including the normal forms of Belgian *pavé*. It provides a taut, well-controlled ride; there is very little roll on corners, a feature that is further improved by the use of transversely inclined telescopic dampers for the rear suspension. Rack and pinion steering, a type well known for its general excellence for a car that is designed to be "driven" rather than "used," is well suited to this car. With 2¾ turns from lock to lock it is a little heavy at low speeds, but this is more than offset by the positive feel and absence of back-lash.

The Riley corners well and can be placed with precision on bends of all types; the steering has a useful degree of self-centring action, while the car as a whole has a desirable degree of understeer with a two-up load that provides it with a directional stability of a very high order. There is no suspicion of vagueness in the steering, of the type that is often found when a large number of rods, levers and bearings is used—all with their own share of spring and back-lash. Nor is there an excessive amount of kick-back through the steering wheel—a criticism often held against units of this type—but there is that lively feel that gives the driver a good impression of what is taking place between the front wheels and the road.

Hydraulically operated brakes are now fitted to all four wheels (as distinct from the hydro-mechanical system fitted previously). They are both powerful and progressive, yet during performance testing a very noticeable amount of fade was experienced, while some very slight fade was noticed under hard driving conditions on the road. An umbrella type of hand brake control is conveniently positioned to the right of, and slightly below, the steering column.

The driving position is very good; in true sports car style

The Riley has an air of quality about it which is accentuated by the use of leather upholstery and polished wood cappings in the body interior. Two ashtrays are provided in the front compartment and there are pockets in the front doors, as well as a useful tray below the facia. Another very convenient fitting is a dipping type of non-glare rear view mirror.

The rear compartment is well arranged and very comfortable. There is a folding central armrest, while outside armrests are mounted on the doors, low down in which ashtrays are recessed. Two interior lights are fitted, one at each side, mid-way above the rear doors.

The luggage locker is of useful capacity. A separate lower compartment contains the spare wheel, and to gain access to this it is necessary to remove the cover on which is mounted the rear number plate. The luggage locker lid is pivoted on external plated hinges. Two fuel filler caps are provided, one on each rear wing.

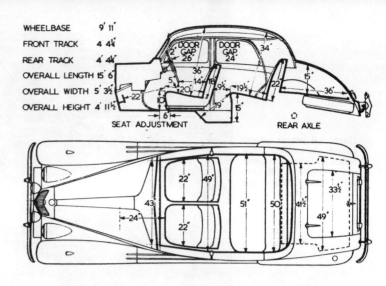

| WHEELBASE | 9' 11" |
| FRONT TRACK | 4' 4¼" |
| REAR TRACK | 4' 4¼" |
| OVERALL LENGTH | 15' 6" |
| OVERALL WIDTH | 5' 3½" |
| OVERALL HEIGHT | 4' 11½" |

Measurements in these ⅛in to 1ft scale body diagrams are taken with the driving seat in the central position of fore and aft adjustment and with the seat cushions uncompressed.

two seats are provided in the front compartment, as distinct from a single bench-type seat, and they are well proportioned, yet a little more support for the driver's left leg would be appreciated—an impression produced by the space for the left foot when it is not operating the clutch pedal being limited by the central tunnel. The cover is suitably shaped to form a footrest, but it would be better if it were placed a little farther forward. A well-proportioned backrest provides comfort and supports the driver in just the right places. Also the positioning of the pedals and steering wheel relative to the seat is well arranged. The spring spoke steering wheel is adjustable on its column, which is suitably raked, with the result that the adjustment really means something. Although the throttle pedal is well placed, this control, like the clutch, has an unusually large range of movement.

From the driving seat there is very good forward visibility, and both front wings, complete with their externally mounted side lamps, can be seen, whilst the dummy radiator filler cap forms a useful "sight." Visibility to the rear is also very satisfactory, and night driving comfort is increased by the provision of a rear view mirror that tilts and brings into use a smoked glass to reduce dazzle from behind at night.

### Galaxy of Minor Controls

In the minor controls the theme is, no doubt, one switch for one circuit or item of equipment. There are no fewer than twelve separate knobs, including those used to operate the heater, but excluding radio controls as being part of an optional equipment. The majority of these controls are mounted in a row on the facia below the centrally placed instruments. There are arguments for and against such a layout and the use of multiple knobs, but during the test it was found that the driver quickly became acquainted with the relative position of any particular control, and then it was a simple matter in the dark to feel for the first on the left or third from the right, as the case may be. Although it is an optional extra, the heater is worthy of mention, as apart from the usual adjustments such as the variation of the air flow to the windscreen and the interior of the car, it is possible to supply air to either the right or the left side of the front compartment to suit the individual requirements of driver or passenger. Also, this heater earns full marks as being one of the few that warm the interior and de-ice the screen without contaminating the car with the familiar heater smell sometimes experienced.

Presumably because of limited toe board width, a foot-operated head lamp dip switch is not used, but this operation is performed by a hand-operated switch mounted on the extreme right of the facia. This is quite convenient to use, but it does necessitate the removal of one hand from the steering wheel. Among the group of controls are two that

are seldom found today; an adjustable slow running control and an ignition advance and retard. The throttle control is useful during the warming-up period to enable the engine to be set at a fast tickover. During tests, when the engine was running on premium grade fuel, the ignition was set in the full advance position, while on British Pool fuel it was found advantageous to retard it very slightly.

### Sound Body Features

Construction of the Riley body results in a quiet and boom-free car, and coachwork noises, even over stone setts and rough surfaces, are at a very low level. The rear compartment is well appointed and, for a sports saloon, quite roomy. Because of the low build there is a quite deep propeller-shaft tunnel running through the rear compartment, but even so there is ample room for the rear passengers' feet. On the model tested some of the electrical equipment did not seem to be up to the general high standard of the rest of the car; for example, although the head lamps gave a reasonably good beam and spread of light, they were not up to the high-speed potentialities of the car. The windscreen wipers, too, were not able to cope with the mud and slush thrown on to the screen from other vehicles. On the other hand, the horns, operated by a centrally placed button on the steering wheel, are both pleasing and effective.

Some slight hesitation was experienced in cold starting at temperatures around and slightly below freezing point, and it was found necessary to open the throttle slightly while the mixture control and starter switch were operated.

The 2½-litre Riley saloon is a quality car, with sports car performance, coupled with very good road manners. It responds well to being "driven," and is one that conveys its occupants in high-speed comfort.

Oil, water and battery levels can all be checked from the left side of the longitudinally hinged two-piece bonnet. With its two plated valve gear covers the engine is satisfying to look upon.

Unspoiled period houses lining its canals are relics of the ~~bygone~~ prosperity of Bruges as a great commercial centre.

**By Gordon Wilkins**

# 5,000 Miles on 1,500 c.c.

## CONTINENTAL EXPERIENCES WITH A FORD CONSUL AND 1½-LITRE RILEY

NOWHERE is the difference between the living standards of North America and the rest of the Western World more strikingly illustrated than in the amount of horse-power which is considered desirable to move a man and his family about in a car. In the United States a figure of 100 b.h.p. is now widely regarded as the minimum, and a self-respecting family with a social position to maintain dare hardly be seen during 1953 in a car which has an engine smaller than 4½ litres and delivers less than 190-200 b.h.p. In Europe, for obvious reasons, this trend has no counterpart, and for the great majority of people an engine of one third or one quarter the American size, delivering something between 25 and 55 b.h.p., is the maximum which can be considered. It is not solely a question of fuel consumption, because some American cars can be surprisingly economical, but car size and weight are closely related to the engine power, and the tyre bill, repair costs, insurance premiums and garage charges are greatly influenced by the size of the engine.

It is difficult to regard this comparative poverty of horse-power as a very great deprivation, and a personal liking for the 1½-litre engine, as one capable of offering a satisfactory measure of performance and economy, already reinforced by a few successes in competitions where performance, stamina and fuel economy were severely tested, has recently been strengthened by essential motoring which has provided extensive experience with two representative examples in this category, the 1½-litre Riley and the Ford Consul.

The Riley was used in the late spring and early summer of 1952 for a European trip which included several Road Tests and coverage of both the Turin Show and the Mille

Miglia race. The car carried two people, plus their luggage for three weeks and all *The Autocar* Road Test impedimenta, which now represents quite a bulky and weighty load in itself. Starting in Belgium, the route led through Germany, Switzerland, Liechtenstein, Italy and back through France. As usual, the schedule was a crowded one and full throttle was used for most of the time.

After testing another car on the Belgian *autoroute* there was time for a quick look at some new 500 c.c. racing cars in construction in Brussels, besides an interesting van to carry them, powered by a flat-four air-cooled engine from a Pilot Cub aircraft. Then it was time to depart eastward for Malmédy and over the vile frontier roads leading to Aachen and the Western Zone of Germany.

At the German frontier post, there is none of the casual informality so familiar elsewhere; everyone is polite, but correct. Passengers are not allowed to stay in the car while the driver attends to the formalities; everyone has to get out and present his own passport for verification. It is unwise to attempt to enter with any large quantities of cigars,

Four lines of traffic and two tram tracks are carried over the Rhine by this vast suspension bridge at Cologne. It was completed within the past two years.

# 5,000 Miles on 1,500 c.c.

tobacco, coffee or tea, as these are subject to heavy duty.

It was two years since I had been in Cologne, and the progress in reconstruction in that time was astonishing. In 1950 a vast vista of ruin stretched on all sides of the cathedral, very like that which surrounds St. Paul's Cathedral today. There was only one road bridge over the Rhine, a British Bailey bridge, and one railway bridge patched up to allow single-line traffic. Now there is a vast suspension bridge carrying six lines of traffic (the cables were made locally and dragged through the streets by tractors); near by is a fine steel bridge carrying four lines of traffic, and the railway bridge is fully restored, with multiple tracks capable of carrying several hundred trains a day. And the Bailey bridge? It was presented to Western Germany by Britain to help the economic reconstruction of the country, but they say it was pulled down soon afterwards and sent back to Britain as scrap.

### Late Work

New department stores have sprung up round Cologne cathedral, and at ten o'clock on a Saturday night workmen were busy on the foundations of a new bank. Big business is running the reconstruction and banks and insurance companies are pouring vast sums into the building of offices, shops, hotels and blocks of flats. Credit for building operations appears to be plentiful, but is said to be tight on consumer goods such as radio, cars, washing machines and refrigerators. No one seems to spend much time puzzling out how to ensure fair shares, but the tempo of activity is hectic, and bricklayers working in teams with a system of jigs reach output figures which are not contemplated in Britain.

To get people under cover quickly, houses have been built on old foundations, using rubble, or new materials, or a mixture of both, and it is not uncommon to see a new top storey in brick, built on a blitzed sandstone building. One day they may pull them down and rebuild, or they may put on a facing of stucco to make the whole thing presentable, but meanwhile they have somewhere weatherproof to live and to work. They maintain the shape of their cities, and on the whole the method seems preferable to the British habit whereby the blitzed centres of some cities have been virtually abandoned to the weeds, and large areas of valuable agricultural land torn up to make sites for new council houses and workers' flats.

The old German pride in work is reasserting itself and in a car factory the assembly line hardly seems to have stopped for the lunch break before the hooter has signalled a resumption of work. The break is only twenty minutes and there are no stops for morning or afternoon tea. There is, of course, good and nourishing food for everyone who is able to earn it. Good beer and sausages full of meat for the working man; lavish meals and fine wines in the elegant new restaurants for the plump and prosperous business chiefs and executives.

From Cologne, the Riley was turned on to the *autobahn* for the run to Stuttgart. One good feature of the *autobahn* is the freedom from advertisements, contrasting strongly with the dreadful rash of advertising signs which defaces the Italian *autostrada*. The *autobahn* has not escaped entirely, however; there are frequent large direction signs in English and American for the guidance of the Allied forces, and on the way to Heidelberg it is a little disconcerting to be

The litter of advertising signs and models which is almost continuous along the Italian autostrada contrasts sharply with

confronted with a vast hoarding which proclaims the fact that one is "now approaching Java Junction, hot coffee day and nite." Heidelberg itself seems to have become a replica of a United States mid-Western city and of its former glories little can be discerned by the passing traveller save the baroque castle still standing on its crag above the Neckar. Bombarded by the troops of Louis XIV, struck by lightning and set on fire more than once, the old castle has seen many strange disturbances in its hundreds of years of history and will probably see many more. In the vaults, the fabulous wine tuns are still intact and so is the famous booby trap clock which catches at least one visitor in every party.

After a few days in Stuttgart, the Riley sped southwards to Frederikshaven and then turned to cross a tiny neck of Austria in driving round the lakeside into Switzerland, but there was no great loss of time before reaching St. Margarethen, in Switzerland, where the Riley was warmly housed underneath the hotel while its crew enjoyed a couple of vast steaks.

The Consul by Lake Como.

The next day's motoring took us southwards through a country gay with blossom of tulip trees, cherry and apple to Liechtenstein, where the Prince and Princess and their children in the remote castle on the mountain seem to have suffered from the attentions of tourists, judging by the notices which emphasize that the gardens are private. In this democratic age there were, however, no armed sentries in sight to reinforce the warning.

At Chur, the snow had long since departed and Lenzerheide had that forlorn, deserted village air which comes to ski resorts when the season is over, but there was still one tea shop open to provide brief refreshment before the climb over the Julier Pass, where work was in progress on a vast new reservoir for the city of Zurich; we took a last look down at the doomed village of Marmorera. It was evening when we reached Italy and the drive down past the lakes was

the clean and unspoiled appearance of the German autobahnen. Farmland comes right to the road edge.

punctuated by the crash of the may-bugs, those immense flying beetles, which hit the car in swarms and smack the windscreen with such resounding impacts that one ducks involuntarily, even in a saloon car.

During the week which followed, the Riley worked hard, shuttling backwards and forwards over the 80-85 miles of *autostrada* between Turin and Milan, with several trips farther afield to Bergamo and Brescia. The period culminated in a satisfactory run back from Milan to Turin in a heavy storm of rain, keeping company with one of the very fast and light Fiat 1400s, with Superleggera coachwork, which had run in the Mille Miglia. It was full throttle the whole way and for more than thirty miles the average was about 70 m.p.h., but at the end of the *autostrada* the two cars were still together.

Leaving Turin the next evening, the Riley hummed its way up through the late snow on the Mont Cenis Pass and on through miles of forbidding frontier country to an overnight stop at Chambéry. The next morning brought a warm and brilliant sun which had been conspicuously absent so far and provided a perfect early summer day for the final run back to the coast, which was just as well, as there was some serious motoring to be done, 38 miles in the first hour; the second hour, over tortuous mountain roads, accounted for 49 miles. Thereafter, the average was round about 50 miles for each hour.

There was time for a lavish lunch at Dijon, followed by a brief sleep in the sun when the effects of much eating began to tell on the driver, but after that there were no more stops. Troyes, Château-Thierry, Soissons and Arras all passed by as the Riley kept up its happy, effortless cruising, and finally it pulled into Dunkirk with plenty of time in hand before we rolled on to the night ferry and ate a late supper. A satisfactory day's motoring of 525 miles with no particular fatigue as a result.

The Riley's S.U. carburettor had been adjusted for economy before the journey began, but it will be apparent that the performance had not been allowed to suffer appreciably, and the overall consumption of just over 26 m.p.g.

for 2,900 miles is creditable for a car driven hard, over very varied roads. It was a most satisfactory demonstration of the capabilities of a 1½-litre quality car, which is both graceful and practical. It was one of the last, and certainly one of the best-looking cars ever designed to the old formula, with separate wings and running-boards. It would be no light task to evolve a worthy successor in the modern flush-sided manner.

Two troubles have to be recorded. One was the loss of a tiny drain screw from the fuel pump, a trivial incident which magnified itself into a delay of about four hours, as it took place at night on the Belgian *autoroute,* where there are no filling stations, garages or telephones, and where the rural population speaks only Flemish. As the cause of the stoppage was not discovered on first inspection, it was concluded that the car had run out of petrol, and it was only after hitch-hiking several miles and walking miles back again that it was discovered that the petrol did not solve the problem. By the time the tiny vacant hole in the pump had been located and a replacement screw improvised, the night was well advanced.

The only other untoward occurrence was the blowing of an exhaust flange gasket after many hours of full-throttle driving. The spare in the tool kit appeared to be made out of a sort of brown paper, and it was no particular surprise when that, too, failed after about 40 miles. After a few days of noisy motoring with an open exhaust a proper replacement in copper and asbestos was fabricated by an Italian mechanic, and no further bother was experienced.

### British Consul

The second car, a Ford Consul, is an excellent example of the modern popular car in the 1½-litre category, although for some inexplicable reason the designers have seen fit to give its engine a swept volume of 1,508 c.c., thus imposing a needless handicap on owners who, with factory approval, enter their cars in competitions. With its chunky outline and astonishing carrying capacity, the Consul simply asks to be heavily loaded, and this is the treatment it received on a late summer expedition to Belgium, Switzerland, Italy and France, undertaken for the purpose of carrying out a series of Road Tests, visiting foreign car factories and covering the Monza Grand Prix.

With four adults, luggage for three weeks and, once again, the Road Test equipment, every bit of the Consul's carrying capacity was utilized, and when it left Ostend it was carrying nearly 900lb of load. For the first few days it was based on Bruges as a centre while road testing proceeded, with the delays inseparable therefrom. There was time for an evening run over to Knocke and Le Zoute, where there are some rather fine and elegant villas among the sand dunes, contrasting with the rather tasteless and shapeless coloured brick buildings that disfigure so much of the Belgian coast. There was a chance, too, of exploring the canals of Bruges by boat, of watching the old ladies sitting at their cottage doorways making lace, and of climbing the 365 steps up the belfry tower. The famous belfry was built in 1619, but the bells were added later. There are 47 of them, which can be rung by hand or played automatically by a kind of mammoth, creaking pianola. Unfortunately, the Passion Play of the *Sanguis Christi*, with its 2,500 actors performing in a floodlit setting in the great square before the belfry, had taken place a few days before, and the open-air stage was just being dismantled. One aspect of Bruges at that time of the year was the extraordinary persistence of the mosquitoes. Not for nothing do the hotels provide gauze on the windows, and British visitors remove it at their peril.

### The Ghost

Road testing completed, the road lay through the rolling Ardennes on an evening run which was memorable for the astonishing sight of a pair of gloves and a hat walking across the road without any visible means of support. It turned out to be a new employment for Scotchlite, the luminous material which is being used by the Belgian police, in common with some others on the Continent, to render their signals more visible at night. After an overnight stop

German improvisation in Stuttgart : new houses are built with rubble and new materials on old foundations.

at Marche, where the crew was replenished from the efficient kitchen of the *Rôtiserie de la Famenne* and the Consul was refilled from one of the new electric pumps which shuts itself off when the tank is full, we turned southwards for a heavy day which was to take us most of the way to Italy.

The first hour led through the scenes of the bitter fighting of the German Ardennes offensive in the winter of 1944. Bastogne now has a Sherman tank in the town square, guarding a bust of the American commander whose colloquial and monosyllabic response to the German demand for his surrender is commemorated in a large sign which invites the visitor "Visitez la musée 'Nuts'!" While it was still morning we were in France, passing the fountains and the delicate wrought ironwork of the Stanislaus Square in Nancy and later stopping for a brief picnic lunch in a wood before crossing the frontier into Switzerland. So far it had been a brilliant sunny day, but rain lashed down as the Consul sped through Lucerne, round the north side of the lake, past the Queen Astrid memorial with its ever-present throng of visitors, through Altdorf, and on over the twisting roads to Andermatt.

### Mountain Mist

By the time the St. Gotthard Pass was reached it was a black stormy night and a thick mist blocked out the surrounding peaks. Eventually the road itself became lost in the clouds and near the top of the pass extensive road reconstruction was taking place. The Consul droned up in second gear over muddy tracks reminiscent of a British trials hill with the added perils of the white mist to hide the unprotected edges. At last the long descent began and eventually the lights of Airolo could be discerned twinkling far below. I had previously been there in the spring of 1951, just after the disastrous avalanche which obliterated part of the town and killed many of its inhabitants. Flood, fire and bombing each have a horror of its own, but an avalanche has a specially sinister aspect, contrasting so sharply with the sparkling snow around it, and Airolo has still not fully recovered.

That night the Consul reached Bellinzona, in Switzerland's Italian-speaking Ticino, to conclude another good day's motoring. Despite the heavy load and the holiday weekend traffic on the roads, the total was 447 miles; the total time was 14 hours, from which stops of approximately 75 minutes have to be deducted to give an average running speed of 35 m.p.h., with a best hour of 47 miles. In all that time the Consul had been passed only once, by an Alfa Romeo 1900, the driver of which emphatically disliked the fog on the St. Gotthard and dropped back, never to catch us again.

The run down through Lugano to Milan next morning provided a reminder that the Italian frontier at Ponte Chiasso is to be avoided in the summer. What with the long queue of waiting cars, two deep, the inspection of

documents, the changing of money and the purchasing of petrol coupons to obtain the special tourist rate, the frontier crossing cost a delay of nearly 1½ hours. It is much better to go round by Ponte Tresa and descend via Varese into the Plain of Lombardy.

We went via Como to begin more work in Milan, and the Consul spent its next few days in high-speed running on the *autostrada* between Milan, Turin, Monza, and Como. These were long, hard days of road testing and interviewing often for 12 hours at a stretch, with blazing sun all day, but there were brief relaxations at night when one could drive out for a late dinner in the open-air restaurants in the city squares of Milan and Turin or run up for a breath of cool air to the restaurants in the hills, with terraces from which one can see the whole of Turin twinkling like a star-spangled map under a velvet sky. And no visit to Turin is complete without a climb up to the Superga, the graceful basilica where the Kings of Savoy are buried, or to the neighbouring landmark, the vast winged victory which forms Turin's memorial to the fallen of the 1914-18 war.

The Milanese are fortunate in summer, for a short run on the *autostrada* takes them to the lakeside resorts of

## 5,000 Miles on 1,500 c.c.

Varese or Como for swimming, sailing or speed-boating, and at the weekends the roads are crowded with scooters, often with wives or girl friends on the pillion and not infrequently carrying additional burdens in the form of dogs or small children. The performance they deliver from engines of a mere 125 c.c. is quite astonishing.

The Consul's weekend retreat was a few miles away over the hills, at Cernusco, where Count Lurani had his usual gay house party for the Monza race meeting and where the garage walls are covered with the autographs of both the pre-war and post-war periods. Then it was soon time to turn northward again, on the long run to Paris. Starting from Turin early in the morning, the car had reached Macon by lunchtime. From then conditions rapidly deteriorated, for the main road up to Saulieu was undergoing the most extensive grading and widening operations, with bulldozers in fours and fives still hard at it long after 6 p.m. The scale of these operations necessitated long detours with slow processions of traffic running bonnet to tail round narrow by-ways just like a happy English holiday crowd on the summer run to the coast. This played havoc with the average speed and the arrival in Paris was long behind schedule. It had been a hard day's driving, but by no means a tiring one. The total from Turin to Paris was 485 miles, with filthy weather for much of the way and the running average was just over 40 m.p.h. with 56 miles in the best hour.

The Ford had proved itself as practical and functional as its looks suggest. It had carried a very heavy load for most of the time and had not been specifically tuned for economy. Moreover, it was an early example of the type, which had already had quite a hard life, but over a total distance of 2,400 miles of hard driving its fuel consumption averaged a fraction above 20 m.p.g. Mechanical trouble was confined to a delay caused by dirt on the quick thread of the starter pinion, a predicament which is admittedly aggravated by the modern tendency to abolish the starting handle. Otherwise the only fault to be found is the inadequacy of the petrol filler, which makes it almost impossible to fill the tank without an excessive rate of loss. This means that on a long Continental run one tends to stop for petrol at least three times a day and may have to pay for it in three different currencies.

Both cars proved untiring to drive, and both are clearly capable of energetic day-to-day service, with a capacity for covering long distances under heavy loading worthy of bigger vehicles. Differing widely in style, design and price, they cover between them a big range of motoring requirements.

# *More attractive than ever!*

2½ litre Saloon

# at the new low price

£925 plus £386.10.10 Purchase Tax

You can shortly realise your ambition to own this superb car which more than lives up to the great name it bears. Its highly successful engine with the exclusive hemispherical head is matched by steering and suspension to warm the heart of motoring enthusiasts. Its tireless power and zest are a revelation in fast, safe motoring. And every detail in chassis and coachwork is craftsman-built to give you years of proud ownership.

*Arrange a trial run today with your Dealer.*

**ACCENT ON THE ENGINE**

The great-hearted 2½ litre Riley engine puts 100 m.p.h. safely at your command, and high average speeds in long distance travel.
Much more than swift, comfortable transport, 'Riley Motoring' is always a delightful experience.

*For the sheer pleasure of driving choose a Riley.*

## *Yes indeed!*
# RILEY *for* MAGNIFICENT MOTORING

**NUFFIELD SERVICE IN EUROPE**

All Riley Owners, planning a Continental Tour, are invited to see their Dealer for details of a Free Service to save foreign currency.

**RILEY MOTORS LIMITED**, *Sales Division*, COWLEY, OXFORD
*London Showrooms:* RILEY CARS, 55-56 PALL MALL, S.W.1    *Overseas Business:* Nuffield Exports Ltd., Oxford and 41 Piccadilly, London, W.1

# 1½-LITRE RILEY SALOON

OF the large variety of cars produced by the recently formed British Motor Corporation, the two Riley models retain a considerable measure of individuality that is often completely lost in satisfying the demands made by rationalized production. Since these models were introduced (as the result of complete redesigning soon after the war), very few changes have been made in them; consequently, although the 2½-litre was tested for the second time a few months ago, it is now five and a half years since the 1½-litre car—the subject of this test—was put through a Road Test. During that time the chief alteration to the appearance has been a modification of the bumpers to provide better protection. A larger rear window has also been fitted to improve rearward visibility. Mechanically, the most significant change is that made to the final drive, which now employs the Hotchkiss drive open propeller-shaft arrangement in place of the torque tube used on the *marque* for many years. The interior has also been modified since the last test was carried out and there is a new instrument layout, while detail changes have been made to the trim.

A 1½-litre car is large enough to provide an interesting performance—above that obtained with the average small family car—yet it can produce the desired result without an excessive thirst for fuel. The Riley is just such a car. Compared with the results obtained when it was last tested by this journal, there is a noticeable increase in some of the performance figures owing to a change in the rear axle ratio and, no doubt, the present use of first-grade fuel; for example, 3 sec improvement from 0-50 m.p.h. through the gears, while on top gear from 30-50 m.p.h. it is over 1 sec faster than on the earlier occasion. The mean maximum speed is similar to that recorded in the previous test in spite

of the higher overall ratio, which is 5.125 to 1 compared with 4.89 to 1 on the previous model. The general running on this car on the present occasion included a Continental trip of about a thousand miles, and more than two thousand miles in all were covered. The engine was not specially tuned to run on the better fuel and would perform in a satisfactory way on the ordinary grade of fuel, with perhaps a slight sacrifice in smoothness and slight pinking under acceleration from very low speeds on top or third.

It is very pleasing to record that on some of the fast Continental roads the Riley could cover fifty miles in the hour and fully laden, too. Obviously with the power-to-weight ratio existing under these conditions, averages of this order would be difficult to obtain on crowded British roads owing to the constant need for acceleration and deceleration, yet even in this country, under normal give-and-take driving conditions, averages of around the 40 m.p.h. mark were frequently obtained, and at no time did the car feel that it was being over-driven. This is, in fact, a car to swing along at high speed on the open road, compensating its owner by its solidity and good furnishings for any shortcomings in split-second acceleration.

In spite of its sporting nature, the use of twin camshafts and hemispherical combustion chambers, the engine does not suffer from the effects of temperament associated with high tune; it is, in fact, a tough, robust unit built to stand up to hard work without losing its tune. It has a degree of comparative silence in keeping with the character of the car, together with a satisfactory degree of smoothness. The transmission is conventional with a dry single-plate clutch and a four-speed gear box with synchromesh on top, third, and second gears. The clutch is smooth in operation, but

Both front seats are individually adjustable for leg length ; they are covered in leather upholstery piped at the edges in a contrasting colour. Rubber heel mats are fitted to both sides of the front compartment.

In the centre of the rear seat is a folding arm rest and there are combined arm rests and pulls on the rear doors, which also contain swivelling ash-trays placed low down and towards the leading edge. The polished wood cappings are formed to provide finger grips on all the doors. The traffic signals are placed well back on the body.

The Riley has pleasing curves from this view. Roof and locker lid contours blend together very well. Twin fuel filler caps are provided, one in each rear wing, and the protective strips on the running boards extend a little way up the front wings.

the required pedal pressure is rather heavy for the full depression that is desirable; it also has a short arc of effective movement. The gear change is very well suited to the car; the short, stiff lever is well placed centrally. It is very positive and has an easy action, although some slight difficulty in engaging second gear was experienced at times. The synchromesh fitted to top, third, and second gears is quite effective for normal driving, but can easily be beaten if anything approaching a fast change is made or if the clutch pedal is not fully depressed.

The Riley is very much a "wheel at each corner" type of car, and thus possesses many desirable features that are appreciated by the owner who is really interested in driving his car and in getting from place to place quickly. First, it is a very stable car because of its low build, resulting from a generous wheelbase; it also has a satisfactory degree of under-steer which gives it very good directional stability. It holds the road well and can be cornered fast without risk of " peculiar developments with unpleasant results." Rack and pinion steering provides a means of control that is seldom bettered; it is precise, sufficiently light for a car of this type, and gives the driver the satisfying feeling that he is accurately controlling the movements of the road wheels, without the use of a large number of rods, links, and levers and their resulting bearings that must wear. There is some slight transmission of road shock back through the steering wheel when traversing the rougher type of road surface, but this is more than offset by the general accuracy and positive feel. There is good self-centring action of the steering.

In both front and rear compartments the riding is good; the suspension is firm without being harsh, and sufficiently flexible to prevent high-frequency vibrations when traversing rough surfaces. There is very little roll on corners and the car provides a level ride free from pitching. The 1½-litre Riley has a particularly pleasing sense of balance.

The general noise level on top gear on main roads is low; the engine can be heard to some extent and there is a slight passing vibration—or, rather, noise—period at a little below 40 m.p.h. on third gear, but it is not excessively noisy. The transmission, too, is quiet, although there is audible evidence of the indirect gears, but this, again, is not unpleasant. Wind noise is of a low order; on the particular car tested some noise was noticed locally around the top of the right-hand front door. A considerable amount of noise was trans-

mitted to the body via the suspension when traversing Continental stone setts. Generally, there was very little tyre noise or squeal.

The hydraulically operated brakes are well up to the requirements of the car. No fade was experienced either during the severe conditions imposed during the performance testing, or when the car was driven fully laden on the road. It was necessary to adjust the shoes after more than a thousand miles of fast driving to reduce the free pedal movement, although the brakes were still effective. During the brake tests a fairly heavy pedal pressure was required for maximum stopping power, but on the road this tendency was not very evident. For normal check braking the pedal pressure is satisfactory.

The driving position generally is very good and the driver has a clear view of the front wings and side lamps showing the width of the car. With the V-type windscreen the pillars are well back and although they are fairly wide they do not form a serious obstruction. Rearward vision is satisfactory and the dipping driving mirror, for anti-rear dazzle purposes at night in the absence of a rear window blind, is well positioned. The steering wheel, adjustable on its column, is well raked, and the driving seat is well positioned relative to both the wheel and the pedals. The seat cushion is rather hard and could, in the test driver's opinion, with advantage provide more support for the driver's leg muscles on long runs. The squab is well sprung and of ample height.

Both clutch and brake pedals are well positioned, yet more space for the driver's left foot between the central tunnel and the clutch pedal would be appreciated by those wearing a large shoe. The throttle pedal is nicely placed; it has a wide arc of movement. A pistol-grip type of hand brake control is placed under the facia, on the right; it is convenient to operate and does not get in the way when it is not in use. The hand-operated dip switch is mounted on the facia to the right of the steering wheel. A considerable array of minor controls is placed in a row below the instruments. As well as the essential switches, these include an ignition control and a valuable and now rare slow-running throttle control. Owing to the similarity of these controls they are apt to be a little confusing at night. An unusually comprehensive interior heater distribution control is within the driver's reach, but it is placed out of sight, half under the facia, in a position where it could easily be completely

Left : The compartment just in front of the bulkhead contains the battery on one side and the jack and tools on the other. Although the engine bay is well filled, the sparking plugs, together with the oil, water, and brake fluid filler caps, are all accessible.

forgotten. A warning light is fitted in the heater fan circuit; it would be better for night driving if this were less bright. The instruments are centrally grouped on the facia; they include a clock, ammeter and water temperature gauge on the left side, with the speedometer, oil pressure and fuel gauge on the right. The instrument lighting is good and is controllable by a rheostat switch; it does not cause reflections in the screen at night but there is some reflection from the plated traffic signal control.

In spite of the low overall height of the car there is a good amount of headroom in both front and rear compartments. Wells in the rear floor increase the leg-room for the passengers. Twin sun vizors are fitted in front, and are neatly flush mounted in the head trim when not in use, but it is necessary to move the rear view mirror to permit the vizors to pass into the lowered position. If a radio is fitted, provision is made for a rear loudspeaker, which can be regulated by a rheostat on the facia. The luggage locker floor is covered with rubber to insulate and protect the luggage, and a single strut holds the lid in the raised position for loading. There is a small parcel tray under the facia, and there are pockets in the front doors.

Double-dip head lamps are fitted; they have a good spread of light and a satisfactory beam for normal driving. During the test starting from cold was at all times very good, and the car warmed up quickly and required very little use of the mixture control. The chassis has nineteen grease points, thirteen of which require attention at intervals of 1,000 miles. The horn note is penetrating and yet not raucous.

The 1½-litre Riley is a medium-sized car by British standards; it has a good performance, fine road characteristics, and good detail finish. It is a car which, above the ordinary, inspires confidence and affection.

## 1½-LITRE RILEY SALOON

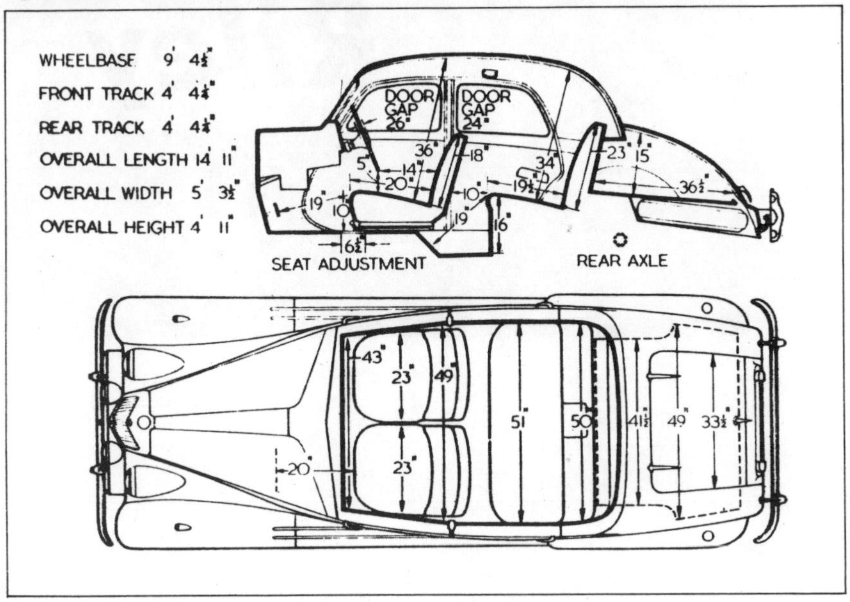
WHEELBASE 9' 4½"
FRONT TRACK 4' 4¼"
REAR TRACK 4' 4¼"
OVERALL LENGTH 14' 11"
OVERALL WIDTH 5' 3½"
OVERALL HEIGHT 4' 11"
DOOR GAP 26"
DOOR GAP 24"
SEAT ADJUSTMENT
REAR AXLE

Measurements in these ¼in to 1ft scale body diagrams are taken with the driving seat in the central position of fore and aft adjustment and with the seat cushions uncompressed.

### PERFORMANCE

**ACCELERATION :** from constant speeds.
Speed, Gear Ratios and time in sec.

| M.P.H. | 5.125 to 1 | 7.585 to 1 | 11.736 to 1 | 20.372 to 1 |
|---|---|---|---|---|
| 10—30 | 11.9 | 8.5 | 6.2 | — |
| 20—40 | 12.5 | 9.2 | — | — |
| 30—50 | 14.1 | 10.7 | — | — |
| 40—60 | 17.3 | — | — | — |
| 50—70 | 25.9 | — | — | — |

From rest through gears to :

| M.P.H. | sec |
|---|---|
| 30 | 6.2 |
| 50 | 15.9 |
| 60 | 25.1 |
| 70 | 41.0 |

Standing quarter mile, 22.8 sec.

**SPEED ON GEARS :**

| Gear | | M.P.H. (normal and max.) | K.P.H. (normal and max.) |
|---|---|---|---|
| Top | (mean) | 74.25 | 119.5 |
| | (best) | 75.5 | 121.5 |
| 3rd | | 44—52 | 71—84 |
| 2nd | | 26—31 | 42—50 |
| 1st | | 14—19 | 23—31 |

**TRACTIVE RESISTANCE :** 23 lb per ton at 10 M.P.H.

**TRACTIVE EFFORT :**

| | Pull (lb per ton) | Equivalent Gradient |
|---|---|---|
| Top | 193 | 1 in 11.5 |
| Third | 265 | 1 in 8.4 |
| Second | 359 | 1 in 6.1 |

**BRAKES :**

| Efficiency | Pedal Pressure (lb) |
|---|---|
| 73 per cent | 130 |
| 60 per cent | 100 |
| 31 per cent | 60 |

**FUEL CONSUMPTION :**
24 m.p.g. overall for 1,603 miles (11.8 litres per 100 km).
Approximate normal range 23–27 m.p.g. (12.3–10.5 litres per 100 km).
Fuel, First grade.

**WEATHER :** Fine, dry surface ; very slight wind.
Air temperature 48 degrees F.
Acceleration figures are the means of several runs in opposite directions.
Tractive effort and resistance obtained by Tapley meter.
Model described in *The Autocar* of October 10, 1952.

**SPEEDOMETER CORRECTION : M.P.H.**

| | | | | | | | | |
|---|---|---|---|---|---|---|---|---|
| Car speedometer | 10 | 20 | 30 | 40 | 50 | 60 | 70 | 80 |
| True speed | 10.5 | 19 | 28 | 38 | 48 | 57 | 66 | 75.5 |

### DATA

**PRICE** (basic), with saloon body, £860.
British purchase tax, £479 5s 6d.
Total (in Great Britain), £1,339 5s 6d.
Extras: Radio £34 12s 10d.
Heater £27 10s 0d.

**ENGINE :** Capacity : 1,496 c.c. (91.25 cu in).
Number of cylinders : 4.
Bore and stroke : 69 × 100 mm (2.72 × 3.94in).
Valve gear : Overhead ; push rods and twin side camshafts.
Compression ratio : 6.8 to 1.
B.H.P. : 54 at 4,500 r.p.m. (B.H.P. per ton laden 36.8).
Torque : 76 lb ft at 2,500 r.p.m.
M.P.H. per 1,000 r.p.m. on top gear, 15.26.

**WEIGHT** (with 5 gals fuel), 25⅝ cwt (2,870 lb).
Weight distribution (per cent) 50.5 F ; 49.5 R.
Laden as tested : 29¼ cwt (3,284 lb).
Lb per c.c. (laden) : 2.2.

**BRAKES :** Type: F, 2-leading shoe. R, Leading and trailing.
Method of operation : F, Hydraulic. R, Hydraulic.
Drum dimensions : F, 10in diameter, 1¾in wide. R, 10in diameter, 1¾in wide.
Lining area : F, 67.2 sq in. R, 63.05 sq in (89 sq in per ton laden).

**TYRES :** 5.75-16in.
Pressures (lb per sq in) : 22-24 F ; 24-26 R.

**TANK CAPACITY :** 12½ Imperial gallons.
Oil sump, 10 pints.
Cooling system, 13 pints (plus 1 pint if heater is fitted).

**TURNING CIRCLE :** 30ft 0in (L and R).
Steering wheel turns (lock to lock) : 2¾.

**DIMENSIONS :** Wheelbase 9ft 4½in.
Track : 4ft 4¼in (F) ; 4ft 4¼in (R).
Length (overall) : 14ft 11in.
Height : 5ft 0½in.
Width : 5ft 3½in.
Ground clearance : 7½in.
Frontal area : 20.85 sq ft (approx.).

**ELECTRICAL SYSTEM :** 12-volt. 51 ampère-hour battery.
Head lights : Double dip, 42-36 watt.

**SUSPENSION :** Front, Independent ; wishbones and torsion bars.
Rear, Half-elliptic springs.

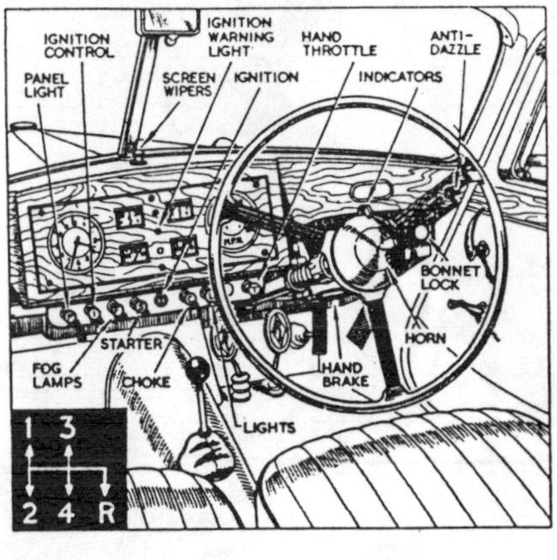
IGNITION CONTROL
IGNITION WARNING LIGHT
HAND THROTTLE
ANTI-DAZZLE
PANEL LIGHT
SCREEN WIPERS
IGNITION
INDICATORS
BONNET LOCK
HORN
STARTER
FOG LAMPS
CHOKE
HAND BRAKE
LIGHTS
1 3
2 4 R

# I Still Love My Riley

by H. Ray Baker

Foreign car mechanic tightened nut so tight, it was pulled completely through rocker arm cover, welded, but not replaced.

I DIDN'T rush heedlessly into buying a 2½ Litre Riley drophead coupe. First I read everything I could find about them. One American motoring magazine referred to the marque as a "connoisseur's car." Another called it the "reliable Riley." Still another found it to be a "truly fine automobile." Yet another claimed it to be the "best bargain in an English car."

Every time a Riley effortlessly passed me on a winding Rocky Mountain road, I mentally compared my Detroit land barge with it and said land barge came off second best. I admired the Riley's excellent coachwork and the luxurious leather upholstery. I liked its sleek, low-slung look and the absence of unnecessary bulges and overhang.

Finally, when I could no longer bear the agony, I put myself out on a financial limb and bought one. But if I had it to do over again, I'd remember the guarantee.

Not that the reports weren't right. They were—almost. The quick responsive steering on a mountain road is a delight. The car goes like a scared antelope. When I need to stop in a hurry, it *stops*. Although I bought tire chains for it, I've never used them because, due to the excellent weight distribution, the car has never shown any inclination to slide or skid, even when stopping or starting on icy roads.

As for comfort, I find myself less tired at the end of a day's driving in the snug bucket seat than I did

114

All photos by H. Ray Baker

This Riley climbs mountains like a jet-propelled goat.

. when "enjoying the baby buggy ride" of my former cars.

There is, however, another side to the picture that isn't so pretty. In the first place, I bought the Riley in November, 1951, from a dealer who lost his dealership shortly afterwards in a local scramble for franchises. For some reason I never received my certificate of guarantee from Nuffield Exports Limited of England who export the Riley. That's my own fault really—I should have asked for it.

A recurring miss showed up in the early life of the engine. It became increasingly worse as time went on.

Finally, at about 12,150 miles, after the local dealers told me that I would have to have a valve job and that the clutch throwout bearing was worn out, I wrote the Riley Motor Company in England. I explained that since I had neglected to insist that a certificate of guarantee be sent me, I didn't expect to regain any expenditures; I only wanted to know if I had a "lemon."

A reply from Nuffield Exports Limited courteously stated that such troubles are not typical of the Riley marque and that they were referring the matter to their American concessionaires for further investigation. They indicated a continued interest.

By that time, the Riley

(Above) MG valve adjustment bolt amateurishly altered to fit Riley.

(Below) This spring and bailing wire device was attached to carburetor.

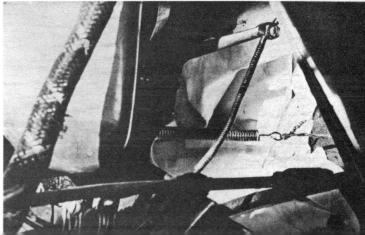

# I Still Love My Riley

had been in the shop for the valve job and I was sure I had something that would interest the Riley's manufacturers.

I mailed them a second letter which follows in part:

### The Letter

To Mr. J. G. Harris
Service Technical Department
Nuffield Exports Limited
Cowley, Oxford, England

". . . your local representatives decided that the miss in my Riley was caused by faulty carburetion. Consequently, the carburetors were dismantled and cleaned. When they attempted to tune them again, they decided that there was a warped valve on the front cylinder.

" 'How much will a valve job cost?' I asked.

"Your dealer, who manages his own repair department, referred to a cost chart. 'Thirty dollars—plus any parts that have to be replaced,' he said. 'And I can loan you a car to use while we have yours apart.'

" 'Do you have the parts in stock if any need to be replaced?' I asked.

"On being assured that they did, I agreed that they should do what was necessary and asked them to also tighten the front fender.

"Three days later I picked up the car and the bill. The charges were $63.46 ($15.10 plus tax for parts, $47.50 for labor). Included was a charge for a set of spark plugs. (The others had been in three weeks.)

"When I protested, the new plugs were taken off the bill.

" 'You told us to make it run right,' the dealer stated. 'Now take it out and drive it for a couple of hundred miles and bring it back for the final tuneup. That won't cost you anything. And, incidentally, what was wrong was that one of the Riley's valve adjustment bolts was defective. We had to make one out of an MG valve adjustment bolt.'

"When I started the motor, I remarked that it was idling quite fast.

" 'Bring it back after a couple of hundred miles,' your dealer said. 'We'll adjust it then.'

"So I took it back at the appointed time. They tightened the head bolts. They adjusted the valves.

"The carburetors wouldn't return to slow idling position. They solved this by attaching a coil spring between one end of the carburetor interconnecting bar and a bolt on the starter motor to hold the slow idling adjustment down. Somewhat amateurish, don't you think? (There should be a better remedy . . . Editor.)

"But here are the final back-breaking straws. When replacing the rocker arm covers, they tightened one nut too tight and pulled it clear through the cover. They welded the cover but are *not* going to replace it. (Imagine how a man feels who takes pride in a shiny pair of rocker arm covers.)

"I've purchased a complete set of wrenches in Whitworth sizes and have arranged for space to work on the Riley.

"One other item of interest for you. Your local dealer had told me that the clutch throwout bearing was worn out; that the engine would have to be pulled out so that it could be replaced. Well, I can announce a happy ending for that, at least. I adjusted it myself (by trial and error) so that for the first time since I've owned it, the gears no longer grind when I shift. And there's still room for further adjustment."

I heard from Nuffield's American concessionaires a short time later. So, to be fair, I wrote Nuffield's a final letter.

### Another Letter

"Dear Mr. Harris:

"The following is the body of a letter just received from your concessionaires:

" 'Nuffield Exports Limited have passed on to me a copy of your letter to them with reference to various troubles you have had with your 2½ Litre Riley.

" 'I have by today's post written to the dealers in your area asking them to give you every assistance.

" 'I sincerely hope they will be able to clear up your difficulties and get your Riley running to your complete satisfaction.' "

\* \* \*

And that's the other side of the picture.

Several of my friends have not had to pay for any parts during the six months warranty period.

As for the Riley, I've had to pay for both parts and labor, since I never received a certificate of guaranty. In spite of that, I would *not* trade the Riley for Detroit's finest—when it comes to sheer fun of driving. With a fine dealer and a competent service department, I now look forward to better times with my Riley which truly is a marvelous car.

(*EDITOR'S Note:* Reports such as this reach us occasionally about our own *domestic* as well as foreign cars. Sometimes foreign car dealer service is not all that it should be, but in all fairness the same must be said of domestic dealer service in many instances. To boil it down, there are honest dealers as well as those whose interest in the customers' satisfaction ends with a sale. Such a regrettable experience as the one suffered by our author should *not* be taken as a general indictment of all foreign car dealers. Rather such a report serves to quicken the senses of all concerned to bother themselves to know something of the reputation of any dealer when a purchase of a car is contemplated. Suffice it to say, honest dealers generally stay in business while their miserable opposites usually wind up behind the 8 ball. Also, foreign cars, and British cars in particular, have excellent guarantees and we know personally of many fine dealers all over the country who back those guarantees to the utmost.) ●●●

## CORRESPONDEN

OPINIONS EXPRESSED ON THESE PAGES ARE THOSE OF OUR CORRE-
SPONDENTS, WITH WHICH "THE AUTOCAR" DOES NOT NECESSARILY
AGREE. LETTERS INTENDED FOR PUBLICATION SHOULD BE
ADDRESSED TO THE EDITOR, "THE AUTOCAR," DORSET HOUSE.
STAMFORD STREET, LONDON, S.E.1.

### LONG STROKE

Negligible Oil Consumption After 50,000 Miles

[64850.]—In reply to letter [64793] from Mr. G. H. Oddy may I
say that I have a 1948 1½-litre Riley which has covered 50,000
miles and the oil consumption is still negligible? No engine
overhauls have been undertaken with the exception of decarbonizing every 12,000 to 14,000 miles.
What is a reasonable mileage to expect from an engine of this
type?                                              P. M. CLAYTON.
Wisbech, Cambridgeshire.

New Big-ends Only, in 128,000 Miles

[64851.]—I have been running a 1949 1½-litre Riley and have
just fitted a replacement engine. The mileage covered by the
original engine was 128,000 miles. The only replacement
during this mileage was one set of big-end bearings.
The car has given every satisfaction and was serviced only
as the makers recommend. No troubles have been experienced and the
I might add that no troubles is just as good as new in every way.
with the new engine ...dshire.               A. S. DAVEY.

Mr. A. S. Davey's
Riley in winter
trim, with the
radiator muff
adjusted.

# 128,000
# Miles before Rebore

## AN OWNER'S EXPERIENCES AND METHODS WITH A BRITISH 1½-LITRE

WHEN any human being reaches the age of 100, even doctors pay serious attention to that person's views on diet and habits—even if they are odd! So it is with a car that reaches a great mileage; one wants to know what the owner did with it to get such good results.

The 1949 1½-litre Riley owned by Mr. A. S. Davey, which figured in the Correspondence columns of *The Autocar* recently, covered 128,000 miles with no replacements of engine components except a new set of big-end bearings, and new piston rings. Throughout his ownership, Mr. Davey made full use of the performance of the car, and even ran in two speed trials, in one of which the car gained an award. He is on the technical staff of the de Havilland aircraft company, and business trips all over Britain accounted for much of the big mileage which was covered between September, 1949, and March, 1953; the distance between his home and his factory is considerable, so that the Riley had very little short-distance work. The normal cruising speed, maintained whenever conditions permitted, was 60-65 m.p.h., and even when four persons and luggage were carried a high average speed was maintained on journeys.

In cold weather, a 250-watt electric heater was placed under the sump at night so that, all the year round, when first starting in the mornings, it was possible to return the choke almost the instant that the engine fired, and to avoid washing the cylinder walls with wet petrol mixture. The car was allowed to warm up before moving off, even if ten minutes were required, so that the lubrication system was in full play. Redex in the recommended proportions (double when running in) was added to the petrol, as an upper cylinder lubricant, but no additives were used in the sump; the oil used was Energol S.A.E. 30, both summer and winter. A blank was used over the radiator when necessary, but the engine was on the whole run rather cool—at 70 deg C—to keep up the viscosity of the oil, which was changed at the recommended intervals of 2,000 miles. Every 10,000 miles the oil filter element was replaced and it was usually very dirty. One of these filter changes was allowed to become overdue by almost 50 per cent, and this was almost certainly the reason for the only serious engine trouble experienced when, at 60,000 miles, the big-end bearings ran.

### Unworn Crankpins

New big-ends were fitted—it was noticed that the crankpins were almost completely unworn at this mileage—and these bearings went on to the full 128,000 miles, when neither they nor the main bearings required renewal; the manufacturers of the car said that only a rebore was necessary.

While the engine was dismantled for renewal of the bearings, new Macrome chromium-plated piston rings were fitted, and the scraper rings were renewed. Throughout his ownership,

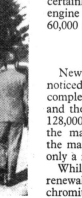

The car did not have a lazy life, and it was twice entered in speed trials.

117

# 128,000 Miles before Rebore

Mr. Davey, who does his own servicing, decarbonized the engine every 10,000 miles and ground in the valves. It was, he thinks, the maintenance of perfect seating which most helped the valves to remain in good condition for 128,000 miles, having been spared the corrosive scouring which takes place when burning gases escape past a badly seating valve. The aircraft world is much more particular about this point than is the car world. At 128,000 miles, the bores were much worn, there was piston slap, No. 2 plug had a tendency to oil up, and oil consumption had risen to 1,500 miles a gallon, but the road performance was still there and oil pressure remained normal.

### Free Use of Gear Lever

The owner's careful warming up was no doubt good for the bearings, as also were his driving methods. It was his custom to use the indirect gears freely, and to accelerate at part throttle; he continued in each gear, when accelerating, to the following speeds: first, 10 m.p.h.; second, 20 m.p.h.; third, 40-50 m.p.h. At all times, labouring the engine was avoided, the idea being to keep it turning briskly but lightly. That his progress must have been smooth and easy, in spite of his high cruising and average speeds, is indicated by good mileages from tyres. A set of ordinary Dunlops (not the heavier-duty Fort tyres) were fitted and balanced by the tyre makers, and did 24,000 miles front, 20,000 miles rear. Then a set of India Super heavy duty tyres gave 30,000 miles. The initial front tyres wore remarkably rapidly, and although a garage certified the toe-in of the wheels as correct, the owner was doubtful, and himself carried out a check; the toe-in was a full $\frac{1}{4}$ in wrong.

He regards the difficulty of having

" When the mileage stood at 90,000 a tour of the Highlands was undertaken "
—the Riley in Hell's Glen.

any defect traced at garages, unless it is an obvious one, as serious. A squealing front brake had four different linings fitted without success and was written off as "one of those things," but the owner traced the trouble to a sloppy fit at the fork holding one end of a shoe, and made a permanent cure by nipping up this fork in a vice. He makes no claims for his own servicing of chassis lubrication points, except that of absolute cleanliness, and at the full mileage it was found that the swivel pins were good and that the steering ball joints had no appreciable wear.

Early in the car's life a rear axle was found to have imperfect splines, and this was replaced under guarantee. The clutch linings were burnt out in

one of the competitions entered—the car is quite a heavy one, and when it is started violently a number of times the clutch has a lot of work to do. Apart from this mishap, and the bearing failure previously mentioned, the car was an economical one to run, with its good tyre life and moderate petrol consumption. When the mileage stood at 90,000, a tour of the Highlands of Scotland was undertaken with four adults and all their baggage on board; even in those unfavourable circumstances the m.p.g. over 2,000 miles averaged 28.4. Mr. Davey has a new, $1\frac{1}{2}$-litre Riley now, and is pleased with the redesigned transmission introduced last year, and with the finish which, satisfactory on the older car, he regards as greatly improved.

## offers you
# 'MAGNIFICENT MOTORING'
## and Double Saving

### *Lower Basic Prices  *Lower Purchase Tax

**OLD PRICES**

1½ litre saloon £860, plus £359.9.2d. Purchase Tax.    2½ litre saloon £1055, plus £440.14.2d. Purchase Tax.

# NEW PRICES

1½ litre saloon £825, plus £344 . 17 . 6d. Purchase Tax.
2½ litre saloon £925, plus £386 . 10 . 10d. Purchase Tax.

These important price reductions place this car of rare character, with its superb performance and fine craftsmanship, within the reach of a wider circle of motoring enthusiasts.

## RILEY MOTORS LIMITED, SALES DIVISION, COWLEY, OXFORD

London Showrooms: RILEY CARS, 55-56 PALL MALL, S.W.1.    Overseas Business: Nuffield Exports Ltd., Oxford & 41 Piccadilly, London, W.1

# By SIMON CRANSTON

# "Are we nearly there

## A RILEY, A FAMILY, AND A HOLIDAY

Leaving Princetown firmly behind with the family still intact—on the way home.

WRITERS of motoring articles seem to have a code which decrees that they may only refer to anyone travelling with them in the most vague terms. "My passenger" is the nearest they ever get to a description and one is left to wonder, somewhat tantalisingly, what sort of company such gentlemen keep. These notes are essentially about motoring with the family and become downright domestic from the start.

The family in question consists of four males and three females. Taking the males first, there is Jeremy ($9\frac{1}{2}$), Peter (6), Anthony ($3\frac{1}{2}$) and me. On the feminine side we have my wife (whose age is no business of yours), Glen—a 14-month-old Welsh sheepdog who wasn't travelling anyway—and our eight-month-old $2\frac{1}{2}$-litre Riley. And, with the exception of my wife and the car, we were all taking a holiday under doctor's orders to recover from ailments various—a pleasant way of making you feel that your journey is reasonably necessary. What it also meant was that we were doing in April what thousands of other families would be doing from June to September, which gave us just something of that superior feeling one always enjoys when out and about before the crowd.

## Perpetual Problem

Most family preparations must be the same. Each member spends a good deal of time dithering about which 10 per cent of their total wardrobe they might be able to do without. The children are quite prepared to sacrifice everything useful if they can only take a model aircraft with a 3 feet wingspan and a large toy yacht which won't fold up properly since Uncle John got the mast stuck last Whitsun. The paternal problem is simple—he just needs everything he doesn't wear at the office except perhaps the old battle-dress trousers he keeps for painting in. Mum listens sympathetically to each in turn—then goes away and packs what *she* considers to be the minimum necessities for the family. She is usually about right after Pop has insisted upon throwing out just enough to allow the back wheels of the car room to revolve. When you go away in April, the whole problem is merely more acute. It's colder, but there is always the possibility that it might be warmer.

The safest thing to do with the car is to catch it unawares and set off without so much as cleaning the windscreen. Put it in for a thorough service before you go and, when you're roughly half-way there, the most frightful noises develop. The same gremlin breaks the main-spring in your watch a few days after it returns from having a broken glass replaced. On this occasion we refused to be intimidated and gave Old Mother Riley, as the children sometimes irreverently call her, a 1,000-mile service and a good wash and polish.

I cannot abide a dirty car, particularly on a sunny morning, and we were so hoping for one of those. I also had a couple of extra pounds put into the tyres to cope with the additional weight and remembered to blow up the spare. Finally the tank was filled up to a mark I had made on the filler pipe to help check petrol consumption. What a lot of extra petrol you can get into those pipes (the Riley has double filler caps—a great boon).

Our destination was a small farm a few miles from the coast near Ivybridge, South Devon. I had calculated the distance to be 188 miles, assumed an average of 40 m.p.h. actual running time, told myself not to be stupid, knocked it down to 32 or 33 m.p.h., added $1\frac{1}{2}$ hours for picnic lunch and other stops and told the family that we ought to leave $7\frac{1}{2}$ hours before our intended time of arrival—teatime. We always say we'll arrive at tea-time—like the Army term "forthwith" it means practically any time!

We had been in complete agreement about two things. First, that we would get away promptly at 9 a.m. and secondly, that an early night was essential to our invalid state. There wasn't a hope of achieving either—there never is—but we kept up a brave pretence. In fact, 9 a.m. next morning found the Riley parked expectantly near the front door completely empty save for Jeremy reading a comic. The other two were nowhere to be seen. There followed 30 heated minutes at the end of which five bad-tempered humans and one asthmatic vehicle seethed out of the front gate and headed westwards. This particular Riley of ours has a most unfortunate habit in the mornings; within a few minutes of the engine starting, a wheezing high-pitched whine appears above the engine note; five minutes later all traces of disorder disappear and the unblemished gentle purr takes over until next morning when it all begins again. The cause? The experts said it would disappear after 4,000 or 5,000 miles. The young lady is now 8,000 miles old.

So the whine and the bad-tempers moved off to join A30 where at Bagshot they both disappeared at the sudden colour of the flowering trees and shrubs of a well-known roadside nursery. Even A30 looked pleasant and deceptively like a good road. The right foot went down a little further, Anthony switched on the radio and the sun began to advertise the new brand of car polish I was experimenting with.

Camberley was now approaching at the 50-60 m.p.h. mark, at which speed the Riley ambles along in delightful fashion. Your foot merely rests on the throttle pedal and your hands toy with a motionless wheel through which the road can still be felt but from which the tendency to heavy steering experienced at lower speeds has now disappeared. It is the completely relaxed motoring that can be enjoyed only in a car which is really direct and completely manageable. Perhaps it is best illustrated by a remark recently made to me

*Daddy ?"*

and mother had slipped him an aspirin to relieve the slight headache which was also present.

Ten minutes beyond Andover we stopped for elevenses, and I lifted the bonnet to have a closer look at what turned out to be merely a slight overflow from a too-full radiator. At the crucial moment an A.A. scout passed, slowed at the sight of a raised bonnet, turned and came back. Three minutes later he had confirmed my diagnosis and I was joining the A.A. It was good to be back in the family. My earlier membership had lapsed and only laziness had kept it that way. We gave him a cup of tea and he showed the children, all five of us, what really is kept in those bright yellow sidecars. I also gathered that his weekly mileage was 800, on a 10-mile stretch of road.

We were soon off again, with a paper A.A. sign pasted inside our windscreen and a lovely new game watching for flashes of yellow in the distance and then waiting for salutes which the boys returned with the self-conscious nonchalance of newly commissioned subalterns. Mere and Wincanton were quickly overtaken and 1 o'clock arrived simultaneously with Ilminster and a welcome picnic lunch which was eaten in the sunshine we had all hoped for so much.

### Tea Time

At 2 p.m. we removed the last traces of ice-cream and moved off with 118 miles on the trip-meter and 70-odd still to do. A303 soon became A30 with Honiton and the Exeter by-pass coming smoothly along to meet us and we were just approaching Ashburton at about 50 m.p.h. in third when a small flat voice behind the driver's ear said "I'm going to be sick." A squeal of brakes and a hurriedly opened door and Jeremy was mal-de-car all over the rather surprised grass verge. We were off again in five minutes, feverishly playing "I-spy" and it was not long before somebody's little eye found Buckfast Abbey.

The misty treeless heights of Dartmoor were now rolling past on our right and Ivybridge suddenly came round a bend to greet us. Out came the one-inch map and parents changed seats again in order to allow father to map-read. Why are women so defeatist about such a simple art? Five miles of those delightful high-banked lanes along which you soon begin to drive with undue faith in horn and brakes and—we were there. Four o'clock (it really was tea-time) and 191 miles on the trip-meter which on investigation produced a mileage per gallon a point or two over the 20 mark. Despite our initial gloomy estimates we had averaged 38 m.p.h. actual running time, poor in relation to the car's ability but fair enough when driving had been a mere side-issue to one long series of parlour games. Who said the Riley wasn't a family car?

by an attractive female who, in casual conversation, was complaining about the need to "climb up" into her new family-type car which then proceeded to sway somewhat vaguely about the road. On learning of my new purchase she said "Ah, well there you are—you don't climb up into a Riley. You put it on!" She was so right.

We crammed a lot into that first hour. Housewife's Choice, Camberley, a boiled sweet apiece, Blackbushe airfield (whose scattered huts and hangars might have been dropped from a great height by the strangely varied aircraft parked in disarray about the place), the village cricket delight of Hartley Wintney, the first wide sweep of open Hampshire and 43 miles.

We were now on the narrow, winding, uneven surface of A303, enjoying its rolling countryside and revelling in the absence of practically any other vehicle—in particular the procession of broad-beamed tarpaulin-clad matrons who trundle interminably down A30. Their driving manners are usually impeccable but their exhausts provide a poor diet for children with queasy tummies and we had one of those. Normally all three travel any distance without trouble, but this morning Jeremy had for some reason faced breakfast with a slight nausea. It didn't stop him from eating huge quantities; few things do, but parents had raised eyebrows

The end of the road—this one anyway.

The new wing and body style blend well with the familiar 1½-litre Riley coachwork. The hinged ventilator — an optional extra—is fitted to the front doors.

# RILEY TRANSFORMATION

Traditional features are fully retained in the smaller car in the Riley range—the very successful 1½-litre. This car is a traceable descendant of the Riley Nine, and has such classic features as a separate chassis frame of side- and cross-members, coachbuilt bodywork and traditional appearance. The overhead-valve engine—a willing performer capable of holding its tune over many thousands of miles—develops 55 b.h.p. and is notable for its ability to revolve at very high rates without valve bounce; it is an engine in which the connoisseur delights.

Transmission is through a four-speed synchromesh gear box and an open propeller-shaft to a hypoid semi-floating rear axle. The latest modifications to this model (before those at present being reviewed) were concerned with the transmission, the torque tube being dropped and the gear ratios raised to give lower gearing overall. Rack and pinion steering, quite high-geared, is notable for its precision and the hydraulic brakes are ample for the performance. Torsion bar independent suspension is employed.

Described by the manufacturers as the "New Look 1½-litre," the car has now been given a face-lift and, although it still retains its well-known rakish line, detail modifications have been made to the body to improve the appearance. At first glance it is difficult to see just what has been altered, as the modifications have been well blended into the original basic style, but closer examination reveals that both the front and rear wing treatment has been altered; in place of the sweeping front wings and built-in running boards, a shorter and more rounded wing pressing is used, while the sill pressing, now used in place of the running board, permits easier access to the car as well as providing a cleaner appearance. Detachable panels have been added to enclose the rear wheels.

The body interior makes no pretence to seat more than five at the outside, and is really a comfortable four-seater. The separate front seats are upholstered in leather, as is the back seat, which is capable of division by a wide folding arm rest. There are folding arm rests on the doors. Woodwork is extensively used on facia and door cappings and the instrument layout is complete in terms of oil pressure gauge, ammeter and coolant thermometer.

Luggage is stowed in a locker of large capacity in the long tail, though the shape of the locker is shallow and the owner needs to bear the fact in mind when purchasing his suitcases. Under the floor of the locker the spare wheel is stowed and is extracted through a separate lid between the bars of the duplex rear bumper.

Optional triangular ventilating panels for the front window can improve the ventilation control, and door pockets have been provided on the front doors at the bottom.

Optional extras also include radio and a badge bar. A fresh-air heating unit is fitted as standard.

### RILEY PATHFINDER SPECIFICATION

**Engine.**—4 cyl, 80.5 × 120 mm (2,443 c.c.). Compression ratio 7.25 to 1. 102 b.h.p. at 4,400 r.p.m. Maximum torque 136 lb ft at 3,000 r.p.m. Three-bearing camshaft. Hemispherical combustion chambers. Overhead valves operated by short push rods, rockers and twin camshafts.

**Clutch.**—Borg and Beck dry single plate; 10in diameter; 12 springs. Mechanical withdrawal mechanism, incorporating progressive ratio device.

**Gear Box.**—Overall ratios: Top, 4.1; third, 5.88; second, 8.446; first, 13.59; reverse, 18.42 to 1.

**Final Drive.**—Hypoid bevel (10:41). Ratio 4.1 to 1. Two-pinion differential.

**Suspension.**—Front: independent (8 deg semi-trailing wishbones, links and torsion bars). Telescopic spring dampers. Rear: coil springs, radius arms, and Panhard rod. Telescopic spring dampers. Suspension rate (at the wheel): front, 158 lb in; rear, 184 lb in. Static deflection: front, 5.5in; rear, 4.5in.

**Brakes.**—Hydraulically operated, servo assisted. Two trailing shoe, front. Leading and trailing shoe, rear. Drums: 12in diameter, 2¼in wide front; 12in diameter, 2¼in wide rear. Total lining area: 202.5 sq in (103.5 sq in front).

**Steering.**—Bishop cam.

**Wheels and Tyres.**—6.70—16in tyres on 5.00—16in rims. Five-stud steel disc wheels.

**Electrical Equipment.**—12-volt; 64-ampère-hour battery. Head lamps, 42-36 watts.

**Fuel System.**—13-gallon tank. Oil capacity 12¼ pints.

**Main Dimensions.**—Wheelbase 9ft 5½in; track, front 4ft 6in, rear 4ft 6½in. Overall length 15ft 3½in; width 5ft 6in; height 4ft 11½in. Ground clearance 6⅝in. Frontal area: 20.5 sq ft. Turning circle 34ft 9in. Weight (with 13 gallons fuel) 30½ cwt. Weight distribution, 53.5 per cent front, 46.5 per cent rear.

**Price.**—Basic, £975; British purchase tax, £407 7s 6d. Total, £1,382 7s 6d.

### RILEY 1½-LITRE SPECIFICATION

**Engine.**—4 cyl, 69 × 100 mm (1,496 c.c.). Compression ratio 6.8 to 1. 55 b.h.p. at 4,500 r.p.m. Maximum torque 78 lb ft at 2,500 r.p.m. Three-bearing crankshaft. Hemispherical combustion chambers. Overhead valves operated by push rods, rockers and twin camshafts.

**Clutch.**—Borg and Beck dry single-plate 8in; 6 springs. Mechanical withdrawal mechanism.

**Gear Box.**—Overall ratios: Top, 5.125; third, 7.585; second, 11.736; first, 20.372; reverse, 20.372 to 1.

**Final Drive.**—Hypoid bevel (8—41). Ratio 5.125 to 1. Two-pinion differential.

**Suspension.**—Front: independent, wishbones with torsion bars; telescopic spring dampers. Rear: half-elliptic; telescopic spring dampers. Suspension rate (at the wheel): front, 140 lb in; rear, 130 lb in. Static deflection: front, 4.96in; rear, 5.85in.

**Brakes.**—Hydraulically operated two-leading shoe, front. Leading and trailing shoe, rear. Drums: 10in diameter, 1¾in wide front; 10in diameter, 1¾in wide rear. Total lining area: 130.4 sq in (68.3 sq in front).

**Steering.**—Rack and pinion.

**Wheels and Tyres.**—5.75—16in tyres on 4.50—16in rims. Five-stud steel disc wheels.

**Electrical Equipment.**—12-volt; 51-ampère-hour battery. Head lamps, 42-36 watts.

**Fuel System.**—13-gallon tank. Oil capacity 10 pints.

**Main Dimensions.**—Wheelbase 9ft 4½in; track, front 4ft 4½in; rear 4ft 4½in. Overall length 14ft 11in; width 5ft 3½in; height 4ft 11in. Ground clearance 7½in. Frontal area: 19.8 sq ft. Turning circle 30ft 0in. Weight (with 13 gallons fuel) 26 cwt 16 lb. Weight distribution: 48.5 per cent front, 51.5 per cent rear.

**Price.**—Basic, £850; British purchase tax, £355 5s 10d. Total, £1,205 5s 10d.

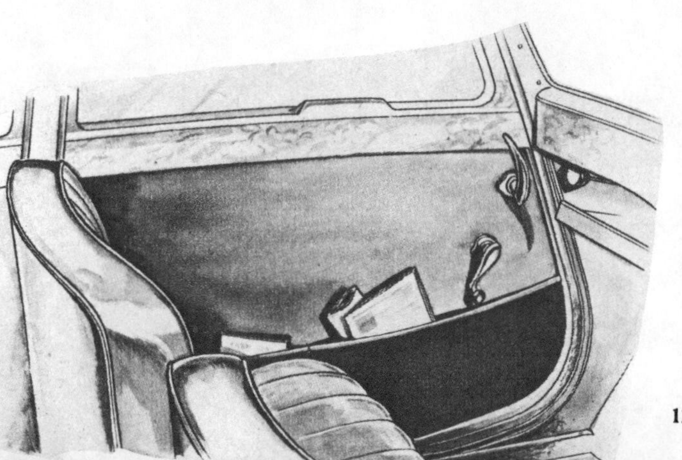

Originally the lower parts of the front doors of the 1½-litre were covered with carpet material. These have now become useful map pockets.

# USED CARS ON THE ROAD

## No. 77 : 1950 2½-litre Riley Roadster Two-three-seater

| Price New £985 plus £266 17s 2d purchase tax | Acceleration from rest through gears | | Fuel consumption 20 m.p.g. | Speedometer reading 43,216 |
|---|---|---|---|---|
| **Price Secondhand** £645 | To 30 m.p.h. ... ... 6.2 sec | | **Oil** consumption negligible | **Car First Registered** February, 1950 |
| | To 50 m.p.h. ... ... 17.0 sec | | | |
| | To 60 m.p.h. ... ... 23.1 sec | | | |
| | 20-40 m.p.h. (top gear) 11.7 sec | | | |
| | 30-50 m.p.h. (top gear) 12.1 sec | | | |

ORIGINALLY introduced as a left-hand drive export model, in which form it was subjected by *The Autocar* to a complete Road Test in September, 1948, the 2½-litre Riley roadster was later released for the home market. Now it is out of production, and Riley enthusiasts who prefer open car motoring must seek used examples of the model. It was not intended to be an out-and-out sports car, as its title implies —and much attention was paid to comfort. But despite a weight of about 27 cwt, the model, when tested new, proved to have a very useful performance.

The car that is the subject of this test was provided by Webb Motors (Watford), Ltd., 232-234, St. Albans Road, Watford,

Hertfordshire. It was finished in light metallic green, and even a brief inspection was enough to show that the car had been looked after unusually carefully. Closer inspection indicated that the highly polished surface of the cellulose was impaired by only one very small dent, and that the chromium plating was in excellent condition. The upholstery was good and the carpets had obviously been protected, as they were in virtually new condition. The Vynide hood and tonneau cover were also well preserved, and the side screens were intact.

The engine started at once, hot or cold, and it pulled well. It did seem that the power was not all that it should be, and this was borne out by the performance figures, and particularly by the top speed of 78 m.p.h., compared with a speed little short of 100 m.p.h. achieved when the model was tested new. However, the engine was quite free from mechanical fussiness and it never seemed to be stressed. It was felt that the lack of performance resulted from no more than the need for careful ignition and carburation adjustment. As tested, the performance was such as to enable high point-to-point average speeds to be made, and at its near-80 m.p.h. maximum it would travel quite happily for as many miles as conditions permitted.

The suspension was firm to the point of being a little bumpy, but it provided a very stable ride, adding much to the pleasure of driving the car. The steering was accurate, although it was heavy at low speeds. The column was adjustable for length. The main criticism centred on the operation of the steering column gear change. There was some wear in the linkage, and although third and top were readily obtainable without difficulty, the same could not always be said of first and second gears, particularly as the lever was very close to the steering wheel in either of those gears when the wheel was adjusted to its farthest forward position. There was also a tendency for third gear to jump out on the overrun.

With the exception of the spare, the tyres were sound; the battery appeared to have been fitted recently, and the body was free from rattles. Accessories included a windscreen washer with a very large container, twin driving mirrors on the front wings, fog lamps, and no fewer than eight bumper over-riders.

This Riley was a most pleasant car to drive, and the condition of the mechanical components and of the body was unusually good in view of age and mileage, even for a car of this initial quality.

---

# TWO CARBURETTERS FOR RILEY 1½-LITRE

A STANDARDIZED twin carburetter conversion kit for post-war Riley 1½-litre models, designed for the benefit of owners requiring improved performance for trials and rallies, is now available from the Service Department of Riley Motors, Ltd., Abingdon-on-Thames, Berks, at a price of £30. It is claimed that the conversion improves acceleration by 10 to 15% with only a moderate increase in fuel consumption.

The major components of the conversion kit comprise a twin carburetter manifold, two S.U. 1¼-in. carburetters, air cleaner elbow and an air cleaner assembly of the 2½-litre model type.

The inlet manifold of the standard 1½-litre engine is heated by pipes which pass through the cylinder head from the exhaust manifold to the inlet manifold and return through the block. It will be found when fitting the twin carburetter manifold that this blanks-off the hot-spot conduit in the head without obstructing the return pipes through the block. As the hot-spot system is no longer required the three holes in the exhaust manifold must be blanked off

and this can be done by brazing. The three outer tubes or conduits may, however, be left in place.

Other minor modifications required include the removal of a small quantity of metal from the manifold stud hole bosses to clear the edge of the head, and the fitting of longer inlet manifold studs to accommodate the twin carburetter manifold.

With the new manifold in position it will be found that a slight alteration is required to the throttle control linkage. The position of the lever at the outer end of the throttle countershaft, to which the rod from the pedal is connected,

should be reversed so that the hole in the arm of the lever is at the top but, owing to the proximity of the steering column and the handbrake intermediate lever, the countershaft lever will require a slight " set." The control rod between the lever and the pedal should be adjusted accordingly and the rod from the countershaft to the carburetters should be replaced by the modified rod provided in the kit.

**CONVERTED.**—The appearance of the 1½-litre engine after the twin carburetter conversion has been carried out.

**Make: Riley**   **Type: 1½-Litre Saloon**

**Makers: Riley Motors Ltd., Cowley, Oxford**

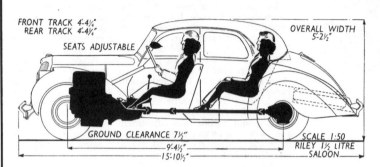

FRONT TRACK 4'-4½"
REAR TRACK 4'-4¼"
OVERALL WIDTH 5'-2½"
SEATS ADJUSTABLE
GROUND CLEARANCE 7½"
SCALE 1:50
RILEY 1½ LITRE SALOON
9'-4½"
15'-10½"

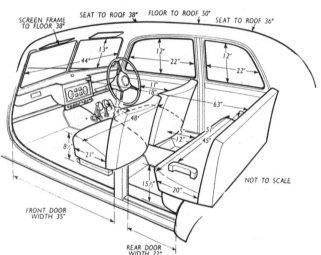

SCREEN FRAME TO FLOOR 38"
SEAT TO ROOF 38"
FLOOR TO ROOF 50"
SEAT TO ROOF 36"
13"   12"   12"
44"   22"   22"
11"
18"
63"
48"
8½"   21"
15½"   20"
5"   5"
12"   45"
NOT TO SCALE
FRONT DOOR WIDTH 35"
REAR DOOR WIDTH 22"

## Test Data

**CONDITIONS.** *Weather: Fine, Warm, little wind. Surface: Dry tar macadam. Fuel: Premium grade.*

### INSTRUMENTS
| | |
|---|---|
| Speedometer at 30 m.p.h. | 2% fast |
| Speedometer at 60 m.p.h. | 6% fast |
| Distance recorder | Accurate |

### MAXIMUM SPEEDS
**Flying Quarter Mile**

| | |
|---|---|
| Mean of Four Opposite Runs | 74.7 m.p.h. |
| Best Time equals | 76.3 m.p.h. |

**Speed in Gears**

| | |
|---|---|
| Max. speed in 3rd gear | 53 m.p.h. |
| Max. speed in 2nd gear | 36 m.p.h. |

### FUEL CONSUMPTION
39.5 m.p.g. at constant 30 m.p.h.
36.5 m.p.g. at constant 40 m.p.h.
33.0 m.p.g. at constant 50 m.p.h.
26.0 m.p.g. at constant 60 m.p.h.
Overall consumption for 1186.5 miles, 46.6 gallons, equals 25.4 m.p.g.
Fuel tank capacity 12½ gallons.

### ACCELERATION TIMES Through Gears
| | |
|---|---|
| 0-30 m.p.h. | 7.2 sec. |
| 0-40 m.p.h. | 11.7 sec. |
| 0-50 m.p.h. | 18.6 sec. |
| 0-60 m.p.h. | 31.8 sec. |
| 0-70 m.p.h. | 59.5 sec. |
| Standing Quarter Mile.. | 24.3 sec. |

### ACCELERATION TIMES on Two Upper Ratios
| | Top | 3rd |
|---|---|---|
| 10-30 m.p.h. | 11.8 sec. | 8.1 sec. |
| 20-40 m.p.h. | 12.2 sec. | 9.3 sec. |
| 30-50 m.p.h. | 14.7 sec. | 12.0 sec. |
| 40-60 m.p.h. | 21.6 sec. | — |
| 50-70 m.p.h. | 40.9 sec. | — |

### WEIGHT
| | |
|---|---|
| Unladen kerb weight | 26 cwt. |
| Front/rear weight distribution | 49/51 |
| Weight laden as tested | 29½ cwt. |

### HILL CLIMBING (At steady speeds)
| | |
|---|---|
| Max. top gear speed on 1 in 20 | 55 m.p.h. |
| Max. top gear speed on 1 in 15 | 47 m.p.h. |
| Max. gradient on top gear | 1 in 11.1 (Tapley 200 lb./ton) |
| Max. gradient on 3rd gear | 1 in 7.6 (Tapley 290 lb./ton) |
| Max. gradient on 2nd gear | 1 in 5.5 (Tapley 400 lb./ton) |

### BRAKES at 30 m.p.h.
0.94 g retardation (= 32 ft. stopping distance) with 140 lb. pedal pressure
0.82 g retardation (= 37 ft. stopping distance) with 100 lb. pedal pressure
0.63 g retardation (= 48 ft. stopping distance) with 75 lb. pedal pressure
0.42 g retardation (= 72 ft. stopping distance) with 50 lb. pedal pressure
0.26 g retardation (= 116 ft. stopping distance) with 25 lb pedal pressure

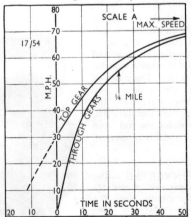

SCALE A — MAX. SPEED
17/54
¼ MILE
TOP GEAR
THROUGH GEARS
M.P.H.
TIME IN SECONDS

SCALE A
17/54
POWER AVAILABLE
FUEL CONSUMPTION
POWER REQUIRED
APPROX. H.P. AT REAR WHEELS
FUEL CONSUMPTION AT STEADY SPEED—GALLONS PER 1,000 MILES
M.P.H.

| | |
|---|---|
| Drag at 10 m.p.h. | 40 lb. |
| Drag at 60 m.p.h. | 170 lb |

**Specific fuel consumption** when cruising at 80% of maximum speed (i.e., 59.8 m.p.h.) on level road, based on power delivered to rear wheels .. 0.68 pints/b.h.p./hr.

## Maintenance

**Sump:** 10 pints, S.A.E. 30. **Gearbox:** 2 pints, S.A.E. 90 (hypoid). **Rear Axle:** 2½ pints, S.A.E. 90 (hypoid). **Steering gear:** Grease. **Radiator:** 13 pints (2 drain taps). **Chassis Lubrication:** By grease gun every 1,000 miles to 13 points. **Ignition timing:** 8° B.T.D.C. (with hand-control at full advance). **Spark plug gap:** 0.025 in. **Contact breaker gap:** 0.014-0.016 in. **Valve timing:** Inlet opens 7° B.T.D.C. and closes 48° A.B.D.C. Exhaust opens 48° B.B.D.C. and closes 20° A.T.D.C. **Tappet clearances:** (Hot) Inlet 0.015 in. Exhaust 0.015 in. **Front wheel toe-in:** Nil. **Camber angle:** 1°. **Castor angle:** 3°. **Tyre pressures:** Front 22 lb. Rear 24 lb. **Brake fluid:** Girling. **Battery:** Lucas 12-volt, 51 amp./hr. **Lamp bulbs:** Head lamps, 42/36 watt (Lucas No. 354); side, tail, stop and roof lamps, 6 watt (Lucas No. 207); reversing lamp, 36 watt (Lucas No. 57); fog lamps, 48 watt (Lucas No. 162); ignition, panel and fuel gauge lamps, 2.2 watt (Lucas No. 987); trafficators, 3 watt (Lucas No. 256).

Ref. B/15/54.

# The RILEY 1½-litre Saloon

### A Well-built and Excellently-finished 1½-litre Car with Notably Good Handling Qualities

MODERNIZED by the removal of running boards and the fitting of new front wings and spatted rear wheels the Riley 1½-litre nevertheless retains its classic outline.

## In Brief

Price: £850 plus purchase tax £355 5s. 10d. equals £1,205 5s. 10d.
Capacity ... ... ... 1,496 c.c.
Unladen kerb weight ... 26 cwt.
Fuel consumption... ... 25.4 m.p.g.
Maximum speed ... ... 74.7 m.p.h.
Maximum speed on 1 in 20 gradient ... ... 55 m.p.h.
Maximum top gear gradient ... ... 1 in 11.1
Acceleration:
  10-30 m.p.h. in top ... 11.8 sec.
  0-50 m.p.h. through gears 18.6 sec.
Gearing: 15.4 m.p.h. in top at 1,000 r.p.m.; 58.3 m.p.h. at 2,500 ft. per min. piston speed.

WHILST the latest 1½-litre Riley was recently in our hands for an extended road test, we were approached by a stranger who pointed to his own identical model standing a few yards away and informed us that it was his sixteenth Riley. This fact (which we were subsequently able to check from another source) seems singularly apposite as an introduction to this road test report, because it epitomizes the user-enthusiasm and affection that has for so long been inspired by the marque Riley.

There are 1½-litre cars that are livelier, or roomier, or more economical, but the Riley couples a happy mean in these respects with such a sterling blend of all that is in the best British traditions of good engineering, excellent finish, good looks and notably roadworthy behaviour that its appeal is not hard to understand.

The 1954 model represents the latest example of a type which was one of the first completely new post-war designs to be launched in this country. Subsequent experience in the hands of the public has suggested the need for no major changes, although various detail improvements have been incorporated from year to year. The latest of such changes (incorporated for the London Motor Show last year) took the form of new wings and the elimination of running boards to provide a more modern appearance without disturbing the good lines of the car as a whole; these changes also enabled the twin fog lamps to be built in at the front and wheel spats to be introduced at the rear.

The full mechanical specification is reproduced in a data panel, but one or two characteristically Riley features should be mentioned here. The engine, for example, is notable for the use of hemispherical combustion chambers with inclined valves operating from a pair of highly placed camshafts, one on each side of the block, to give many of the advantages of twin overhead camshafts without any timing complications during top overhauls. This car was also one of the first British makes to employ independent front suspension embodying torsion bars and the now-widely-used wishbones of unequal length. Also notable in this age of quantity-produced pressed-steel bodies, is the retention of coachbuilt construction.

As one would expect, the performance of this latest Riley is closely on a par with that of the 1953 type tested (on Pool petrol) a little over a year ago, the maximum speed of 74.7 m.p.h., in fact, differing by a mere 0.1 m.p.h. The latest model did, however, show distinct gains in constant-speed fuel consumption recordings, confirmed by an improvement of 5% in the overall figure, despite the fact that the latest test was taken over a high mileage which included not only the performance tests but also a considerable distance over hilly West Country roads.

In the main, it is true to describe the 1½-litre Riley performance as lively rather than startling, but the combination of its response to the accelerator and its essential roadworthiness makes it a car in which good averages can be put up over long distances with a pleasing absence of strain.

More will be said of handling qualities later. So far as the engine is concerned, the Riley unit has always been a willing performer and the current example proved no exception. A genuine 60 m.p.h. seems to suit the car particularly well and the engine is, in fact, quieter at this speed than at 50-55 m.p.h., at which the noise level —never high—is at its maximum. At low speeds there is a very reasonable degree of flexibility for a four-cylinder unit and it is notable that there is no trace whatever of pinking or running-on when premium fuel is used; it was never found necessary, in fact, to use the ignition control, but this now-rare feature should be a useful adjunct where, through choice or necessity, low-grade fuels are used.

Reference has already been made to the improvement in fuel consumption and, in the light of the points just mentioned, the engine obviously takes well to the present economical setting; for those who place more importance on performance than economy, however, alternative settings giving more emphasis on the top end of the range might prove an advantage as shown by the fact that, on the model tried, the acceleration tailed off noticeably above 65 m.p.h. in top gear, whilst 53 m.p.h. was maximum

DISTINCTIVE lines are allied with such practical features as twin fuel fillers, widely spaced bumper bars and a large rear window.

HIGH-GRADE leather is used for the seats and this combined with the real wood used for facia and fillets gives the interior an air of quality and refinement. Notable points are the centre and side armrests at the rear, the very adequate roof lights and a telescopically adjustable steering column.

in third, with 40 m.p.h. as a natural changing-up speed. For those who use their cars in competitions, a twin-carburetter induction system is available.

Starting at all times proved easy, but the engine is not so sweet as some at tick-over speeds. A very good point is the way hard driving produced very little rise in engine temperature, and it was noticeable that the tops of both Porlock and Countisbury hills were reached with the needle still at 175 degrees F., on a warm spring day.

Access to the engine for routine maintenance via the centrally split bonnet top is quite good, and a sensible point is that both hinged portions can be opened together and retained in the open position by convenient catches.

### Central Gear Lever

There is a very positive action about the clutch but it is, nevertheless, sufficiently smooth for easy starts to be made in second gear on the level. The pedal travel is comparatively long and, on the car tried, it was necessary to depress it fully to free the drive completely. Provided this was done, the gear change proved both easy and straightforward, and the neat central control lever is of the type which so many enthusiasts prefer. Competition-minded drivers will find snatch changes comparatively easy between first and second and between third and top; the through-the-gate movement between second and third makes this technique a little more difficult in this instance, but still quite possible. Upward changes are, however, pleasantly rapid in any case without resort to trick tactics. Gear noise is commendably low.

Owing to the transmission tunnel, there is no room for the driver's clutch foot at the side of the pedal, but this difficulty has been partially overcome by shaping the casing of the tunnel to form a rest which

CLEAR, plain-faced instruments, a central gear lever and efficient heater make for driving ease, but not so good is the use of eight identical knobs at the base of the facia panel which are open to confusion.

takes the weight of the driver's foot off the pedal. There could, however, be more room for the pedal itself with advantage, the present spacing being barely adequate for those wearing wide-fitting shoes.

As will be seen from the accompanying data, the brakes provide good stopping power with moderate pedal pressures, and to this comment may be added the information that Porlock hill was deliberately descended in top gear in order to throw all the work of this two-mile descent on to the brakes; no signs of fade were apparent when the car was brought to a standstill on the still-steep gradient below the bottom corner.

The hand-brake is of the pistol-grip type to the right of the steering column and, whilst it is quite satisfactory, a pull-up lever between the seats and close to the gear lever would obviously offer greater convenience.

Suspension on the current models is rather softer than on the original 1½-litre type with a corresponding improvement in general riding comfort. There is very little roll on corners and damping is normally very satisfactory, but fast drivers might

### The Riley 1½-litre Saloon - - - - - - - - -

prefer slightly more restraint for fast cornering on bad surfaces. The Riley remains, however, a car which inspires very notable confidence on give-and-take roads, the steering being accurate and the general cornering qualities above average. The effort required on the wheel is moderate rather than light and there is some road reaction through the wheel. A much-appreciated refinement is an extensible steering column.

From the driver's angle, the general layout of the controls and seating gives instant confidence, but the array of identically shaped knobs beneath the facia requires learning before one's hand automatically finds the right knob at the right moment—especially at night when the instrument lighting provides no help. The instruments themselves are comprehensive and clear-faced, with black markings on a gold background. At night they are illuminated by rheostat-controlled indirect lighting which, even when dimmed to the maximum, is rather bright for some tastes, the more so as the illumination of the central group is augmented by escaped light from the warning lamps for the heater and the headlight main beam.

The confidence which the 1½-litre Riley inspires is undoubtedly augmented by the excellent view of both front wings obtained from the driving seat and a useful detail is the provision of transparent ruby "pips" on the tops of the side lamps. All-round visibility is also good, although the top of the screen causes some restriction of upward view for a very tall driver and the tapered upper portions of the screen pillars are also slightly obtrusive in such cases. In wet weather, larger areas of wiped screen would be welcome.

Rearward, the back window gives a good view and the anti-dazzle mirror is appreciated at night. Those who like to drive with an elbow on the door sill or to put their heads out of the window for reversing will note with approval that the windows disappear completely into the doors. A neat detail is the provision of a pair of flush-fitting vizors which give protection from a head-on sun.

An adequate heater and demister of the recirculating type is provided as standard in countries where it is considered necessary, but the provision of draughtless ventilation in cold weather calls for a rather careful adjustment of windows because hinged ventilating panels are not part of the normal equipment. In hot weather, side ventilators in the scuttle are a distinct aid to a cool interior. The Riley is, incidentally, commendably free from excessive wind noise.

The front bucket seats are well shaped to give support on corners and their high squabs provide a restful but fairly alert position. At the rear, the seat cushion might be shaped to give a little more sup-

TWIN fog lamps are built into the revised front of the latest 1½-litre car

the seats is in keeping with the whole. Both interior and exterior, in fact, have that distinct air of quality which is so satisfying to motorists who want more from a car than mere transport.

On the electrical side, the headlamps provide a very good range and are supplemented by a pair of built-in fog lamps, whilst a good interior detail is the provision of roof lamps which are really adequate for map reading. An unusual detail is a push-button dipper on the facia, which is quick, although not particularly comfortable, to use and gives no indication of whether the lamps have been left dipped or otherwise. The radio equipment, when provided, is notable for the use of two speakers.

Stowage space for luggage and oddments is well planned, with useful parcel shelves

## - - - Contd.

A FLAT FLOOR and plenty of unobstructed room make the stowage of luggage an easy task in the Riley, the spare wheel being housed separately beneath and being extracted between the bumper bars.

port to the thighs with advantage, but, even so, the general standard of comfort is very good and is aided considerably by fixed arm rests on the doors as well as the usual central folding arm rest.

In general finish and appointments, the Riley reaches a high standard, and the provision of what the Americans have been known to call "genuine tree wood" for the main portion of the facia board and the window mouldings and door cappings, is a most pleasing feature, whilst the use of beautifully trimmed high-grade leather for

under the facia and behind the rear squab, map pockets in the front doors and a really excellent boot offering a clear floor for luggage, with tool receptacles in the wing recesses and a separate compartment for the spare wheel below.

With its many traditional British features, its good road manners and its excellent build and finish, this latest 1½-litre Riley will continue to appeal to discerning drivers whose tastes run to an individual car of very pleasing up-to-date, but not ultra-modern, line.

# Mechanical Specification

**Engine**

| | | |
|---|---|---|
| Cylinders ... ... ... ... | 4 |
| Bore ... ... ... ... | 69 mm. |
| Stroke ... ... ... ... | 100 mm. |
| Cubic capacity ... ... ... | 1,496 c.c. |
| Piston area ... ... ... | 23.2 sq. in. |
| Valves ... Pushrod o.h.v. (2 camshafts) |
| Compression ratio ... ... | 6.8/1 |
| Max. power ... ... ... | 55 b.h.p. |
| at ... ... ... | 4,500 r.p.m. |
| Piston speed at max. b.h.p. 2,960 ft. per min. |
| Carburetter ... ... S.U. horizontal |
| Ignition ... ... ... Coil |
| Sparking plugs ... ... Champion L10S |
| Fuel Pump... ... ... AC mechanical |
| Oil filter ... ... Vokes external full-flow |
| (throw-away element) |

**Transmission**

| | | |
|---|---|---|
| Clutch ... ... | 8-in. Borg and Beck |
| Top gear (s/m) ... ... ... | 5.125 |
| 3rd gear (s/m) ... ... ... | 7.585 |
| 2nd gear (s/m) ... ... ... | 11.736 |
| 1st gear ... ... ... ... | 20.372 |
| Propeller shaft Divided Hardy Spicer, open |
| Final drive... ... ... Hypoid bevel |
| Top gear m.p.h. at 1,000 r.p.m. | 15.4 |
| Top gear m.p.h. at 1,000 ft./min. piston |
| speed ... ... ... ... | 23.3 |

**Chassis**

| | | |
|---|---|---|
| Brakes ...Girling hydraulic (2LS on front) |
| Brake drum diameter ... ... | 10 in. |
| Friction lining area ... ... | 131 sq. in. |
| Suspension: Front ... ... Torsion bar |
| Rear... ... Semi-elliptic |
| Shock absorbers: Front and rear |
| Telescopic hydraulic |
| Tyres ... ... ... ... | 5.75-16 |

**Steering**

| | | |
|---|---|---|
| Steering gear ... ... Rack and pinion |
| Turning circle: Left ... ... | 30 ft. |
| Right ... ... | 30 ft. |
| Turns of steering wheel, lock to lock ... | 2⅞ |

**Performance factors** (at laden weight as tested):
| | |
|---|---|
| Piston area, sq. in. per ton ... | 15.7 |
| Brake lining area, sq. in. per ton ... | 88.8 |
| Specific displacement, litres per ton mile 2,000 |

Fully described in *The Motor*, October 14, 1953, and October 15, 1952.

# Coachwork and Equipment

Bumper height with car unladen:
Front (max.) 20 in., (min.) 12 in.
Rear (max.) 23¼ in., (min.) 11¾ in.

| | | |
|---|---|---|
| Starting handle ... ... ... | Yes |
| Battery mounting ... ... ... | On scuttle |
| Jack ... ... ... ... | Bevelift |
| Jacking points ... ... ... | Four |
| (below bumper over-riders) |

Standard tool kit: Pump, grease gun, 3 double-ended set spanners, 3 double-ended box spanners, tommy bar, brake bleeding tube, adjustable spanner, hammer, screwdriver, 2 tyre levers, pliers, type valve spanner, distributor screwdriver, and gauge.

Exterior lights: Two headlamps (double dipping), two built-in fog lamps, two side lamps, two combined tail, number plate, reversing and stop lamps.

| | |
|---|---|
| Direction indicators | Semaphore type, self-cancelling |
| Windscreen wipers ... | Electric, two blades |
| Sun vizors ... ... | Two, flush fitting |

Instruments: Speedometer (with total trip mileage), clock, ammeter, water thermometer, fuel gauge and pressure gauge.

| | |
|---|---|
| Warning lights ... | Ignition, headlamp main beam, heater fan |

Locks:
| | |
|---|---|
| With ignition key | Driver's door and boot |
| With other keys ... ... | None |
| Glove lockers ... ... ... | None |
| Map pockets ... ... | In front doors |
| Parcel shelves ... ... | Below facia and behind rear squab |
| Ashtrays ... ... ... | Four (two in facia and two in rear doors) |
| Cigar lighters ... ... ... | None |
| Interior lights ... | Two (above rear doors) |

Interior heater: Re-circulating type with screen demisting, fitted as standard in territories where required.

| | |
|---|---|
| Car radio ... ... ... | Optional extra |

Extras available: Rev. counter, ventilating air scoops to front windows, badge bar, H.M.V. radio.

| | |
|---|---|
| Upholstery material ... ... | Leather |
| Floor covering ... ... ... | Carpet |

Exterior colours standardized: Black, maroon, green, blue, grey and ivory.

| | |
|---|---|
| Alternative body styles ... ... | None |

# PROFILE: 1952 1½-LITRE

## A CAR OF CHARACTER WITH A KNACK OF INSPIRING AFFECTION

I SUPPOSE I know MYL 596 better than any car I have owned. Of the 60,000 miles now showing on the mileometer, the owner must have been at the wheel for 59,000; he will be content to stay there for a long time still if this product of Riley Motors, of Abingdon in Berkshire, will let him, for it is a happy association. A car is not readily relinquished that has covered, amongst many lesser events, Holland's Tulip Rally, and chased two Tours de France between the Mediterranean and the Channel. Such runs hold memories. And an eye for the shapely does not willingly contemplate the substitution of a contemporary convexity for the concavity of yesteryear. The Riley, like Cassius, has a lean and hungry look; today's cars have been over-eating suet pudding.

When engine V118206E is ultimately stripped down, that will be the time to talk about it; for the present it suffices to recall its four cylinders and their overhead valves operating, with the aid of twin high camshafts and short push-rods, in hemispherical combustion chambers. The bore is 69mm and the stroke a long one at 100mm. With the aid of $\pi r^2 \times S \times N \div 1,000$, the resultant capacity of 1,496 c.c. is discovered (or you can look it up in the handbook). And to comply with the unwritten mathematical laws, let me remind you that r = half the bore in millimetres, S = the stroke (mm), and N the number of cylinders.

In these high-octane days, the compression ratio of 6.8 to 1 is nothing out of the ordinary. Abingdon's M.G. Magnette, another 1½-litre, boasts 7.15 to 1. So with the relatively low figure, the Riley revels in the premium spirits, not producing a pink under any sensible circumstances; and the affectionate driver will see to it that the circumstances of his driving remain sensible. It is an engine to sing with the poets: a little noisily, perhaps, but with a melodious noise, in which the ear picks out the musical instruments; valve gear, timing chain, exhaust, carburettor intake, and nowadays a descant of water pump bearing, periodically silenced by a renewed injection of one of the many **Doug** Holt preparations for the aged. And a starter of great willingness, even if mollycoddled by the owner with rugs and lamps. On two occasions only has the Riley failed to start; each time the cork washer of the petrol pump (AC mechanical on the 1½, S.U. electric on the 2½) had perished so that the cap fitted loosely and permitted air to enter, seemingly a common fault.

The rarely used choke may be pushed in immediately, and the hand throttle is set to about 1,200 r.p.m. while garage doors are closed and the rug removed and folded, by which time the engine has picked up to about 1,700 r.p.m. In about a quarter of a mile the thermometer needle leaves the stop at 90 deg F and about four miles later it is safely on 170; the oil pressure gauge is as likely as not to be registering 100 lb per sq in if the morning is cold, and it

*" All black except for the chromium and the wine-red wheels "*

# RILEY

## By MICHAEL BROWN

is many miles farther before it is down to the normal 50 to 60 of the 1½-litre concerned. The r.p.m. figure will not have exceeded 2,500 unless the owner is in a hurry.

Enough of that wonderful engine, which shall receive its full tribute in due course. The profile is of the car as an entity—a slim, ascetic outline to the eye, a sensitive personality to the hands that control it. Who styled the 1952 Riley? Let him be brought forward to receive a metaphorical laurel wreath, for he managed to retain the appearance of Rileys down through the ages in a line of such eternal grace that the eye mourns the incidental departures of the latest models. They are confined mostly to the wings at the moment, but the trend is obvious; asceticism is disappearing in the bulges that suggest the flesh and the devil. *Sic transit. . . .*

Mind you, I have been known to execrate the running-boards that help the older lines so much. No one but a dwarf could use them to enter the carriage; topping six feet, I should have to insert myself in a hairpin bend or suffer a blow from the roof at waist level. Also, my clumsy shoes (size ten) have a habit of knocking paint off the running-board as I leave the car. But what man who has ever held a palette in his left hand is prepared to sacrifice beauty to utility? Not this one, anyway. It is this elongated line that results in a luggage locker, of vast floor area but limited height, under which is the spare wheel. To get at the latter is a joke, to stow kit in the former a work of art; but again, I would not change the line for the sake of an extra pair of pyjamas.

### Hard-top ?

The Riley is one of the earliest "hard-top convertibles." That is to say, it is a saloon with a fabric-type roof, and if the fabric is maintained with some of the gloss of a fireman's high boots the effect is very smart indeed. My car is all black except for the chromium and the wine-red wheels, and although the finish seemed poor in 1952 it has stood up to the intervening years exceedingly well and looks to the casual glance as good as ever. Black, say my critics, is inverted snobbery on my part; or snobbery. Snobbery if it is intended to recall the gloss of the earl's coach of the last century, inverted if I feel that anything else might rob my own personality of colour. I leave that one to Freudians, merely insisting that my next car shall be black. The upholstery—good leather—is wine-red, and the wheel discs were matched up to it because the black refused to stay on ill-suited surfaces. So did one coat of wine-red, but after that the coachbuilder gritted his teeth and said "or else."

The roof lining is fawn, and there are roof lights at each side. In the course of two and a half years, the white plastic of the lamp shades has warped so that they drop out of the slots; this is the kind of failing that only prolonged ownership will reveal, and stimulates my hatred of plastics in many of the contexts in which they are used. I remember discovering that my old friend Donald Osmond, *The Autocar*'s head photographer, shared that dislike. We sat down to dinner in a Continental hotel. The bright red chequered tablecloths were covered with an insipid plastic, through

*" A slim, ascetic outline to the eye . . ."*

which the colour was muted, however clean the cloth was kept. Donald made an impassioned speech against all that was synthetic in life, and after that we enjoyed our meal the more.

Seats are separate in the front of the 1½-litre, with the single rear seat divided by a wide arm rest. There are arm rests which fold into the front doors, the one on the driver's side having only nuisance value. He is compensated by a yellow curtain ring just above the door, which more modern motorists will not have encountered, for it operates a rear blind, a splendid though anachronistic fitting. Glare from the rear is eliminated at a single pull, and the effect of walling the rear eye is salutary in reminding the unmannerly that it is gentlemanly to dip at close quarters in the rear. The quarters of the car itself cause blind areas, as they usually do on four-light saloons, but I have schooled myself to keep them always in mind. They are, in any case, not half so dangerous as is sometimes maintained, and often as I

*" It is a V-screen and the driver's view out front is satisfying in the extreme "*

listen to drivers inveighing against blind areas I think of the old French proverb, *qui s'excuse, s'accuse.*

No one would say that a low-built saloon like the 1½ was the easiest car in the world to enter or leave, particularly as the footwells are deep, the prop-shaft tunnel a Massif Central. The owner's view here is that a car is a vehicle, something for transporting people from one place to another with maximum efficiency. That need must have precedence over passenger ease of exit and entry, and the low centre of gravity of the Riley is a big factor in its efficiency in motion. Once settled in such an interior, there is a cosiness, a compactness, that makes for good humour, assisted by the hardwood and handsome styling of the surroundings. You do not get the same feeling in a flat floored dance hall of a car with juke box facia and tartan seat covers. I like to see my passengers nodding, and my only regret is that the very poor heater of the 1952 Riley means that they must be tucked in with rugs on a cold night.

## No Rattles

Bodywork troubles have been almost non-existent. There isn't a rattle on the car; there never has been. An entry on the car's work card reminds me that at 34,200 miles there was door lock trouble, and in certain conditions of rainfall there is a little leakage at the non-opening screen, on the passenger's side. It is a V-screen and the driver's view out front is satisfying in the extreme. The tapering bonnet reaches ahead, tautly rising and falling as the dampers fight the springs. Both wings are visible, and at night there is a ruby glow on each side from the separate side lamps. It isn't the best outlook in a world of fog, the eye meeting the left-hand kerb too far ahead and just where the central strip of the V-screen adds confusion. Still, I get along as well as most in fog, aided by yellow dipped head lamps unless it is really thick, when I use the left-side Butler fog lamp, turned

well to the left and with its original bulb replaced by the lowest powered one I could get short of a festoon type. The other fog lamp I have never used, and have often reproached myself for laziness in not taking it off and taping up the lead; why cart unnecessary weight round?

Driving the 1½-litre Riley is a pleasure that has grown with the miles, and I always feel an absurd reluctance to leaving the driving seat for that of another car. A Riley owner sits well up to the job, head high, but with legs fully stretched out to reach substantial clutch and brake pedals, and an organ-pedal accelerator. He will not find much room for his left foot off the clutch, and he will never grow to love the nasty little hand brake handle under the facia, saving all his affection for the short central gear lever, which he can thrust here and there to the accompaniment of a swinging needle on the rev counter and the consignment of automatic transmissions to the other side of the Atlantic. This is one of the few skills left in car handling and the 1½ owner can legitimately indulge it, for the small engine hauls a considerable weight of car about (2,716 lb) and should be helped to do so.

Item two for driver affection is the large sprung steering wheel. The high gearing permits the car to be swung round all but the sharpest bends without shifting the hands on the rim—a fine, swinging gesture, perhaps liable to be construed as showing-off, but making, all the same, for a smooth negotiation of bends, especially as the castor action of the 1½ is fairly strong. That row of switches about which I complained in "Interim Assessment" a couple of years ago remains a matter of counting, in the dark, to the east or west of the Greenwich meridian of the ignition key, and the hand dipper still displeases this driver, whose hand is rarely at the requisite spot on the wheel rim (about two o'clock). My wheel hold remains twenty to four and, in any case, roads have bends. The dip-switch is located on the facia near the base of the screen pillar, an unusual spot.

The cornering ability of the 1½ is outstanding. The car runs on Michelin X tyres, the first set of Xs having been replaced at 27,000 miles. This was considerably less mileage than expected, though 7,000 up on the previous tyre mileage and thus more than covering the extra cost. There were three other factors involved; one was the increased cornering ability (which was made full use of), the second the replacement of two left-hand front wheel bearings during the life of the tyres. Their failure to stay put on the stub axle had resulted in flats starting on the tyres before the loose wheel was discovered. Thirdly, the front spring dampers needed renewal by the time the tyres were discarded. Anyway, the new X tyres, of the correct size where the previous ones were oversize, give the car the same limpet hold. They run at 23lb per sq in front, 27 rear, and if the car speed is high enough, and the road wet enough, for adhesion to be lost, it goes into a four-wheel drift with the front seats occupied. With weight at the rear there is a rear wheel slide. Guiltily enjoying himself with such tactics, the driver assuages his conscience by being positively demure on the straight, rarely taking the car above 70 m.p.h. or the engine above 4,500 r.p.m. It is, after all, getting on in years. Even so, it is surprising how many pedestrians will glower after it these days; one is reminded of Goebbels' tactics. Never mind whether it is a lie or not; hammer away long enough and the mob believes you. Anyone who drives fast is dangerous. Yet those same pedestrians, given a lift in the Riley, would delight in the speed and urge one to go faster.

## Braking

Brakes are excellent. Only once, in wet weather, were they found to be less efficient than those of a rival. We were following a Javelin quite fast. Ahead on the right of the road there had been an accident. The Javelin's stop light went on, so did mine. Then a rubberneck from the opposite direction stopped his car opposite the accident and blocked the road. The Javelin, a light car, took full braking without sliding, but the heavier Riley began to snake, and for some moments it was doubtful if the 1½-litre would succeed in not shunting the Jowett. It did, however, and we commiserated by grimace at the foolishness of some motorists.

A paragon, says a colleague, has a slightly sarcastic ring about it. But for that I might have used the word to describe the Riley from the purely driving angle. One drawback does enter into its driving, however, so perhaps the term is unjustified. The transmission vibration in this model is considerable at certain engine revs (the 1952 model had the torque tube, since dropped). I have heard many "explanations" of this vibration, but incline to believe that it is a crankshaft period that has to be felt somewhere, and, logically enough, comes out and down the prop-shaft. On MYL 596 it has led to clutch trouble, the cushioning springs having chewed outwards towards the linings. One new plate was fitted at 25,230 miles. Curiously enough, the only failure on the road was a clutch failure, the linkage having fractured at 40,000 miles; close inspection revealed an old crack near a drilling. Other failures have been of the speedometer drive (four of 'em), rear spring dampers, renewed at 40,000 miles, battery (44,900) and front spring dampers (56,933 miles). The brakes have been relined twice. The car is well looked after by service staff who, under the cynical wisecracks which they make about MYL 596 and its owner, have hearts of gold that are beating with excitement at the thought of getting 100,000 miles out of the car before the oil consumption rises. At the moment it is negligible, and the petrol consumption (Esso Extra) remains 30 m.p.g.

Dear me, how affection for a car makes one run on. I had meant to say so much more about the 1½, and to dwell on so many of its other virtues. Is the profile revealed? I hope so. To me it is a sensitive one, and aristocratic. This is a quality product by virtue of its engineering and design. At £750 list price it was first-class value; the purchase tax added £418 3s 4d, so that the resultant figure was under £1,200. For anything that makes you feel good every time you drive it, that pleases the eye, excites the admiration of others, and restores your faith in the ingenuity of man for peaceful ends, it was cheap enough.

*" The quarters of the car itself cause blind areas, as they usually do on four-light saloons "*

*Cylinder head as lifted off. All photographs in this article are unretouched*

# RMA 10558 AFTER 77,600 MILES

*Report on a 1½-litre Riley Engine After the First Removal of the Cylinder Head : A Test of Multigrade Oil*

AT 77,600 miles my Riley 1½-litre lost the compression in one cylinder and the moment had come to remove the cylinder head for the first time. Let me re-emphasize that—*for the first time*. This engine had lost nothing detectable in the way of performance, nor had it shown any sign of pinking, and as the service manager and I were both agreed on a policy of leave well alone, we waited for trouble instead of going out to meet it. You will recall, also, that this car has, for the whole of its life, had Q5500 oil in the sump. This is a multigrade oil made by Alexander Duckham and Co., Ltd., and the measurements of wear can be related to use of the oil as far as is legitimate. How far that is I do not pretend to judge, but I would emphasize one negative certainty: the use of this oil obviously involved the engine in not the slightest risk whatsoever.

The car has been driven fast but, I trust, intelligently. It is not often used for taxi work, most of its journeys being of over twenty miles. Rugs and, in winter, a miner's lamp, keep the engine just perceptibly warm overnight and the hand throttle is used to warm up for at least a minute or two. The choke has been necessary only for winter starts, and even then it can go in almost the moment the engine fires. The fuel is invariably Esso Extra in this country, mostly Azur Super abroad, for the Riley has seen quite a lot of France. It has climbed high passes and undergone full summer heat in Provence. The engine has stopped

*Cylinder block immediately after head had been removed*

# HARD DEPOSITS

*Below : Carbon deposit on piston crown: maximum thickness was forty thousandths and the carbon was flaky*

*Above : Exhaust valves, showing the burn that caused the dismantlement.*
*Below : Inlet valves, lightly coated and with limited build-up on the back of the heads*

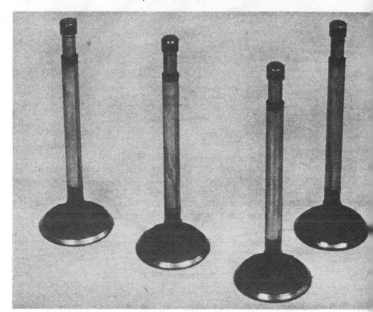

on the road twice, and on both occasions the nut securing the cap of the mechanical petrol pump needed tightening.

The record is, I submit, enviable, and I had every confidence that the figures for wear would back it up; oil consumption—always slight, though always good for a visible wisp of blue at the gear change—had remained constant and so low that it was regarded as negligible. What about carbon? What about additive action? What about detergency? The cylinder head came off without difficulty and some of the answers to these questions were evident.

Loss of compression was caused by a burned-out exhaust valve in No. 1 cylinder; No. 3 had five small burned flats and the other two were somewhat pitted. Elsewhere there was nothing to suggest that this was the first removal of a cylinder head after nearly eighty thousand miles.

First the deposits: the exhaust valves were fairly heavily coated on the head and neck with the usual white to fawn deposit. Inlet valves were lightly coated on the heads with a soft carbon film and there was a build-up of flaky carbon on the necks to a maximum depth of about one sixteenth of an inch, not considered sufficient to interfere with the engine's breathing.

Pistons had a crust of black on the crowns, ranging from a mere film in places to a maximum of about 0.040in thick. On the skirt relief areas and in the ring grooves was a light soft film, but there was no lacquer or staining on other skirt areas.

The combustion chambers had a carbon layer with a general thickness varying from 0.010in to 0.030in; the peak thicknesses were about 0.050in. Valve ports were coated by a very light, dry carbon not more than 0.010 to 0.020in thick and easily removed by a solvent and rag. So much for carbon deposits, and it was generally agreed that there was insufficient accumulation anywhere to justify dismantling purely for decarbonization.

Oil deposits were equally slight. The rocker gear and covers, crankshaft and sump carried a very thin, moist, black film which could be cleaned right down to the metal by the finger; there were no signs of adherent sludge.

The wear figures proved, as hoped, to be very good. First, the bores: maximum wear was 0.005in on Nos. 1 and 2, 0.006in on Nos. 3 and 4. Working surfaces were perfect

and there was no staining. Similarly the pistons were free from scuffing, scoring or staining, and the wear here was 0.0095in on No. 1 and 0.010in on the other three.

All the piston rings were free, bright and clear of scuffing or scoring. The oil control rings carried a moderate film of soft deposit but were quite free from clogging. Maximum average wear was suffered by the top ring of No. 3 piston, and was calculated as follows:

| | | | | |
|---|---|---|---|---|
| Measured gap | .. | .. | .. | 0.038in |
| Nominal gap | .. | .. | .. | 0.010in |
| | | | | 0.028in |

Divide by 3 to obtain total diametral wear:

3)0.028

0.009in

Subtract mean bore wear:

0.009in
0.005in

0.004in

Piston ring wear therefore equals 0.004in on diameter, or 0.002in on radius. The ring gaps were measured with each ring in a position approximately corresponding to top

# SOFT DEPOSITS
# AFTER 77,600 MILES

*Valve gear : The third pushrod has been cleaned, as has the rocker shaft between the pedestal brackets.   The left-hand valve cover has been wiped also.   Cleaning was a double rub with a rag*

*Below : Sump detail, showing how the base was easily cleaned down to the bare metal*

dead centre; that is at the point of maximum bore wear for the compression rings.

Valve stems and guides maintained the good record, and wear figures are worth quoting in full along with the comment of the technicians in their report: "The figures," they say, "speak highly for the materials and workmanship as well as the lubricant.  It should be noted that no valve stem oil seals are used and the good fit of stem and guide is relied upon to control the supply of lubricant."  Working surfaces were very good indeed and free from scoring or scuffing.

| INLET VALVES | | | | | | |
|---|---|---|---|---|---|---|
| | | Nominal | 1 | 2 | 3 | 4 |
| Guide .. .. | end | 0.3125±¼ | 0.3130 | 0.3130 | 0.3135 | 0.3135 |
| | mid | " | 0.3130 | 0.3128 | 0.3130 | 0.3130 |
| Stem .. .. | end | 0.3125 | 0.3115 | 0.3118 | 0.3118 | 0.3115 |
| | mid | " | .0.3118 | 0.3118 | 0.3118 | 0.3115 |
| Clearance .. .. | end } | 0.001 to | 0.0015 | 0.0012 | 0.0017 | 0.0020 |
| | mid } | 0.0015 | 0.0012 | 0.0010 | 0.0012 | 0.0015 |

| EXHAUST VALVES | | | | | | |
|---|---|---|---|---|---|---|
| | | Nominal | 1 | 2 | 3 | 4 |
| Guide .. .. | end | 0.3125±¼ | 0.3135 | 0.3135 | 0.3130 | 0.3130 |
| | mid | " | 0.3130 | 0.3135 | 0.3130 | 0.3132 |
| Stem .. .. | end | 0.3125 | 0.3125 | 0.3118 | 0.3115 | 0.3118 |
| | mid | " | 0.3120 | 0.3120 | 0.3118 | 0.3118 |
| Clearance .. .. | end } | 0.001 to | 0.0010 | 0.0017 | 0.0015 | 0.0012 |
| | mid } | 0.0015 | 0.0010 | 0.0015 | 0.0012 | 0.0014 |

Finally the bottom end bearings.  Here the wear was consistent on all four and was 0.0005in on the thrust side

*Oil control rings—free of clogging but carrying soft deposit*

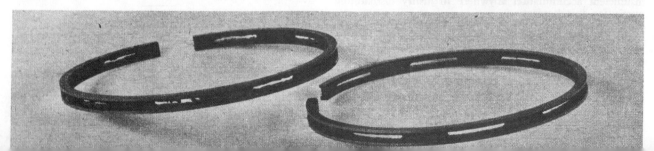

*Thrust faces of the pistons: maximum wear was ten thousandths*

*Left : Big end bearing shells and cleaned con-rod*

(none elsewhere). Journals were free from scoring and the surfaces of the white metal shells was very good for the mileage. No. 4 had a tiny portion broken out, Nos. 1 and 2 had one or two small surface cracks, while No. 3 had a small suspected crack. There was no sign of sludge build-up in the oilways.

The final comment of the examiners pays tribute to the materials and workmanship used in this engine and points out that the lubricant was able to develop its full contribution to a good record. They do not attempt to assess the size of that contribution, but I think it can be agreed that it was no small one. RMA 10558 is now reassembled with new exhaust valves and new piston rings of standard size. Needless to say, the sump still contains the emerald green Q5500 and there should be little difficulty in covering 100,000 miles before a rebore is necessary. However, that is likely to be in other hands than mine.

I am indebted to Mr. J. R. Fenwick and Mr. A. D. Stone, of Alexander Duckham and Co., Ltd., for their examination and report on the engine, from which the material in this article is extracted.

MICHAEL BROWN.

*Below : Non-thrust piston faces. The pistons have since been reassembled with new standard sized rings*

 **Riley** *A joy to own —
a dream to drive*

With its long, low lines and elegant new styling, the Riley 1½ litre Saloon proclaims its good breeding and your own good taste wherever it goes. Its special appeal is to the discriminating motorist who expects 'all round' excellence in a car. The Riley has one of the most successful engines ever designed, matched by incomparable steering, superb road-holding, suspension and braking. See and test the Riley 1½ litre for yourself.

For the sheer pleasure of driving there's nothing quite like a Riley—it's a car of rare character.

*The New Riley 'Pathfinder'.*
*Ask your Riley dealer for full information about the brilliant new Riley 'Pathfinder'.*

**Yes indeed!**
### RILEY FOR MAGNIFICENT MOTORING

**RILEY MOTORS LIMITED,** *Sales Division,* **COWLEY, OXFORD**

*London Showrooms:* RILEY CARS, 55-56 PALL MALL, S.W.1   *Overseas Business:* Nuffield Exports Ltd., Oxford and 41 Piccadilly, London, W.1

The chromium was in excellent condition, with the exception of the door handles, and the black and green finish was practically up to the standard of a new car. The double-dipping head lights were excellent

# Used Cars on the Road–102

## 1953 RILEY 1½-LITRE

| | | | |
|---|---|---|---|
| Basic price new | £850 | 0s | 0d |
| Total price new | £1,205 | 5s | 10d |
| Price secondhand | £695 | 0s | 0d |

| Acceleration from rest through gears: | |
|---|---|
| to 30 m.p.h. | 7.4 sec |
| to 50 m.p.h. | 18.8 sec |
| to 60 m.p.h. | 30.6 sec |
| 20 to 40 m.p.h. (top gear) | 11.3 sec |
| 30 to 50 m.p.h. (top gear) | 13.7 sec |

| | |
|---|---|
| Petrol consumption* | 22-30 m.p.g. |
| Oil consumption | negligible |
| Speedometer reading | 31,161 |
| Date first registered | December, 1953 |

*The need for petrol economy led to a necessary reduction in the mileage usually covered on these tests, and the fuel consumption calculation is based on the original test of the model in *The Autocar*, and checks over short distances.

APART from its main purpose of providing a guide to cars actually offered for sale on the used car market, this series gives a welcome opportunity to recall the qualities of the cars which were really good in their day, but have since ceased production; few deserve a "second look" better than the well-known Riley 1½-litre. This example was provided for test by Clarke and Simpson, Ltd., 49, Sloane Square, London, S.W.1, and it was soon obvious that its one owner must have looked after it with fastidious care.

The car's four-cylinder engine has push rods on both sides operating inclined overhead valves in hemispherical combustion chambers, and the unit is efficient and willing; but it has to work hard in this 26cwt car. Quiet at tick-over, and when running on small throttle openings, it became clearly audible—though not obtrusively so—when accelerating and at high revs. The driver was reminded of the low power-to-weight ratio, and in normal use acceleration was somewhat leisurely. It was understood that no repair work had been carried out on the engine, yet it appeared remarkably sound, and showed few indications of the mileage which had been covered. Starting was immediate at all times, and the choke was needed only once throughout the test, after a night of severe frost.

For a three-year-old in this class, the car's mechanical condition was outstanding. The back axle was silent, and there was very little free rotation in the propeller shaft. The four-speed gear box was also silent, and the synchromesh was still efficient; the pleasant, positive change encouraged use of it. Clutch action was smooth and viceless. The brakes were progressive and powerful, in response to light pedal pressures, but were approaching the time for adjustment. The umbrella-type handbrake was very effective.

Lost movement in the rack-and-pinion steering was virtually negligible, yet few road shocks were transmitted to the steering wheel. The suspension, although on the hard side, was well damped, and the car gave a splendid ride. There was, it is true, a certain amount of firm but limited vertical motion on bad surfaces, but this was minimized by the relatively long wheelbase and the comfort of the seats. Particularly commendable was the silent action of the torsion bar and wishbone front suspension, even when the wheels were aimed into one or two atrocious potholes.

An efficient and well-made recirculatory heater, a dipping mirror, and Tudor's useful windscreen washer, were among the accessories fitted to the car. The standard equipment included twin built-in fog lamps, manual ignition control, hand throttle, two interior lights, automatic reversing light, and a comprehensive and neat array of instruments which included a trip mileometer, but lacked a rev. counter.

All the tyres were Dunlops, those on the front wheels being tubeless, about a third worn; on the rear wheels were practically new remoulds and the spare was an original cover, about three-quarters worn. The toolkit was in good condition and appeared complete.

Switches, lights, instruments and controls were all in good working order, and the car was very well prepared for sale.

In spite of a slightly limited performance and a fairly low final drive ratio, the car was most enjoyable to drive. Very good forward visibility over the straight bonnet, and first-class stability and cornering, in addition to the good brakes and steering already mentioned, made swift, safe progress possible. It would cruise happily with the unusually accurate speedometer indicating 65 m.p.h., and should be capable of a maximum speed in the vicinity of 75 m.p.h. Good seating and sensible planning of the controls added to the pleasure of driving the car.

This car is a good example of a case in which the obsolescence

of a model, and its date of manufacture, have led to a price depreciation from the original cost when new, completely out of proportion to its actual deterioration. This is also owed in part to the present petrol troubles, which have led to a considerable price reduction from the amount which was being asked for it a month or two before.

Against this have to be considered three years' use and a mileage of over 30,000; but in *The Autocar's* experience of the model the existing speedometer reading should be doubled at least before any major overhaul work should become necessary.

This Riley will be remembered among the several very desirable used cars which have been tried by *The Autocar* this year, and it was returned to the owners with some regret.

Headlinings and wood and leather trimmings were all in remarkably good condition, and the floor carpets showed little sign of wear. The leather seats, however, had not lasted as well as the rest of the car, although some well-worn green seat covers (removed for this photograph) were fitted front and rear. The steering column was adjustable

On this page is abbreviated a Test Report on a car conducted by the Automobile Association for one of its members. We submitted the facts to a qualified service engineer well acquainted with the particular model concerned and in the text below he shows the cost of making the car fully reliable if (a) the work is undertaken by a garage or (b) done by a competent private owner. Reference is made in the Test Report only to assemblies and components found to be in an unsatisfactory condition.

# No. I—RILEY I½-litre Saloon

FIRST REGISTERED—1947
RECORDED MILEAGE—37,094
PRESENT VALUE—about £380

IN view of the Riley reputation for withstanding hard driving over many thousands of miles without wilting, some readers may be surprised at the amount of attention required by this particular specimen after only 37,094 miles. It should be stressed, however, that the figure quoted was taken from the speedometer and the evidence would seem clearly to indicate that the car has covered at least double the indicated figure and has therefore some 80,000 miles behind it.

If the car were to be taken into the service station of a Riley agent and the service manager instructed to carry out the work required to make it a roadworthy and reliable machine capable of passing the "Hendon" test and not likely to fail by the roadside, then the total cost would probably be in the neighbourhood of £91 if the paintwork was touched in, and £116 if the car was resprayed.

Work on the engine would cost about £12. For this sum the engine would be decarbonized, the valves ground in, the sparking plugs cleaned and adjusted and the distributor points attended to, after which the car would be road-tested to ensure that all was well.

Attention to the front suspension, steering and front hubs would account for £25 of the total, for both nearside and offside front suspension units would have to be removed and new rubber bushes fitted where necessary. The front hubs would require dismantling in order that new bearings and seals could be fitted if required, and the inner and outer track rod ends examined for undue wear and the steering rack adjusted. The setting of the torsion bars might also require adjustment.

The rear-spring shackles need their rubber bushes replacing, which would cost £2. The brakes, obviously, require overhauling, and all the brake drums would, therefore, have to be removed, the shoes replaced by relined brake

## TEST REPORT

### COACHWORK

**Condition of paint**—Faded and flaking off in parts due to the presence of rust beneath the surface.

**General comment on bodywork**—The roof fabric shows signs of deterioration and the front number plate is damaged.

### ENGINE

**Functioning of valve and timing mechanism**—Acceptable.

**State of Compressions (where practicable)**—Almost nil when engine is hot.

**Signs of knocking (if any)**—None during the road test.

**Are there any external defects?**—The flywheel undershield and two of the clutch bell housing bolts are missing—no other defects visible but engine is very dirty.

**Does oil pressure indicator function?**—Yes.

**Any general comment?**—The amount of general wear does not appear to be unreasonable. There are indications that the loss of compression is due to sticking and/or burnt valves.

### ELECTRICAL EQUIPMENT

**Condition of ignition system**—The manual advance and retard control is immovable, the distributor requires servicing.

**Condition of lamps and wiring**—Appear to be serviceable but interior lamp cover is missing and the glasses of one side lamp and one number plate lamp are damaged.

**Does lighting installation function?**—Not efficiently—the reversing light and offside headlight do not function and the nearside headlight is extinguished by operation of the dipping switch.

### CARBURETTER AND FUEL SYSTEM

**Make and condition of carburetter**—S.U. The piston damper oil requires replenishing.

### BACK AXLE

**Is there any undue leakage of oil?**—Indications of leakage from the nearside hub into the brake drum.

### FRAME AND SUSPENSION

**Condition of springs**—Very dirty—no defects visible. The rear shackle bushes appear to be worn.

**Condition of frame**—Sound so far as can be seen—frame is coated with weather-proofing compound. The radiator undershield is loose and the front jack socket rubbers are missing.

### FORECARRIAGE

**Is there any undue rock or play in hub bearings?**—Yes, in the offside.

**Is there any undue wear in the front suspension units?**—Yes.

### STEERING GEAR

**Was steering satisfactory on road test?**—No—unduly heavy.

### BRAKES

**Functioning of brakes (foot)**—Poor.

**Functioning of brakes (hand)**—Not fully efficient.

**Condition of external actuating mechanism**—The hydraulic flexible connections to master cylinder and front brakes show signs of appreciable deterioration, the fluid reservoir is loose and the clevices, etc. are devoid of lubricant. The linings should be checked.

### RUNNING OF CAR

**General pulling and acceleration**—Below standard.

**Quietness of running**—Acceptable except for a rattle emanating from the offside front door.

### TYRES

| | | | | |
|---|---|---|---|---|
| N/S front tread | .. | .. | .. | 40% wear |
| O/S front tread | .. | .. | .. | 45% wear |
| N/S rear tread | .. | .. | .. | 100% wear |
| O/S rear tread | .. | .. | .. | 80% wear |
| Spare tread | .. | .. | .. | 100% wear |

## Repairs Recommended by A.A. Engineer

Renovate the paintwork as desired. Repair the front number plate. Fit new tyres to the nearside rear and spare wheels. Restore the engine compression and performance to standard. Fit a flywheel undershield and bolts where required in the clutch bell housing. Attend to the electrical equipment as indicated. Replenish the carburetter piston damper oil. Overhaul the rear spring shackles. Tighten the radiator undershield. Fit rubbers to front jack sockets. Eliminate oil leakage from nearside rear hub. Eliminate play in offside front hub bearings. Overhaul the front suspension assemblies and ensure that vehicle steers satisfactorily. Restore the braking efficiency to standard. Carry out complete lubrication service. Eliminate rattle from offside front door.

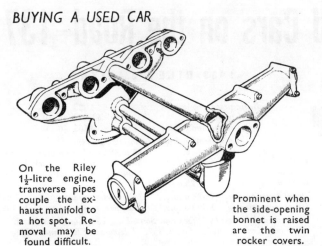

On the Riley 1½-litre engine, transverse pipes couple the exhaust manifold to a hot spot. Removal may be found difficult.

Prominent when the side-opening bonnet is raised are the twin rocker covers.

shoes, the wheel cylinders dismantled and cleaned and the brake hoses replaced. Reassembly, bleeding, balancing and the required adjustment would bring the charge for this vital piece of restoration to about £18.

Servicing the electrical system and replacing such missing or damaged items as the interior lamp cover and the glasses of one side lamp and one number-plate lamp would cost about £5.

Attention to the numerous small items such as the rattle in the offside front door, the missing flywheel undershield and the damaged front number plate, together with the replacement of the two badly worn tyres would cost some £24, the bulk of this figure, of course, being accounted for by the two new tyres.

If the new owner is content for the paintwork to be touched in where it has flaked off, then the job would cost about £5. A complete respray of the whole car would cost some £30, however.

Most of the work required on the car is well within the capabilities of an owner who, in the past, has been accustomed to carrying out his own decarbonizing and who possesses a set of ordinary hand tools. Such an owner will save himself a considerable sum of money, for he should be able to carry

out all the work for about £48 spent on new parts, including the two new tyres.

Before beginning operations, an instruction manual will prove to be a worthwhile investment, even should the car's instruction book still be available. The manufacturers publish an excellent workshop manual covering both the post-war 1½-litre and 2½-litre cars. Part number of the manual is AKD630 and it is available from the stores of official Riley distributors and dealers, and *not* from Abingdon, price 21s. Another useful book is " The Riley Maintenance Manual," by S. V. Haddleton, which deals with all Riley models from 1930 to 1956. It is published by G. T. Foulis and Co., Ltd., at 35s. and the sections dealing with the post-war 1½-litre car are based on the workshop manual.

Owners who have hitherto tackled the decarbonizing only of normal side-valve or pushrod-operated overhead valve engines need have no fear that the unusual Riley engine, with its two camshafts mounted high up on the cylinder block, will present any special difficulties. The only point at which trouble is likely to be encountered is in the removal of the hot spot elbow and two hot spot pipes which have to be extracted before the inlet manifold can be removed.

Owing to the formation of carbon, these items may prove somewhat stubborn, in which case it may be advisable to borrow or buy two special tools, namely, a hot spot elbow extractor (Part No. 18G336—£7 15s. 6d.) and a water tube extractor (Part No. 18G340—£1 2s. 2d.). Apart from these two items, the total cost of decarbonizing the engine and grinding in the valves will be about £4, allowing for the replacement of all the old exhaust valves.

By stripping down the front suspension himself, the owner will reduce the cost of overhauling it from £25 to £12, even though he fits new shock absorbers and hub bearings, and replaces all seals and bushes. He will, however, require two special tools, a front hub extractor (Part No. 18G358—£3 17s. 9d.) and a special spanner for the front hub bearing retaining ring (Part No. 18G357—£3 3s. 10d.).

Attending to the brakes himself will also reduce the cost considerably, from £18 to £9, including the cost of new hoses and relining the brake shoes.

Just how much of the work the new owner tackles himself will, of course, to a considerable extent be governed by his ability and the facilities he has available. People do overhaul their cars in the street outside their house, but this is not a practice to be recommended owing to the likelihood that considerable quantities of dirt and dust will be built into the car when its components are being reassembled.

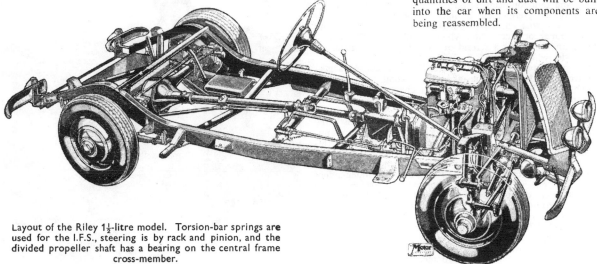

Layout of the Riley 1½-litre model. Torsion-bar springs are used for the I.F.S., steering is by rack and pinion, and the divided propeller shaft has a bearing on the central frame cross-member.

## 1953 RILEY 2½-LITRE

| | | |
|---|---|---|
| Basic price new | | £925 0 0 |
| Total price new | | £1,311 10 10 |
| Price secondhand | | £565 0 0 |

*Acceleration from rest through gears:*

| | | | |
|---|---|---|---|
| to 30 m.p.h. | 6.7 sec | 20 to 40 m.p.h. (top gear) | 11.4 sec |
| to 50 m.p.h. | 14.7 sec | 30 to 50 m.p.h. (top gear) | 11.5 sec |
| to 60 m.p.h. | 18.8 sec | Standing quarter mile | 22.4 sec |
| to 70 m.p.h. | 23.6 sec | | |

| | | | |
|---|---|---|---|
| Petrol consumption | 18-23 m.p.g. | Mileometer reading | 11,241 |
| Oil consumption | 1,500 m.p.g. | Date first registered | July 1953 |

*Provided for test by Offord and Sons, Ltd., 154, Gloucester Road, South Kensington, London, S.W.7. Telephone: FREmantle 3388*

*This Riley, as often happens with this make, has been very well preserved, and the condition of the interior and exterior is splendid. The low mileometer reading is no indication of the total distance run; Offord say this is believed to be in the region of 50,000 miles*

OF all cars made since the war, probably among the surest to buy from the used car market are Rileys. Not only do they last well, but it is quite general to find that their owners have looked after them, and this 2½-litre is the third Riley we have tested in just over two years which has been proved to be—with certain reservations—in outstandingly good condition.

Both inside and out, its appearance is much above the standard normally expected after nearly six years, and close inspection of the body revealed few blemishes and no signs of repaired accident damage. The car is finished in black which, at first glance, appears to be up to new car standards, and which on careful examination proved to be marred only by a few tiny chips or scratches on the wings and running boards. The chromium is scratched in some parts, but the general appearance is of unmarked chromium—particularly on the radiator grille—which has resisted rust attacks unusually well.

Green is used for the interior finish. The carpets show minimal wear, and the leather of the comfortable bucket front (and bench rear) seats is creased but sound and very clean. On the polished wooden facia and door trim the varnish has cracked somewhat, but the overall impression is of quality construction and careful preservation. Unusually clean and unspoilt cloth roof linings play their part in this.

This same attention which has obviously gone into the bodily condition of the Riley is reflected in its mechanical shape, but the pleasure of driving the car is spoilt to some degree by an unpleasant vibration—intermittent and rumbling—which is loudly audible when the engine is pulling. On the over-run it disappears, and the car is very quiet, which can scarcely be said of it when the vibration is occurring. Offord and Sons have been unable to trace the cause of the noise, and all that can be said is that some expensive dismantling probably would be necessary to trace it to its source and rectify it.

This fault is particularly unfortunate in view of the much above average condition of the rest of the car. Nevertheless, some minor attention is also needed to the engine. Starting from cold was not as good as it should be for a Riley, suggesting need for adjustment of the ignition or mixture, which was confirmed by hesitation when accelerating at low revs. The engine is also running far too cold; a piece of cardboard insinuated between the grille and radiator made a considerable improvement in the behaviour of the engine, but a higher temperature thermostat is needed as a permanent cure. As it is, the engine pulls well and provides a range of acceleration which is still lively by modern standards, and is within a second or two of the times recorded by the model when new.

Some clutch drag makes it a little difficult to engage a gear quietly from standstill, but the take-up is smooth, and there is no clutch spin. The stubby central gear change lever remains precise and extremely pleasant to use; some weakening in the synchromesh is the only indication of wear.

The Riley serves as a worthy reminder that few substantial advances in steering and suspension have been made by manufacturers in recent years. The rack-and-pinion steering on this car is unusually light, yet high-geared and almost entirely free from lost movement. The steering alone makes the car a delight to handle. Fairly firm suspension is fitted, using an independent torsion bar layout at the front and normal leaf springs at the rear. The front dampers have weakened noticeably, but the ride is still extremely good; it is comfortable, yet transmits a solid feel of the road to the driver.

An unusually effective hand brake is fitted, and the brakes themselves came as a mild surprise by being powerful and dependable in return for light pedal pressures. They give confidence for use of the high performance of which the car is capable. Its easy 70 m.p.h. cruising speed corresponds to just under 3,500 r.p.m.

A notable absence of rust may be noted under the Riley, all the important parts of the chassis being in good condition. The engine compartment is also commendably clean. A small exhaust leak has started from the silencer box, but this is a fault which is to be rectified by the vendors before sale.

Throughout the test a considerable charge was indicated on the ammeter, and this with the sluggish behaviour of the self-starter on cold mornings, implies that the battery is feeble and may need to be replaced.

The comprehensive array of instruments provided includes a clock (keeping good time), ammeter, fuel gauge, thermometer, oil pressure gauge, and speedometer (steady and reasonably accurate) with trip mileometer. The car has also a dipping rear mirror, two wing mirrors, a hopelessly inadequate heater, Trico screenwasher, cigarette lighter, and a Motorola radio of which the tone and general reproduction were outstandingly good. There are also two Lucas fog lamps giving a flat and a pencil beam, which are controlled together with a map-reading lamp from an auxiliary switch panel on the left of the facia.

Four practically new Michelin X tyres are on the wheels, and they suit the car perfectly. Cornering and directional stability are first class, and there is none of the lateral movement of the car on straight roads which is sometimes associated with Michelin tyres. The spare is a well-worn Goodyear. A comprehensive tool kit is still with the car.

This Riley 2½-litre is a good car which deserves to have another considerate owner to follow the four who have looked after it during its life so far. But his first job will be to trace and rectify the transmission vibration which, incidentally, has been noted to a lesser degree in other examples of this model.

*Impressive features of the Riley were the ways in which the doors still closed with a positive "clunk", and the window winders worked easily. The car gives the impression of being one on which the owner has kept pace with the rectification of any minor faults as they developed*

# 2 ½ RILEY DROPHEAD, 1950

S.C.W. Classics Salon

# RILEY 2½

ANY self-respecting vintage enthusiast might be excused for wondering what in tarnation a 1950 Riley 2½ litre drophead coupe is doing in SPORTS CAR WORLD'S Classic Salon. But take it easy. No classic need necessarily be old to qualify. A degree of exclusivity, of well-preserved rarity is enough. A Riley drophead is a very rare bird, in spite of its comparative youth. Good examples are hard to come by.

The extremes of Australia's climate combine with our impossible roads to make for rapid deterioration in traditional coach-built bodywork like the Riley's. Constant pampering is necessary if the car is to be maintained at any sort of pitch. Unfortunately few motorists in Australia have either the time or the inclination to devote themselves over 10 full years to that sort of pastime.

Rareness alone, you say, is not sufficient claim on a place in Salon. You might be arguing correctly, but who among us will contest that the Riley, no matter how pedestrian it might have grown today, had its share of classic forebears?

The 1950 2½ springs directly from the 1926 Riley Nine — most famous of all Percy's brainchildren. The revolutionary (circa 1926) twin high-camshaft engine was varied only in detail in the 2½ litre unit first introduced in 1946. Extra capacity was achieved by adopting the alarming dimensions of 80.0 x 12 mm to give a swept volume of 2443 cc.

Perhaps that justifies the presence of this lovely car in this month's Salon spot. Now let me outline to you the effort and conniving that went into locating it.

Several months (or was it years?) ago editor Doug Bain expressed his desire to feature just such a car. My job? Find one! I looked and I looked. Finally gave up hope of ever finding a really good example, undamaged and unmarked and unmodified. I even started watching for something a little less rare to photograph—a Squire maybe.

Then, one day, there it was—standing right outside my office in the heart of Sydneytown. It reposed in dignified yet rakish glory, early morning sunbeams

# LITRE DROPHEAD COUPE, 1950

dancing on its gleaming panels, while all around the mundane monsters of This Atom Era trundled past on their weary way to the junkyard.

Investigation showed that the Riley belonged to Mr John C Duval. A quick phone call and Mr. Duval (who turned out to be an adman of some note) expressed his willingness to have the car subjected to the glassy gaze of my Rollei.

Closer and more detailed examination has failed to reveal any serious flaw in this delightful car. With 50,000-odd miles to its credit, the body remains as straight as a die. It rattles so little that I was constantly obliged to remind myself that this was a *coachbuilt* convertible with 10 summers at its back. The iridescent green enamel — most of it entirely original — still has about it the pearly sheen of a real quality paint job.

The car has been in Mr. Duval's careful hands for six years, during which time it has covered around 30,000 miles. It's the second 2½-litre Riley drophead coupe he has owned. He had the first for about a week before this one turned up. The second car was the better, he thought. Result: a swap. Since then, apart from some minor paint respraying on the front wings and bonnet, the only real work done on the car has been a rear-end overhaul. When a trunnion went, owner Duval decided to get the job done properly. Too, one of the first things he did after buying the car was to have a new hood made. It remains today in very nearly new condition. What

is more important (and unusual, in a full four-seater drophead) it provides perfect weatherproofing.

Surprisingly enough, Mr Duval is not a Riley-lover. Among other things he objects to the 2½'s overly heavy steering — a point other Riley users before him have found time to complain about! What Duval *does* like is fresh-air motoring.

Major basic difference between the 2½ of 1950 and the original 1926 Nine is the dimensions. That tremendous 120 mm stroke was, during the 2½'s day (1946 to 1954) the longest of any commercially produced car. In spite of this long stroke, high piston speed has not been a major cause of mechanical breakdown — possibly because the engine allegedly peaks at only 4400 rpm. On the standard compression ratio of 6.9 to 1, the 2½ litre turns out 100 honest bhp. At roughly 21 mph per 1000 rpm, that gives it a theoretical maximum of about 93 mph.

Discussion with various owners (not to say my own experience —I once owned a 2½ saloon) confirms that the big four-cylinder will churn quite happily to 5000, at which speed a genuine ton should be on the clock.

According to *The Autocar* of February 25, 1949, the 2½-litre Riley was a car for "the real motoring enthusiast, the type of driver who wants to go far and fast, who appreciates and can obtain the utmost from steering, braking and handling qualities all designed to fit exactly the demands made on a car when high averaging is required."

There is no doubt in my mind that the 2½-litre Riley is, for its time, a first class high-speed touring car. Pottering along, the rack and pinion steering *is* noticeably heavy. On the other hand it becomes increasingly light as speed rises — without becoming less precise.

The same issue of *The Autocar* lists a number of trip times for the Riley. They compare more than favourably with the times you might expect to put up today in hardware of comparable class. One of the 2½'s most endearing characteristics is its tremendous performance in second and third gears. Starting off in second is so easy, you're tempted to try it in third!

This is the same torquey engine that Donald Healey used in the Silverstone Healeys. Although the Silverstone distinguished itself in British and Continental sports car events, the Riley saloon was precluded from serious competition by its heavy (nearly 30 cwt) body. Undoubtedly the hot Riley was — and still is — a fast road car. Yet even in Australia, where competition is not so intense, it has never been conspicuously successful. Used as the factory intended — as a high-speed touring car — the 2½ often reigned supreme in English and Continental rallies.

Suspension is very firm — you could almost call it uncompromising. The independent front end is suspended on torsion bars. the rear by semi-elliptics. I well remember a nightmare journey I undertook in my own Riley a few years ago. Driving from Sydney to Melbourne for the Olympic Games. I was forced to journey over the Hume Highway at a time when floods and semitrailers had wrought almost unbelievable havoc on the road surface. The Riley was all at sea in the terrible conditions, and promised to pound itself to pieces unless I took it easy. Slowing down certainly lessened the burden on suspension and body work, but it made the journey even more tiresome for driver and passengers. It was a pretty huffy lot that eventually reached Melbourne that year.

The braking I never found to be particularly outstanding, although the years may have dimmed my memory a little. The stoppers were Girlings—a hydromechanical system operating hydraulically on the front wheels and through a mechanical linkage on the rear. *The Autocar* says the setup was equal to the car's performance.

Top gear pulling ability was sufficiently useful to suit even the laziest drivers. My car, had I encouraged it, would have slugged happily uphill day after day without suffering visible stress.

Various small devices on the drophead coupe make it an interesting car. Erection of the huge hood is made easy by concealed hydraulic cylinders. The job takes only a minute or so. All models have a blind in the rear window which can be operated from the driver's seat.

A great dal of my interest in this Riley stems from the fact tha it is the product of a transitional period. That becomes increasingly obvious as you grow more familiar with its mechanical specification. The hydro-mechanical brakes could have come from a car 10 or 15 years older; the heavy front suspension, coupled with rack-and-pinion steering, gives the car a true vintage feel; a massive chassis, while ensuring rigidity, also adds unnecessarily to all-up weight. Obviously the Riley's styling is that of a car from the late pre-war period.

The 2½-litre, particularly the coupe model, remains a car of **great charm and. I think, one with a very real claim to the title "classic."**

In stature it is to me as a **bearded giant against the shamefaced youths which today bear** the hallowed diamond nameplate.　　　　　　　　#

# You're right ahead –

## with the New  1½ litre Saloon

## You're right ahead with *POWER* and that in the long run contributes most to your motoring enjoyment

*The brilliant New Riley* **'PATHFINDER'**

It's the most powerful, roomiest Riley ever. Your Dealer will be pleased to tell you all about this great-hearted car.

No other 1½ litre car gives you the same spirited performance with such consistent reliability. You're right ahead with safe, sure road-holding at speed, and incomparable steering. These are part of the Riley tradition. And the long, low lines of the luxurious body proclaim to all that this is one of England's outstanding cars.

For the sheer pleasure of driving, there's nothing quite like a Riley 1½ litre Saloon—built to give you years of *Magnificent Motoring.*

*Service in Europe—*
Qualified Riley owners planning a Continental Tour are invited to see their Riley Dealer for Details of a Free Service to save foreign currency.

## *Riley for Magnificent Motoring*

**Riley Models are fitted with safety glass all round.**

**RILEY MOTORS LIMITED,** *Sales Division,* **COWLEY, OXFORD**

*London Showrooms:* RILEY CARS, 55-56 PALL MALL, S.W.1    *Overseas Business: Nuffield Exports Ltd., Oxford and 41 Piccadilly, London, W.1*

# Three Ages of

ON the introduction of the current Riley 4/Sixty-eight comment was made in *The Autocar* that, in some of its features, it closely resembled and was a worthy successor to the 1½-litre Riley which was in production from 1946 until 1956. This comment must have started a train of thought in the Editor's mind, for in due course he suggested that a little research into this resemblance, and a comparison with one of the pre-war 1½-litre Rileys, might produce some interesting results.

To make a direct comparison of three cars from three distinct periods of motoring obviously is meaningless since, at each stage, motorists' requirements have varied, and different standards proved acceptable; accordingly, some more just basis of assessment must be devised. An attempt has been made, therefore, to see these cars through the eyes of an individual who in 1937, 1948 and 1959 bought himself a new Riley. As he sits for the first time in his 4/Sixty-eight, we will jog his memory, and see if he can recall some of the features of his two previous Rileys. It is more than possible that some readers have done just as this imaginary owner has done, but perhaps they would like to refresh their own recollections of how a vehicle, bearing the same name, has changed over twenty-two years.

Obviously any change that has occurred has not resulted merely from the designer's whim, but because his thoughts have been influenced by advances in automobile engineering, and tempered by market demands which are, in turn, the assumed requirements of the buyers.

In 1937 our hypothetical owner bought himself an Adelphi Light Four saloon; this was possibly one of the less well-known of several 1½-litre Rileys then available. This particular model will suit our purpose well, since it existed also in two larger-engined forms. It was, therefore, rather heavy and overbodied for its 1½-litre engine; possibly this could be said also of the 1948 model, and even to a certain extent of the new model. Basic price in 1937 of the Adelphi was £375; adjustment of this figure with the change in the Board of Trade's cost of living index gives an equivalent of over £1,000 today. The price of the 1948 car was £675 in that year, and gives an adjusted price of almost exactly £1,000. The basic price of today's model is £725.

Of course, one has to remember, in making such comparisons, the limited sales of the pre-war Riley when made by the Riley Company, the rather curious market situation which existed in 1948 when the car was made by Nuffield, and the industrial position today when it is, of course, a British Motor Corporation product. This decline in the cost of the vehicle can be taken as reflecting directly the advantages of improved mechanical assembly, mass production, rationalization of the motor industry and large sales.

A quick glance round the latest Riley will remind our owner of many features which he liked on his two previous models of the same name. The interior finish is still of high quality, with polished wood facia—now surmounted by safety padding—natural leather upholstery, comfortable individual front seats, a centrally mounted gear-change lever to which the hand drops readily (although with the Adelphi there was the option of a self-change gear box), and a comprehensive array of instruments.

Certain controls have fallen by the wayside, however; advance-retard ignition control and hand throttle have gone, the steering column is no longer of the adjustable telescopic variety, and the fuel gauge does not now indicate the engine oil level as well. He has gained a rev counter, retains a combined oil-pressure gauge and water thermometer, and instruments are hooded to prevent reflection in the windscreen. Over the years, the hand-brake lever has moved steadily round him in a clockwise direction; in 1937, he had a lever comfortably mounted between the front seats; in 1948, it tucked itself awkwardly under the dashboard; today it is conveniently sited between the driver's door and his seat.

Additional items the 4/Sixty-eight now offers as standard equipment are windscreen washers and a built-in heater and ventilating system—both evidence of the increased comfort which modern motorists consider to be a necessity, and of the great development of the motor car as a means of transport. Introduction of synthetic materials has meant that a washable roof-lining is incorporated today. The old cloth lining, while excellent when new, soon became dirty and dusty, and very difficult to clean.

It is indeed a surprise to discover how little the seating space has changed over the years, although designers have altered to some extent their ideas about what shape we are. There has been a steady increase in the distance between the back of the front seat and the steering wheel, but the most marked alteration has been in the actual seat size, particularly between 1937 and 1948. Backrests and seat cushions have shrunk, but the width has increased. The distance from the leading edge of the seat

| Model | 10-30 m.p.h. in 3rd | 20-40 m.p.h. in top | 30-50 m.p.h. in top | | 0-30 m.p.h. | 0-50 m.p.h. | Max Speed m.p.h. | | Fuel Consumption approx. | Overall weight approx. |
|---|---|---|---|---|---|---|---|---|---|---|
| | sec | sec | sec | 1937 | 8.7 | 23.1 | 70.5 | 1937 | 26 m.p.g. | 25 cwt |
| 1937 | 10.1 | 15.8 | 18.1 | 1948 | 7.8 | 19.0 | 74.0 | 1948 | 27 m.p.g. | 24½ cwt |
| 1948 | 8.6 | 13.3 | 15.3 | 1959 | 5.6 | 14.3 | 83.6 | 1959 | 27 m.p.g. | 22 cwt |
| 1959 | 9.2 | 12.5 | 13.7 | | | | | | | |

# the Riley

*Considered by many to be one of the finest medium-size cars built after the war, the 1½-litre Riley remained in production with few alterations for ten years (1946-1956)*

*Latest in a long line. The Farina-bodied 4/Sixty-eight is one of several British Motor Corporation cars with similar body styling. It carries its tradition lightly*

to the pedals was only 13in in 1937; today 16in is accepted as normal. The front seat of the Adelphi, however, did have 2in more fore-and-aft adjustment.

Back-seat passengers in the Adelphi were much better off for room than in either of the two later models, except for overall width. They had more to sit on and lean against, and considerably more room for their knees; the width of the back seat was certainly adequate for two, and it is questionable that the extra inches the newest model offers in rear-seat width have made it into a really practical three-seater. Modern requirements have also greatly increased the area of glass in a car; door and window pillars are slimmer, rear windows larger and windscreen wrap-round greater. This is a great boon to the passengers, besides adding greatly to the safety of driving the car.

One disadvantage that our imaginary motorist suffered with his earlier Riley was the lack of space for all those things one carries in a car besides oneself and one's passengers. The boot was rather small by modern standards, and, except for a lockable glove pocket, there was a complete absence of those shelves and pockets with which most cars of today are so liberally endowed. The Riley owner has never had his boot full of spare wheel, since a separate compartment has always been provided for this article. In conjunction with this, therefore, he has never had that curse of having to remove all his luggage to take the spare wheel out, although in the 4/Sixty-eight, if the boot is very full, it may be necessary to remove some items before it is possible to turn the handle to lower the underslung spare wheel carrier.

Exterior dimensions are particularly interesting; there is a good chance that the same garage has conveniently accommodated

each of the Rileys in turn, only 4in difference in overall length existing between all three models. The 4/Sixty-eight, which has the greatest overall length, strangely enough has a wheel-base shorter by over a foot than the other two models, on which this measurement is identical. Overall width has remained unchanged for all 22 years, which is an excellent commentary on the way in which designers have learnt to get more into the same space. Turning circle has also remained much the same, at around 38ft, but the number of turns from lock to lock on the steering wheel increased from 2½ to 2¾, and now is 3. Reversing on the Adelphi, with the wheels near the back of the car, should theoretically be easier than with a car with considerable overhang at the rear. On the 4/Sixty-eight the body designer has come to the aid of the driver and the pair of tail-fins give an excellent indication of where the car ends.

With regard to performance, the table reproduced gives an idea of these three different cars' capabilities. The 30-50 m.p.h. top-gear figure for the Adelphi must be considered rather poor, but otherwise the performances offered in the different years are fairly closely comparable. One cannot imagine that an owner would have been at all disappointed by any of them in this respect. The post-war motorist has probably demanded better performance from everyday cars than did his pre-war counterpart; certainly he gets increased power and better acceleration. His petrol consumption is not likely to have varied much over all the years, and an average figure of 26 m.p.g. could be anticipated then as now.

One of the most evident differences is in road behaviour; the Adelphi certainly gave a far firmer ride than the two post-war models. The suspension of the 1937 car was by half-elliptic leaf springs all round, and although Rileys still use half-elliptics at the rear, the 1948 version had wishbones and torsion bars on the front; in 1959 the torsion bars were replaced by coil springs.

Steering on the latest version will certainly be lighter, but lacks something of the sensitivity and precision of the earlier model, which would probably be our motorist's favourite from this aspect. The road-holding of the former Rileys set a high standard. One important feature that the Adelphi did not have was hydaulic brakes, but the Girling mechanical ones with which it was fitted were very difficult to fault, and quite as good as many hydraulically operated systems of that time. Drivers who have never experienced rod-operated brakes would not have been immediately happy with the feel of the pedal on the pre-war car.

In summary, it may be said that our owner will have had in each of his three Rileys a motor car for fine motoring by the standards of its time. Perhaps he will not have in his present model that distinctiveness which set the Riley owner apart, but he will have many of a Riley's innate good qualities and traditions. Although engineers and designers are offering him today features in many ways similar to those they offered in 1937, these have been improved so that he can now drive with greater ease, much better vision, and in a higher degree of comfort.

PETER RIVIÈRE.

# Riley Roadster

Brian Lecomber tries his own car seven years on.

I WALKED down the line of gleaming Rolls-Royces – and there she was. My old Riley Roadster.

But she was very different, now. When I had her she was black and tatty and the wings rattled: now she shone in white coach-paint and her chromework was whole and glinting. I'd expected to greet her as a long-lost love – but I couldn't. The seven years had changed her too much: now she was someone else's baby.

Perhaps, even, I was resentful because she'd come up in the world more than I have. In '66 I bought her for 50 or 60 pounds, and about a year later, sold her for much the same. And now . . . she sat complacently a couple of years back in a Rolls-Royce showroom with a price of £1650 on her head, while I'm still an itinerant writer-cum-pilot without two pennies to rub together.

She was born in 1949, four years after me. She, too, was a war baby in a way, produced by Riley as a gesture of defiance against the austerity of the immediate post-war years and with the hope of picking up some much needed dollars in the American market.

Exhibiting a rather touching optimism, Riley marketed the car both in Britain and the US. I think they actually sold some in America, too – although they couldn't have exactly flooded the market, since I understand they produced less than 1000 Roadsters all told between '48 and '50.

In all, the beast must have been one of Riley's ugliest-ever motor cars – so much so that its very ugliness gives it a sort of anti-hero charm. Not £1650 worth of charm, though – not when you could get a very nice XK120 or two immaculate Healeys for the same sort of outlay. This is very definitely a case of pure rarity inflating the tag. Not that I mind particularly, since this is the way of the world – but I wouldn't like anybody to go away with the impression that a 1949 Riley Roadster is worth that kind of money for any *other* reason than rarity. It's really the last word in un-classic classics.

Nonetheless, when I owned her I loved her dearly – and so it was painful to meet her again as a near-stranger. I stroked her wing and wanted to tell her that *I'd* have done this for her if I'd had the money – but, remembering some of the things I *did* do to her, she probably wouldn't have believed me. She might have recalled the day I lowered her hood and screen, donned a pair of goggles – and knocked out her elderly big ends in a frenetic dash from Cornwall to Buckinghamshire. Or she might have held against me the time when one of her brake rods parted company with the expanding-type master cylinder, causing both of us to hurtle across a busy blind junction in the middle of a rush hour. We mercifully missed hitting anything, but both lost a lot of cool. Or, possibly more than anything else, she could still have been resentful of the part I made her play in a flying circus I was involved with. Belting along a grass strip with a Tiger Moth's wheel in the driver's ear and me trying to step off the wing into her cavernous, lid-less boot might well have left scars on her memory which will never be erased. It certainly left scars on *me*.

According to her logbook, the chap I sold her to, kept her right through until she was purchased by a Rolls-Royce and Bentley dealer in Fyfield, Ongar, Essex which is where we met. So it must have been this gentleman who did the restoration – and, body-wise in particular, he did a very good

job. I had to sit in the Riley for several minutes, running my hands round the enormous steering wheel and letting my fingers find the knobs and switches, before I really started to recognise her again.

But gradually, it all came back. I closed my eyes, and the smell of leather and linseed oil from the woodwork took me back seven years – and I found I could put my hands straight onto the steering column dip switch, the obscure bonnet catches, and the nearly-out-of-reach gear lever. I remembered that the steering would be incredibly heavy, largely due to a gearbox half way down the column which was designed to remove the top half of same from the vicinity of the carburettors. And I remembered, too, that the gearchange was long and slow, and that the bench seat provided no lateral keying at all during cornering. The first few Roadsters had a column gearchange – which must have been *really* ghastly – and Riley fitted this bench seat so that they could advertise the car as a three-seater. After a while the gearstick moved down to the floor – but the bench seat remained, so that the beast was still a three-seater providing the driver was more than just good friends with the centre passenger.

Unlike the body, the engine didn't appear to have been touched. The twin alloy rocker covers, looking for all the world like overhead cam boxes, were lightly corroded and the gaskets looked old. A shame, I thought – but I couldn't really blame the man from Cardiff if he decided to leave the clockwork. The old 2443cc Riley engine is no small lump: it's a tall, heavy long-stroke four which does not come out of the car easily – and then when you've got it out, there's a lot of it to work on. It has two camshafts, mounted high in the block, and early post-war models like this have metalled con-rods instead of bearing shells. The oilways in the crankshaft are badly designed, and prone to becoming greatly restricted by sludge – so much so that you have to watch out for *high* oil pressure in a Riley 2·4 engine. If the crank is clean the oil sits at 40psi or just under. But if it's well sludged up, the pressure hits 80 quite easily, while very little oil actually gets to the bearings.

And sure enough, when I started it up the pressure leapt into the late eighties: I was moved to wonder whether the bottom end had ever been down since I took out the rods and had them re-metalled with the engine *in situ*, leaving the concrete sludge of ages in the crankshaft oilways and selling the car soon afterwards. Furthermore, the valve gear rattled more than I remembered it – although that may just be the years colouring things quiet, since the big Riley unit was never renowned for mechanical silence.

Once on the road, however, I forgot such trifling matters to some extent. The car is a beast – always was, and always will be – but she is a charming, evocative beast for all that. You sit high and haughty with the big wheel in your stomach, while the long bonnet points the way. The engine ambles easily, and she'll cruise for ever at 65–70. In my day she'd occasionally hit 100 on a long downhill – but now she feels less lively, and I doubt if she'd wind up more than 85 or so. Perhaps the ignition timing is a bit out: she's very critical of her ignition timing.

She's a straight-line car. Providing you don't wish to change her heading she sits stable and four-square at any speed. Even bumps and cats'-eyes, which make her front wings shake gently, call for

no directional correction. I find I am fascinated by this discreet nodding of the wings. All Rileys do it – but when I owned the Roadster they didn't just shake, they *clattered*.

She loses her dignity on the bends, however. Two factors play a major part in this – firstly, her saloon car length, which makes her naturally very reluctant to change heading, and secondly, the enormously heavy steering. That gearbox half way down the column is quite well worn, and the more cornering force you have to apply, the stiffer it gets. In my day she always had balding back tyres, so she would slide quite easily – but now, for some obscure reason, she had Town and Country's at the rear, and the weight of the car seemed to dig these deep into the road. So instead of breaking away at the back she goes into a sort of squealing, ponderous understeer regime, in which the steering becomes rock-hard and very reluctant to transmit feel back to the driver's hands. I much preferred her when she would break away at the back – that way there wasn't so much load on the steering box, and you could "feel" what was happening.

The brakes are quite good: someone must have been working on them. They're hydraulic front, mechanical rear – and they're *always* going out of adjustment. I am amused to find that after a few minutes I am hardly using them at all: even after seven years the traumatic memory of that total failure still haunts me, and I can't bring myself to rely on them utterly. You see, if the expanding master cylinder rod breaks you lose *everything* – including the handbrake. That sort of things leaves its mark on a chap.

But in spite of this, I am enjoying it. The whip

*Above, the Riley looking very tidy and below, the former owner being re-united with his Roadster.*

*Above, right, a pleasant and purposeful front end. Below, left, what we trust some of the other drivers saw; centre, the twin rocker boxes much in evidence; right, three passengers were just possible in the Roadster.*

*The Roadster, pictured with raised hood.*

of the wind takes me back over the years, and as we whirr through the Essex countryside I fancy I can smell new-mown summer grass and the tang of dope on a biplane's wings. I feel a ridiculous urge to drop off the salesman, fold the screen flat on the bonnet, put on my old flying goggles, and elope with the Roadster back to a small, sunny airfield out of the carefree past.

But of course, it could not be. I don't have £1650 to pay for her, so I took her back to the rich man's showroom and bade her a very last farewell.

I hope you found a good home, Roadster. I should've loved you better when I had you – but maybe you'll remember me, like I'll remember you, for the *good* times . . . ●

**Riley Roadster**
– Specifications:
Engine capacity: 80 × 120mm, 2443cc
Brake horse power: 100 at 4500rpm
Compression ratio: 6·85:1
Weight (without passengers): 27cwt 2qr
Tyre size: 600 × 16 on bolt on steel disc wheels
Tank capacity: 20 gallons
Turning circle: (R), 36ft; (L) 27ft. Minimum ground clearance: 7in
Main dimensions: wheelbase, 9ft 11in, track, 4ft 4½in (front and rear); overall length, 15ft 6in; width, 5ft 6in; height, 4ft 7in.

# THE ROO-SHOOTER'S RILEY ROADSTER

*Above: Peter Hocking's restoration job has occupied four years and $3000. He says the car's almost mint again — complete with standard squeaks, rattles and "other funny noises".*

*Right: Hocking's Riley is a 1949 model, landed in a batch of 50 in Brisbane and sold to its first owner there. How it turned up in Geraldton, WA, is a mystery.*

**What this country needs (we say) is more people like Greg Milner and Peter Hocking, a pair of West Australian Riley nuts. Hocking, who owns this Riley 2½-litre roadster, and Milner, who drove it and wrote this story, both acknowledge the car as magnificent, yet they can also talk with affection about squeaks, rattles, clutch judder and a gearchange throw "as long as the legs of a Kings Cross stripper".**

LIKE THE CRIMINAL driven by the irresistible urge to return to the scene of his dastardly crime, I knew I'd have to do it some day.

Ever since I sold my Riley 1½ all that time ago, given the thing a last loving kick and a contemptuous bash on the crooked bonnet panels, the sudden outbursts of maniacal laughter that afflict Riley owners had been growing in intensity. I was an addict in need of a fix.

So it was with a relieved sense of guilt that I approached Peter Hocking's magnificent deep blue 2½ litre roadster (from behind, to catch it unawares) and

gave it a tentative pat on the boot-mounted spare tyre.

Hocking, a stalwart of the WA Riley Club, says his is the only roadster running in WA. He's heard of the remains of another, but with any luck nobody will find it.

Restored classic cars in Australia don't seem to deserve a seal of approval unless they spend a certain qualifying period slowly rotting in a disused barn somewhere in the outback, after doing the usual stint of several years rounding up sheep or racing at the outer-Widgiemooltha speedway on Sunday afternoons.

Hocking's is no exception.

Chassis number 59 SS 4866 started life in Brisbane in 1949, one 50 to be imported from Britain. Twenty-five went to Queensland and the other half to Victoria. The car's history between Brisbane and WA is blurred, but in WA the car took up the true thread of Australian classic car destiny.

Hocking found the car in a sorry state on a farm near Geraldton, 480 kilometres north of Perth. It had arrived there from a property at Mullewa, to the east, where two brothers had used it for some time as a paddock-hopping chariot for their kangaroo-shooting expeditions.

It had been stripped of body panels back to the engine bulkhead and the bootlid was off.

That was in May 1972. Now, four years, $3000 and several thousand hours later, it is almost back in its original mint condition.

And that includes all the squeaks, rattles, bumps and other funny noises that any Riley owner will tell you are absolutely impossible to remove.

"I stripped it down completely — every nut, bolt, washer and split pin," says Hocking.

"Then the rebuild started — chassis sandblasted, all new wood (all the wood had rotted), new panels, with rubber between the joins, complete engine rebuild and a new clutch and transmission.

"And STILL the damn thing rattles, and the new transmission hasn't gone anywhere near curing that good old Riley clutch shudder."

Unlike the many nuts who insist that if the factory installed it, it's impossible to do better, Hocking is not an originality freak.

For example, the instruments are Pathfinder, and the dash layout is his own design, incorporating tachometer, speedometer, water temperature, oil pressure and generator charge, as well as the usual switches for lighting and accessories.

The 2½-litre roadster was designed for the American market, with offset steering, bench seat for three (yuk) and a column change (double yuk).

Thankfully, somewhere in Australia, the gearstick was put back on the floor where it belongs, but the job was not a good one. The floor change now has a throw about as long as the legs on a Kings Cross stripper, and you have to lean so far forward you almost toot the horn with your nose.

The version for the home market had bucket seats and the normal floorchange. Both versions had a 90 litre (20 gallon) fuel tank, giving an incredible range of almost 800 kilometres! Hocking's roadster joins his stable of a "hack" 1½ saloon, a 2½ litre drophead he is restoring, and a Humber Super Snipe. ("The Humber is my civilised car. It has a heater and it's automatic.")

The roadster, despite its admirable qualities, was a monumental failure for the Coventry company. Five hundred and seven of them were built between 1948 and 1950, and right in the middle of that, William Lyons introduced his Jaguar XK 120.

Most people casting around for a sports car of that type knew which they preferred, particularly since the Jaguar was £100 cheaper than the Riley on the home market.

And to make matters worse, apart from the engine and running gear, not a single body panel or fitting was interchangeable with any of the company's other models.

Anyway, I drove the great, raunchy, truck-like monster. Clunk, into first, way down in the depths of the footwells, and slip out the clutch ever so gently, but oh, no, the damn thing refuses to get moving without shuddering in anger, and the bloke behind laughs as he watches your face become a blur in the rear vision mirror.

Quickly into second and the shudder disappears, give it squirt on the heavy accelerator and that great, lumbering four-cylinder engine comes to life. The Riley roadster really comes into its own on the open road. No matter what anybody says, it is not a pleasant car in city traffic, but given the room to stretch its legs, it is fast, the tight rack-and-pinion steering nippy, and the vast acreage of bonnet exhilarating.

The 2½ litre Riley sedan had a top speed of around 160 km/h and the roadster is supposed to be capable of 175, with its lighter body.

A roadster finished 17th out of 60 starters in the 1950 Le Mans, at an average speed of 118.8 km/h (74.22mph). The car reached 160 km/h on three points of the circuit, and a couple of times reached 175.

The flexibility of the big twin-cam four is amazing. Once, being unfamiliar with the car, I slowed down almost to a stop to round a normal right-angled bend, and inadvertently dropped it into top instead of second. With a slow squeeze on the throttle, the roadster pulled away smoothly without a grunt from the engine, nor a snatch from the transmission.

I'd been wondering what I'd missed most about Rileys. Driving this big, boisterous roadster, I found out. I missed that beautiful blonde bird standing on the corner, giving a wide chic smile and a little wave as we drove by. That fix should last another couple of years. ☐

*This beautiful Riley 2½-litre roadster was once a 'roo-shooter's paddock-hopper in the WA inland. Who'd have thought the shooters had taste like that?*

# Riley 1½ litre

# No. 4

*The Mini-Manual is based on the original survey of the car conducted by Motor Trader when the model was still current*

*Manufacturers: Riley (Coventry), Ltd., Foleshill, Coventry.*

ALTHOUGH bearing a strong family resemblance to the pre-war Twelve, with identical engine dimensions, the post-war 1½-litre model has been completely redesigned and differs in almost every detail. Most notable change is the adoption of "Torsionic" independent front suspension with torsion bars, and the body is now of composite construction. The engine has a timing chain instead of gears, and the transmission, though similar in principle, is altered in detail.

Between the 1½-litre and 2½-litre models the only visible external difference, apart from the longer bonnet on the larger car, is the colour of the radiator badge, which is dark blue on the 1½, pale blue on the 2½-litre.

Chassis and engine serial numbers correspond, but the chassis number is prefixed by two figures indicating year of production (36=1946, 37=1947) and a letter (S for saloon) indicating body type. The chassis number is stamped on top of the nearside chassis frame member alongside the engine, and the engine number is on the nearside top

## ENGINE DATA

| No. of cylinders | 4 |
|---|---|
| Bore and stroke: mm | 69 × 100 |
|     in | 2·72 · 3·94 |
| Capacity: c.c. | 1496 |
|     cu. in | 91·3 |
| R.A.C. rated hp | 11·9 |
| Max. b.h.p. at r.p.m. | 55 at 4500 |
| Max. torque (lb/ft) at r.p.m. | 76 at 2750 |
| Compression ratio | 6·7:1 |
| Compression pressure: | |
|     at 1,000 r.p.m. | 125 lb/sq in |
|     at cranking speed | 112 lb/sq in |
| Firing order | 1 2 4 3 |
| Tappet clearance (hot): | |
|     inlet | 0·003in |
|     exhaust | 0·004in |

## INSTRUMENTS

1 Screenwiper control
2 Oil pressure gauge
3 Ammeter
4 Hand throttle
5 Panel light switch
6 Starter switch
7 Speedometer
8 Choke
9 Pass light switch
10 Ignition control
11 Petrol gauge
12 Water temperature gauge
13 Screenwiper control
14 Trafficator switch
15 Windscreen winder
16 Lighting and ignition switch
17 Ignition warning light
18 Horn push
19 Handbrake lever
20 Electric clock
21 Accelerator pedal
22 Brake pedal
23 Gear lever
24 Clutch pedal
25 Dipper switch

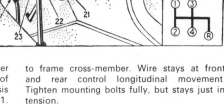

of the bell-housing flange. The chassis number is also stamped on a plate on the nearside of the bulkhead under the bonnet. Chassis numbers in this series started from 35S 10001.

Changes during the currency of the model are listed later in the article. The only visible changes which may date the car are the horn mounting and control box type.

Certain special tools, listed here, are available from the Riley Company. Although not absolutely necessary they greatly facilitate certain service operations. All threads are B.S.F. Simmonds self-locking nuts are widely used.

## ENGINE
### MOUNTING

At front two moulded rubber blocks are bolted to timing cover and to front cradle. At rear single block bolted to rear of gearbox and to frame cross-member. Wire stays at front and rear control longitudinal movement. Tighten mounting bolts fully, but stays just in tension.

### REMOVAL

Engine and gearbox should be removed together. Take off bonnet and undo two nuts below radiator shell. Lift shell straight up. Detach radiator stays and remove two nuts below. Disconnect water hoses and lift radiator straight up. Remove coil. Undo nut at lower end of front wire stay. Take out six $\frac{5}{16}$ in bolts holding tubular cross-member to front cradle, and slide out cross-member (forked ends fit on cradle lugs). Disconnect exhaust manifold. Detach starter and lay aside on frame. Disconnect all pipes, wires and controls, and remove air cleaner and carburettor. Place rope sling round middle of engine. Disconnect both front mountings from frame, and remove

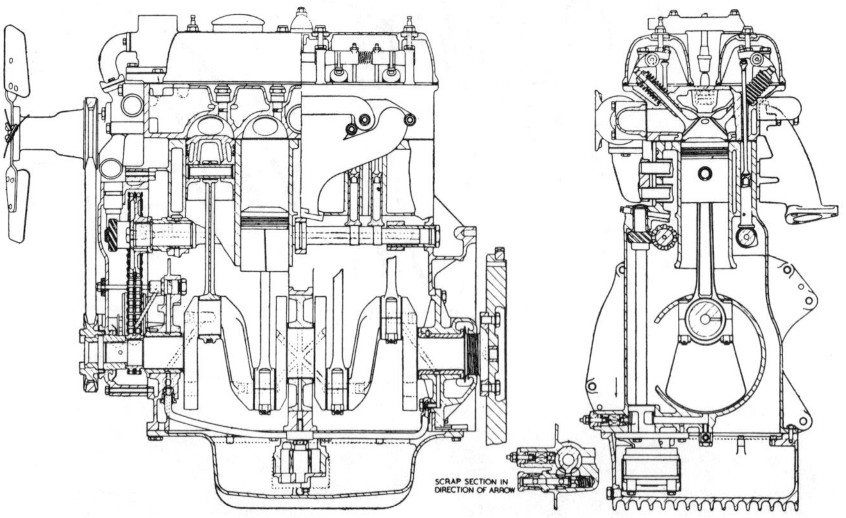


Cross section and side view of the RME's engine. Note the classic Riley twin underhead camshaft design.

nearside mounting from timing cover. Take weight of engine on sling.

Slide both front seats right back and take up carpets. Screw off gear lever knob and remove gearbox cowl and floor boards. Disconnect propeller shaft front end, speedo drive and reverse lamp wire. Undo wire stay nut behind cross-member. Detach rear mounting from cross-member and gearbox, and take away. Extract pin from clutch cross-shaft universal joint. Detach gearbox top cover. Engine-gearbox unit can then be tilted and drawn out to front.

When reassembling note rubber radiator buffer washers, thick above, thin below bracket. Tighten Simmonds nuts only enough to nip rubber.

## CYLINDER HEAD REMOVAL

Hot spot tubes connecting inlet and exhaust manifolds pass through cylinder block. Before removing cylinder head take out two setscrews holding hot spot elbow below inlet manifold. Detach manifold and draw out elbow with tubes. If tubes are stuck in exhaust manifold, lever elbow gently. If this fails use special extractor.

## CRANKSHAFT

Three main bearings. Front bearing is flanged bronze bush, white metal-lined and pressed into crankcase from front with dowel locating in flange.

Centre bearing is white metal-lined split housing which is spigoted in centre web of crankcase and located by key, and setscrew inserted from nearside of crankcase. Rear bearing is white metal-lined bronze bush flanged both sides for end float control, and dowelled in top half of split housing which is flange-bolted to register in rear wall of crankcase.

**ENGINEERING CHANGES**

| Change | Date | Chassis No. |
|---|---|---|
| Serrated clutch cross-shaft introduced .. .. | April 1946 | 36S 10157 |
| Clutch pedal stop added .. .. | Sept. 1946 | 36S 10632 |
| Clutch centre springs, all black to black and green .. | Feb. 1947 | 36S 11000 |
| Reamered torque tube centre bearing added .. .. | April 1947 | 37S 11360 |
| Horn mounting raised .. .. | April 1947 | 37S 12053 |
| Balanced propeller shaft adopted .. | April 1947 | 37S 12070 |
| Gearbox tunnel altered .. .. | June 1947 | 37S 12560 |
| Tighter differential star pinions adopted | June 1947 | 37S 12646 |
| Front number plate strengthened .. | Sept. 1947 | 37S 13127 |
| RF95 Control box replaced RF91 .. | Sept. 1947 | 37S 13259 |

**SPECIAL SERVICE TOOLS**

C-spanner for timing chain adjuster pinion
Hexagon key for chain adjuster sprocket spindle
Spanner for lock nut on chain adjuster spindle
Extractor for crankshaft oil thrower
Extractor for crankshaft timing sprocket
Extractor for front main bearing bush
Drift for cylinder head spot tube
Extractor for hot spot outlet
Rear axle bevel pinion setting gauge
Extractor for front hubs
Front suspension setting gauge

Replacement bearings supplied with fitting allowance for line-boring.

Flywheel, with shrunk-on starter ring gear and Oilite clutch spigot bush, spigoted on crankshaft flange and retained by six setscrews. Flywheel may be refitted in any position.

Timing sprocket keyed on front end of crankshaft with Woodruff key. Oil thrower sleeve pressed on outside sprocket on smaller diameter, keyed with separate key and retained by taper pin. Starting handle engaging pin in front of sleeve, retained by pulley, which is screwed on sleeve with left-hand thread.

To remove crankshaft, after stripping timing gear, pistons and con-rods, and flywheel, slacken centre bearing housing locating set-screw and drift out housing. Alternatively drive crankshaft to rear with hide mallet.

**CRANKSHAFT AND CONNECTING ROD DATA**

| | Main Bearings | | | Crankpins |
|---|---|---|---|---|
| | No. 1 | No. 2 | No. 3 | |
| Diameter | $1\frac{3}{4}$in | $2\frac{3}{4}$in | $1\frac{3}{4}$in | $1\frac{7}{8}$in |
| Length | $2\frac{1}{2}$in | $1\frac{7}{16}$in | $2\frac{3}{8}$in | $1\frac{1}{4}$in |
| Running clearance: | | | | |
| main bearings: front and rear | | | | ·0015in |
| centre .. | | | | ·0025in |
| big ends .. .. .. .. | | | | ·0015in |
| End float: main bearings .. | | | | ·004—006in |
| big ends .. .. | | | | ·002—004in |
| Undersizes: main bearings .. | | | | ·010, ·020in |
| big ends .. .. | | | | ·025, ·050in |
| No. of teeth on starter ring gear | | | | 93 |
| Con-rod centres .. .. .. | | | | 8·0in |

## CONNECTING RODS

Big ends white-metalled direct. Replacements supplied with fitting allowance for hand scraping or boring.

Small ends bronze bushed.

## PISTONS

Split skirt. Gudgeon pins fully floating, located by spring rings.

Big ends will not pass through bores, nor will pistons pass crank throws. Push piston up, drive out pin and draw rod down.

When reassembling warm pistons in oil. Fit pistons with split towards exhaust (near side) and numbers on big end bosses towards inlet (off side).

## CAMSHAFT

Duplex roller endless chain drive with tensioning sprocket.

Two separate camshafts, inlet on offside, exhaust on nearside. Inlet camshaft has skew gear behind centre bearing for oil pump drive, and extension for distributor drive gear.

Each camshaft carried in three bearings. Rear bronze bushes pressed into crankcase from rear, centre bearings direct in crankcase, front bronze bushes provided with long ears retained by common stud. Extra location by setscrews from outside.

Each sprocket keyed on camshaft with Woodruff key and retained by setscrew in end of shaft. Distributor drive gear keyed on inlet camshaft.

End thrust taken by front bearings between shoulder on shaft and split thrust washer, located by recessed collar and retained by sprocket.

Timing chain tensioner consists of sprocket on eccentric bush between two quadrant plates, mounted on spindle screwed into crankcase, and retained by castellated nut. Outer quadrant plate has toothed sector engaging with pinion on stud, locked by Simmonds nut. When brass cap in timing cover is removed, end of pinion is exposed and can be turned with special C-spanner after locknut has been slackened. Turn pinion until chain is tight, without forcing, and slacken back slightly before locking.

*To remove camshaft* engine must be taken out of chassis and turned upside down after removal of rocker gear and push rods. Release tension from timing chain and unscrew tensioner spindle (hexagon socket). Timing chain can then be lifted off. Remove sump, oil pump and petrol pump. Take out front bearing locating setscrews. Camshaft can be drawn out with front bearing.

When reassembling adjust chain tension to give $\frac{1}{8}$in slack on long run, before fitting timing cover. Before tightening cover nuts check that there is clearance all round oil return thread on crankshaft oil thrower sleeve. Do not omit cork washer on centre stud.

Timing marks on camshaft sprockets should be adjacent and in line with crankshaft keyway at T.D.C.

## VALVES

Overhead, inclined at 90 deg from each other. Inlet and exhaust are interchangeable. Split cone cotter fixing, double springs. Valve guides shouldered, interchangeable.

## TAPPETS AND ROCKERS

Mushroom tappets sliding direct in block. Camshaft must be removed before tappets can be extracted.

Push rods can be extracted singly by depressing valve spring and sliding rocker aside.

Each rocker shaft carried on four pillars, located by setscrew in front pillar. Front pillars are drilled left- and right-hand for elbow feeding oil from hollow stud. Other pillars interchangeable. Nos. 2 and 4 have boss

## PISTON DATA

| | | |
|---|---|---|
| Clearance (skirt) | ·0015—·003in | |
| Oversizes | ·020, ·030, ·040in | |
| Weight (*without* rings or pin) | 10 oz. 4 dr. | |
| Gudgeon pin: diameter | 19 mm ($\frac{3}{4}$in) | |
| fit in piston | Light drive | |
| fit in con. rod | Push | |
| Compression height (to top of crown) | 50·5 mm | |
| | Com-pression | Oil Control |
| No. of rings | 3 | 1 |
| Gap | ·008in | ·008in |
| Side clearance in groove | ·00075—·00125in | ·00075—·00125in |
| Width of rings | $\frac{5}{64}$ | $\frac{5}{32}$ |

## CAMSHAFT DATA

| | No. 1 | No. 2 | No. 3 in | No. 3 ex |
|---|---|---|---|---|
| Bearing journal: diameter | 1,2598in | $1\frac{1}{2}$in | $\frac{7}{8}$in | $\frac{7}{8}$in |
| length | $2\frac{1}{4}$in | $\frac{5}{8}$in | $1\frac{25}{32}$in | 2in |
| Bearing clearance | ·001—·0025in | | | |
| End float | ·0025in | | | |
| Timing chain: pitch | $\frac{3}{8}$in | | | |
| No. of pitches | 82 | | | |

## VALVE DATA

| | Inlet | Exhaust |
|---|---|---|
| Head diameter | $1\frac{7}{16}$in | $1\frac{7}{16}$in |
| Stem diameter | $\frac{5}{16}$in | $\frac{5}{16}$in |
| Face angle | 45 deg | 45 deg |
| | Inner | Outer |
| Springs: length: free | $2\frac{9}{16}$in | $2\frac{13}{32}$in |
| loaded | $1\frac{9}{16}$in | $1\frac{5}{8}$in |
| at load | $22\frac{3}{4}$lb | $34\frac{3}{4}$lb |

## IGNITION DATA

*(All degrees on flywheel rotation)*

| | |
|---|---|
| Advance range: manual | 15 deg |
| centrifugal | 32-35 deg |
| Advance starts at crank r.p.m. | 1000 |
| Max. advance at crank r.p.m. | 4000 |
| Firing point (hand control adv.) | 8 deg. before TDC |
| Contact breaker gap | ·012—·015in |
| Plugs: make | Champion |
| type | L 10 S |
| size | 14 mm |
| gap | ·030in |

## FUEL SYSTEM DATA

| | |
|---|---|
| Carburettor: make | S.U. |
| type | H.2 |
| needle | No. 3 |
| jet | 90 |
| Air cleaner: make | AC |
| type | E/AC 2280 F |
| Fuel pump: make | AC |
| type | T 1524137 |
| pressure | $2\text{-}3\frac{1}{2}$ lb/sq in |

to front, No. 3 boss to rear. Rockers offset left- and right-hand, each pair separated by spring.

### LUBRICATION

Gear pump in sump, spigoted and flange-bolted to bottom of crankcase. Lower end of shaft runs in bush in pump body, upper end in flanged bush pressed into crankcase. To renew upper bush extract Welch plug and press bush downwards.

Skew gear keyed on upper end of shaft with Woodruff key, and located by taper pin. Pump driving gear keyed and pressed on lower end of shaft. Pump cover bolted to body with two dowels.

Remove pump with shaft and skew gear, detach cover and push shaft through until driving gear can be drawn off and key extracted.

Gauze intake strainer bolted to pump cover. Oil delivered through drilling in crankcase and external pipe to full flow Wilmot Breeden filter.

Adjustable relief valve on offside of crankcase behind oil pump tunnel and just above sump flange. To adjust, slacken lock nut and turn screw. To remove valve for cleaning unscrew bush and extract washer, spring and valve. Seat is renewable.

Additional non-adjustable relief valve, which comes into action if filter is choked, located in crankcase behind oil delivery union leading to filter.

Minimum oil pressures are:—

| | |
|---|---|
| 15 mph | 19 lb/sq in |
| 20 mph | 22 lb/sq in |
| 30 mph | 26 lb/sq in |
| 50 mph | 35 lb/sq in |

### IGNITION

Lucas coil. Distributor with centrifugal, advance, spigoted in timing cover and located by movable clamp plate, connected to hand control, and spring-loaded nut on stud which retains fixed plate. Set contact points to break 8 deg before T.D.C. with hand control fully advanced (pushed right in). This is equivalent to two flywheel teeth, visible through trap in bell-housing.

### COOLING SYSTEM

Pump, fan and non-adjustable thermostat bolted to adapter on cylinder head. Water delivered from pump through manifold on nearside to ports in side of cylinder head. Thermosyphon circulation to block. Pump has carbon and rubber seal.

To remove pump detach fan and remove pulley and bearing housing assembly, with seal and impeller, from pump body. There is enough clearance for this, but not to get pump body off cylinder head studs.

To dismantle pump remove brass Simmonds nut and draw off impeller. Pick off spring, collar, rubber seal, carbon disc and sealing plate. Remove pulley nut and draw off pulley (Woodruff key). Extract felt washer behind pulley and press shaft out to rear. Two ball bearings pressed into housing with distance pieces between inner and outer races. Lipped oil seal and spring ring behind rear bearing.

Adjust fan belt by swinging dynamo until there is $\frac{1}{2}$in slack either way on top run of belt.

# TRANSMISSION

### CLUTCH

Borg & Beck single dry plate, spring centre. Carbon thrust release bearing.

Adjust on pull-rod at bottom of cross-shaft lever to give $\frac{3}{4}$in free movement at pedal pad. After this adjustment set pedal stop (setscrew and lock nut behind relay shaft) to allow pedal $\frac{1}{2}$in further movement when clutch is quite free.

Clutch cross-shaft is articulated, with universal joint outside bell-housing. Free end of shaft supported in spherical bearing in split housing bolted to frame. Universal jaw on outer shaft serrated and clamped on shaft. This makes it possible to set lever at correct angle (5-$7\frac{1}{2}$ deg. forward from vertical). To disconnect cross-shaft extract universal joint pin.

Access to clutch for service after removal of gearbox.

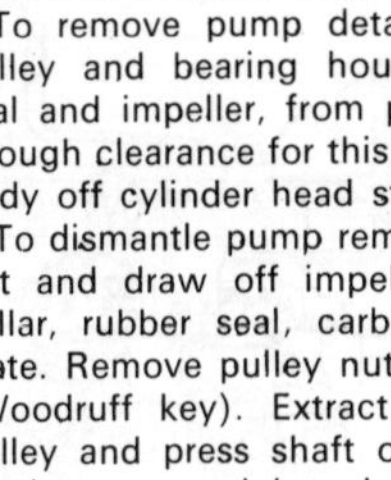


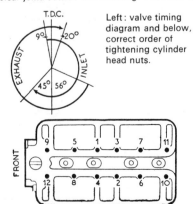

Left: valve timing diagram and below, correct order of tightening cylinder head nuts.

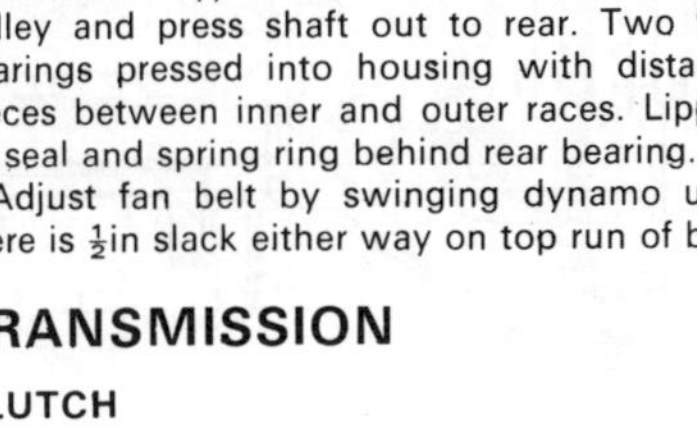


### GEARBOX

Four-speed, synchromesh on 2nd, 3rd and top gears.

**To remove gearbox,** leaving engine in place, slide both front seats right back and take up carpets. Screw off gear lever knob and remove gear box cowl and floor boards. Disconnect propeller shaft front-end, speedo drive and reverse lamp wire. Undo wire stay nut behind cross-member. Jack up engine under rear of sump. Detach rear mounting from cross-member and gearbox, and take away. Disconnect clutch cross-shaft. Detach plate in front of bell-housing (three bolts). Detach starter and lay aside. Take out bell-housing setscrews. Draw box clear of clutch plate and lift out.

To dismantle gearbox, detach clutch release bearing from fork, and remove bell-housing from gearbox. Pick out two steel washers in bearing register. Detach top cover with remote control.

Draw off driving flange with speedo drive gear, and remove rear cover with speedo drive pinion, and mounting plate.

Remove setscrews from forks and stops and drive out each rod to rear catching selector balls and interlock balls as they are released.

Make up dummy layshaft spindle with $\frac{3}{4}$in dia. rod $7\frac{9}{16}$in long. With this tap layshaft out to rear after removing setscrew from lower rear corner of box.

Drive out primary shaft with ball bearing by tapping rear end of mainshaft. Extract needle roller spigot bearing. Drive mainshaft back until rear bearing is clear of box and can be drawn off. Lift out mainshaft assembly through top of box, guiding front end past cut-away in box. Lift out layshaft cluster. Detach reverse gear rocking lever from side of box, and take out $\frac{3}{16}$in and $\frac{1}{4}$in setscrews which retain reverse fork slider rod and reverse gear spindle, and draw out rod and spindle to rear. Remove fork and bushed reverse gear.

To dismantle mainshaft assembly slide off synchromesh assemblies. Third gear is located on shaft by splined locking washer, locked by spring-loaded plunger. Depress plunger (exposed by slot in washer) and turn washer until male splines are in line with female splines in shaft, and slide washer off. Slide off gear and catch needle rollers.

Second gear is located by splined collar locked by spring-loaded plunger, with split thrust washer behind. Depress plunger with thin wire through holes in synchro cone and collar, turn collar and slide off. Extract split washer and slide off gear.

**To reassemble gearbox** assemble reverse gear (fork grooves to front), fork and slider rod, fitting setscrews to retain them. Assemble rocking lever.

Insert long distance-piece in layshaft cluster, with small thrust washers at each end. Smear thick grease inside bores and insert dummy layshaft spindle. Feed in 15 needle rollers at each end, followed by stepped thrust collars (large diameter inwards). Place large plain thrust washer on front end, followed by pegged washer. Smaller thrust washer goes on rear end with slotted washer. Lower assembly into box.

Reassemble mainshaft by inserting spring

and plunger in front end of shaft and assembling 3rd gear with 36 needle rollers. Slide on splined thrust washer, depress plunger through hole in gear, push washer home and turn to lock. Assemble 2nd gear with 22 needle rollers after inserting plunger and spring. Place split thrust washer against gear so that tab is in line with plunger. Slide on collar, making sure that slots are in line with tabs on split washer.

Depress plunger through hole in cone; push collar home and turn, listening for click as plunger registers. Slide on synchro assemblies.

Place mainshaft in box through top opening and assemble dished oil thrower washer (inner edge to bearing) and rear bearing on rear of shaft, with circlip on outer race to rear. Tap bearing home.

Assemble front bearing with dished oil thrower washer (inner edge to bearing) on primary shaft and tighten nut (left-hand thread). Using a length of $\frac{5}{8}$in dia. bar as a guide, assemble 13 needle rollers in spigot bearing, retaining them with thick grease. Assemble primary shaft in box and tap home.

Lift layshaft cluster carefully so that thrust washers are not displaced, and gently tap in layshaft spindle.

Insert selector rods, starting with reverse (nearside) rod, which has steady fork and selector jaw. Before inserting top and 3rd gear rod (centre) tilt box to nearside and insert interlock ball in cross-drilling in rear wall. Insert second interlock ball before 1st and 2nd gear rod.

Before fitting rear cover and mounting plate check end float of speedo drive pinion, which should be ·002in. Excessive float may cause oil pumping up cable. If no float is present, file end of bearing. Where rear cover fits over oil return thread on driving flange there should be ·003—·005in clearance. Burrs or paint should be cleaned off. Flat and dished washers fit between rear cover and bearing. Flat washer goes next to bearing and disher washer with inner edge towards flat washer. Assemble bell-housing with same arrangement of bearing washers.

### PROPELLER SHAFT

Two-stage. Short Hardy Spicer shaft with fixed needle roller bearing universal joints (nipples for lubrication), bolted to flange end of enclosed solid shaft. Rear end of enclosed shaft splined in muff coupling pinned to bevel pinion shaft. Centre bearing is bushed housing pushed into torque tube, and located by setscrew from outside. Front end of shaft supported in ball bearing carried in torque tube. Earlier type had bearing located in trunnion housing, which screws into torque tube. Shaft, with bearing, can be drawn out of torque tube when axle assembly is removed from car.

On some cars trunnion housing is clamped in torque tube. Clamp bolt must not be tightened enough to grip trunnion.

### REAR AXLE

Three-quarter floating shafts, spiral bevel final drive. Rear cover welded to banjo casing. Torque tube riveted to final drive housing.

**To remove axle from car** block up under chassis in front of rear spring hangers. Disconnect front end of open propeller shaft and draw shaft out with rear sliding flange. Take out $\frac{3}{8}$in setscrews and washers from trunnion ends, and eight $\frac{1}{4}$in bolts holding rubber bearing bushes in split housings. Disconnect brake rod from relay lever, and shock absorber links. Remove rear wheels and spring U-bolts, and drop rear ends of springs. By moving axle forward and twisting trunnion it can be released from frame brackets, which must not be prised apart.

Hub flanges are pressed on to splined axle shafts (interchangeable) and serviced as assembly. Inner ends of shafts splined in differential gears. Hubs run on ball bearings retained on axle casing tubes by ring nuts. Lipped oil seal behind bearing in each hub, lip towards bearing.

To withdraw shaft remove wheel and drum brake, and split flange joint by screwing $\frac{5}{16}$in Whit. bolts (or brake drum screws) into dummy holes.

Bevel pinion shaft carried in double row ball front and double row roller rear bearings. Distance-pieces between inner and outer races. Bearing assembly retained on bevel pinion shaft by nut. Shaft and bearing assembly retained in housing by ring outside outer race of rear bearing, held by three Allen-head setscrews inserted from outside. No bearing adjustment.

Bevel pinion mesh adjustment by screwed ring inside housing. with access through trap in top of housing. Rear retaining ring setscrews must be slackened off for bevel pinion mesh adjustment, which should be done, if possible, with special gauge.

Crown wheel spigoted on split differential cage and retained by 10 setscrews. Differential assembly carried in semi-thrust ball bearings in split housings. Bearings and mesh adjusted by large nuts on differential cage extensions.

Adjust bearings until there is no play and no drag. Move both adjusting nuts equally after bearing adjustment to adjust mesh until backlash is ·006in.

Before remounting axle on car, screw trunnion housing into torque tube until distance between rear face of final drive housing flange and rear face of trunnion lug is $52\frac{7}{16}$in, or as near as possible with grease nipple at top of trunnion housing.

## CHASSIS

### BRAKES

Girling hydro-mechanical (hydraulic front brakes, mechanical rear brakes).

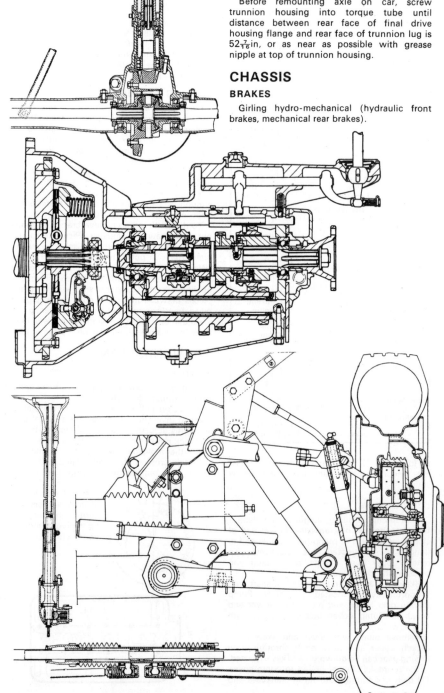

Front brake adjustment is by snail cams on backplates for each shoe. Tighten each adjuster until shoe binds, and back off until quite free.

Rear brakes have square-ended adjusters on backplates. Tighten until resistance is felt, and back off one click. Check that wheel is free.

If front brake hose is disconnected it must be refitted with banjo on backplate pointing forward at about 30 deg. from horizontal. If too horizontal hose will stretch and foul suspension. If too vertical it will foul wheel rim.

### REAR SPRINGS

Semi-elliptic, shackled at both ends. Rubber shackle bushes. Shouldered bolts. Tighten self-locking nuts fully.

### FRONT SUSPENSION

Independent, torsion bars. Built-up tubular triangulated upper and lower links. Inner ends pivot in rubber bushes, outer ends in bronze bushes.

Complete suspension and steering assembly can be removed as a unit from frame. Remove radiator shell and core, and front wings. Disconnect all front end wiring, including steering column wires, at push-in connectors. Slacken union nut below steering box and draw out control column. Slacken wheel clamping nut, extract spring ring and draw off wheel. Slacken steady bracket and column

clamp at lower end, and draw column tube up, exposing nut which retains column in muff coupling. Remove column. Drive out ten ½in bolts holding front cradle to chassis frame (eight long, two shorter). Two lowest bolts enter from front, and can be extracted when lower link is moved down. Cradle can then be removed.

Upper and lower ends of king pins, with outer bearing assemblies of suspension links, are identical and interchangeable. Lugs have flanged bronze bushes for king pins and link bearings. Link bearing spindles are shouldered, dowelled in links and retained by Simmonds nuts. Tighten nuts fully. If link bearing brushes are renewed they should be spot-faced after assembly to 3·248—3·246in between faces. King pin pressed into stub axle against shoulder and located by steering arm, acting as cotter. King pin thrust taken by screwed bushes at top and bottom, located in lugs by grub screws.

Inner end of upper link has rubber bushed eyes. Spindle located in cradle by locking plates, one serrated.

Inner eyes of lower link serrated and retained on externally and internally serrated sleeve by ring nuts. Sleeve works in rubber bushes in cradle, separated by distance tube and squeezed up by link eyes. Torsion bar fits in internal serrations in sleeve, and is retained by bolt and cup washer.

Setting of torsion bars is important. Height of inner ends of lower links from ground must be 1½in more than height of outer ends, measured at centres of spindles, with front tyres at correct pressure (22 lb), and car on level ground.

If dimension is less than 1½in jack up front until all weight is off wheels, and tighten adjuster setscrews at rear ends of torsion bars. One full turn of adjuster makes ⅜in difference in dimension. Lower car and test again. If dimension is now more than 1½in adjusters can be slackened off without car being jacked up. Car should be rocked up and down between measurements to settle suspension.

For track adjustment wheels should be parallel with suspension set to 1½in. Car should then be raised to 1½in setting. *Note: Torsion bar setting must never be increased while weight of car is on wheels.*

### STEERING GEAR

Helical rack and pinion. Ball pins attached to lug on centre of rack, and connected to two identical track rods.

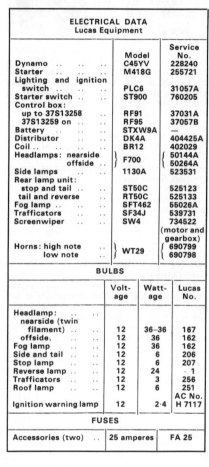

| ELECTRICAL DATA | | |
|---|---|---|
| **Lucas Equipment** | | |
| | Model | Service No. |
| Dynamo .. .. .. | C45YV | 228240 |
| Starter .. .. .. | M418G | 255721 |
| Lighting and ignition switch .. | PLC6 | 31057A |
| Starter switch .. .. | ST900 | 760205 |
| Control box: | | |
| up to 37S13258 | RF91 | 37031A |
| 37S13259 on .. | RF95 | 37057B |
| Battery .. .. .. | STXW9A | — |
| Distributor .. .. | DK4A | 404425A |
| Coil .. .. .. | BR12 | 402029 |
| Headlamps: nearside offside .. } | F700 | 50144A 50264A |
| Side lamps .. .. | 1130A | 523531 |
| Rear lamp unit: | | |
| stop and tail .. | ST50C | 525123 |
| tail and reverse .. | RT50C | 525133 |
| Fog lamp .. .. | SFT462 | 55026A |
| Trafficators .. .. | SF34J | 539731 |
| Screenwiper .. .. | SW4 | 734522 (motor and gearbox) |
| Horns: high note low note .. } | WT29 | 690799 690798 |

| BULBS | | | |
|---|---|---|---|
| | Voltage | Wattage | Lucas No. |
| Headlamp: | | | |
| nearside (twin filament) .. .. | 12 | 36—36 | 167 |
| offside .. .. | 12 | 36 | 162 |
| Fog lamp .. .. | 12 | 36 | 162 |
| Side and tail .. | 12 | 6 | 206 |
| Stop lamp .. .. | 12 | 6 | 207 |
| Reverse lamp .. | 12 | 24 | 1 |
| Trafficators .. .. | 12 | 3 | 256 |
| Roof lamp .. .. | 12 | 6 | 251 |
| | | | AC No. |
| Ignition warning lamp | 12 | 2·4 | H 7117 |

| FUSES | | | |
|---|---|---|---|
| Accessories (two) .. | 25 amperes | | FA 25 |

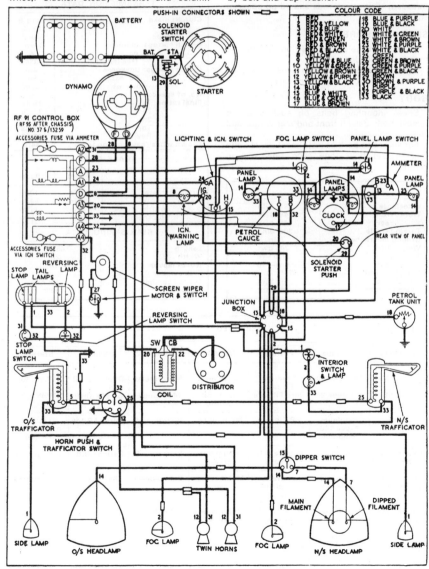

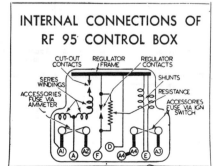

## INTERNAL CONNECTIONS OF RF 95 CONTROL BOX

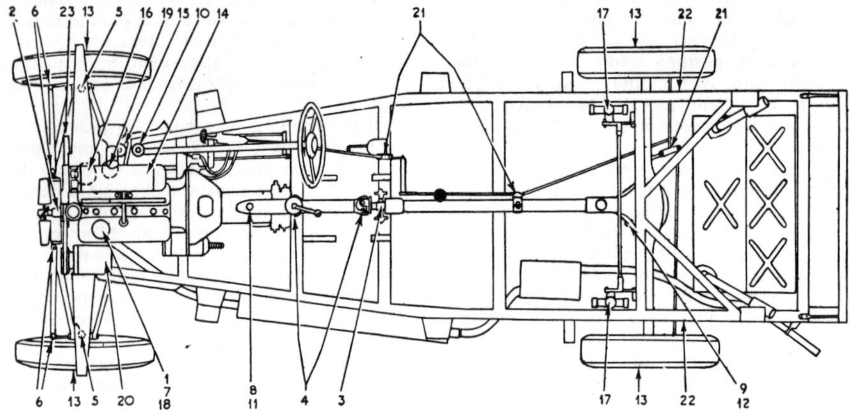


EVERY 250 MILES
1. Engine sump—top up

EVERY 1,000 MILES
2. Water pump bearings (1)
3. Torque tube front bearing (1)
4. Propeller-shaft universal joints (2)
5. King pin bearings (4)
6. Steering ball joints (4)
} grease gun

EVERY 1,500 MILES
7. Engine sump—drain and refill
8. Gearbox
9. Rear axle
10. Brake fluid reservior
} top up

EVERY 5,000 MILES
11. Gearbox
12. Rear axle
} drain and refill
13. Front and rear hubs—grease gun
14. Air cleaner—clean in petrol and re-oil
15. Carburettor—few drops oil in dashpot
16. Distributor—machine oil in oiler and under rotor arm. Light grease or engine oil on contact breaker pivot
17. Rear shock absorbers—top up

EVERY 10,000 MILES
18. Engine sump—remove and clean
19. Engine oil filter—renew complete
20. Dynamo—refill lubricator
21. Control joints, brake linkage—machine oil in oilcan
22. Rear springs—clean with paraffin and apply grease

EVERY 30,000 MILES
23. Steering gear—remove cap and spring in box and repack with grease

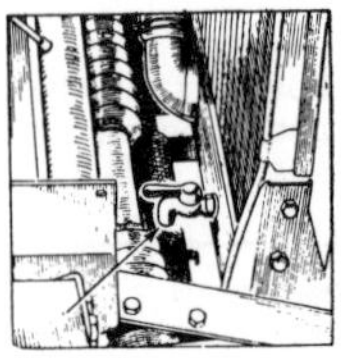

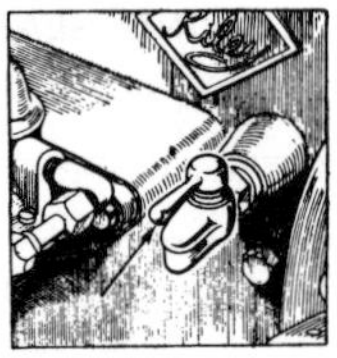

| FILL-UP DATA | |
|---|---|
| Engine sump .. .. .. .. | 10 pints |
| Gearbox .. .. .. .. | 2 pints |
| Rear axle .. .. .. | 2¾ pints |
| Cooling system .. .. | 13 pints |
| Petrol tank .. .. .. | 12½ gallons |
| Tyre pressures: front .. | 22lb |
| rear .. | 24lb |

To remove steering gear from car remove control column, steering wheel, column tube and column. Disconnect outer ball pins of track rods and detach front tray. Take out setscrews (below) and two nuts (above, on cradle bolts) attaching steering cross-tube clamp brackets to cradle, and draw out steering gear assembly.

Pinion shaft runs in taper roller bearings in housing. Shims for bearing adjustment.

Mesh of rack with pinion maintained by spring-loaded plunger below cap at top of housing. Shims under cap to adjust pressure.

To dismantle gear slacken and pull off nearside clamp bracket, exposing countersunk screw retaining collar and nearside extension tube on centre tube. Draw these off, with spherical bush in end of tube. Detach meshing plunger and cap assembly with shims, and slide out rack with track rods. Rack can be screwed out of ball pin lug with spherical bush between.

Track rod inner ball joints are screwed end plug type, reversed. Order of assembly of ball joint is; short spring with stop piece inside, ball socket, long spring and screwed plug.

Outer ball joints are screwed side plug type, with renewable ball seats. Washer between ball seat and spring.

To adjust track slacken track rod clamps and tuen tube (sockets left- and right-hand threaded). Both track rods should be adjusted equally.

## SHOCK ABSORBERS

Front Girling telescopic. No adjustment, no topping up needed.

Rear Luvax Girling piston type, linked by anti-roll torsion bar. Top up in place.

## BODY

Seven mounting bolts on each side. To remove body detach front and rear wings, and steering column.

For access to back of instrument panel undo four bracket bolts—one each side, two in centre.

| GENERAL DATA | |
|---|---|
| Wheelbase .. .. .. | 9ft 4½in |
| Track: front .. .. | 4ft 4¼in |
| rear .. .. | 4ft 4¼in |
| Turning circle .. .. | 30ft 0in |
| Ground clearance .. | 7½in |
| Weight (dry) .. .. | 24¼ cwt |
| Tyres: front .. .. | 5·75—16 |
| rear .. .. | 5·75—16 |
| Overall length .. .. | 14ft 11in |
| Overall width .. .. | 5ft 3½in |
| Overall height .. .. | 4ft 11in |

| TRANSMISSION DATA | |
|---|---|
| Clutch: make .. .. .. .. | Borg & Beck |
| type .. .. .. .. | 8A6°G |
| Clutch springs: colour .. .. .. | Brown |
| no. .. .. .. | 6 |
| free length .. .. | 2,334in |
| Clutch linings: thickness .. .. | ⅛in |
| dia. ext. .. .. | 8in |
| dia. int. .. .. | 5¼in |
| No. of speeds .. .. .. .. | 4 |
| Final ratios: 1st .. .. .. .. | 19·42 |
| 2nd .. .. .. .. | 11·20 |
| 3rd .. .. .. .. | 7·23 |
| Top .. .. .. | 4·89 |
| Rev. .. .. .. | 19·42 |
| Crown wheel/bevel pinion teeth .. | 44/9 |

BRAKE DATA

| | Front | Rear |
|---|---|---|
| Drum diameter .. .. | 10in | 10in |
| Lining: length .. .. | 9¾in | 9⅜in |
| width .. .. | 1¾in | 1½in |
| thickness .. | 3/16in | 3/16in |

| REAR SPRING DATA | |
|---|---|
| Length .. .. .. | 45½in |
| Width .. .. .. | 2in |
| No. of leaves .. .. | 13 |
| Free camber .. .. | 4in |
| Loaded camber .. .. | 1¾in *neg.* |
| at load .. .. .. | 750lb |

| | RECOM-MENDED | LUBRICATION | | | APPROVED | | | | |
|---|---|---|---|---|---|---|---|---|---|
| | Duckham's | Duckham's | Wakefield | Essolube | Filtrate | Vacuum | Price's | Shell | Sternol |
| Engine Summer | N.O.L. Thirty | Adcol NPXX | Castrol XL | Essolube 30 | Medium Filtrate | Mobiloil A | Motorine M | Double Shell | W.W. 30 |
| Winter (below 32°F) | N.O.L. Twenty | Adcol NPX | Castrolite | Essolube 20 | Zero Filtrate | Mobiloil Arctic | Motorine E | Single Shell | W.W. 20 |
| Gearbox, rear axle | N.O.L. E.P. transmission oil 140 | Adcol NS Press 140 | Castrol Hi-press | Essoleum Expee 140 Compound | EP Filtrate | Mobiloil EP | Motorine EP | Spirax EP 140 | Liquid Ambroleum EP 140 |
| Wheel hubs, fan bearings | Adcol H.B.B. grease | Adcol H.B.B. grease | Castrolease heavy | Esso grease | Filtrate R.B. grease | Mobil hub grease | Belmoline C | Retinax R.B. | R.B. grease |
| Chassis nipples, springs, steering gear | Laminoid Soft | Adcol HPG grease | Castrolease medium | Esso fluid grease | High pressure solidified Filtrate | Mobil grease No. 4 | Belmoline D | Retinax C | M.M. grease |
| Cables and control joints | ZNOL K.G. 16 grease | ZNOL K.G. 16 grease | Castrolease brake cable grease | Anti-freeze grease | Filtrate AF grease | Mobil grease No. 4 | Belmoline H | Retinax C | Anti-freeze grease |
| Oil can, Carburettor dashpot | N.O.L. Twenty | Adcol NPX | Castrolite | Essolube 20 | Zero Filtrate | Mobiloil Arctic | Motorine E | Single Shell | W.W. 20 |

# BUYING AN RM RILEY

*In their publicity Rileys promised their customers "Magnificent Motoring" and this well-restored example — a 2½-litre RMF — is clearly one of the outstanding cars of the early post-war period.*

**V**ery soon after the end of the Second World War Rileys announced a range of 1½ and 2½-litre cars which are now appreciated by classic car enthusiasts for much the same reasons that attracted their first owners. They are cars for the discerning people who appreciate fine materials and engineering elegantly presented in cars which are a pleasure to look at, maintain and drive, providing long lasting satisfaction and pride of ownership in a way that few of their contemporary rivals can.

So far I have owned six Riley RMs and I have enjoyed all of them, furthermore I have met very few people who have owned an RM and been less than complimentary about the cars. Yet there are those who feel that the post-war Rileys were not *real* Rileys at all and so we must look briefly at the background story of these distinctive cars.

Riley made their first four-wheeled cars in 1907 and established a good reputation for the design and quality of their Coventry made products.

During 1926 the Riley Nine appeared and it set new standards for high quality, lively motoring in the small to medium sized car market. The power unit was a notably good one and established the pattern for all Rileys made up to the introduction of the BMC C-series six-cylinder Riley 2.6 in 1957, and served in a wide range of saloons, tourers, sports-cars and racing cars — in six-cylinder form it served as the starting point for the very successful ERA single-seaters.

This engine gained practically all the advantages of a twin overhead camshaft layout but avoided the expenses, complication and maintenance drawbacks by having its two camshafts high in the cylinder block operating short pushrods linked by rockers to valves opposed at ninety degrees in a classic hemispherical combustion chamber. This layout was efficient, economical and reliable and Rileys gained considerable popularity, but in 1938 the risks of a large and complex model range which was aimed at a fairly narrow section of the market caught up with Rileys and they were taken over by the Nuffield Group.

William Morris, later Lord Nuffield, believed in making a little go a long way and had actively pursued a policy of common parts and badge engineering within Morris, Wolseley and MG and not without success.

*Michael Brisby enthuses over one of his favourite model ranges.*

*The side view (above) of this lovely 1948 Riley 2½ (RMB) shows to full advantage the superbly balanced lines of the post-war Rileys. The 1½-litre versions were the same from the windscreen back but had a shorter wheelbase and bonnet. The 1½ and 2½-litre Rileys are difficult to distinguish from the rear but the short bonnet and line of the front wings and running boards (left) show this is the smaller version — a large rear window and bars linking the rear over-riders indicate it is an early RME.*

Riley supporters feared the worst and felt that at the very least Rileys would lose their quality of engineering and construction and their individuality. Some diehards insist that this is exactly what did happen but I think they were wrong.

As the Second World War approached the development of new models was proceeding rapidly and they were not glorified Morrises because revised versions of the four cylinder Riley engines in 1½ and 2½-litre form were adopted and the new chassis was equally exclusive to Riley.

While very few British manufacturers ignored the trend towards providing

*In 1950 the interior of the RMs was revised. The earlier cars (above) had a very elegant traditional instrument panel with the "umbrella" handbrake on the left below the panel and features included an opening screen for the driver and hand parked wipers — the heater is a period extra. The later panel (below) went "modern" with rectangular minor gauges, and a row of switches below them. Note that the handbrake was now on the right and that the panels were common to 1½ and 2½-litre cars. Those very big steering wheels do not make the excellent steering particularly light, though.*

independent front suspension in the late thirties some efforts were crude, slightly better versions followed American practice and a select band of engineers studied the front wheel drive Citroens very closely. Rileys engineers plumped for the Citroen recipe — parallel, unequal length wishbones with torsion bars as the suspension medium. They did not miss the point that independent suspension is a waste of effort unless the car's structure is rigid, they appreciated that rack and pinion steering (another Citroen feature)

*The Riley Roadster was a shortlived attempt to win sales overseas. The styling is a bit debatable and this example lacks part of the brash bumper arrangement.*

*The final version of the Riley 1½-litre was the later RME which was given completely different wings and lost its running boards in a facelift which was not as unsuccessful as some would suggest.*

was desirable and did not undo their work by following the American trend towards shoving the engine ahead of the front wheel centre line to increase passenger carrying space. Overcoming a reluctance to trust hydraulics, Rileys gave the new car hydraulically operated front brakes but, like Rolls Royce for several years to come, retained rod operated rear brakes.

It seems likely that from the outset a 1½-litre and a 2½-litre were planned to share many components with only a longer front end, ahead of the front bulkhead, on the 2½ to differentiate between the cars. The body and interior owed nothing to other Nuffield Group products. If there was any outside influence it came from the immediate pre-war BMWs and was shared with the post-war Bristol 400 which had a similar general outline and wing form with sweeping running boards, but carried its spare wheel externally on the boot lid and did not have that distinctive fabric covered roof which so identifies the Riley RMs.

Constructional details of the Riley body were a mixture of ancient and modern with

## What to Pay

Riley RMs moved out of the bargain basement some time ago and you may have to look quite hard to find a sound basis for restoration at around £400 — unfortunately quite bad examples do not go significantly cheaper, and it is very important to make sure that you are not paying good money for an almost derilect wreck. If anything the 1½-litre saloons are more common and cheaper, but the poorer Roadster and Dropheads probably only start at around £1,000 if you can find them!

The top 1½-litre saloons cost around £3,000 and the 2½-litre prices approach £4,000, a Roadster could go to around £6,000 and a Drophead might fetch £7,500-£8,000 but all these prices apply to outstanding examples.

timber in the screen pillars, around the rear window, in the door frames and in the sills. The bodies were not, strictly speaking, coachbuilt but the attention to details, the panel fits and the way the doors 'click-chopped" shut reflected superb quality and while it is unfortunate that the fabric of the roof and the use of timber have spelt restoration problems in recent years, the bodies have generally lasted well.

After the saloons went into production some variants were produced, including some exposed woodwork estate cars built by outside concerns on the 1½-litre chassis, the unsuccessful 2½-litre Roadsters which failed to impress the export markets but now command high prices, and the extremely elegant (and now valuable) two door drophead coupe which was almost exclusively built on the 2½-litre chassis. There were some detail

*The poor relation — the 2½-litre Riley was replaced by the Pathfinder in 1953 and while this still had the four-cylinder Riley engine and was given the factory code RMH it was quite a long way removed from what had gone before.*

## R.M. Roundup

Basically the Riley RM range centred around the 1½- and 2½-litre saloons but to identify the changes incorporated and the drophead and roadster variants it becomes useful to refer to the factory type codes. These included three letters and it is the third letter which is significant.

**RMA** — This refers to the 1½-litre in its original form, a saloon with quarter bumpers front and rear, round instruments, opening driver's screen, small rear window, hydro-mechanical brakes, torque tube rear axle.

**RMB** — The 2½-litre saloon had much the same identification points.

**Note** — Various changes were made to the RMA and RMB including a change from external bonnet locks to internal ones, the deletion of cloth seat panels, improvements to the brakes and dampers, and alterations to the ratio of the steering rack to reduce effort. 1950 models and their successors lost the opening screen and were provided with a revised instrument panel with rectangular faces on the auxiliary guages.

Because bare chassis were supplied to outside coachbuilders it is possible to find shooting brakes and drophead coupes with RMA chassis numbers.

**RME** — In mid-1952 the 1½-litre was fitted with a continuous front bumper and the rear quarter bumpers were linked by plated bars above and below the rear number plate panel. The rear window was also enlarged. The brakes were now all hydraulic and the torque tube rear axle was replaced by a two piece prop shaft with a conventional hypoid axle and the final drive was altered to improve acceleration and low speed flexibility.

**RMF** — At the same time (1952) the bigger car was similarly revised and the new rear axle eliminated a weakness in the earlier half-shafts which could break in adverse conditions. This was the final version of the 2½-litre and a series of minor changes to the engine increased power to 100 b.h.p.

**RME** — No, we are not repeating the RME by mistake — in 1953 there were a further batch of changes for the 1½-litre saloons but the RME identification was retained!

Externally the running boards were deleted and the front and rear wings replaced by "helmet" ones — the front ones with the side and spotlights built in and the rear ones with spats.

**RMH** — While we may consider that the Riley RMs have a timeless grace to customers, they did look old-fashioned by the end of their run. The RMH, known as the Pathfinder, had a new chassis and body which allowed much more interior space and window area and a smooth (perhaps bland) outward appearance. The 2½-litre four-cylinder engine was retained until 1957 and the gearbox now sprouted a right-hand gate change. Most Riley supporters have strong reservations about these "non-RM" RMs but they are now becoming quite rare.

**RMC** — Intended for export the RMC is the Riley Roadster, and it was based on the 2½-litre. Just over 500 were built between 1948 and 1951 and the early ones had a steering column gear-change to permit three-abreast seating — later cars had the same floor change as the saloon. The body was lower and wider than the saloons and had a foldflat screen and cutaway doors, with bumpers more suitable for catching cows and fending off kangaroos. Now expensive despite their questionable proportions.

**RMD** — The D stands for drophead and this is considered the most desirable RM — prices reflect this and although Roadster and Drophead production figures are almost identical the Drophead is now much rarer. Only the 2½-litre Drophead was catalogued but it should be remembered that while only a couple of 1½-litre dropheads were built by the factory some were made by outside coachbuilders. The factory dropheads are extremely elegant.

# BUYING AN RM RILEY

*The engines were placed well back in the chassis on both the 2½ (above) and the 1½ (below) and that probably contributed to the cars' reputation for excellent handling; access might appear to be a problem until you realize that the bonnet sides are easily removed.*

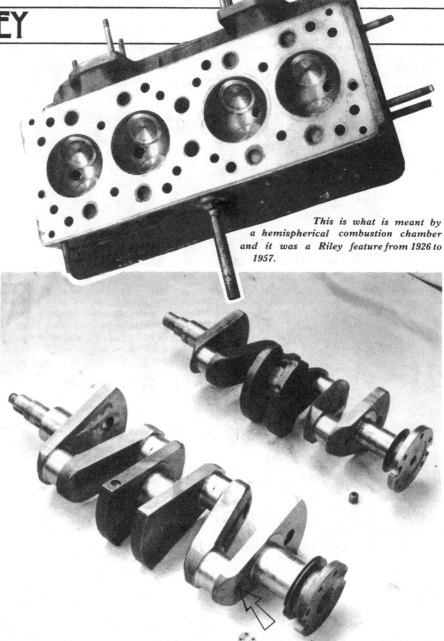

*This is what is meant by a hemispherical combustion chamber and it was a Riley feature from 1926 to 1957.*

changes to both 1½ and 2½-litre Rileys affecting both the mechanical and body details prior to 1953 when the 2½-litre was dropped and the 1½-litre was given a "facelift" which deleted the running boards and substituted "helmet" front wings for the original flowing ones. Fuller details of these production changes are provided in the accompanying table which also explains the Riley model code applications.

*Taking the grille, bonnet assembly and wings off is not a five minute job, but it can be done since they are all bolted on. This view of the 1½-litre engine shows the two rocker covers — the engine is a twin cam, but the camshafts are below the cylinder head.*

*Despite the robustness of the crankshafts (1½ top, 2½ in foreground) they can give trouble if the oil passages through the crank-pins (arrowed) clog causing bearing starvation — dirty oil and long spells of idleness aggravated the problem but once dealt with the engines will last for years.*

## THEN AND NOW

The 1½-litre saloon was the first Riley RM to appear and was widely applauded by the motoring press who spoke in glowing tones about the car's quality, its road behaviour and its performance. Even allowing for the fact that the motoring press were uniformly polite about almost anything put in front of them and the motoring public's enthusiasm for all new cars (despite the difficulty of getting them and the petrol to run them immediately after the war) the Riley deserved its praise although I would have been a bit more reserved about the performance — a car with 55 b.h.p. and over

*The independent front suspension incorporating torsion bars was very sturdily made and played a great part in the RM reputation for good road behaviour. On many cars the suspension bushes are now due for replacement and the steering rack is worn. On very early cars the bottom wishbones can crack.*

27 cwt to pull was working very hard to do 75-80 m.p.h., took a long time to get there and did not like attempts to maintain that speed.

The Riley 2½-litre was announced within months of the smaller car and was even more enthusiastically received by the press. Weighing 3½ cwt more (quite a lot of that was engine!) and with a 6½-inches longer wheelbase the bigger car had 90 b.h.p. (later increased to 100 b.h.p.) and could do between 95 and 100 m.p.h. A much longer legged high speed tourer, it is generally accepted that the 2½ is less agile than the 1½-litre cars but both could run rings around the opposition in terms of stable, predictable road manners. You will see reports that the steering is heavy (not surprising with 2½ turns lock to lock) but it is also very precise.

I had four 1½-litre Rileys and found them a pleasure to own and my first reaction to the 2½-litre was that I had bought a lorry but the better visual proportions, much easier and relaxed performance and the discovery that on long fast journeys fuel consumption was only two or three miles per gallon worse, soon convinced me that the bigger car was the one for me. However, as the owners of both cars share the same interiors and enjoy the same quality of engineering and materials the choice must depend upon what car is available, personal taste and how much fast, long distance work you want to do.

## THE MECHANICS

With the exception of the half-shafts on the early 2½-litre cars the Rileys had no obvious weaknesses in their engines, transmissions or chassis. The cars were designed by engineers and built by people who did things properly and no corners were cut — I have been told that when the Nuffield Group was absorbed into BMC cost-accountants visited the engine line; they calculated what each engine cost to build and gave urgent instructions that this would have to stop!

Unfortunately, by the time the youngest RM engine was twenty years old it became clear that there were some "built-in" problems in the bottom end of the engines. These are a combination of a) oil starvation due to sludge in the crankshaft oilways, b) over-revving increasing the loads on bearings coping with the strains of long stroke engines, c) problems getting white metal bearings re-metalled satisfactorily or on the bigger cars of obtaining suitable shell bearings either to replace the originals or to convert white metal bearings to shells.

When a Riley RM crankshaft oilway clogs up it occurs at the journals and the only way to overcome the problem is to remove plugs at each crank pin journal (much easier said than done!) and remove the solid accumulation that prevents oil circulation. If there are no signs of

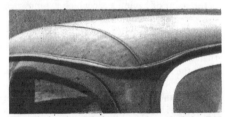

*The distinctive fabric covered roof of the RM saloons can be a major source of trouble when the seams part and the fabric shrinks and splits allowing water to penetrate. The pimples on the roof of this car indicate rust on the expanded metal below the fabric and layer of felt.*

*With the fabric and felt removed to expose the expanded metal it becomes clear that water leaks around the rear window can play havoc with the timber in that area — discoloured or rotten headlining around the rear window are indications of trouble.*

trouble (low or high oil pressure) regular use and oil changes will keep you in the clear.

I revved my 1½-litres and paid the price — to the man who did the white metalling. With the bigger engines I don't think I used over 40 m.p.h. in third let alone the 70 m.p.h. some people insist is possible and at sensibly modest revs those engines will pull and pull and last very well indeed.

Because of the bearing problems described (which are curable and preventable) many

*The timber screen pillars can suffer at the top from roof leaks and at the bottom from road dirt and water thrown up where they protrude below the wings and running boards. Replacing the pillars and the metal covered wooden sills (which secure the running boards) are major undertakings.*

*Rust attacks the body adjacent to the rear also be examined, as this stripped 1½ litre seen at the Riley Centre indicates.*

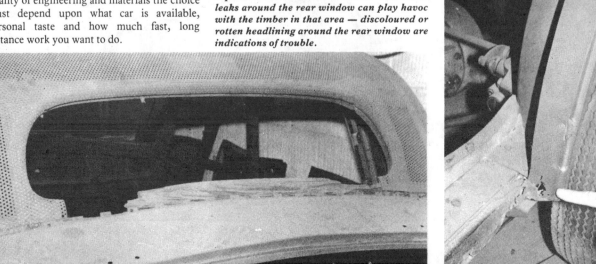

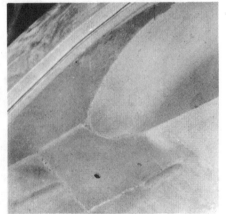

*Although the chassis is very strong the boot floor and wheel arch around the rear body mounting (indicated on a car where the body has been raised off the chassis) can rust and allow the entire rear body to settle.*

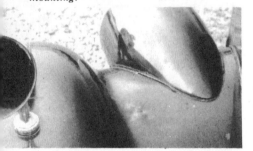

*This is where the boot floor often requires repairs — the bolt hole for the body mounting.*

*The dimpled metal on the front wing, halfway between the wing mirror and headlamp pod indicates a common problem caused by a mud-trap between the wing and the supporting bracket. Failure of the wing mounting is not completely unknown.*

RMs that started out with white metal big end bearings have since had their con-rods modified to take non-standard (modified lorry) bearings. Perhaps it is carrying originality a bit far but I argue that as long as you can get the white metalling done properly and then run the car in nicely white metal big ends last well and are kind to the crankshaft.

Top-to-bottom engine overhauls by professionals are frighteningly expensive at between £700 and £900 until you consider that some very average engines are now becoming unexpectedly costly and these are not any old engine. Even if you decide to "do-it-yourself" you will need some expert assistance and will have to allow for pistons that might cost £25 each and sets of piston rings at between £40 and £50. However, there is the consolation that the engine should, barring accidents, and given a reasonably sympathetic driver last nearly 100,000 miles which is a long time if the car is for pleasure use.

## SUSPENSION AND STEERING

We have said it before — many classic cars are let down by suspension and steering which may well function safely but does not perform as it did when new. Time expired front suspension bushes (particularly the rubber ones), poor rear springs and inefficient dampers will spoil even the best cars and what is the point of having a car which is renowned for its excellent steering, ride and road-behaviour and handicapping it by not making sure that everything is "as-new" I have found that weak rear springs and tired dampers can make the Riley RMs pitch to the point where a ride in the rear seats is decidedly uncomfortable and it is worth mentioning that on pre-1951 cars the lever arm rear dampers present a problem — later cars with telescopic dampers all-round are much easier to deal with.

The excellent rack and pinion steering unfortunately remains excellent long after

*Later Riley RMs had their sun visors recessed into the headlining which is a nice touch but underlines the fact that restoring the interior of one of these cars can be a major, and expensive, undertaking.*

serious wear is likely to have alarmed the MoT tester and the main problem is likely to be a worn guide in the rack tube.

In my opinion both the 1½ and 2½-litre Rileys are at their best on 600 x 16 Avon Turbospeed cross-plies and if you consider using the cheaper alternatives, bear in mind that these are quite heavy cars and while the smaller car is happy at 50-55 m.p.h. the 2½-litre can cruise comfortably at 70 m.p.h.    □

*The RM Rileys were a remarkably successful design in almost every respect combining the best of pre-war quality and elegance with advanced and well executed modern features. Michael Brisby recently drove this one and looks forward to the next excuse to borrow it.*

# "As Old as the Industry As Modern as the Hour"

# 1950 RILEY 2½ LITER

**by Arch Brown**
**photos by Vince Manocchi**

I T'S ONE of the joys of this line of work that a person gets to drive a lot of different automobiles. Most of them are choice examples of whatever make and model they represent.

Some are styled so well that their beauty is undimmed by passing years and changing fancies.

A few feature engineering achievements far in advance of the era from which they came.

Many offer performance beyond the norm.

Some cradle their occupants in superb comfort.

And a handful provide such crisp handling qualities that driving becomes, once again, an exhilarating experience.

But only very, very rarely does one find a single automobile that manages to combine in generous measure *all* of these qualities!

Such a motorcar is the 2½-liter Riley.

Based on its sheer, classic beauty, we've suffered the anguish of unrequited love with respect to this gorgeous vehicle for 35 years—ever since we saw some fortunate family touring Yosemite in a bronze-finished saloon. (See glossary.) Now, in Yosemite National Park one is expected to admire the beauty of the falls, the grandeur of Half-Dome, the

magnificence of El Capitan. But we couldn't take our eyes off that Riley!

So much for the confessional. We really didn't know a great deal about the car, and when someone informed us that the Riley was powered by a four-cylinder engine, and sold, on this side of the Atlantic, for a price approaching that of the Cadillac, we pressed the investigation no further.

Kind of a dumb notion anyway, maybe. The Riley, after all, was styled like something straight out of the late thirties. Couldn't hold a candle, when it came to aerodynamics, to the step-down Hudsons that were just beginning to appear. And what kind of performance could one expect, for heaven's sake, out of a four-cylinder engine?

Little did we suspect!

Three things came together, many years later, to rekindle our interest in the Riley.

For one thing, following the advice of our son we had purchased a four-cylinder European sedan which, we found, could hold its own very nicely

with many American cars firing twice as many barrels.

So much for any doubts we had about four-bangers.

For another, we learned two or three years ago when we interviewed Donald Healey (see *SIA* #67) that he had used the 2½-liter Riley engine in a number of his early sports cars.

Hard to find a better recommendation than that!

And then, while in southern California on an assignment for *SIA* we caught sight of Varlie Gordon's Riley drophead. We called Editor Dave Brownell, back in Vermont, and verbally twisted his arm. "Dave," we pleaded. "This car is so beautiful I don't care if the damn thing won't get out of its own way, we've got to do a driveReport on it!"

Six months later, his arm dangling from a bloody socket, the editor capitulated!

The Riley family was known, in the nineteenth century, for its prominence in Britain's weaving industry. But in 1890 the family firm, then under the direction of William Riley, Jr., purchased Bonnick and Company, builders of fine bicycles. Six years later William liquidated the weaving operation and placed all his chips on the bicycle factory, changing its name to the Riley Cycle Company.

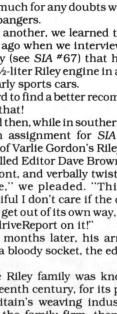

William Riley had five sons, each of whom would in the succeeding years play an important role in the family's business enterprises. It was Percy Riley, the middle son, for instance, who first became involved in building automobiles. By 1898, working independently of the family concern, Percy had designed and built his first car, a 2½-horsepower one-lunger that featured mechanically operated valve gear (a "first") and a steering wheel in place of the then-customary tiller.

A year later the Riley Cycle Company displayed, at the National Cycle Show, the "Royal Riley," a single-cylinder quadricycle. In 1901 the subsidiary Riley Engine Company was established, to produce a range of engines employing Percy Riley's patented valve gear.

For the 1906 season Riley introduced a V-twin, the first car in the world to be fitted with detachable wire wheels. It was a fast little number for its day, and over the next few years the two-cylinder Riley scored a string of successes in a variety of competitive events. Team drivers included three of the Riley brothers, Victor, Allan and Stanley.

For a time the demand for Riley's patented detachable wheels was so great as to overshadow the automobile enterprise, but in 1913 a monobloc four-cylinder Riley was offered. The coming

of World War I then diverted the company's attention to the production of military hardware.

The diamond-shaped Riley badge made its initial appearance on a new 11-horsepower Riley, first displayed at the 1919 Olympia Motor Show. Its side-valve four developed a respectable 35 horsepower, giving the car a moderately lively level of performance. An aggressive marketing program was soon underway, under the direction of William Riley's youngest son Cecil. As part of this effort the slogan "As Old as the Industry" was adopted in 1920. Five years later it was expanded to read "As Old as the Industry—As Modern as the Hour."

By 1926 there were several Riley enterprises. (The group included Riley Coventry, Ltd., the parent concern, presided over by William Riley's eldest son Victor; the Midland Motor Body Company, directed by second son Allan Riley; and the Riley Engine Company, Ltd., headed by Percy Riley.) The big event of the year was the introduction of the Riley Nine (see sidebar, page 19), powered by an engine so advanced that with periodic modifications it remained in production for more than 30 years. Once again, the designer was Percy Riley.

Features of this remarkable engine

# 1950 RILEY

included hemispherical combustion chambers and overhead valves inclined at an angle of 45 degrees. The latter were operated by twin camshafts set high in the engine block, in order that short pushrods might provide the efficiency of an overhead camshaft design combined with the serviceability of a pushrod engine. A hot-spot induction system provided exhaust gas heating of the induction manifold in order to insure the most efficient gas flow into the combustion chambers.

Equally advanced was the four-speed transmission of the Riley Nine. Crisp and precise, it boasted a silent third gear—highly unusual for that time, and a welcome relief from the dismal whine typical of most gearboxes.

Nor was styling neglected. The Nine was a handsome little car, particularly when fitted with Stanley Riley's "Monaco" saloon body. And prices for this ex-

cellent automobile started at only £235. Even the celebrated "Monaco" was only £285!

The Nine remained in production through 1938—refined and updated from time to time, to be sure, and joined in 1929 by a six-cylinder version employing the same bore and stroke as the four. Both models added luster to the Riley name in a variety of competitive events.

Nineteen-thirty-five brought the next major Riley development, a new, 1½-liter four. Powered by an enlarged version of the Riley Nine engine (1496 versus 1087 cc), this one actually outperformed the six-cylinder Riley, while undercutting its price by £30. Styling was assuming greater importance, and a number of handsome bodies were offered.

But the 1½-liter was only a foretaste of what was yet to come!

Riley, like most motorcar manufacturers—especially the smaller ones—had been hard-hit by the Depression, and by the mid-thirties the company was very nearly on the ropes. The subsidiary companies, Midland Motor Body and Riley Engine, had been absorbed by the parent organization in 1931. Yet, oddly enough, a new subsidiary was spun off a few years later, producing for a short time (1937-1938) an expensive V-8 called the Autovia. It was an impressive machine, but it was clearly the wrong car for the times, and only a comparative handful were sold.

Meanwhile the parent company had introduced, in 1935, a V-8 of its own, the 8-90. Very much less expensive than the Autovia, its engine was similar to the latter, but smaller of bore. On the face of it, this one should have been a winner, but it wasn't. Only a few dozen were built before production was halted.

Perhaps in desperation, Riley brought forth in 1938 one more new car, the 2½-liter Big Four. Basically an enlarged version of the 1½-liter car, it too was a

direct descendent of (and from an engineering standpoint, little changed from) the remarkable Riley Nine of 1926.

But then the curtain fell. In February 1938 the company went into receivership, and seven months later control was acquired by Lord Nuffield, who in turn sold it to Morris Motors Limited for the munificent sum of one pound sterling. It seemed that the end had come, at least for the Riley as Britain and the world had known it.

But the end had *not* come! Lord Nuffield, who of course was the power behind Morris Motors, appointed Victor Riley as managing director of the newly reconstituted Riley (Coventry) Successors, Limited; and both the 1½- and 2½-liter models continued in production. Retitled as the Riley Twelve and Sixteen, respectively, the 1939 models wore coachwork that smacked distinctly of two of Lord Nuffield's other products, the Morris and the Wolseley. Seven models were produced, four on the Twelve chassis and three on the Sixteen, all selling at sharply reduced prices.

But then war came again, and once more Riley turned its attention to the production of munitions.

Late in 1944, with victory in Europe seemingly within reach, Riley advertisements began to speak of "Magnificent Motoring," promising a new chassis and new styling, but retaining the familiar Riley powertrain in the company's postwar cars. Riley enthusiasts might be forgiven a touch of cynicism; they had little faith that under its new ownership the company would be permitted to offer anything distinctive.

How wrong they were! In the summer of 1945, with Germany brought low at last, a new Riley 1½-liter saloon was released. It was long and low and sleek, featuring a fabric-covered hood (British terminology), yet its styling echoed the classic era of a decade earlier. Walnut veneer covered the dash and capped the doors and covered the dash fascia, and fine leather was employed for the seats. The engine was little changed, except that a duplex chain replaced the previous gear-drive of the camshafts. And beneath was a superb new independent front suspension, employing torsion bars—nearly a decade before Packard introduced them in this country. Rack-and-pinion steering replaced the worm-and-wheel design of the prewar Rileys, and the brakes were now Girling hydromechanicals. The latter may have been a bit unusual, at least to the American eye, and the long-stroke engine may have been somewhat dated, but taken all-in-all, this postwar Riley was an advanced piece of automotive design.

The new car was enthusiastically received, and within a few months it was joined by a 2½-liter version, nearly identical in appearance except for its longer bonnet.

*Above:* Riley's design is handsome, balanced and distinctive, but in 1950 it was perceived as dated when compared to new US "slab-side" school of styling. *Left:* Even the delicate trunk handle has an old-time look to it.

## The 2½- And 1½-Liter Rileys Compared

|  | 2½-Liter | 1½-Liter |
|---|---|---|
| Engine displacement | 2443 cc | 1496 cc |
| Bhp @ rpm | 100 @ 4500 | 55 @ 4500 |
| Torque @ rpm | 134 @ 3000 | 76 @ 2500 |
| Carburetor | 2 SU (H4 type) | Single SU horizontal |
| Transmission ratios (:1) | 3.65/2.15/1.42/1.00 | 3.98/2.29/1.48/1.00 |
| Final drive ratio | 4.11:1 | 4.88:1 |
| Turn circle | 36' 0" | 30' 0" |
| Brake drum diameter | 12 inches | 10 inches |
| Brake lining area | 136.5 square inches | 126.5 square inches |
| Wheelbase | 119 inches | 112.5 inches |
| Overall length | 182.5 inches | 179 inches |
| Unladen kerb weight | 29½ cwt | 26 cwt |
|  | (3304 pounds) | (2912 pounds) |
| Weight distrib. (front/rear) | 51/49 | 49/51 |
| Maximum speed | 90.1 mph | 74.7 mph |
| Acceleration (seconds) |  |  |
| 0-30 | 4.65 | 7.2 |
| 0-40 | 7.55 | 11.7 |
| 0-50 | 11.90 | 18.6 |
| 0-60 | 16.85 | 31.8 |
| 0-70 | 24.30 | 59.5 |
| Standing quarter mile | 21.1 | 24.3 |
| 30-50 | 11.85 | 12.0 |
| 40-60 | 13.45 | 21.6 |
| 50-70 | 15.95 | 40.9 |
| Hill-climbing (top gear) |  |  |
| Maximum speed, 1 in 20 | 75 mph | 55 mph |
| Maximum speed, 1 in 15 | 65 mph | 47 mph |
| Fuel consumption (average)* | 19.6 mph | 25.4 mpg |
| *Imperial measure |  |  |

## Riley Price List (1950)

| | |
|---|---|
| 1½-liter Saloon | £714 ($1999.20) |
| 2½-liter Saloon | £958 ($2682.40) |
| 2½-liter Roadster | £958 ($2682.40) |
| 2½-liter Drophead | £970 ($2716.00) |

(All prices f.o.b. factory, Abingdon, England.)

Note: The rate of exchange in 1950 put the value of the pound sterling at $2.80 U.S.

# 1950 RILEY

Britain was especially anxious, at that time, to expand its overseas markets, especially on this side of the big pond, and in 1948 two variations on the 2½-liter theme were introduced, both intended primarily for export: a lovely two/three seat roadster and the gorgeous four/five seat drophead coupe. Both were targeted for the American market, where Lord Nuffield's smart (if quaint) little MG roadster was beginning to score.

But the American public evidently failed to understand what the 2½-liter Riley was all about. Here was a car, roughly the size of a Chevrolet, powered by a four-cylinder engine that was 25 percent smaller than that of a Model A Ford, selling in this country for at least as much money as a Buick Roadmaster.

It didn't wash! In four years of production (1948-51) only 502 dropheads and 507 roadsters were built. Such a fine automobile deserved a better reception!

The two Riley saloons—1½- and 2½-liter—remained in production for some years after the open models were dropped—the 1½-liter through 1955 and the 2½-liter until 1953, when it was replaced by a new model called the "Pathfinder." The latter retained the familiar Riley engine and driveline, but its coachwork—once again—was that of the Wolseley.

By this time the merger of the Morris and Austin interests had resulted in the formation (in 1952) of the British Motor Corporation. Further integration of the corporation's many product lines was inevitable. And so, with the passing of the 1½-liter in 1955 and the Pathfinder two years later, Riley's links with the past were severed. To all intents and purposes the Riley was gone. Oh, to be sure, cars bearing the distinctive grille

and the diamond-shaped nameplate of the Riley continued in production. But they weren't really Rileys any more. They were re-badged, upscale versions, in assorted sizes and shapes, of the various other cars in the BMC line: Morris, Austin, Wolseley, even MG.

And then came the British Leyland merger. With Riley production down to less than 10,000 units annually, and with so many marques under the new corporation's umbrella, it really wasn't worth the effort. Late in 1969 the decision was made to discontinue the manufacture of automobiles under the Riley name.

Given the undistinguished nature of the product by that time, perhaps it was a mercy.

## Driving Impressions

When the time came for us to slip behind the wheel of Varlie Gordon's Riley drophead, we experienced a sensation reminiscent of the feeling we had, years ago, as we approached our first date with the girl we eventually married. We were, after all, already in love. In both instances!

And as in that earlier experience, we weren't disappointed. Quite the contrary!

Boarding the Riley is easy. The big, "suicide" doors swing wide enough to give ready access to the back seat as well as the front. Seats are comfortable, though lateral support could be improved. Leg room is ample up front and adequate to the rear—better than many an American ragtop we've known. The boot is similarly commodious, with a separate compartment for the spare tire. Since the hood was down, we had no opportunity to judge the drophead's visibility factor, but our guess is that with the hood raised, the twin mirrors

# specifications

Illustrations by Russell von Sauers, The Graphic Automobile Studio

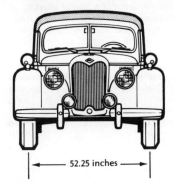

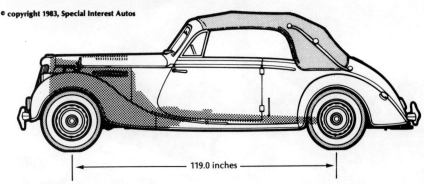

← 52.25 inches →

← 119.0 inches →

## 1950 Riley 2½-Liter

| | |
|---|---|
| **Price** | $2716 f.o.b. Abingdon, England, with standard equipment |

### ENGINE

| | |
|---|---|
| Type | 4-cylinder; overhead valves, hemispheric combustion chambers, dual camshafts located high in block |
| Bore & stroke | 80.5 mm x 120 mm (3.169" x 4.725") |
| Displacement | 2443 cc (149 cubic inches) |
| Max bhp @ rpm | 100 @ 4500 |
| Max torque @ rpm | 134 @ 3000 |
| Compression ratio | 6.8:1 |
| Number of main bearings | 3 |
| Induction system | Twin SU type H4 carburetors; electric fuel pump |
| Lubrication system | Gear-driven vertical oil pump |
| Cooling system | Pump, thermostat and fan |
| Electrical system | 12-volt Lucas coil |

### CLUTCH

| | |
|---|---|
| Make/Type | Borg & Beck single plate |
| Diameter | 10 inches |
| Actuation | Mechanical, foot pedal |

### TRANSMISSION

| | |
|---|---|
| Type | 4-speed, synchronized top three gears; center remote control floor-mounted lever |
| Ratios: 1st | 3.65:1 |
| 2nd | 2.15:1 |
| 3rd | 1.42:1 |
| 4th | 1.00:1 |
| Reverse | N/a |

### DIFFERENTIAL

| | |
|---|---|
| Type | Spiral bevel |
| Ratio | 4.11:1 |
| Drive axles | Semi-floating |

### STEERING

| | |
|---|---|
| Type | Rack and pinion |
| Turns, lock to lock | 2½ |
| Ratio | N/a |
| Turn circle | 36' 0" |

### BRAKES

| | |
|---|---|
| Type | Girling hydro-mechanical (hydraulic front, mechanical rear) |
| Drum diameter | 12 inches |
| Total swept area | 136.5 square inches |

### CHASSIS & BODY

| | |
|---|---|
| Frame | Box section with box and tubular cross members |
| Body construction | Steel and aluminum over hard-wood framing |
| Body style | 5-passenger drophead coupe |

### SUSPENSION

| | |
|---|---|
| Front | Torsion bars |
| Rear | Semi-elliptical leaf springs |
| Tires | 6.00 x 16 |
| Wheels | Dunlop steel disc |

### WEIGHTS AND MEASURES

| | |
|---|---|
| Wheelbase | 119 inches |
| Overall length | 186 inches |
| Overall height | 59 inches |
| Overall width | 63.5 inches |
| Front tread | 52.25 inches |
| Rear tread | 52.25 inches |
| Ground clearance | 7 inches |
| Shipping weight | 3304 pounds |
| Weight distribution, front/rear | 51/49% |

### CAPACITIES

(Imperial measure)

| | |
|---|---|
| Crankcase | 7 quarts |
| Cooling system | 10.5 quarts (plus 1.25 pints for heater) |
| Fuel tank | 12.5 gallons |

### PERFORMANCE*

| | |
|---|---|
| Top speed (avg) | 90.1 mph |
| Acceleration: 0-30 | 4.65 seconds |
| 0-40 | 7.55 seconds |
| 0-50 | 11.90 seconds |
| 0-60 | 16.85 seconds |
| 0-70 | 24.30 seconds |
| 0-80 | 36.75 seconds |
| Standing ¼-mile | 21.1 seconds |
| Fuel consumption | 19.6 mpg overall (Imperial measure) |

*From road test by *The Motor*, as reported in the July 5, 1950, issue.

*Riley is fun to drive, handles well and cruises easily at 60 mph or better.*

REPRINTED WITH PERMISSION FROM
**Special Interest Autos #79 February 1984**
Box 196, Bennington. Vermont 05201

special interest
**autos**

A Publication from Hemmings Motor News

## Glossary

Whether or not the British and their former colonists on this side of the Atlantic really do speak the same language has always been a debatable matter. Certainly we express ourselves in different ways with respect to our automobiles!

The following is a partial glossary of British automotive terms with their stateside equivalents. Some of these expressions are used in the accompanying driveReport.

| British term | American equivalent |
| --- | --- |
| Cwt. (hundredweight) | 112 pounds |
| Bonnet | Hood |
| Boot | Trunk |
| Drophead | Convertible |
| Gearchange | Gearshift |
| Hood | Top |
| Kerb | Curb |
| Petrol | Gasoline |
| Saloon | Sedan |
| Strangler | Choke |
| Tyres | Tires |
| Wings | Fenders |

*Above:* For a "small" convertible, there's plenty of rear seat leg room. *Right:* Directional signals operate from little flip lever on steering wheel. *Far right:* Full instrumentation was standard. Tachometer was an option; it filled hole where clock dwells. *Below:* Louvered hood panels were standard on export cars.

# 1950 RILEY

mounted atop the front wings would be a virtual necessity.

We happen to be especially fond of fine woods, so the Riley's rich walnut veneers have a special appeal for us. The leather upholstery is another delight.

With a little help from the manual strangler, the engine lights off promptly at the push of a small knob, located just below the instrument panel. It's not a

particularly quiet engine; you wouldn't expect it to be, in a car of this character. There's an eager, throaty quality to its sound, which we interpreted as meaning, "Let's Go!"

The clutch is rather stiff. No legbreaker, you understand; it's simply the clutch of an automobile that's meant to be driven! Engagement is smooth, and acceleration is quick. Gear-change action is easy and precise, with a rather long throw to the non-synchro first gear. It's not difficult to override the synchronizers on the top three gears—a

Riley characteristic, we've been told—but shifts can still be accomplished swiftly. This is a car that fairly begs to be wound out through the gears. The Riley engine evidently thrives on vigorous exercise!

A little notch to the left of the clutch provides a convenient footrest, once the car is cruising along in top gear. The driving position, enhanced by the flexibility of the adjustable steering column, is very comfortable. The ride is firm, well-controlled, in marked contrast to the mushiness typical of most American cars of the Riley's vintage.

In the hills above Varlie Gordon's Whittier, California, home, the car reveals its strength, as well as the flexibility of its long stroke engine. We took some pretty stiff grades at 40-plus, using the 1.42:1-ratio third gear. And in the turns the Riley's stance, thanks to its advanced torsion bar suspension, remains comfortably flat.

This is, in short, a driver's automobile, intended for and surely appreciated by the enthusiast. The rack-and-pinion steering, while rather heavy in parking maneuvers, is sheer joy as one guides the car through twisting mountain roads. Even the brakes, despite the con-

siderable pedal pressure they require, are excellent. Unusual brakes they are, hydraulic to the front, mechanical at the rear wheels. An odd combination, replaced by full hydraulics on later Riley models. But no matter; they get the job done!

This is a great tour car. At 60 it seems to have acceleration to spare; indeed, Varlie Gordon has driven it at 80 miles an hour with no complaints coming from beneath the louvered Riley bonnet. (Those louvers, by the way, were intended primarily for the export market.)

It's a well-equipped car, with such features as Butler pass lamps and flip-out turn signals supplied as standard equipment. A tachometer was a Riley option, taking the place of the dashboard clock. Varlie Gordon's car doesn't have this feature, and we missed it.

Gordon, secretary-treasurer of the Riley Motor Club USA, purchased the drophead a dozen years ago. The previous owner had burned a rod bearing, having failed to keep his sludge traps clean. Discouraged at the prospective cost of rebuilding the engine, he let Varlie have the car at an incredibly

reasonable figure. Varlie's mechanical overhaul was accompanied by refinishing the Riley in its original Autumn Red with black wings, a combination that is both unusual and highly attractive.

It's a rare automobile. The original production was 502 dropheads. Several of these venerable automobiles are still in the hands of their original owners, Varlie Gordon reports. There are people, it seems, who, having acquired a very good thing, are not about to let it go!

It was with genuine reluctance that we returned the Riley to its proud owner. This one, far more than most, we'd like to keep. □

**Acknowledgements and Bibliography**

*R.M. Clark, editor,* Riley Cars, 1950-1955; *Cecil Clutton and John Stanford,* The Vintage Motor Car; *G.N. Georgano, editor,* The Complete Encyclopedia of Motorcars, 1885-1968; *Riley Supplement to* The Motor Trader, *February 9, 1949; David G. Styles,* As Old as the Industry; *Joseph H. Wherry,* Automobiles of the World.

*Our thanks to Eric Killoran, Andover, Massachusetts; Don Milligan, Andover, Massachusetts. Special thanks to Varlie Gordon, Whittier, California.*

## "The Grandfather": Riley's Nine

There had been some notable Riley automobiles in the company's earlier years. As far back as 1905 Riley Tricars were racking up records for both speed and reliability.

And there were some superb Rileys later on. Our driveReport car clearly qualifies as one of these.

But the most significant Riley of them all, the one responsible for putting Riley (Coventry) Limited on the map, was a modest little machine introduced in 1926 and called the Riley Nine.

Rated at nine horsepower for tax purposes—hence its model designation—the Nine actually developed 34 horsepower at 4000 rpm. Fitted to an automobile of comparatively modest size and weight, it readily outperformed most of its competitors, and it sold for as little as £235.

In a number of respects that first Riley Nine was simple, almost primitive. Cooling was by the thermo-siphon method: Petrol was fed by gravity from the tiny (5½-gallon) fuel tank; a fabric-faced cone clutch was used on the earliest cars (though it was soon

replaced by the single dry plate type); and there were only two main bearings.

But it worked! Of course, in a number of respects the little Riley was a comparatively sophisticated piece of machinery. The hemispheric combustion chambers with valves inclined at a 45-degree angle; the twin camshafts mounted high in the block, providing unusually short pushrods; the fine four-speed gearbox with its "silent third," all marked the Nine as a car ahead of its time.

At first, cylinder and crankcase blocks were separate castings, but within a year the two were cast as a single unit—a short, wide, rather tall and exceedingly sturdy block. Water jackets extended downwards for only half the length of the barrels, providing a midway stiffening of the latter, while the bottom ends of the cylinders were reinforced by a strong cast rim. As thousands of owners were to learn, it was a very tough little engine indeed.

Among the first to see the potential of the Riley Nine were J.G. Parry Thomas and Reid Railton. They tweaked the engine, extracting from it 55 brake horsepower at 5500 rpm,

and in 1928 the resulting "Brooklands Nine" established a world six-hour record by averaging just over 85 miles an hour. Two years later the modified Nine won the Irish Grand Prix, and as late as 1935 this remarkable little automobile was still racking up victories in races as far away as New Zealand.

Railton had, it must be confessed, substituted an electric fuel pump for the gravity feed, and a vertical water pump for the thermo-siphon setup. Riley itself followed suit in one respect: A vacuum tank was introduced in 1930, followed by an electric fuel pump for the 1933 season. But to the end of its production the stock Riley Nine retained its thermo-siphon cooling. And not until 1938—the very last year for the Nine—was a third main bearing added.

One Riley owner, writing of his Nine when it was already more than 30 years old, said, "This Riley Nine was—no, let us say is—an excellent little sporting car of robust construction with good handling qualities."

To which one of Britain's leading automotive journalists added, "It's such fun to drive!"

# DIAMOND LIFE

### The Riley 1½- and 2½-litre were the jewels in Nuffield's post-war crown. But do they come up trumps as a classic buy today? Jon Pressnell profiles the cars; photos by Phil Rudge

"It is a car which, above the ordinary, inspires confidence and affection". The car was the Riley 1½-litre, and *The Autocar* were writing of it in 1953, a full eight years after its introduction. Then, as now, the post-war 1½- and 2½-litre Rileys were cars of enduring appeal, born with classic status rather than having it thrust on them in old age.

It's not difficult to see why: the low-slung elegance of the well-appointed coachwork bridged pre-war and post-war trends with an assured wheel-at-each-corner poise, while a race-bred twin-cam engine and a chassis with torsion-bar independent front suspension and rack and pinion steering appealed to the sporting driver appreciative of fine machinery.

With such a thoroughbred combination of virtues, the cars have always been sought-after, yet prices remain realistic.

The story of the 1½- and 2½-litre Rileys goes back to 1938. This was a sad year for the proud family firm of Riley, with its fine heritage of technical and sporting achievement, as several years of overstretched financial resources had culminified in the appointment in February of an official receiver.

After an abortive attempt to merge the company with Triumph, it was Lord Nuffield who picked up the pieces, personally buying the company in September 1938 and then selling it to Morris Motors Ltd – allegedly for the sum of £1.

Every effort would be made, said Lord Nuffield, to preserve the Riley character and to make sure that "the company may add to the great reputation it has so deservedly won". Understandably, this statement was greeted with a fair degree of scepticism, and this was not allayed by the following month's announcement of the hurriedly redesigned 1939 Riley range, blandly styled and with plentiful evidence of cost-cutting to be found. To make matters worse, the cars proved less than reliable in service.

Was this the beginning of the end for Riley? Would the marque end up like Wolseley, as a badge-engineered Morris? Such agonising tended to obscure the fact that the new cars were principally conceived by Riley's design team, rather than by Nuffield men.

It was all academic. War stopped play, and then German bombing raids destroyed the body drawings and at least some of the jigs. The Coventry firm had the opportunity to redeem itself by designing a fresh range of cars for the post-war market, drawing on the strengths of the 1939 cars and discarding their weaknesses. Under the direction of the long-serving and much respected chief engineer, Harry Rush, work appears to have begun in 1942 or 1943, and the final result emerged in August 1945 – a striking new 1½-litre saloon, with a 2½-litre derivative promised.

Foundation of the car was the simplified chassis of

the 1939/40 cars, re-jigged to take advantage of wartime advances in welding technology. The front of the chassis, however, was cut away, to be replaced by a bolt-on cradle bearing twin-wishbone independent suspension, in conjunction with longitudinal torsion bars and telescopic dampers. The torsion bars were mounted at their rear to the chassis's first tubular cross-member. Rack and pinion steering was fitted, the Riley being the first British car to enter production with such an arrangement.

The whole set-up, dubbed 'Torsionic', evoked that of the *Traction Avant* Citroën, out of expediency as much as out of imitation, but with a fair element of the latter: two Citroëns are known to have been at the Riley works in 1937, and to have been closely studied.

At the rear, the suspension was much as before, with semi-elliptic springs and with the axle located by the traditional Riley torque tube, aided by an anti-roll bar. To facilitate removal of the gearbox, and, indeed, of the axle, as well as to cushion drive-train harshness and vibration, the torque tube was linked to the gearbox *via* a short open propshaft, an imaginative interpretation of Riley tradition first seen on the '39/40 models.

The gearbox itself was the same four-speed unit as used on those cars, a Nuffield product with

174

*Clockwise from top: 2½-litre saloon with smart but non-authentic split to duo-toning; 1947 2½ interior – note early dash, fabric seat inserts, storage pouches; Roadster, bumpers modified; 2½-litre drophead displays slightly teutonic profile; drophead interior, showing revised dashboard, deep windscreen header rail, and high standard of appointments*

synchromesh on the top three ratios.

The only point of chassis design where the Riley perhaps lagged, at least on paper, was in the fitment of Girling hydro-mechanical brakes. In remaining loyal to their long-time supplier, they had to content themselves with this system until such time as Girling came up with an all-hydraulic arrangement to rival that offered by Lockhead.

The 1496cc engine was the pre-war 12hp unit, a development of the original Riley Nine engine of 1926. First seen in 1934, and modified for the 1939 model-year, the new car's engine, with its high-set twin camshafts and short pushrods, was given chain rather than gear drive for the camshafts. With its hemispherical combustion chambers, 90-degree valve angle, and cross-flow head, it was still an impressive power unit, although its long 100mm stroke and its white-metal bearings gave away its age; with a single SU, power was 55bhp at 4500rpm, with torque of 76lb ft at 2500rpm.

All this fine engineering would have risked going un-noticed, had it not been for the body. Designed by Riley's stylist, Bert Holmes, it drew both on previous Rileys and on an expropriated Nazi legation BMW 327 which during the war had found its way to the factory.

A key feature of the timber-framed body, built by Morris Motors Body Branch, was the roof, fabric-covered over a wooden frame and an expanded steel base. Echoing earlier generations of Riley, the

wadding-padded roof cut down on the body resonances which had affected the '39/'40 cars, and was also held to reduce up-high weight.

One story, of dubious authenticity, is that this form of roof was arrived at quite by accident. Victor Riley allegedly visited the bodyshop one day, to enquire about progress on the prototype, and to ask if the car could be ready for the end of the week, for showing to his distributors. On being told that this was out of the question, as the car hadn't yet received its roof, he is said to have retorted "oh, for goodness sake, make a roof of expanded metal, and cover it with fabric, just so that we can show the car". The story goes that this is exactly what happened, and that the distributors so liked the feature that it was adopted for production...

When the car was first shown to the press, in August 1945, it seems unlikely that the production lines had fully been laid down. It also appears that there remained doubt over the design and manufacture of the torsion bar springing; certainly in late 1945 the company recruited Bob Aves, a former Bentley, MG and ERA man, on the strength of his brief involvement with the development of Citroën's 15/6 model.

Production finally began in early 1946, with the press being able to report more fully on the cars towards the end of February.

During the Motor Industry Golden Jubilee celebrations of summer 1946, Riley showed the promised 2½-litre variant, although the car's formal announcement had to wait until November. Two factory-built dropheads, on the 1½-litre chassis, also appeared in the jubilee parade, and one of these became the personal car of Nuffield vice-chairman Sir Miles Thomas; Bob Aves recalls delivering the car to Thomas, and making embarrassed apologies for the scuttle shake from which it suffered.

The 2½-litre was 7in longer than the 1½-litre, measuring 15ft 6in. This was on account of a 6½in stretch in the wheelbase, to allow the larger 16hp 'Big Four' engine to fit under a lengthened bonnet; the passenger compartment was identical

Delivering 90bhp at 4300rpm, the twin-SU 2443cc engine had the longest stroke – 120mm – of any four-cylinder on the market, and was largely unchanged from its final pre-war specification. It still retained white-metal bearings. The gearbox was also basically the pre-war 16hp unit, and to take this considerably more weighty combination, the 2½ chassis was of heavier gauge and the torsion bars were uprated; the rear axle and torque tube assembly were also more substantial. An easy recognition point for the 2½-litre is that its radiator badge is pale blue, as against the dark blue of the 1½'s badge.

By 1947 both the 1½-litre (RMA) and 2½-litre

(RMB) saloons were in production, although not the 1½-litre drophead, which never made it to the market. The press loved the new cars, especially for their high standards of roadholding and handling.

"The way this car can be taken round curves is astonishing", wrote *The Autocar* of the 2½-litre, while *The Motor* spoke of "sports car performance with town carriage manners". The 1½-litre was dubbed "a capital all-rounder" by *The Autocar*, with "such qualities as to lift motoring far above the plane of transport alone".

As for performance, *The Motor* extracted 78mph from the 24½cwt 1½-litre and 94.8mph from the 2½-litre, figures *The Autocar* could not quite match. This made the 2½ near-unbeatable as a four-door saloon, and only the much lighter Jowett Javelin bettered the 1½ in its class.

March 1948 saw the introduction of the 2½-litre Roadster, coded RMC. Built on a full-length chassis, initially only with left-hand drive, it was a bizarrely long and flamboyantly-bumpered vehicle, with three-abreast seating on a bench seat and with a lengthy rear deck incorporating a sizeable boot; doors were cutaway and the screen folded flat, over a scuttle 1½in lower than on the saloon.

To seat three, a column gearchange was fitted, to the outrage of enthusiasts, and a transfer box was installed to the steering mechanism, to move the wheel further to the driver's side. To lessen the not inconsiderable effort needed to steer the 2½-litre at low speeds, the steering was also made lower-geared than the normal 2⅓ turns lock-to-lock.

Launched with the standard 90bhp engine, the Roadster soon received a revised unit, with a modified cylinder head and enlarged inlet valves pushing power up to 100bhp and improving low-speed flexibility; this engine quickly found its way into the saloon.

For the 1950 model year the RMC was introduced to the home market, purely as a two-seater with floor-change and standard steering. The whole confection, though, was really aimed at the Americans.

Indeed, the story goes that the Roadster had its origins in a sketch on the back of a grubby envelope brought back from the States by a member of the sales force, the man claiming that this was the sort of car for which Americans were clamouring. It apparently transpired that the enthusiastic salesman had only talked to around a third of the American dealers...

Whatever the truth of this story, the Roadster was not a success, despite the sales brochure trumpeting that it was 'acclaimed everywhere as the supreme sports car'. When production ceased in January 1951, the Americans had taken only 77 of the 507 made, as against 134 taken by the Australians, out of total exports of 314 RMCs.

The final production variant of the series was the 2½-litre drophead (RMD). First shown at the 1948 Motor Show, although manufacture did not begin at least until May 1949, it has a fully-lined mohair hood with a glass rear window and external irons. Wind-down rear quarter lights were fitted, and the car weighed approximately 1cwt more than the saloon. Initially there was a very shallow header rail to the windscreen; by the time the car entered production this had deepened, to limit scuttle shake.

The drophead was evidently more to American

*Top: prototype 1½-litre. Horn grilles were not used on production cars. Final roofline was arrived at after Sir Miles Thomas had persuaded Riley to chop 1½in from pillars. Bottom: 2½-litre chassis, showing substantial construction and torque-tube*

tastes than the Roadster, as of the 417 exported, out of a production of only 502, no fewer than 177 went to the States – including one to Clark Gable. No other bodystyles were to be produced by the factory, although a prototype, steel-roofed, six-light saloon was built in 1947/48.

Chassis were made available to outside coachbuilders, however, with 227 1½-litre and 16 2½-litre chassis being supplied to such firms. Estates were the most popular style of body, this form of coachwork enjoying a vogue in the late forties and early fifties, but a fair number of dropheads were also built by coachbuilders such as the Bonallack and Epps concerns. One of the most striking special-bodied cars, though, was the streamlined coupé displayed at the 1948 Geneva show by the Basel firm of Köng.

Bearing in mind the lack of a sports model, Riley didn't do too badly in holding onto their sporting image – mainly through the efforts of private owners in national and international rallies, but with some limited works participation.

In rallies, Lyndon Sims was the most consistent entrant, and he competed in the Monte Carlo right through to 1955 in 2½ litres; best result was 22nd, in 1954. As for racing, Harold Grace was the Riley-man to beat, but the cars also did well when raced as a team, with a three-car *equipe* winning the 1953 Production Touring Car races at Silverstone. Finally, let's not forget the privately-entered but works-prepared Roadster which finished 17th at Le Mans, 1950.

The story of the 1½ and 2½ Rileys is one of progressive development rather than radical change. In fact the most radical change was not to the cars but to the production facilities: in early 1949 these moved to the MG factory at Abingdon. First announced in December 1948, the switch was completed by May 1949, after a short period when cars appear to have been made at both factories. It seems that at one stage the move might have happened in reverse, with MG moving to the Riley factory in Coventry, but this was a political battle Riley lost.

The first round of noteworthy modifications occurred around June 1948, when twin-leading-shoe front brakes were fitted to the 2½-litre, a move doubtless inspired by the slightly earlier introduction of the 100bhp engine. Changes to the interior followed, announced at the 1949 Motor Show and including a new dashboard, with the pre-war design of round dials replaced by a combination of round and rectangular gold-faced instruments, while 1950 saw the introduction of smaller diameter rear brake drums with broader shoes.

Without the distraction of constant product changes, during these years the factory could get on with satisfying export demand – at least for the 2½-litre, which by 1949 had supplanted the 1½ as the mainstay of Riley exports, with 70 per cent of production exported in 1948.

The peak year for exports of the cars was 1950, and in 1951 figures fell away – only slightly for the 1½, but by more than a half, from 1613 to 788, for the 2½, resulting in a dramatic fall in production of the larger car. From 1952, exports collapsed.

It's worth observing Australia was Riley's main export market, and that there were never that many exports to the States, and none at all of the 1½. In the peak year of 1950 only 261 2½-litres were sent to the US, out of a total 1950 production (1½ and 2½ combined) of 3588 cars and total exports that year of 2273 – and that 261 was a massive jump from the pitiful 13 cars sent to the Americans in 1949! By 1952 the figure had slumped to six cars…

Faced with this fall in production, effort was concentrated on making the cars simpler and cheaper to assemble, as well as more appealing to home-market buyers.

## Australia was the Riley's main export market, and there were never that many exports to the States, and none at all of the 1½-litre

1951 saw the first stage in this process. By the time of the Motor Show, telescopic dampers, angled to improve axle location, had replaced the rear lever-arm units, and the anti-roll bar had been deleted, thereby simplifying assembly. Seats were improved, and so was the cars' ventilation. These 1952 cars can be identified by the two cross-pieces added to the rear bumpers and by a one-piece front bumper. They were only available as saloons, the January 1951 deletion of the Roadster having been followed in October by the disappearance of the drophead.

The fun really started in 1952. The year began with the fitment of lower-geared and thus slightly lighter steering, in around February, and in October a whole package of modifications was announced. Foremost among these was the substitution of an orthodox open propeller shaft for the previous torque tube, this move bringing with it the fitment of a new hypoid bevel unit. On the 1½ there was also a lower-ratio final drive, and on both models the rear brakes gained hydraulic actuation.

Both engines were also modified, with a repositioned water pump and dynamo allowing the pump and the fan to share a common spindle and thus a single drive-belt to be used. On the 2½-litre the compression ratio was raised and the cams and valve gear revised, the resultant more powerful engine being dubbed RMB/2.

Bodywork was revised, too, with a higher roofline at the rear incorporating a larger rear window, and the cars were coded as the RME in the case of the 1½-litre, and as the RMF in the case of the 2½.

The snag is, though, that while these many changes were first revealed at the 1952 Show, some had already been implemented before then, while others only filtered through during 1953. Not for nothing does Riley RM Club Spares Secretary John Byron regard the year 1952 as the bane of his life! Things did eventually settle down, but not before the 2½-litre, in around 1953, had received a final and most desirable modification, namely the fitting of shell bearings to the engine.

The end came for the 2½-litre in October 1953, when it was replaced by the controversial RMH Pathfinder, but the 1½-litre RME underwent one final round of modifications, while the Nuffield management pondered over its replacement with a 1½-powered Pathfinder – a project firmly knocked on the head when it became apparent that the one prototype, known as the Wayfarer, was *extremely* slow…

The revised RME was essentially a facelifted car, with reshaped wings, incorporating faired-in fog-lamps and sidelamps, part-spats to the rear wheels, and the replacement of the running boards by a

*Claimed to be a saloon rather than a utility, this shooting-brake by Massey was typical of many of the special bodies on the 1½-litre Riley*

shaped sill panel; more radical proposals, involving headlamps flush with the wings and front wings faired into the doors were not implemented, perhaps thankfully. Mechanically, the car was much as before, though the cam was slightly less sporting and the clutch had been made lighter. The recipe seemed to appeal, as the 1954 production figure of 1747 cars was 608 vehicles up on the 1953 total.

The Riley was looking pretty dated by this time, however – not least one presumes, in terms of its production costs, especially as the deletion of the 2½ had left it rather out on a limb. It thus came as no surprise when it was discontinued in January 1955, after a total of 13,950 1½-litre cars and 8960 2½-litres had been produced.

## BUYERS SPOT CHECK

The first spot-check you have to make is on your own inclinations: do you fancy a 1½-litre or a 2½-litre? The received wisdom is that the two models have completely different characters, and we can bear this out from our own experience of the cars.

The 1½ is a milder, more civilised vehicle, especially in its slightly softened post-1953 form. Steering is not over-heavy, the car bowls along happily at 55-60mph, and there is a feeling of refinement and balance in its behaviour. The 2½ is a little bit of a brute, with stiffer and far heavier steering and a more rugged feel to the engine, but with performance which makes cruising at the legal limit an effortless process, with plenty in hand.

Common to both are delightfully precise steering, a firm and roll-free ride, effective brakes (hydro-mechanical or otherwise), and crisply responsive power units – together with a very pre-war gear-change with distinctly leisurely synchromesh!

How to choose? If you want to use the car regularly for long distances, the 2½ may be a sounder bet, while if your driving is more rural pottering or urban communing, the more sedate but easier-handling 1½ may make better sense; its thirst is also much more modest.

With your basic decision made, what next? The first thing to remember is that these Rileys have a

timber-frame body. This makes them a far less safe buy, in bodywork terms, than a Rover P4, for instance, on account of the wood's propensity to suffer from wet-rot. In extreme cases the top of the body has been found to be barely attached to its bottom ...

In particular, beware the high-priced car with seductively fine new paintwork, as all too frequently this can hide a badly decayed wooden frame. Often it's the regularly-used Riley with the tatty paint which is the sounder car, as its owner will have carried out the essential structural work while leaving the inessential cosmetics until a later date.

Start your inspection of a potential purchase by checking for over-wide and uneven door apertures. This is a sure sign of deterioration of the body at its mounting points, generally as a result of decayed timber.

The most crucially vulnerable point is at the rearmost body mounts: serious rusting of the boot floor directly over these mounts throws the body out of kilter and deranges the hanging of the doors. Bad rusting should be easy to spot inside the boot, but the real giveaway is if the rear body is resting on the bumper irons, having sunk past its in-boot mounts.

Deterioration of the 'L' section wooden sills is another cause of grave body maladies, as it can result in partial collapse of the coachwork at the mounting point by the central pillar; this can lead to the pillar dropping, and with it the roof. It's worth noting that sill-rot is more likely on the offside than on the nearside, which is baked by the exhaust, but the exposed timber on both sides should be carefully examined for rot, prodding it with a penknife.

The mountings forward of the rear wheelarch are another weak point. Water can run down the inside of the body from a poorly-sealed rear window, and in combination with water collecting at the end of the running board and with that thrown up by the rear wheels, it can rot out the timber at this spot, together with the metal of the door jamb bottom and of the body mount itself.

Check by looking for a rusted door jamb by the wheelarch, and for rotten wood both at the end of the sill and inside the arch, and then lift the rear seat to inspect the mounting point itself.

The front pillar also merits close examination. Loose roof guttering or a leaky windscreen will let in water, with predictable effect on the timber pillar. The first sign of rot is the door striker-plate pulling loose, and generally also the pillar's finishing trim; if the latter is not loose, it can be unscrewed to inspect the wood behind. Note that on spatted RMEs the striker-plate test does not apply, owing to a different mounting of the plate. Look instead for the mountings for the bonnet release mechanism pulling loose. Another giveaway, on all models, is rust bubbling at the scuttle – and obtrusive scuttle-shake!

The bottom of the pillar is exposed and thus at least equally vulnerable, and in addition capillary action sends damp from the lower section of the member into its upper reaches; we have inspected cars where the pillar bottoms, visible through the wheelarch, have rotted completely away.

Needless to say, the roof can also be a source of problems, so look especially for splits or decayed stitching which may have allowed water to get under the covering. Loose guttering should also raise your suspicions, notably at points vulnerable to water collection, such as above the windscreen and at the bottom of the rear pillars, while the area around the rear window is also a trouble-spot. Test for a decayed wooden frame by pushing firmly on the roof at these spots. Finally, if there are bumps in the roof, it is likely that the expanded steel base is rusting.

Roof repairs and replacement of the covering are perfectly feasible for the amateur, but are no picnic, so think very carefully about taking on a car where both the lower body and the roof appear less than sound. Bear in mind, too, that with the body's scope for extensive deterioration it is likely that a car which has been standing outside for some years could be a high-risk purchase.

If the foregoing all sound a bit dire, there is some consolation in that thanks to the robust chassis, it is possible to keep the cars running in a fairly decayed condition, while body repairs are progressively carried out – so long, that is, as the roof is not as rotten as the rest of the body. All ash framework for the saloon and drophead is available from specialist Ernie Mould, who can also provide most of the Roadster's wood, and it is possible to replace one sill in a weekend.

It's worth noting that in the RM Club are a number of members with no previous coachwork experience who have carried out first-rate body rebuilds – basic woodworking skills and infinite patience are the main requirements.

The body's metalwork doesn't really pose problems, beyond those points already detailed, although you should check for rust behind the headlamps and by the spot welds securing the front wing to the mounting bracket for its stay. On the spatted RME, look out for rust around the sidelamp housings and in the sill cappings, as well as in the doors, which have a slightly different, more rust-prone construction.

The mechanical side of the car is rather less of a minefield, while the only ailment likely to be afflicting the sturdy chassis is a dose of accident damage,

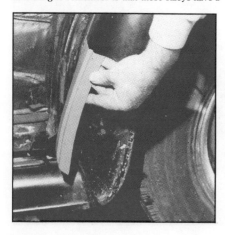

*Left: Both metal and wood are prone to rot at this point, forward of the rear wheelarch. Repair panel is available. Right: Leaks at the rear window can spell trouble. Water can also enter at base of the roof or at open seams. This is a very bad example!*

*A certain amount of the wooden framing is visible – if it hasn't already rotted away! Bottom of front pillar, shown, is vulnerable*

generally revealed by an ill-fitting bonnet.

The engines suffer from one particular problem, that of bearing maladies brought on by sludging up of the fairly narrow oilways supplying lubricant to the crankshaft journals, and/or by poor white-metalling. The remedy is to clean out the oilways and either re-metal the bearings or convert to shells, a straightforward operation involving either BMC 'B' Series shells (1½-litre) or Bedford diesel ones (2½-litre).

As a guide to engine condition, 1½-litre and white-metal 2½-litre units should register 40-50 psi at 40mph, and at idle 10-15 psi on the 1½ and 0-10 psi for the 2½; shell-bearing 2½s should give a zero reading at idle, 50 psi at 40mph when cold, and 30-40 psi at 40mph when warm.

You should always be wary of a car with a seized or long-unused engine. If water has been left to freeze in the passages, the block could have split. In the case of the 2½ unit, the cracks are often internal, at the centre bearing for one or both of the camshafts, and the first you'll know of this is when you find water in your oil. To check for external cracks, shine a torch onto the block by the hot-spot tubes, as this is a common place to find damage.

On the 2½-litre, the exhaust manifold is prone to metal fatigue, so check for cracks; the RM Club can supply replacement manifolds, cast in a superior metal, for £105 plus VAT.

The gearbox is a robust old beast, and suffers from no more than the usual ageing problems of fading synchromesh and popping out of gear. Secondhand 'boxes are easily found. One weakness particular to the 2½ is a tendency for the halfshafts to fracture in old age.

The rest of the running gear is pretty bullet-proof, and it is not uncommon to find cars still on their original wheel bearings, and with king-pins

appearing to have a long life. Steering, which should have no more than 1in of play at the rim, is trouble-free, as are the brakes. Don't be put off by the thought of a hydro-mechanical system – the retardation is well up to scratch and you have two fewer wheel cylinders to seize!

Spares? Thanks to the enterprise of the Riley RM Club's Spares Secretary, John Byron, virtually everything is available to keep a car on the road. A good selection of trim parts and 'shiny bits' can also be obtained, while Ernie Mould can provide the all-important timber components.

Exterior panelwork is of less pressing concern than on many other cars, so efforts have been concentrated on supplying repair panels for the common rust-points, but the next year or two could see items such as the spare wheel compartment cover being remanufactured.

## PRICES

You can buy a really grotty 1½-litre, or one partially dismantled, for £200 or less and a 2½ in similar condition for £250-£350. At these prices, in all likelihood you're buying a rolling nightmare, unless you know the cars backwards.

Far better to pay more – up to £750-£1000 (1½) or £1000-£1250 (2½) – for a basically sound car, perhaps one which has been laid up for some years.

A good useable car, MoT'd and in regular use, will start at around £1500 for a 1½, or around £2000 for a 2½ – once 2½s are in this category, prices start to take off as a result of the larger Riley's scarceness and desirability. Top-notch cars are in the £2000-£5000 bracket, and good, spatted RMEs seem to attract a slight premium over earlier 1½s.

Drophead prices tend to be a bit silly: a kit of parts, if complete, could come with a £4000 price-tag, while a complete and properly stored example will run to £5000 or more. Useable dropheads are around the £6000 mark, and a really good example can command £10,000. As for Roadsters, subtract £1000 from these prices.

## CLUBS

**Riley RM Club:** Long-established club with excellent spares back-up. Magazine, *R. Memoranda*, published eight times yearly. 1400 members, many from overseas. National Rally August 8/9, Littlecote Manor, nr Marlborough, Wilts. Subscription £14 (£7 half-year); £3 joining fee. Contact: Bill Harris, 57 Cluny Gardens, Edinburgh EH10 6BL.

**Riley Motor Club:** Established 1925, and formerly the official, factory-backed club. Caters for all Rileys, so the club to join to put your RM in its historical context. Magazine, *The Record*, published six times yearly. 1000 members. Subscription £9.50; £1 joining fee. Contact: John Hall, Treelands, 127 Penn Road, Wolverhampton WV3 0DU.

## SPECIALISTS

**John S. Foster**, 1A Leeds Old Road, Heckmondwike, W. Yorks WF16 9AA (tel: 0924 409319).

**J.B. Walker**, 18 De Clare Close, Nottage, Porthcawl, Mid-Glamorgan CG36 3JH (tel: 065-671 5760).

**Lundegaard Spares Co**, Unit B, Boarshaw Industrial Estate, Middleton, Manchester (tel: 061-653 3579).

**Gavin Lumsden**, The Red House, Bowsers Lane, Little Walden, Essex (tel: 0799 22330). Secondhand spares.

**E.B. Mould**, 31 Sandbach, Gt Lumley, Chester-le-Street, Co Durham DH3 4LL (tel: 0385 881191 after 6.00pm). Wood framework; body restorations.

## BOOKS

**As Old as the Industry** by David G. Styles (out of print). Weighty volume, with emphasis on pre-war Riley history.

**Riley Cars 1945-50; Riley Cars 1950-55.** Brooklands Books compilations, out of print.

## ACKNOWLEDGEMENTS

This feature would not have been possible but for the many kindnesses of John Byron, Alan Dixon, Steve Hope, Simon Kinder and Nigel Trotman, all of the Riley RM Club. An equal debt of gratitude is owed to Arnold Farrar, of the Riley Motor Club, and to Bob Aves, Ernie Mould, and David Styles. Thanks also to Historic House Hotels, for allowing us to use Hartwell House as a photographic location.

| SPECIFICATION | RILEY 1½-LITRE (1949) | RILEY 2½-LITRE (1949) |
|---|---|---|
| Engine | In-line four | In-line four |
| Construction | Iron block and iron crossflow head | Iron block and iron crossflow head |
| Bore/stroke | 69 × 100mm | 80.5 × 120mm |
| Capacity | 1496cc | 2443cc |
| Valves | Overhead, twin high-set camshafts, short pushrods | Overhead, twin high-set camshafts, short pushrods |
| Compression ratio | 6.75:1 | 6.9:1 |
| Fuel system | Single SU carburettor | Twin SU carburettors |
| Power | 55bhp at 4500rpm | 100bhp at 4500rpm |
| Torque | 76lb ft at 2500rpm | 134lb ft at 3000rpm |
| Transmission | Four-speed manual, synchromesh on top three gears | Four-speed manual, synchromesh on top three gears |
| Final drive | 4.89:1 | 4.11:1 |
| Brakes | Girling hydro-mechanical drums | Girling hydro-mechanical drums |
| Suspension front | Ind by wishbones and longitudinal torsion bars | Ind by wishbones and longitudinal torsion bars |
| Suspension rear | Torque-tube, leaf springs, anti-roll bar | Torque-tube, leaf springs, anti-roll bar |
| Steering | Rack and pinion | Rack and pinion |
| Wheels/tyres | Steel disc, 4in × 16in | Steel disc, 6in × 16in |
| Body/chassis | Separate chassis, timber-framed mainly steel-panelled body | Separate chassis, timber-framed mainly steel-panelled body |
| **DIMENSIONS** | | |
| Length | 14ft 11in | 15ft 6in |
| Width | 5ft 3½in | 5ft 3½in |
| Height | 4ft 11in | 4ft 11½in |
| Wheelbase | 9ft 4½in | 9ft 11in |
| Kerb Weight | 24.25cwt | 28.56cwt |
| **PERFORMANCE** | | |
| Max speed | 74mph | 92mph |
| 0-60mph | 31.2sec | 18.4sec |
| 30-50 in top | 15.3sec | 11.9sec |
| 50-70 in top | n/a | n/a |
| Fuel consumption | 25-30mpg | 18-25mpg |

**August 1945:** Riley 'Twelve' announced.

**February 1946:** Formal launch of Riley 1½-litre.

**November 1946:** Riley 2½-litre announced.

**October 1947:** Bedford cord inserts to seats – until mid-1948 only.

**March 1948:** Roadster introduced.

**April/May 1948 (approx):** 100bhp engine standard on 2½-litre.

**June 1948:** Twin-leading-shoe front brakes, 2½-litre.

**October 1948:** Narrower transmission tunnel and lowered floor; armrests on doors; plastic ('Melleroid') replaces leathercloth for roof; detachable bonnet sides for 2½-litre. Drophead (2½) announced.

**May-October 1949:** New dashboard; opening driver's screen deleted; folding door-armrests; revised door trims; door pockets replace rear-of-seat pouches; centre armrest; recessed sunvisors.

**October 1949-January 1950:** phasing into production of rhd Roadster – floor change now available.

**October-December 1950:** Phasing in of improved brakes for 2½ – 1in smaller (11in), with broader shoes.

**January 1951:** Roadster production ceases.

**October 1951:** Drophead deleted. Two-bar rear bumpers and one-piece front bumpers; telescopic rear dampers (anti-roll bar deleted); larger-bore front dampers; revised door trims and seats; air-scoop panes optional.

**February 1952:** Lower-geared steering rack.

**July 1952:** Hypoid bevel rear axle; torque-tube deleted; hydraulic rear brakes; twin-leading-shoe front brakes (1½); lower rear axle ratio (1½).

**October 1952:** Repositioned water pump and dynamo; RMB/2 engine (2½); raised roofline and enlarged rear window; square-backed seats; front door-armrests deleted. Models designated RME (1½) and RMF (2½).

**Mid 1953:** Shell-bearing engine (2½) – from engine RMB/2 no 945.

**October 1953:** 2½-litre discontinued. 1½-litre restyled; softer cam profile; clutch mechanism improved.

**October 1954:** Wing-mounted rear lights.

**Jan 1955:** 'D' lamps deleted; chrome stoneguards to rear wings; production phased out.

*Note: Dates are generally those of the announcement and not necessarily of the implementation of the changes detailed.*

# OWNER'S VIEW

Simon Kinder has owned both 1½- and 2½-litre Rileys, and now runs a 2½-litre. How practical are the cars as regular transport, and how do the two models compare?

RAF Engineering Officer Simon Kinder bought his 2½-litre in July 1983. It followed a very poor 1½-litre he had acquired cheaply and had planned to rebuild; this had been disposed of when he realised that he needed more experience of the cars before he could tackle a full restoration.

The 2½, bought for £900 with a very rattly engine, was on the road by the end of 1983, after Simon had rebuilt the engine, and was used mainly for weekend and pleasure motoring for the next two years – albeit with the monthly mileage gradually creeping up, as Simon found out how much he enjoyed driving the Riley!

"During that period I spent a lot of time and effort working my way progressively through the car, ensuring that componentry like the steering and suspension was up to scratch.

"About May 1985 I came to the stage where I had bought a 1½-litre, and I had a modern Citroën as well. I thoroughly enjoyed driving the Rileys and decided that with two of them I could really afford to use the 2½ full-time … So I sold the Citroën and started to use the 2½ in earnest.

"Very shortly after this, I changed the cross-ply tyres and put on taxi radials. I think that for anyone who's using the car day in, day out, this is essential – or for anyone who wants to use the car safely, because cross-plies in the wet are appalling. Not only that, but I was getting 8000 miles out of a set of cross-plies and I've still got the radials on the 2½, and I've done 30,000 miles since."

This sort of mileage, with the car "driven almost into the ground", has not thrown up any real problems. "Considering the useage to which the car was put, the fact that I would climb into it virtually every day, I think there were only two occasions when I was unable to do that. Once was when the regulator box packed up … and the second time was when I had a halfshaft fail. On both occasions I was able to get the car mobile again within the day.

But what's the car like to work on – and how about that engine rebuild?

"It isn't a tricky engine to rebuild at all, except that you have to be very methodical with it … It was the first engine that I'd actually rebuilt, and it was a learning process – a learning process helped by the fact that I could ring up someone such as John Byron and say 'what do I do now?'.

"I don't think anything on the car is beyond an amateur home mechanic. The only thing that's difficult – on the 2½, in comparison with the 1½ – is the sheer weight of everything. I remember that I was taking off the cylinder head once … and I found that the only way to lift it was to stand over the engine, with both feet on the chassis members on either side, and then heave up the head. I managed to lift it off the studs and was left holding the head and wondering where to go from there!

The only disappointment Simon has found with his 2½ is how rapidly the body has deteriorated in regular use. "When I bought the car I was aware of how the woodwork wasn't particularly strong, and in fact one of the sills had been replaced by a rather slapdash, home-made plywood sill and a chair leg had been forced into one of the pillars to beef it up …

"The front pillars have become progressively weaker … and I've noticed more and more scuttle movement. I've also had to dig out quite a lot of dead wood from underneath the rear window, where, as a

horrendous bodge, I've made repairs with chopped glass-fibre, really just to keep the car on the road and to keep the water out.

"The car had a reasonably good roof when I bought it. It had been replaced at some stage, but not particularly well, as it wasn't very tight and so tended to 'balloon' a bit. But I really spent some time working my way around the guttering and around the rear window, making sure that the roof was watertight … and I've had no problems.

"My car is quite a good example of where the Riley can rot … All that's happened is that I've actually caught the rot and tried to slow it down. I bought the 2½ with the knowledge that eventually I'd have to rebuild it. Depending on the use to which I put it, I could, however, keep it going for quite a few more years … A car like mine just goes to show, I suppose, that you can actually use the cars with problems in the woodwork."

How about his 1½? This was bought through the RM Club, from an enthusiast who had owned the car since the early sixties and had expended some effort on the car before laying it up in the mid-seventies.

"I drove the car for about three months … and then had the big-ends fail. It was a consequence of

## "The 2½ is much more of a man's car. It's a rorty beast … very much faster, and more suited to motorways …"

old white metal and a lack of oil feed to the bearings, and – dare I say it – being driven fairly hard! The symptoms I noticed were dropping oil pressure and, when I started the engine and the oil was very thick, a patter from the big-ends because the oil feed wasn't sufficient.

"I converted that engine to take shell-bearings, and found that I could slot a set of BMC 'B' Series shells straight in, without having to do anything to the crankshaft … You line-bore the con-rods, cut slots to accept the little slots in the shells, and reassemble the engine without doing much more than cleaning everything. And that includes cleaning out the crankshaft by taking out the Allen-key plugs and cleaning out the sludge."

Beyond this engine overhaul, Simon had to do very little to the 1½, over and above such minor jobs as re-rubbering the brakes, and the car served him well on three extensive continental trips, during one of which he notched up 1500 miles in one week. How does the 1½, now sold, compare with the 2½?

"It's very boring on motorways, but very satisfying if you come to windy roads … The 2½ does tend to become a bit of a handful on winding roads. It doesn't have the nimble, sure-footed feel of the 1½.

"The 1½ was a good car for use on holidays, when I wasn't in a rush to get anywhere and I could potter about the place. My 1½ would cruise quite merrily at 60mph, and on radial tyres would outcorner most modern cars, and was so very enjoyable if I just wanted to go down country lanes and so on.

"The 2½ is much more of a man's car. It's a rorty beast, in comparison, and it's very much faster, and more suited to motorways and modern traffic … It's a very, very reassuring car to drive fast.

"The other advantage of the 1½, however, is that its fuel consumption is much better than on the 2½. I know lots of people who claim to get over 25mpg from the 2½, but I find it very difficult to get more than 20mpg. Generally I am getting 15-20mpg … whereas on the 1½ I got 30mpg quite happily."

After three cars, and four years of experience, what advice does Simon offer to those tempted to buy a 1½ or 2½?

"I'd suggest to anyone who is new to the cars that they do as I did – buy one that's roadworthy, albeit with a little bit of work needed, rather than do as I did earlier, which was to buy a basket-case for rebuilding … You need to know what you're doing with a rebuild, and it's a painful way to learn with a wreck. Whereas if you're actually driving the cars for a while you know more about it before you start."

# RILEY
## *resurrection*

*The wood-framed Riley RM is a challenging car to restore. Eric Cuss did it on a shoestring – and his 2½-litre is one of the best you'll come across. Story by Jon Pressnell, photos by Julian Mackie*

Eric Cuss has one of the very best Riley RMs in the country. It was judged Best Restored RM at the Riley RM Club's 1987 National, and Best 2½-litre at the 1988 gathering. Yet the full restoration has cost Eric less than £1600, cost of car excluded.

Purchased in December 1980 for £800, as a fairly smart-looking taxed-and-tested runner, it was used as regular transport by Eric until the end of the following summer – by which time he'd come to realise that its condition was appreciably less satisfactory than he'd thought!

"I think that if you'd really torn round a bend, the body would probably have left the chassis," he recalls. "From inside the car you could see right through the rear wheelarch, and you could lift one rear corner of the body clean off the chassis.

"I knew, from talking to people in the club, that you have to start an RM restoration by doing the body. It's no good lifting the shell away and starting with the mechanicals, because the body will just fall apart.

"I started at the back end, because that was the end poking out of the garage, and I tackled the boot floor, the wheelarches, and the lip to the boot aperture.

"This stage took the longest time, because body repair work was new to me. During my apprenticeship [Eric is a maintenance engineer for British Airways] I had been taught to weld, though, and I had some oxy-acetylene welding gear... Still, welding new metal to new metal is one thing – welding new metal to rusty old metal is another!

"Where the bumper irons come through the body is the datum point on the Riley, for accurate alignment of the rear, so I started by making sure

that the irons were straight and were bolted on properly, then I jacked the body up, until the irons came through the centre of the hole. That wasn't difficult, as the rear body mounts inside the boot had rotted through and you could lift the body with your hands...

"Trying to panel-beat sections, weld them in, and take the ripples out – that was hard. And down at the bottom, where the bumper irons come through, it's curved one way, then the other, and there's a flange. It took a long time, working with a wooden dolly, on the bench.

"Most of the wheelarch, which at its forward end forms one of the body mounting points, involved flat sections, or a single curvature, so at least that was fairly straightforward; the boot floor was less easy, as the body-mounts are double-skinned. The hardest bit, though, was trying to remake the boot opening, where it had rotted away particularly badly at the corners. I got a fellow to make up the stepped section, so all I had to do was bend it to shape, but it still took quite a time – and when I'd done it, I discovered that I should have had it made up with two lips, not one. Perhaps I should have taken the time to look at someone else's car first..."

Eric was now ready to get stuck into the real heart of an RM restoration – the wood framing. By this point he'd already stripped much of the body, which proved quite a challenge:

"It took an awful long time, trying to find out how the body comes apart, because where it has been leaded you can't see the body joins. You end up putting heat on a spot, and the lead drops away and you see the screw and nail heads.

"I tackled the wood one side at a time, and began with the sill on my first side. Reproduction sills at the

*Top: Eric Cuss poses with his superb 2½-litre. The culmination of six years' hard work, it is his first go at restoring a car, and it has already won him two major prizes. Left: The Riley as purchased – superficially sound, and a good runner, but with serious structural problems waiting to be uncovered on closer examination*

*Top: Three views of the restored car. Body was resprayed by Eric, using small compressor; duotone colour scheme suits the rakish lines of the Riley. Interior woodwork is a highlight of the restoration, and took much thought. Seats are originals, renovated; rest of interior all remade by Eric. Bottom: Buffing mops and buffing paste brought fine finish to twin-cam engine; chassis was hand-painted. Roof was fitted after primering*

time cost around £32 each, and they were only of marine ply. I said that as they'd used ash in the first place, I'd use ash – in fact, at any point where strength is required, I've used ash.

"So I bought an ash plank, had it planed down, and made up a sill from this. Rather than just screwing the assembly together, I glued it as well, for extra strength.

"Then I did the front door pillar – the 'A' post – on the same side. You have to take the scuttle outer panel off first – it's tacked on along the bonnet edge and inside the door opening, where it's screwed as well, and then it's leaded over.

"There should be a mounting plate at the bottom of the post, but this was completely missing and the one on the other side wasn't much better. So I had to guess the plate's size, and how it should be fixed. I was near-enough right, but even so there's a plywood packing piece there now, because I welded it on a bit too high!

"I then repaired the front wheelarch metal, and the front body mounting, before moving on to the timber 'A' post itself. It was quite good, so I just cut out the dead wood and half-lapped new timber into the post's bottom.

## "When I'd aligned the doors on the second side, I discovered I'd lost alignment on the first side's doors"

"The piece of timber which curves down from the 'A' post to the sill, forming the door aperture, was completely missing, though, so I had to buy a ready-made section – otherwise I wouldn't have known how it all went together."

Putting back the scuttle Eric didn't find too difficult, and he then moved on to the centre pillar. There's no timber involved, so all that he had to do was to grind off the corroded brackets at the bottom of the pillar, and make up new ones and weld them into place.

"That was a bit tricky, trying to find the exact spot to weld them on. Weld them on too low, and your door opening is too big; weld them on too high, and you won't be able to get your doors into the aperture. You have to put virtually everything together as best you can, doors included, and clamp the brackets in place, mark their position, and then weld."

With the centre pillar repaired, Eric now had all four body mounting points – boot floor, rear wheelarch, centre pillar, 'A' post – back together, and could move on to the next operation, accurately locating the sill and hanging the doors. With the sill loosely attached, he realised he had a fresh problem: the outer rail – the cant rail – of the timber roof frame had fractured.

"I bought a ready-made rail, but it wasn't a very good shape, so I had to plane it down at one end, and glue additional wood to the other, before it was right.

"With the cant rail replaced, then came the problem of aligning the doors. I temporarily attached the sill to the centre pillar with wood screws, and slotted the doors in place; they don't need securing, as they won't fall out.

"I could then start playing around, trying to get

the doors to close, moving the centre pillar and the sill in and out, up and down, all over the place. I eventually got it what I thought pretty much right, and went on to do much the same repair work to the other side of the car – including making up my own cant rail this time, out of 4x4 ash cut to shape with a bandsaw.

"But when I'd aligned the doors on the second side, I discovered that I'd lost all the alignment of the first side's doors.

"So I ended up in effect having to align *six* doors, as I had to start all over again. It was terrible. Pure

patience saw me through. A little bit here, a little bit there, then you'd stop and think 'I've lost it *there*, so where do I need to adjust it?' Say it's very tight at a top front corner – it's probably something to do with the back end. If you release a bit of pressure, or jack it up, it'll give you a little more of a gap at the front. It's very flexible, the structure.

"The body was originally mounted with a packing of something like ½in chipboard between the body and the chassis mounting points, so I made up fresh packing pieces in mahogany, which is more durable.

"By adding thickness, or shaving it away, and by

enlarging the bolt holes in the sills so that I could move the sills along a bit or in or out at front or rear, I gradually got there, helped by a certain leeway in the door hinges, which can be bent slightly if the door is touching the frame. With all these adjustments, you're only talking about fractions of an inch – that's enough to make it right."

After this, repairing the timber frame around the rear window was a blessedly straightforward operation, involving cutting away wood where it was soft or where it was peppered with nail holes, and then laminating fresh timber in place; the curved members tying the window to the door post were however replaced with freshly fabricated pieces. More challenging was the front windscreen frame, where the timber had rotted on the upper rail.

"It was a bit of a job trying to get the windscreen frame off, as it sits in round the corner of the 'A' posts and has to be sprung out of place – and first you have to remove the metal cladding, which was very difficult, as the securing tacks are so awkwardly placed that their heads have to be ground off with a very small grinding stone.

"The real problem, though, was when I came to reassembling everything, and had to attach the screen top rail to the roof. after I'd taken off the screen, the whole bulkhead had dropped forward, either under its own weight or because it had been held in tension by the screen and surround. I had to make two big tourniquets to draw the bulkhead back into place."

With the screen frame finally back in position, and the steel screen surround replaced with a better one from a £50 basket-case 2½-litre Eric had picked up, the carpentry side of the restoration was over. Had it been a nightmare?

"My father was a carpenter by profession, so carpentry didn't hold any fears for me. It was just time, because ash is so hard to work, and I didn't have any electric tools powerful enough to cut a plank of ash – my circular saw wouldn't take it. So I did all the work with ordinary hand tools, although a set of rotary files did come in handy for shaping.

"You need a good set of chisels, a good saw, and a good vice, and you must take care with your marking out, and not cut too much off or plane too much away. You must be patient, too, and not rush.

"All the new wood was treated with three or four coats of Cuprinol, dipping the smaller pieces. Somebody told me I shouldn't have Cuprinolled the wood, because it would rot the steel, but I can't see this being a problem, as I've put a self-adhesive linen tape – 'Tank tape', I think it's called – between the steel and the wood, to stop squeaking.

"Yes, the body is complex, but I'd sooner do a body on an RM or another coachbuilt car than a modern car with its spot-welds. That would send me round the bend. At least the Riley body comes apart with nails and screws, and you can work on a small piece at a time – well, except at the rear, where there *are* spot welds…"

With the body structurally sound, Eric taped the doors in position, rolled the car into the garden, and lifted the body from the chassis, raising it off the frame a corner at a time, putting progressively more packing between the two, until he could slide a pair of trestles under the body and pull the chassis away from underneath. He could now set to on the renovation of the chassis, which was fortunately sound enough only to need a little bit of straightforward welding to two of the body mounts.

"The whole car was done on a budget, so rather than spend £70 on having the chassis shot-blasted, I resorted to sanding discs. I found that at work they used an adhesive non-slip tread on their metal steps. It came in a big roll, and I discovered that if I cut circles out of it with a pair of tin-snips, peeled the backing off, and stuck it on my rubber sanding disc, I had a wonderful abrasive!

"Scurfing off the rust, spending hours out in the cold with nothing to show for it, and getting into the shower filthy every night – that was the worst stage

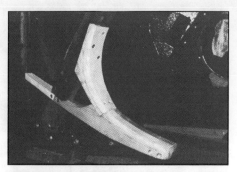

of the restoration. And with everything off the car, I knew that the only way I could sell it would be as a pile of bits, for £50 or something. So I carried on. I'd go to the club meeting that month, see a few shiny RMs, and then I'd go home full of spirits again.

"The club was invaluable, in fact. There's always someone who'll help you out with your particular problem, but just as importantly, the club helps keep up your morale. You go along to a meeting, see a nice car, and you end up thinking 'That's what it should be like; that's how *mine* is going to be.' It definitely kept me going. The spares back-up is excellent, too. Indeed, I don't think I could have done it without the help of John Byron, the spares secretary.

## "The club was invaluable. There's always someone who'll help you out with your problem... It kept me going"

"I hand-painted the chassis, using red-oxide primer and then black Alkyd, which had been recommended by a chap at work – he'd used it on his gutters, and said it had stood up to the weather quite well. It gives a beautiful finish, if you take your time."

At the same time Eric was tackling the underside of the body, using red-oxide primer and Hammerite.

"They say that Hammerite is a wonderful paint. I think it's only as wonderful as the primer you put underneath. They say you can paint it on bare steel or on to rust. That's a load of rubbish. I cleaned up my front floor panels, Hammerite-painted them, and stored them away. When I came to fit them, rust was blistering through…"

Top: Remaking the timber frame at the bottom of the 'A' post was a challenging task, as on one side the lower member had rotted away completely. Centre: Boot floor and wheelarch cut away, to allow repair of the rearmost body mount. Bottom: The Riley part stripped – note the exposed timber of the scuttle/'A' post, and the corroded screen frame. The fabric roof and its mesh base have been removed, but body stays on chassis until strength is restored

As he'd been going along, Eric had been renovating and repainting – with red-oxide and Alkyd – the various running-gear components, and with the chassis repainted he was ready to start reassembly, four years from when he'd begun the restoration.

"I put the back axle on, and wheeled the chassis under the body on a spare set of brake drums. I then let the body slowly down and jacked the chassis into position. With the body-to-chassis packing back in place and the door fit checked, I bolted the body down and trial-fitted the other panels.

"'That's it,' I thought. 'Now I'm getting somewhere!' I could see the light at the end of the tunnel. When you start to put shiny bits back on, with new nuts and bolts, it's wonderful! I think it took me a day to rebuild the front suspension – and what a lovely day that was…

"The engine was advertised as having been rebuilt, and the guy had obviously done some work on it, but I thought 'no, I don't trust this', and so I stripped the whole engine. In fact, I found that the bearings and the pistons were good – all I really replaced on the engine was the timing chain.

"An important job, though, was to drill out the crankshaft plugs and scrape out all the gunge which clogs the oilways on the Riley engine. That was a couple of days' hard work, but it was well worth it, as I got out a lot of gunge. I spent a long time on the block's oilways, too, scraping away with a hacksaw blade and running pipe-cleaners through the passages, in conjunction with a chemical degreaser.

"The rebuild was pretty simple, but it's a heavy engine. I had thought of taking it to be steamcleaned, but I couldn't lift the bare block. When it came to reassembly, I had to keep in on its side on the garage floor, hauling it about."

All the engine ancillaries were rebuilt and cleaned and polished where appropriate, using a buffing mop and buffing soap, and the engine was painted with Hermetite engine lacquer. This last hasn't proved a great success, some blistering having taken place.

Engine and gearbox – the latter untouched, as it appeared sound – could now be installed, and after a successful trial starting-up of the car, Eric moved on to prepare the body for spraying. The doors needed no real attention, but one front wing was so bad that it was replaced by one from Eric's spares car.

"I then started filling over where I'd welded the body. My welding is sound, but I'm no panel-beater, so there is filler in the car, I'll not deny it. But it's not thick filler, and it's not hiding anything.

"One of the places where I had to put a skim of filler was around the boot aperture, and I couldn't get the curve right. I was talking to a chap at work, and he said that the best way was to get a length of 4x2, say about 2ft or 2ft 6in long, tack wet-and-dry to it, and use a gentle sweeping motion across the panel. It worked, and took out all the little unevenesses."

Preparation over – quicker than it might have been, as in general Eric didn't take panels back to bare metal – spraying could begin, in summer 1986, using a small Broom and Wade compressor and cellulose paint.

"I started with the bodyshell itself, because it's all in small sections – you've just got to give a quick blast up and down a windscreen pillar, for example, and it's done. I got quite a good finish with the little gun on the compressor. I was really surprised with myself – but I had played around with the outfit before starting.

"I think the car had about four coats of primer, and in the end at least seven or eight of colour. I put on two or three coats of colour before I bothered letting it dry and then rubbing it down, just so I could gain some idea of what I'd got – I didn't know about the principle of spraying on a black guide-coat.

"With the last two coats, the paint was rubbed down beforehand with something like 800-grade paper. A lot of people use 600-grade at this stage, but I found '600' much too coarse. The last coats were virtually thinners with a little colour.

"I sprayed the main panels off the car, one at a time. The front wings, which I thought I'd have trouble with, trying to keep a wet edge, because they're such an awkward shape, didn't come out too badly. Where I did have problems, though, was spraying up the white, which was mainly on the doors and bonnet sides. I played with the mixture, I played with the pressure, but still I had trouble. I had to keep on rubbing it back…"

Eric fitted the Riley's fabric roof, apart from the guttering, after he'd primered the car.

"I did this to make sure that I'd got paint right up underneath it. John Byron says I should have fully painted the car first, but I was too frightened of scratching the paintwork."

The expanded-metal base had already been blasted and sprayed with powder-epoxy, so it was laid in place and the wadding and hessian spread over it.

"It's a two-man job, fitting the fabric, and it has to be done on a warm day. I laid the roof on the car in the morning, to let it warm up. I think I started off with an inch and a half of excess, yet at the end of the day I cut off three to four inches – that's how much it stretches.

"What they say about the job taking the skin off your knuckles is true. With one guy rolling and pulling and the other putting in tacks, it really is tough going."

Fitting up and trimming began with the installation of a new wiring loom – from Autosparks, whom Eric is happy to recommend.

"I wasn't looking forward to the re-wiring, but it was straightforward enough. The hardest job was around the bulkhead, trying to find out what went through which hole. I then put the dash in, having stripped and cleaned all the switches, and restored the woodwork.

"The first job was to get rid of every trace of the old varnish. I used broken glass to scrape it off. This gets you right back to really good wood, and you can get into all the little corners. I then just had to rub it over with thin glass-paper, and that was it.

"I re-varnished with polyurethane. On the door-

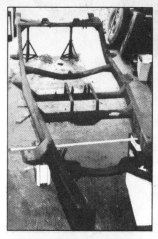
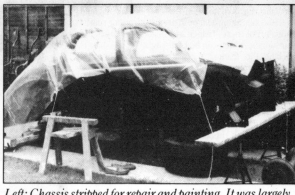

*Left: Chassis stripped for repair and painting. It was largely sound. Above: Body rests on trestles after repair. Below: Wood sill and remade body mount*

cappings, which I'd tackled earlier, this had given me a lovely rich colour, but on the plywood dash it was less satisfactory – I think I should have stained the wood first. I brushed the varnish on, and after the first two or three coats I flattened it with wet-and-dry between each coat.

"I'd thought hard about how to veneer the dash, as the veneer inlay had to take on a curve. I made an aluminium former, prepared the surface of the dash, dampened the veneer to soften it, and then put a sheet of polythene over it, to stop anything sticking to any glue that might seep through. I then put some old thin carpet on top, to give the necessary 'squish', and clamped the aluminium former in place, with a few small blocks of wood to spread the load.

"By now there were shiny bits on the engine, I was pleased with the body finish, and it was becoming all the time something better than just a reasonably sound everyday car. I could see that the end result was going to be something good, and that's when the care and attention really started going into everything.

"Generally, though, my attitude had always been that if I felt a job was 'good enough', that it *wasn't* really good enough – I knew it could be perfect. If I could turn around and say 'that's good, that's perfect – I'm pleased with that', then that was the job finished."

The next major interior task was fitting a new headlining, something Eric was not relishing.

"I'd taken the old one out very carefully, and I used it as a pattern to cut new pieces out of a roll of cloth I'd bought from Paul Beck. I carefully stitched everything together, and tacked it in place with an ordinary staple gun. At the front the headlining is glued to the sunvisor recesses in the header rail, and here I used a 3M aerosol adhesive, as I know that if you brush glue on it will show through.

"I cut out new interior trim panels, in marine-ply, and then I unstitched the old panels, so I could see how they'd been done together. I followed exactly the way they'd been done originally, except where the leathercloth had been stitched through the ply – there was no way I could do that.

"I used an old Singer electric sewing machine which I took to a sewing machine specialist, who

adjusted it so I could sew through thicker material.

"The seats are the originals, treated with a Woolies renovation kit. When I took the seats out, before I put them in the loft I gave them a good dose of saddle soap to clean them, and then fed them with hide food, so that over the years they'd start to soften. Before I began I cleaned them again, and gave them another going-over with hide food.

"I wanted the seats to be a little lighter in colour than originally, to go with the new leathercloth, and Woolies matched their kit to a snippet of this. After three coats of renovator, the colour ended up almost exactly right, but in places it does look a little patchy. But Woolies do say that their kit isn't intended to cope with colour changes.

"The final touch was to bring up the piping on the seats. I used some scuff-coating my wife had bought for a pair of red patent-leather shoes belonging to one of my daughters. It came up quite well!"

August 1987, and the restoration was at last complete, when Eric had made up the carpets. A few teething difficulties – a leaking core-plug, a loose brake union, sticking brakes – were quickly surmounted, and Eric has since then been using the car as his regular 300-miles-a-week transport.

"I'd offer the following advice to anyone contemplating the restoration of an RM: first, join the club; second, go along to the local meetings, and talk to as many people as you can; third, don't rush into it – it's quite a complicated car as a whole, but if you break it down into small sections, it's not really that complex, and because it's an old car, you can take it apart; fourth, don't do too much at once; fifth if you don't know what you're doing, ask, as there's always someone who knows, not least the club's two technical advisors.

**SPECIALISTS USED**

**Auto-Sparks Ltd**, 61a Lime Street, Hull HU8 7AH (tel: 0482 20719).
**Paul Beck Vintage Supplies**, Folgate Road, North Walsham, Norfolk NR28 0AJ (tel: 0692 406574)
**Edgeware Motor Accessories**, 94 High Street, Edgeware, Middlesex HA8 7BN (tel: 01-952 4789/9311).
**John S. Foster**, 1A Leeds Old Road, Heckmondwike, W. Yorks WF16 9AA (tel: 0924 409319).
**Lundegaard Spares Co**, Unit B, Boarshaw Industrial Estate, Middleton, Manchester (tel: 061-653 3579).
**Woolies**, Blenheim Way, Northfields Industrial Estate, Market Deeping, nr Peterborough, PE6 8LD (tel: 0778 347347).

**RILEY RM CLUB**

**Enrolment Secretary:** Bill Harris, 57 Cluny Gardens, Edinburgh EH10 6BL.

| PURCHASE OF CAR | | £800 |
|---|---|---|
| **Body rebuild** | | **£193** |
| …including | ash and ready-made | |
| | ash members | £75 |
| | fabric roof kit | £69 |
| **Brakes and suspension** | | **£110** |
| …including | king-pin kit | £66 |
| | various bushes and seals | £25 |
| **Engine and ancillaries** | | **£184** |
| …including | water pump repair kit | £32 |
| | exhaust system | £89 |
| **Electrics** | | |
| …including | wiring harness | £56 |
| **Trim and fittings** | | **£557** |
| …including | headlining material | £38 |
| | door trim material | £31 |
| | carpet, felt, adhesive | £51 |
| | leather renovation kit | £18 |
| **Paint** | | **£80** |
| **Chroming** | | **£329** |
| **Miscellaneous items** | | **£22** |
| **TOTAL COST OF RESTORATION** | | **£1552** |